THE NEW
ANTI-
SEMITISM

THE NEW ANTI-SEMITISM

by Arnold Forster & Benjamin R. Epstein

McGraw-Hill Book Company

New York   St. Louis   San Francisco
Düsseldorf   London   Mexico   Sydney   Toronto

Book designed by Marcy J. Katz

123456789 DODO 7987654

Library of Congress Cataloging in Publication Data

Forster, Arnold.
    The new anti-Semitism.

    1. Antisemitism. I. Epstein, Benjamin R., joint author. II. Title.
DS145.F67   301.45'19'24   73-22015
ISBN 0–07–021615–0

*For those who have died
because they were Jews—*

Acknowledgments

A grant from the Norman Tishman Memorial Fund—given through the generosity of Mrs. Norman Tishman—made possible the preliminary research essential to the undertaking of this in-depth study.

Extensive data was accumulated and analyzed by a team of experts with a wealth of experience in the field of human relations working under the lay chairmanship of Laurence Peirez. The organization and preparation of this data was the work of Jerome Bakst, Owen Rachleff, Gerald Baumgarten, James Purcell, Mort Kass, Irwin Suall, Abraham Foxman and Morton Rosenthal. Our field research was directed by Justin Finger and Harry Rosenkranz. Mrs. Naomi Rosenbaum coordinated the flow of our massive and complex data, codified it and later organized the footnotes. To all these people, whose strenuous efforts went far beyond their normal assignments, our deep appreciation.

We are also indebted to Susan Glass, who labored ten to twelve hours a day helping the authors reduce more than fifteen hundred pages of the original manuscript to the present volume.

And finally, our sincere gratitude to Ben Levin, of Fargo, North Dakota and Miami, Florida, for making financially possible the approximately three years of work that went into creating the text of *The New Anti-Semitism*.

Contents

Foreword

There is an old Hasidic story about a student who goes to his rabbi and says, "Oh master, I love you!"

The rabbi responds with a question, "Tell me, do you know what hurts me?"

The young man is bewildered, taken aback.

"Why do you ask me such a confusing question when I have just told you I love you?"

The rabbi shakes his head. "Because, my friend, if you do not know what hurts me, how can you truly love me?"

This is a book about anti-Semitism, the oldest hurt of the Jewish people. It is not a history of that painful, pervasive phenomenon, but rather an analysis of anti-Semitism today—here in the United States, and in the world. It goes into the past only to explain the present. It exposes, in all its complexity, a new anti-Semitism that is based on the old but emanates from different and suprisingly respectable sources.

It is a book based on the extensive records of an American agency whose name has been synonymous for sixty years with the fight ·against prejudice, bigotry and discrimination—the Anti-Defamation League of B'nai B'rith. Their weapons have been law, education and public persuasion. And in the years since 1913, when the League was founded "to end the defamation of Jews . . .

to seek justice and fair treatment for all citizens alike," there have been massive, hard-won changes in the status and security of American Jews—and, indeed, of all minorities.

In many circles, the American Jewish community is no longer considered a minority, and certainly not an oppressed minority. In spite of, or perhaps because of, this changed condition, the interests, concerns and well-being of Jews are becoming largely a matter of indifference to the rest of society.

While no Jew has ever been able to convince himself that the roots of anti-Semitism have been ripped out and forever destroyed, he has been able to gain reassurance from its periods of dormancy, each longer than the one before. While the memory of the Nazi Holocaust was fresh in mind, anti-Semitism was silenced. As that memory fades, however, as Jews are more and more being considered a part of the establishment, there are new growths of anti-Semitism. They are being nurtured in a climate of general insensitivity and deterioration in morality and ethics— the kind of climate, history reminds us, in which anti-Semitism grows best.

This book presents the evidence of a new anti-Semitism. It gives a clear picture of facts and anti-Jewish attitudes which are appearing in current American and international life. Although it is a book about anti-Semitism, it is, in the larger sense, a book about the wrongs people do people in the twentieth century.

But this nation is still evolving and is still capable of objective self-analysis and positive change. We firmly believe that America is still willing to improve—and that is what sets it apart and makes it great.

This, then, is a book to hasten change.

We hope it will prod the reader into awareness of what is hurting his neighbor, his country—and, ultimately, himself.

> *Seymour Graubard*
> *National Chairman,*
> *Anti-Defamation League*
> *of B'nai B'rith*

1

The New
Anti-Semitism

Is the post–World War II honeymoon with the Jews over?

This is the question Jewish communities around the world are asking today with increasing frequency.

For most of the nearly thirty years since the end of the war, and especially since the Allied liberation of the Nazi concentration camps and world recognition of the enormity of the crimes committed there by a "civilized" state, anti-Semitism—the defamation, subjugation and persecution of Jews as Jews—was swiftly condemned whenever and wherever it appeared.

Not that all major manifestations of anti-Semitism suddenly disappeared with the war. Nazi racism had little effect on incumbent dictators. Stalin's notorious "doctors' plot," which falsely charged Jewish physicians with conspiracy to murder him, and the anti-Jewish economic trials of late Stalinism were, in fact, postwar phenomena. Nor did an excess of philo-Semitism lower the barriers to immigration that existed in most of the world immediately after the war for survivors of Nazi brutality. For a time it seemed the haunted and haunting Jews of Europe would have to wander the plains and cities of the continent and the waterways of the world before finding a home.

But for a long while after World War II, sympathy for the six million Jewish victims of Nazi genocide not only precluded the more overt and vicious forms of anti-Semitism among all but the lunatic hate fringe, but helped to open doors long closed to Jews here and abroad.

Certainly the State of Israel was one direct beneficiary of world empathy with the Jewish victims of nazism.

Introspection within official Christendom about its own role in the climate that produced the Holocaust brought forth, after a time, the historic Vatican II "Declaration on Non-Christian Religions" whose "Statement on the Jews," if it fell short of exonerating Jews of the charge of deicide (a root cause of Jewish persecution for twenty centuries), served at least to remove the taint of guilt from the Jewish people then and now. Even more fundamentally, it propounded a view of Judaism not as a decadent and defunct precursor of Christianity which the latter had replaced and superceded, but as a lively parent and brother faith that had survived against all the odds and would, no doubt, continue to survive. In its commitment to genuine ecumenism the Vatican pronouncement softened all but the most cynical of Jewish hearts.

In the United States, America's minority groups had begun, with the prewar New Deal, an upward movement that hastened after the war. It was as though the confrontation with the ultimate racist society had shaken America to its underpinnings and made imperative the earliest possible realization of its constitutional promise of equality. Jews, who had never experienced *de jure* discrimination in this country but were victims of social, academic and economic deprivation, benefited from the opening up of the great universities and graduate schools that had long imposed restrictive quotas on Jewish admissions. New careers beckoned in an expanding civil service and in the burgeoning technocracy. And if Jews did not make it to the executive level in older, more traditional industries, they at least had a chance where merit and talent were the criteria—and they took it.

It would be a mistake to believe the great leap forward by American Jewry during the postwar decades toppled all existing barriers. It did not, nor did it usher in the millenium for the Jewish community in the United States. Traditional anti-Jewish prejudices still exist in segments of American society. Jews are demonstrably under-utilized, for example, in the executive and managerial cadre of American business, especially in the insurance, steel and banking fields. And despite the myth of Jewish affluence, hundreds of thousands of Jews in America, especially the elderly, are poor. Nevertheless, in the twenty years after the war, roughly 1945 to 1965, American Jews achieved a greater degree of economic and political security and social acceptance than has ever been achieved by any Jewish community since the Dispersion.

In the aftermath of the war, too, Americans of all religions and races—and American Jews in disproportionate prominence among them—signed on for the great civil rights struggles of the fifties and early sixties, and major legal battles for Negro equality were won. This is not the place to document the unique Jewish contribution to those victories, but it was made in money, in manpower, in skills and, above all perhaps, in organizational experience. And it was made in the closest possible adherence to the injunction of Hillel to be "for myself" but not "for myself alone," and "if not now, when?" American Jews, severely traumatized by nazism, eager to remove remnant barriers to achievement, anxious to protect their new gains and enjoined by the deepest-held traditions of their faith to care for the stranger among them, plunged into the legal battle for civil rights that, secured, would protect us all.

But the domestic achievement has fallen far short of America's promise to blacks and other disadvantaged minorities, and so too the new and hard-won status of American Jewry—which by the early sixties had virtually reached a point of ludicrous enchantment in America with all things Jewish—shows signs of deterioration. And the persecution of Jews abroad continues. In short, the Jewish people, a scant three decades after the annihilation of fully a third of its ranks, is affected everywhere with a profound uneasiness. Is the pendulum swinging back? Is there a new anti-Semitism? Is it the old vinegar in new casks—out of different vineyards, perhaps? Has moral outrage become moral indifference?

Like the surviving members of an ancient species, contemporary Jews have developed extremely sensitive antennae—

genuine survival mechanisms—which warn them in advance
that something is happening that is not good for Jews. History
has taught us that disaster can follow periods of stability, even of
the flourishing of Jewish religious and cultural life: the Inquisi-
tion succeeded the golden age of Spanish Jewry, and the Holocaust
itself descended upon a prosperous, largely assimilated and unsuspecting German Jewish community. This is not to say that a
similar decimation of Jews is around the corner; such is not the
case and should be clearly stated at the outset. Even in Soviet
Russia, perhaps the world's greatest purveyor of anti-Semitism
today, the situation of the Soviet Jews, onerous as it is, is a far
cry from the mass physical destruction of European Jewry in the
thirties and forties. It is a mistake to equate current anti-Jewish
measures in the Soviet Union with those of Nazi Germany, and
those who do badly disserve the cause of Soviet Jews. Their case
for full religious and cultural rights within the USSR and free
emigration to the historic homeland of their people stands on
its own merit and has won widespread sympathy throughout the
world. It can only suffer by exaggerated and unreal comparisons.

Nor can any but the demagogues among us—and there are
Jewish demagogues—fairly assert that a clear potential for Nazi-
like devastation exists in contemporary America; it does not.
Despite the unfinished business of the nation in achieving not
only equality of opportunity but measurable significant progress
for racial and ethnic minorities, despite the real and overwhelming problems of our urban centers—we are still a people that
retains its historic commitment to orderly social progress and
decent treatment for all citizens. Watergate and its attendant
evils, the deliberate corruption of the political process and in-
fringement on the civil liberties of many Americans—a sordid
chapter in the history of the Republic written by many at the
highest levels of our government—are, despite cynics who would
claim otherwise, an aberration in our democracy. That a free
press and independent legislative and judicial branches are, even
as we write, in the process of removing this malignancy in our
midst, reveals the enduring strengths of American democracy.

But anti-Semitism is an insidious disease. It can linger in the
body politic almost invisibly for years without erupting. Its ef-

fects can be long delayed. Moreover, unless expunged it grows. Of all the ills of the world, anti-Semitism is the least likely to die a natural death.

This book represents an attempt to survey the American domestic and world scenes and properly identify the current sources, modes and extent of anti-Jewish behavior. The task will involve, necessarily, some redefining of traditional notions of anti-Semitism and serious reorientation of long-held convictions about the nature of its sources. But more important, we propose to examine as well behavior that can only be properly defined as an insensitivity to these problems rather than anti-Semitic either by the definitions that have existed or by new and more inclusive descriptions. It includes, often, a callous indifference to Jewish concerns expressed by respectable institutions and persons here and abroad—people who would be shocked to think themselves, or have others think them, anti-Semites.

How have we come from there to here? From active sympathy on the part of non-Jews everywhere for the Nazis' victims—contributing to at least two decades of unprecedented opportunity for Jewish communities around the world—to an apparent unconcern about the oldest of the Western world's diseases, anti-Semitism?

In the United States the technological revolution that followed the war caused serious dislocation in the sense of personal status experienced by many Americans, despite the economic benefits it brought most of them. The age of television, of jet travel, of space, of computers, of "the corporate man" and "future shock" may have helped to shrink the continent, the world and the solar system, but it could hardly have failed to have a somewhat diminishing effect as well on people required now to see themselves not as part of small towns and boroughs, or even cities or one nation, but of an enormous humankind reaching for and attaining the moon if not yet the stars. On another level, the rise of immigrant groups—the "hyphenated Americans" as they have been called—seemed to challenge the economic and social supremacy of those who considered themselves native stock. Some were attracted in the mid-fifties and early sixties to right-wing political movements of an extreme nature which attacked all the "big" things that seemed so impersonal and disorienting—big government, big labor, big business, foreign aid, the income tax, welfare measures like social security, the "international Communist conspiracy" and its allies in the United States who were "subverting" traditional American values. Inevitably, because the Radical Right often sheltered or trafficked with the heirs to the isolationist, fascist, anti-Semitic groups that had flourished on the American scene in the thirties, and because the tradition of scapegoating Jews for every evil was a lot longer and stronger than the very recent inclination toward sympathy, some right-wing extremists hinted repeatedly that the international Communist conspiracy was, in fact, a Jewish or "Zionist" conspiracy. Prodded by agencies like the ADL, they made an effort to cleanse their ranks of anti-Semites or to conceal their presence; they never succeeded, and anti-Semitism was never very far from the surface of Radical Right groups. Although the organized Radical Right never encompassed more than a fraction of the American people, millions were drawn to its political outlook with its false promise of a return to an earlier and less complex America. It therefore managed to keep alive, in the decade following the McCarthy hysteria, some of the ancient anti-Jewish canards that might otherwise have died.

In *Danger on the Right* (1964) and *The Radical Right: Report on the John Birch Society and Its Allies* (1967) the authors exposed both the links to anti-Semitism of well-financed right-wing organizations operating under a cover of respectability (and a banner of superpatriotism) and the jeopardy in which their extremist activities placed democratic ideals and institutions. In 1968 an Anti-Defamation League report warned that some of the nation's worst anti-Semites, long Radical Right hangers-on, would be among the presidential electors if George Wallace's American Party did not clean house and repudiate some of its supporters and campaign workers. And in 1972 ADL was required to report that the candidacy of Representative John Schmitz of California, who inherited the American Party standard after the unfortunate wounding of Governor Wallace, was tainted by the support of anti-Semites long connected with the Radical Right and by their continuing unsavory rhetoric.

In the mid-sixties, however, there arose in American life, from the other end of the political spectrum, another extremism containing none of the anachronism that had been a serious problem for the Radical Right in attracting broad-based support among the American people: the Radical Left—which stood for "progress." Moreover, because the Radical Left shared some immediate goals and language in common with mainstream liberalism— advocacy of civil rights for racial minorities and peace in Vietnam, for example—it could not be sloughed off. But soon it became clear that the Radical (totalitarian) Left, embracing both old-line communist organizations and the multifaceted New Left, had taken an anti-Semitic turn away from traditional left-wing opposition to anti-Semitism and today represents a danger to world Jewry at least equal to the danger on the right.

The organized New Left in America as we knew it in the sixties is a dying if not dead phenomenon as a political movement, but the "countercultural" ideas and values it both reflected and promulgated have left a lasting imprint on American and Western European society and especially on the sector Jews have historically regarded as most friendly, the liberal community. Moreover, an entire generation of college students both here and abroad has come of age under New Left influence and is taking its place in the career areas that mold opinion, set the moral tone and style of society and influence or actually make the key policy decisions—from government service and media employment to the teaching and legal professions, the ministry, literature and the lively arts. It is a "now" generation, largely ignorant of the Holocaust; a generation largely unconcerned with, if not hostile to, Jews and Jewish interests, moved deeply—and legitimately— by issues of race, poverty and war, but not by anti-Semitism or Jews as victims. Finally, the danger on the left is intensified by the fact that a majority in the liberal community (but it is hoped, diminishing), including countless numbers of Jews, either fails to see or cannot concede that the Radical Left is a threat at all. Yet anti-Semitism can and does come in many different forms, not all of them openly labeled, and despite the denials by Radical Left organizations that they are anti-Semitic, these groups consistently engage in activity and propaganda in support of policies that are immediately harmful to Jews and in the long run could threaten the very survival of the Jewish people.

It is important to distinguish between the two left-wing movements in the world today: the democratic, liberal left and the totalitarian left. The first is by no means anti-Semitic; indeed, it has been a consistent opponent of anti-Semitism. The Western-oriented social-democratic movement, centered in the Socialist International and led by such figures as Willy Brandt, Giuseppe Saragat, Hugh Gaitskell and Leon Blum, has always been friendly toward the Jewish people. It has supported Israel's right to exist and has included the Israeli social-democratic movement prominently in its ranks. In the United States, where social democracy has not been a major political force, the democratic left has nonetheless also been a friend of the Jewish community. Its major spokesmen — Eugene V. Debs, Morris Hillquit, Norman Thomas — always fought bigotry. Today the organized democratic left in America consists of the Social Democrats, U.S.A. (formerly the Socialist Party) and its youth section, the Young Peoples Socialist League. Both remain true to their traditions, as evidenced by their support of the State of Israel and opposition to anti-Semitism. By contrast, the totalitarian Radical Left — whose major groups include the Communist Party and its youth group, the Young Workers Liberation League; the Socialist Workers Party and its youth organization, the Young Socialist Alliance; the Workers World Party and its youth section, Youth Against War and Fascism; the Progressive Labor Party; Students for a Democratic Society (led today by the Progressive Labor Party); the Workers League, and Spartacus League — fails to eschew anti-Semitism and actively uses hostility against Jews as a weapon in its political struggle. In its outlook the world is depicted as a vast battle plain in which the "socialist" camp is pitted against capitalism and imperialism for hegemony. The camp of capitalism, chiefly the United States and Western Europe, must be defeated through a combined strategy of internal upheaval and opposition in the uncommitted portion of the "third world." It is in this context that the Jewish community finds itself under assault by the Radical Left, not because Radical Left adherents are motivated by religious or racial hatred — the vast majority are not — but because they view the Jews as an obstacle to their revolutionary goals.

In the United States the Radical Left sees the Jewish community and its institutions as part of the "Establishment": an affluent, smug, "liberal" obstacle to the growth of revolutionary consciousness. Indeed, Jewish voting patterns, attitudes, alliances — in short, the political behavior of Jews — has a decidedly liberal cast. But to the Radical Left, especially in recent years, liberalism is the great enemy, the force which sows and perpetuates illusions that progress can be achieved steadily and peacefully through normal democratic processes. Liberalism, therefore, has to be rendered obsolete if society is to be polarized and revolutionary awareness is to replace the tolerant and optimistic attitudes that provide the cement of "the system." In this Radical Left view the Jewish community is seen as part of the problem, not part of the solution.

Moreover, the Radical Left is convinced that because of the unique history and racial composition of American society, its oppressed racial minorities constitute an important explosive potential which can ultimately be a major factor — perhaps the prime factor — in achieving a revolutionary transformation of the society. When the legal victories of the civil rights movement were attained and the movement came to a fork in the road, the directions it took seemed to validate the Radical Left belief that black Americans, Puerto Ricans, Mexican Americans and American Indians — doubly exploited as victims of racism and victims of poverty — had less of a stake than anyone else in American society and were ripe for a revolutionary appeal. In the middle and late sixties, for some objective reasons (the agonizingly slow pace of economic improvement, the squalor of life in the ghetto, the apparent immutability of the welfare cycle) and for some subjective reasons (agitation by "black power" militants, the assassinations of Dr. Martin Luther King, Jr. and Robert F. Kennedy), much of black America went through a period of violence, civil disorder, confusion and a turning inward of black interests and energy toward nationalism. The result was a break-up of the civil rights coalition and the onset of a series of struggles in which blacks were pitted against white America, including many whites who until then had been participants in or supporters of the civil rights struggle. They included a large percentage of Jews.

Black nationalism, with its message of black liberation through racial consciousness, racial unity, racial separatism and unswerving hostility toward the white man, never gained the support of a majority of blacks. But it was loud and got attention, especially from the news media, whose coverage gave it a dimension that was clearly out of proportion to its influence in the black community. From racial pride to racism proved to be a short step and one after another the leaders of black nationalism, with but a few exceptions, began to espouse anti-Semitism. Sometimes it was veiled as anti-Zionism, but the camouflage was transparent since more often than not the target was not Israel but American Jews, viewed now as "exploiters" of the ghetto, whose most recent inhabitants they had been and whose continued presence, virtually alone among white Americans, was highly visible. As merchants, as landlords, as teachers and principals, as social workers and hospital personnel, Jews were seen as blocking the path to "community control" of ghetto institutions.

In this historical context the Radical Left chose to take sides against the Jews. It was not so much a matter of wanting to do battle with the Jewish community as it was a fixed determination to show the blacks, especially the most radical and nationalistic blacks, that in their struggles they could count on the total support of the revolutionary left. As viewed by the left, the outcome of all these racial struggles would be an opportunity to weaken the fiber of American society. The more blacks and other oppressed racial minorities lost confidence in the ability of the system to rectify the injustices from which they suffer, the more ripe they would become for the revolutionary ideology of the far left and the more willing they would be to act as the shock troops of revolution. As for the Jews, they were expendable. Those who were prepared to shed their Jewish identity and throw themselves into the revolutionary movement were welcome. But the great majority, the stiff-necked ones who insisted on anchoring themselves in their Jewishness and their liberalism and demanding *their* minority rights, would have to be prepared to be, in Trotsky's phrase, "swept into the dustbin of history."

Race was seen by the Radical Left as the most vulnerable aspect of American society at home; in foreign affairs the issue became the anti-imperialist struggle of the third world. Indeed, a single term, *third world peoples,* was coined to embrace the mass of humanity involved in both struggles. And just as the Jewish community was viewed as part of the enemy at home, the Jewish nation, Israel, was cast in the same role abroad. Throughout the sixties and early seventies opposition to the Vietnam war was the prime battleground of the Radical Left "anti-imperalist" struggle, with the Middle East, Latin America and Africa playing second-ary roles. With the winding down and eventual settlement of the war in Vietnam, however, the attention of the Radical Left shifted more and more toward the Middle East, where Israel and the Arab world were engaged in a desperate struggle.

The earliest signs that Israel was destined to be a major target of Radical Left hostility occurred during the 1967 Six-Day War, when the left at home, especially the Communist Party, echoed the attacks on Israel that were being leveled in the United Nations by the Soviet bloc delegates. The Soviets, of course, have a vast stake in the Arab world, and they have poured into it huge quantities of military supplies and economic assistance.

To Radical Left organizations in the United States the fact of Soviet and Chinese opposition to Israel confirmed that Israel was a redoubt of Western imperialism while the Arabs were an authentic third-world people struggling for their independence. In vain Israel's supporters pointed out that the Arab world is composed almost exclusively of military dictatorships and re-actionary feudal sheikdoms; that its people are victims of extreme exploitation and poverty; that civil liberties and workers' rights are nonexistent; that it is the Arabs and not Israel who possess the oil and wheel and deal over it with capitalists and communists alike; that the Arabs seek to eradicate Israel and not vice versa. It has been an exercise in futility to talk to the far left of Israel's virtues: that it is a haven of the oppressed and the remnants of Nazi genocide; that it is a highly democratic society; that it is governed by socialists; that its economy is dominated by the public- and worker-controlled sectors; that its wage and salary structure are the most egalitarian in the world; that it won its independence through years of anti-imperialist struggle. The Radical Left is unmoved by these truths because they are irrelevant to its concerns, which are less related to the realities of life in Israel and the Arab world than with the position of the United States in the Middle East. This is crucial for an accurate understanding of the attitude of the Radical Left toward Israel. To the far left, the backbone of world capitalism is America. To weaken and eventually destroy American influence in the world by battering it both at home and abroad is its most fundamental task and the prime requirement for the world victory of "socialism." So the Arabs are the good guys, the Israelis, the bad.

For the Jewish community anti-Semitism from the left, especially the New Left, presented serious problems. The left, in the main, had historically been friendly to Jews. At worst its solution to "the Jewish problem" had been to posit the eventual assimilation of Jews into the larger society once they had all the rights and prerogatives of others; and the left, unlike the historical right, insisted that Jews be given these rights. Liberal-left ideology was enormously compatible with the humanitarian aspects of Jewish religious tradition, with the dominant Jewish view of the world as perfectible and with the religious imperative to strive for such perfection on a daily basis both individually and collectively. Jews, therefore, although never indissolubly wed to either liberalism or conservatism, had a long history of involvement in the left-wing movements that sought to improve not only their economic, social and political position but that of all men. It was hardly a surprise, then, that large numbers of young American Jews in the fifties and sixties were attracted first to the civil rights movement and later to the New Left. Many opted out at the early signs of black nationalist and New Left hostility to American Jews and Israel—but many more did not. The result was a sharp conflict for many Jewish parents. If these parents sided with their New Left sons and daughters; if they remained actively committed to the goal of black equality even after the phenomenon of black nationalist anti-Semitism emerged, if they continued to oppose the Vietnam war arm in arm with some marchers (and often leaders) in peace demonstrations who were hostile to Israel—other Jews and Christian conservatives accused them of selling out Jewish and American interests at home and abroad. If they gave particular Jewish needs first priority the result could be, and often was, the bitter alienation of their children and the accusation alike from their children, other Jews, blacks and the white Christian liberal community that they were fair-weather friends, civil rights proponents in Selma but not in the Bronx, "hawks" on Israel *and* Vietnam. It was, and in some measure still is, an agonizing time for many American Jews; Jewish organizations, religious and secular, were wracked by division almost daily on specific problems the mere discussion of which pitted the "particularists" against the "universalists." You were for one aspect of Hillel or the other unless you strove—as did many, including all the major organizations—to keep in delicate balance the twin dicta, "If I am not for myself, who will be for me? If I am for myself alone, what am I?"

Although these debates within the Jewish community generated much heat, they failed to shed light on some historic truths, especially that Jews have never been secure in societies dominated either by the right or by the left when extremists of either wing assaulted democratic institutions or created a climate in which peaceful democratic reform was thwarted. Moreover, these debates ignored the maxim that a Jewish community divided is a Jewish community even more than usually vulnerable to the hostility of others; that in times of stress, the Jewish minority is the only one against which the majority *and* the other minorities have something in common—latent historic anti-Semitism that can quickly become a powerful political tool and is recognized as such by both the Radical Right and the Radical Left.

At least in part because of its own early failure—despite its normally sensitive antennae—to pay as much attention to the danger signals on the left as it had to those on the right, the Jewish community today, we believe, is the target of a pincers movement from both the right and the left, damned if it does and damned if it doesn't. And the pressure is being applied not alone by anti-Semitic political extremists but by many who consider themselves unbigoted, moderate liberals and conservatives.

As discussed earlier, Jews were the recipients, by and large, of an outpouring of sympathy after World War II that resulted in certain benefits, including establishment of the State of Israel and improvement in the lot of Jewish communities everywhere. But sympathy for Jews, acceptance of their accession to equal and major roles in the society, intolerance of anti-Semitism, all seem to have their limits, limits that are exceeded when the Jew is no longer perceived as victim *whether or not* that perception is accurate. In the postwar world, by any standard of measurement, the time during which the non-Jewish world continued to view Jews as oppressed was incredibly short. Within twenty-five years after the photographs of the bestiality in the concentration camps shocked the world, and while the survivors, some bearing the tattoos of Auschwitz, Dachau, Bergen-Belsen and Treblinka, were still trying to rebuild shattered lives, Jews had ceased being victims. Not only were they perceived as not suffering to any great degree, but the minuscule Jewish state had had the incredible gall to prevail three times—in 1948, 1956 and 1967—against the combined onslaught of neighboring Arab states and their allies in the Arab world and elsewhere. Americans and Europeans gave their admiration, sometimes unstintingly, sometimes grudgingly, to these feats and to the contributions Jews were making to the Western world in science, industry and the arts.

But something simmered just below the surface. In some quarters Israel had been severely criticized for capturing and bringing to justice the Nazi war criminal Adolph Eichmann, and a survey of American opinion shortly after the Eichmann trial showed that despite weeks of intensive television coverage in the United States of the trial, and despite generally favorable impressions of Israel's action, few Americans had absorbed even a minimum of information about who Eichmann was and what he had done. In the 1956 Sinai War, President Eisenhower had brought extreme pressure on Israel to withdraw to borders that had been established in the 1949 armistice and that had proved clearly indefensible; that withdrawal, in which Israel acquiesced, was to set the stage for the 1967 war, in which—for all the brilliance of its victory—the cost to Israel was one Israeli in three thousand, the equivalent of sixty-five thousand Americans on a proportional basis, more than the total American losses in the Vietnam War. Moreover, no sooner had Israel successfully defended itself when the world began to impose on it the novel approach that in war it is the victor who must sue for peace, that the Israelis must be forthcoming and generous, that Israel must yield to Arab demands without so much as a concession from Arab leaders that the Jewish state had a right to exist or a willingness on the part of Arab heads of government—let alone the fedayeen—to desist from their calls for Israel's destruction.

From some government leaders, some church groups and some opinion molders throughout the world—notoriously silent for the twenty years that Jordan had illegally occupied the Old City of Jerusalem and barred entry not only to Israeli Jews but to Jews from anywhere and to non-Jews who had passed through Israel—came the revived notion that perhaps Jerusalem should be internationalized after all. It was as if there were something odious about Jewish sovereignty over a historic Jewish city in which Jews had, in fact, always lived (and in which they had constituted a majority for over a century), often under conditions of severe deprivation and grave danger. That notion emanated from places as high as the American State Department and the Vatican, as well as Protestant circles that had long.had both missionary and charitable interests in the Arab world.

From the president of France—symbol of the French resistance to the wartime Nazi occupation, Israel's ally in 1956 and provider of the Mirage jets that were the backbone of Israel's air force—came a refusal to honor an agreement with Israel for additional aircraft and the supplies to service those on hand, salted with remarks about Jews generally as an "elite" and difficult group. From DeGaulle's successor came the negotiation of a deal to provide those same aircraft to one of Israel's enemies in the Arab world, Libya, with no assurance that they would not eventually come to rest in the hangars of one of the continuing combatants, Egypt. And while all this was going on, the Soviet Union—which in the aftermath of World War II had lent its enormous weight to the Israeli side in the United Nations debate that resulted in the partition of Palestine and the establishment of the state and had been among the first to recognize the infant nation—was supplying heavy military hardware to Israel's enemies and pouring calumny on her in the UN.

Why? Jews throughout the world were indeed hard put to answer the question in rational terms. No amount of sophistication about the influence of self-interest, Arab oil and other hard realities of international political life and intrigue sufficed to explain the rapidity with which major elements in the world shifted gears on the Jews, particularly where Israel was involved. The only answer that seems to fit is that Jews are tolerable, acceptable in their particularity, *only* as victims, and when their situation changes so that they are either no longer victims or appear not to be, the non-Jewish world finds this so hard to take that the effort is begun to render them victims anew.

At the same time a curious phenomenon became apparent in America—an incapacity to hold in consciousness and in conscience more than one victim at a time. No sooner had Jews won widespread sympathy because of their victimization during the Holocaust, no sooner had they begun en masse to climb the economic and social ladder, than they were replaced as principal victim and object of concern by nonwhite Americans. During the civil rights struggles of the early sixties, a subtle change began to take place in the perceptions and attitudes of many Christians, including some of the most liberal, about Jews, the Jewish community and anti-Semitism. It was almost as if the guilt among substantial elements of the Christian community over the treatment of Jews for two millenia was quickly replaced by guilt over the treatment visited upon black people for three centuries. Perhaps it was an easier sin to expiate.

To state this perception so baldly is to overstate it through oversimplification and thus to risk unfairness and a lack of charity. Yet by the early seventies it appeared that major elements of the Protestant churches, both clerical and lay, had become so preoccupied with the problems of blacks in America that they no longer considered anti-Semitism a problem at all but rather a phenomenon of the past. As majority white Americans attempted to deal with the problem of poverty linked to race, there seemed little concern for poor whites, including poor and elderly Jews trapped in increasingly hostile neighborhoods. The pecking order of victims in need of help had changed.

In the wake of the Nazi murders, the question asked by a whole people—"Where are the persecuted to go?"—was answered by the birth of the long-promised Jewish state. In the quarter century since, Jewish communities the world over, and individual Jews whether Zionist or non-Zionist, have acquired a deep and abiding commitment to the survival of Israel. Throughout the Diaspora, Jews believe that whatever legitimate controversies may exist in the Middle East and whatever legitimately differing viewpoints there may be between Israeli and Arab, Israel's continued existence as a sovereign Jewish state is absolutely nonnegotiable. Statements and propaganda manifestoes calling for the destruction or dissolution of Israel, or equating Israeli defense with Arab assault, are seen by Jews as attacks against themselves and world Jewry and, along with other activities supporting those sworn to destroy Israel, are perceived as the ultimate anti-Semitism.

Of course one can be unsympathetic to or oppose Israel's position on specific issues without being anti-Jewish. But many of the anti-Israel statements from non-Jewish sources, often the most respectable, carry an undeniable anti-Jewish message. Some of the public utterances that pass for legitimate discussion mask a real hostility to Jews as Jews; they are often couched in language or contain innuendo that is plainly anti-Semitic.

But gratuitous and illegitimate assaults on Israel—whether they contain true anti-Semitism or betray a gross insensitivity to the profound meaning of Israel to Jews everywhere—provoke Jewish anger and awaken the ancient Jewish anxieties. For excepting the Jewish religion itself, Israel represents the greatest hope and the deepest commitment embraced by world Jewry in two millenia. Just as Israel's survival depends in substantial measure on support from Jews in the United States and elsewhere, Jews in the Diaspora have come to feel that their own security and the only hope for their survival as a people, in a world from which anti-Semitism has never disappeared, depends in large measure on the survival of Israel.

On October 6, 1973—Yom Kippur 5734, the holiest and most solemn day of the Jewish year—Israel's survival was imperiled as never before in the twenty-five years of its modern existence. Armed with the most modern equipment in the arsenal of their Soviet patrons, Egypt and Syria had struck hard blows against

Israeli forces occupying the east bank of the Suez canal and the treacherous Golan Heights, from which, prior to 1967, Syrian artillery had rained down a merciless barrage on Israeli civilian farms and settlements. Within hours, Israel was at war for the fourth time in twenty-five years. And the issue was not, as the attackers were soon to claim, the regaining of occupied territory. It was most clearly and most frighteningly the existence of Israel.

We have outlined the major contents of this book, an inspection of genuine anti-Semitism around the world emanating from some old and some very new and unexpected sources, much of it having distinct political overtones, and a hard look at the negative influence of recent events on the thinking and action of respectable elements in regard to Jews.

The latter, as we have indicated—the respectable community—presents the larger problem; its indifference or antipathy to Jews and Jewish concerns is far more subtle than the blatant forms of anti-Semitism and religious discrimination against which the Jewish community long ago constructed firm defenses, and far more rooted in self-righteousness. It was one thing to "get away with" not hiring a Jew, as too much of corporate America once did; in the positive atmosphere that followed the Holocaust, even when such discrimination persisted it was accompanied by a modicum of guilt or at very least a sense of being out of step with the times. If the times now dictate, among influential sectors of the public everywhere, that Jews are expendable in the name of some high moral purpose; if Jews are now perceived as *legitimate* objects of criticism, scorn and calumny; if Jewish concerns are not regarded at least on a par with those of other minorities—we have either returned to an old and vicious form of scapegoating or there is something very new and potentially very dangerous at hand.

In either case, there is an obligation to alert the Jewish community and the general public. For only when the full information is made available—and the full pattern emerges—can persons of good will here and abroad call a halt to this fresh injustice against history's favorite victim.

2

Gerald Smith's
Road

"Gerald L. K. Smith! My God, I thought he was dead! I remember hearing about him in the forties." But Gerald Smith is, at this writing, alive and well, successfully promoting tourist attractions in Eureka Springs, Arkansas.

This is not the life story of Mr. Smith. It is the story of the corruption of a town, the gullibility of substantial elements of the press and the willingness of government officials to aid in the promotion of bigotry.

A minister and pastor in Shreveport, Louisiana, in the twenties, Gerald Lyman Kenneth Smith in the succeeding decade became an ally of Huey Long, of William Dudley Pelley, head of the native fascist Silver Shirt Movement, and of Charles E. Coughlin, the Jew-baiting "radio priest." Smith has been teacher, mentor or associate of most of the important anti-Jewish propagandists of the past forty years and since 1941 has led the so-called Christian Nationalist Crusade, now headquartered in Los Angeles, a movement that has long defiled the message of brotherhood preached by Jesus.

In 1942 Smith began publishing *The Cross and the Flag*, now America's oldest, most virulent hate publication. Through it he has pumped into the body politic all the ancient poisons employed by anti-Semites throughout the world, including the notorious *Protocols of the Elders of Zion* (a forgery conceived by czarist secret police officials at the turn of the century which set forth a purported Jewish plot by a nonexistant group for world domination, the *Protocols* were spread by like-minded bigots everywhere and were employed as a major propaganda weapon by Joseph Goebbels during the Hitler nightmare in Germany). And although Jew-baiting is its chief topic, Smith's magazine constantly reveals a noxious, racist hatred of black people; according to its November 1966 issue, for example, Negroes are "fundamentally an inferior race" which, without whites, would never have "got past the loin cloth or the G-string."

Smith has been denounced for three decades or more by liberals and conservatives alike, by newspapers and magazines from coast to coast and by political leaders of all parties. In 1944 Governor Thomas E. Dewey of New York, who became the Republican presidential candidate later that year, said publicly:

> The Gerald L. K. Smiths and their ilk must not for one moment be permitted to pollute the stream of American political life. Such would be a betrayal of the sacrifice now being made on the battlefields of the world by millions of Americans who fight for the basic principles which these rodents would undermine.[1]

In 1956, when Smith attempted to attach himself to the vice-presidential campaign of incumbent Richard M. Nixon, the vice-president asserted that there was "no place in the Republican Party for race-baiting merchandisers of hate like Gerald L. K. Smith."[2] And the Manchester (New Hampshire) *Union Leader,* one of the nation's leading ultraconservative dailies, editorialized on March 14, 1969 that Smith was "a man who symbolizes everything all good Americans detest." The *Union Leader* added that it deplored "this man's un-American, anti-Semitic rabble-rousing with all the indignation we can muster." (All this, of course, rolled off Gerald Smith; in November 1972, in a fund-raising letter to his supporters, he was still retorting: "Anti-Semitism, you know, is a vicious word invented by the Jews to describe people who are alert to their machinations.")

It was with shock and disbelief, therefore, that the American Jewish community in mid-November 1969 read news stories announcing a federal grant of $182,000 for the construction of part of a road leading directly to the tourist projects—including an anti-Semitic Passion play—sponsored by Gerald Smith in Eureka Springs. Gerald L. K. Smith, spurned and ostracized by decent people for decades, was to be the recipient of U.S. government largesse. It was inconceivable to most people, but less so to those who had been watching with growing concern the acceptance of Smith by the good Arkansans of Eureka Springs.

Over the decades Smith had developed his propaganda activities into a lucrative business operation that in some years brought as much as a third of a million dollars into the coffers of his so-called Crusade. He maintained a home in Tulsa and one in the Los Angeles area and lived in style, traveling around the country first class, usually with an entourage and often accompanied by his wife, Elna. In 1964, nearing age 66, Smith bought a Victorian home, and later arranged for the purchase of 167 acres of land in Eureka Springs, a beautiful little mountain town in the Ozarks that had been a health spa in the 1890s and that retains to this day the architecture and atmosphere of the Victorian era. Its population of 2,000 included a substantial proportion of elderly people. Smith arranged the deal through a dummy buyer, Charles F. Robertson of Los Angeles, who announced that he was acting for a committee of citizens around the United States interested in erecting a statue to be called the *Christ of the Ozarks.* Robertson was nothing but a front for Smith, whom he had long served as an assistant, and for the Elna M. Smith Foundation, a tax-exempt body Smith set up and named for his wife and which was to be the official sponsor of the *Christ of the Ozarks* undertaking.[3]

Adroitly using the local weekly newspaper, the Eureka Springs *Times-Echo,* as an outlet for a series of press releases, "progress reports" and "open letters" on the *Christ of the Ozarks* project, the Elna M. Smith Foundation—i.e., Gerald Smith—began a subtle and highly successful campaign to undercut potential opposition to the venture, a campaign that built a substantial degree of acceptance for the "sacred project." Constantly emphasizing the spiritual aspects of his plans and promising to avoid commercialism in connection with the statue, Smith nevertheless dangled attractive economic bait before the citizens of genteel, refined, down-at-the-heels Eureka Springs. In one "progress report," dutifully printed by the *Times-Echo*, Smith, vowing to eschew "gross commercialism" as a sacrilege, went on to say: "It is believed and hoped that thousands of people will visit in Eureka Springs just to see the statue, and if this has a constructive influence in the normal business operations of the community all concerned with the statue will be happy."[4]

A few months after the mountaintop acreage had been purchased, the Arkansas *Gazette*—whose consistently forthright coverage of Smith and his activities in Eureka Springs has been a lonely example of journalism at its best—published an article headlined "Christ of the Ozarks Statue Is Project of Anti-Semite Gerald L. K. Smith,"[5] Smith countered with letters to the Little Rock daily and an "open letter" printed by the *Times-Echo*. On behalf of Mrs. Smith and himself, he wrote:

> My life has been a very controversial life. . . . It struck us that nothing could bring us more joy during the sunset days of our lives than to pay tribute to our Lord and Saviour Jesus Christ. . . . It would be sinful and unrefined and un-Christian and un-American for anyone to use such a sacred project to promote any controversial activity.[6]

Smith's skillful public relations campaign worked. By the spring of 1965 it was clear that most citizens of Eureka Springs were not sufficiently concerned about anti-Semitism or Smith's long and notorious record as an anti-Jewish and racist propagandist to oppose his plans, let alone mount a campaign against them or against Smith himself. Many in the local business community and the Eureka Springs Chamber of Commerce saw Smith's "sacred project" as a magnet for the influx of tourists and business for which Eureka Springs had waited half a century.

Astutely spreading their business among the local merchants, purveyors and entrepreneurs, the Smiths soon became part of the scenery as leading citizens of the Springs, while their "sacred project" went forward. The *Time-Echo* contributed to the seduction of its community, offering not a word of criticism and compliantly publishing the canned "progress reports" and publicity handouts manufactured by Smith. Like the Eureka Springs weekly, newspapers in neighboring states, reporting on the statue's construction, identified Smith—when they bothered to do so at all—as merely a "controversial" personality on the American scene in bygone years who had been "accused" of anti-Semitism. None pointed out that Smith was doing much of his anti-Semitic writing for *The Cross and the Flag* then and there in Eureka Springs.

In the summer of 1966 the *Christ of the Ozarks*—seven stories high, with arms outstretched in a span of sixty-five feet and folds of garments fifteen feet deep—was dedicated. Erected of white reinforced concrete (and once described as a "giant milk carton with head and arms"),[7] the statue is floodlighted at night and the atmosphere is reinforced by recorded religious music and hymns. Smith and his wife have announced that they plan to be buried beneath the statue. And while Smith has kept his word to avoid crass commercialism at the statue, visitors are asked to sign a guest book, after which they receive follow-up mail solicitations seeking contributions to the maintenance and upkeep of the statue and the site.

But by 1969 the statue itself was only one of several "sacred projects" initiated by Smith in Eureka Springs. There was, in addition, the "Christ Only Art Gallery." And on July 14, 1968, on one of the Smith Foundation's three mountaintops, there opened a unique Smith version of the centuries-old Passion play, detailing Jesus' last week on earth and the Crucifixion. For the occasion Smith renamed the mountain Mount Oberammergau after the Bavarian village where the Passion play was first presented in 1634 and where it has been staged for a season every ten years since, despite the increasing postwar chorus of protest by people everywhere about its anti-Semitic content.

Smith's "Great Passion Play"—viewed from a natural amphitheater seating 3,000 persons—is presented annually for some one hundred performances between late May and October. It is played on a huge stage containing giant reproductions of New Testament points of reference in Jerusalem during Passion Week, and there are dressing rooms for a cast of some two-to-three hundred persons, many of them recruited from the local citizenry of Eureka Springs. There are live horses, donkeys and several camels. "Invitations" to contribute $1,000 to the creation of the Smith Passion play were sent across the country by the Elna M.

Smith Foundation, the official sponsor. The invitations said that donors would have their names engraved on a plaque; potential contributors were reminded that the foundation enjoys tax exemption.

And once more Gerald and Elna Smith engaged in the economic seduction of their community that had earlier proved so effective. In an "open letter" to the *Times-Echo,* while the Passion play production was in its early stages, they wrote:

> One million people have visited the Christ of the Ozarks statue since it was dedicated on June 25, 1966. What will the motels and hotels do when the Passion Play opens and we release at 11 p.m. on Mount Oberammergau from 2,000 to 5,000 people for 100 nights during the summer . . . ?"[8]

By the 1960s many Christians of good will had recognized that Passion plays have caused great harm to Jews over the centuries. Even when presented with sensitivity and understanding they tend to perpetuate the deicide myth that portrays the Jews as "Christ killers," the root cause of anti-Semitism. In many parts of the world where the Passion play is still presented the script has been corrected to eliminate or soften the anti-Jewish overtones. In February 1968—just months before Smith's "Great Passion Play" opened in Eureka Springs—the secretariat for Catholic-Jewish Relations of the United States Conference of Catholic Bishops had cautioned in a formal statement against the kind of presentation which culminated in a pageant of anti-Semitism. The secretariat warned, for example, against highlighting the controversial line from Matthew in which the crowd before the governor's palace calls for the crucifixion of Jesus, roaring "His blood be upon us and our children." This passage, often quoted by those who would pervert Scripture to justify anti-Semitism, appears only in Matthew—not in the Gospels according to Mark, Luke or John. Nonetheless it had for centuries been emphasized in the script of the original anti-Semitic Oberammergau Passion play.

It was utterly predictable that the script of the Smith Passion play in Eureka Springs would be based on the Oberammergau version, that it would include the line from Matthew (and others that have no Scriptural basis at all) and that it would be redolent with all the other ancient anti-Jewish overtones, including blood-thirsty mob scenes, that have stained the history of Passion plays through the ages. In a perceptive editorial, headlined "In the Name of Jesus and Gerald Smith," published on July 14, 1968, the day Smith's Passion play opened in Eureka Springs, the Arkansas *Gazette* commented:

> Unfortunately for whatever spiritual good might have come out of a religious spectacle of this sort, the script used in the Oberammergau Play has come under increasingly heavy fire in recent years for its part in perpetuating the hateful image of the Jews as being, before anything else, the "killers of Christ." It is the image that from advance indications given by the producer-Christus of the Eureka Springs production—Robert Hyde—will be perpetuated at Eureka, albeit at a level somewhat less elevated than that of Oberammergau —topographically and in every other way. Questioned about changes in prospect for the Oberammergau text, Mr. Hyde would respond only in the cryptic language that "no Committee is going to get me to revise the New Testament."
>
> The new ecumenicity taught by good Pope John has had as a specific goal the purging of any vestigial emphasis upon the Jews as "Christ killers" from the body of Church ritual and from the curricula of the schools in countries . . . where Roman Catholicism is the dominant religion.
>
> It is against this kind of background of world opinion that Eureka Springs embarks today upon its latest adventure in the name jointly of Jesus Christ and Gerald L. K. Smith, the most notorious anti-Semite in America.

By the summer of 1969, after only its first season, the "Great Passion Play" emerged as the most important—and since admissions of $2, $3 and $4 were charged, the most lucrative—of Smith's "sacred projects" in Eureka Springs. By 1973, despite that fact that it had been termed an "atrocity" by at least one Christian clergy-man-journalist who had seen it during the 1972 season,[9] the pageant had become one of Arkansas' top tourist attractions—along with "Dogpatch, U.S.A."

In a comprehensive 1969 *New Yorker* article on Eureka Springs and the Smiths, Calvin Trillin listed the signs of acceptance of

Smith in the community; local high-school girls handed out literature on the Passion play at the booth where visitors registered when viewing the statue; most of the town's stores displayed the same literature as well as reprints of Smith's newspaper advertisements for the play; souvenir programs were for sale at the desk in a local hotel, along with a book on the "sacred projects" by Smith himself. Smith's aide, Charles Robertson (who is listed as editor of the anti-Semitic *The Cross and the Flag*), was elected to the Board of the Eureka Springs Chamber of Commerce, which advertised the Passion play in its brochures and directed Girl Scout groups and Sunday school classes to the box office; Robertson was also named by the mayor to the Town Planning Commission. Gerald Smith appeared before the Lions and the Rotary clubs; Mrs. Smith spoke to the Women's Club; Robertson was able to mobilize support for a testimonial tendered to Smith for his contributions to the town. As for the anti-Semitic Passion play itself, Trillin noted that it was not even an issue in Eureka Springs:

> People in Eureka Springs either do not make the connection between the Passion play and Smith's other activities or have made the connection and prefer to put it out of their minds. It is not unusual for people who refer to Smith as a hatemonger to appear occasionally or even regularly in the Passion play—because its success means business for the town or because "it's something to do." The use of townspeople in the play is sometimes discussed in Eureka Springs as a way to keep teen-agers off the streets in the summertime or a way of giving retired people some activity and a little extra money. (Those who appear receive a share of the gate receipts for themselves or charity—a share that amounts to little more than a token but provides *Times-Echo* headlines like "$2,000 HAS BEEN DISTRIBUTED TO LOCAL CHURCHES AND TO CHARITIES.")[10]

The corruption of Eureka Springs by Smith was pervasive, but it was not universal. Here and there was a voice of dissent. A plan by the Smith Foundation to have the churches furnish the actors for the play and receive the actors' share of the gate was politely turned down by the Ministerial Alliance. The Alliance likewise did not officially sponsor the 1969 Easter sunrise service at the *Christ of the Ozarks* statue—although some ministers took part as individuals. The first public opposition in the town—some five years after the Smiths had arrived in Eureka Springs—was from a plucky fifty-eight-year-old widow, Mrs. Georgia Ziffzer, who operated a dress and gift shop downstairs in her Eureka Springs home and who was treasurer of the Chamber of Commerce. In October 1969, when the Chamber voted 10 to 2 to honor the Smiths for their contribution "to the life, prosperity and prominence of the community," Mrs. Ziffzer, who had objected to the proposed resolution and lost, resigned her post. Her stand triggered expressions of support, both private and public. But the 10-to-2 vote in the Chamber of Commerce was more revealing of Eureka Springs' general sentiment.

Like the good mountain villagers of West Germany's Oberammergau, who have steadfastly resisted efforts to change the script of their commercially successful Passion play to eliminate its anti-Semitism—and perhaps like the other good Germans of an earlier day who went about their business while another fascist anti-Semite went about his—most of the good Arkansans of Eureka Springs just cannot bring themselves to reject Gerald L. K. Smith.

In November 1969 it became clear that Eureka Springs acquiesced in Gerald Smith's anti-Semitism—because his "sacred projects" were significant to the economic growth and expansion of the town. This view was shared at increasingly higher levels of government, reaching through Carroll County, Arkansas; the Arkansas State Highway Department; the Ozarks Regional Commission, a four-state body created by the United States Department of Commerce; and the Bureau of Public Roads of the United States Department of Transportation. Agreeing with it in substantial measure were, in addition to numerous lesser officials, the late Winthrop Rockefeller, then governor of Arkansas, the then-Secretary of Commerce Maurice H. Stans and Senators John McClellan and J. William Fulbright and Representative John Paul Hammerschmidt, all of Arkansas.

Their specific focus at this time was a proposal—germinated in 1968 when Smith's Passion play was first presented to the public—to rebuild about two and a half miles of a county road, Route 1226, leading to the site of the statue and the anti-Semitic Passion play peddled by Smith. The proposal called for an outlay of some

$227,000 in public funds to improve the road, in the name of promoting more tourism, more jobs and the economic development of the depressed area of Eureka Springs. The new stretch of road, of course, would make it easier for tourists to reach the "sacred projects," which—it later became clear—would be the main, perhaps the only direct beneficiary. The plan called for Carroll County to put up $45,000 (20 percent) of the total; for the Ozarks Regional Commission of the Department of Commerce to supply some $68,000 (30 percent), and for the Department of Transportation's Bureau of Public Roads to contribute the remaining $114,000 (50 percent) under the usual 50-50 "matching funds" formula. A total of $182,000 in federal funds was therefore involved, 80 percent of the whole.

The original application to the Ozarks Regional Commission was filed in November 1968—just after the Passion play had finished its first season—by Carroll County Judge Arthur Carter, the county administrator. It was approved by the Arkansas State Highway Department, certified and recommended for federal funding by the State of Arkansas—Governor Rockefeller asserting that it would contribute to the development of the region in his state[11]—and endorsed by the governor's alternate on the Ozarks Regional Commission, Dr. John Peterson. The parlay of public funding for the improvement of Route 1226 was completed in November 1969, when the Transportation Department's Bureau of Public Roads and the Ozarks Regional Commission of the Commerce Department approved the federal grants.

The approval was announced on November 10, 1969 in Washington by Representative Hammerschmidt, from nearby Harrison in neighboring Boone County, Arkansas. United Press International reported the story. Two weeks later, on November 25, syndicated Washington columnist Jack Anderson published the first of several columns denouncing the federal grant. After outlining the details Anderson wrote:

> Instead of the love-thy-neighbor rule taught by Christ, Smith preaches racial and religious bigotry of the most ugly brand.
>
> It is inconceivable that the federal government didn't know who was behind the Eureka Springs project. The literature on the seven-

story high "Christ of the Ozarks" states plainly that the million-pound statue was "originated and instigated by Gerald L. K. Smith, husband of Elna M. Smith." Smith's hate-spouting editor, Charles Robertson, is listed as "coordinator."

Yet without a trace of shame, the Commerce Department announced that the $182,000 in federal funds "will help stimulate growth in tourism and create new jobs."

Anderson's widely-read column triggered a public controversy. The Anti-Defamation League demanded publicly that the Departments of Commerce and Transportation rescind the award as "an outrageous expenditure of taxpayers' money." The ADL asserted that the United States government "should not be a partner to a man whose business has been spreading racial and religious bigotry for more than 30 years."[12] A month later ADL sent a telegram to President Nixon urging him to instruct Secretaries Volpe and Stans to stop the federal funding for the project.[13]

Defending his endorsement of the road project in a public statement a few weeks after the storm broke, Governor Winthrop Rockefeller said his decision to approve the project was based on "traffic counts and other economic data" and that its purpose was to support "the economic growth of the area." He contended that it was not the job of the Ozarks Regional Commission, of which he was a member, to "pass judgment on the political, racial and religious views of either Mr. Smith or the many tourists who use the public roads to get to his attractions." Governor Rockefeller did not claim ignorance of Smith or of his record of bigotry; indeed, he noted that he personally and over many years had disapproved of Smith's philosophy and activities. But the Regional Commission, Rockefeller claimed, could not take into consideration whether Smith's programs were good or bad. "Beyond the question of legality, that is not the government's business," the governor said.[14] A week later, contending that the Arkansas *Gazette* had not reported his full views, Governor Rockefeller, in a letter to the editor, asserted that "when government gets into the business of approving or disapproving of projects on the basis of whether it agrees with every enterprise that might benefit, then the kind of government I believe in and I hope the kind of government you believe in is on the road to ruin."[15] Governor Rockefeller did not indicate what kind of road that government was on which went into the business of financing anti-Semites (nor did he acknowledge that the "road to ruin" in this particular instance might well be paved with government funds). Moreover, Mr. Rockefeller either failed to see or chose not to state the distinction even the most ardent of civil libertarians draw: that there is a difference between acknowledging Gerald Smith's rights to his private beliefs and private projects, abhor them though we may, and supporting him and them with public funds in clear violation of established public policy.

But the late governor was not alone in failing to draw the distinction. The responses from Washington to the controversy over the road project stressed only that the federal grants were legally and procedurally unassailable; that all necessary guidelines and criteria for funding had been met, and that all the procedural rules and regulations had been observed. The federal agencies directly involved developed form letters and by January 1970 these standardized replies were being mailed to the hundreds of people who had protested to Washington.

The Ozarks Regional Commission of the Department of Commerce, which froze its 30 percent of the funding "pending a complete review of the charges," completed its investigation and found no reason to change its mind. On January 6, 1970 it released its share of the funds and made public a study of "Facts and Conclusions" with respect to the project purporting to justify its decision. Its fact sheet said, in part:

> 1. The project in question involves the repaving and regrading of an existing county road, Route 1226, which already serves as a schoolbus and mail route.
>
> 2. The roadway is part of the federal aid secondary system and links U.S. Highway 62 with Arkansas Highway 23 (North).
>
> 3. Funding for the project is being supplied by the U.S. Bureau of Public Roads (50%), the Ozarks Regional Commission (30%) and Carroll County, Arkansas (20%).
>
> 4. The need for repaving is occasioned by the fact that the road is

heavily traveled by visitors desiring to see the statue and play operated by the Elna M. Smith Foundation.

5. The road is an entirely public thoroughfare and does not enter private property at any point along the right of way.

6. None of the federal money in question will go to the Foundation, nor will it be used to improve property owned by the Foundation.

7. The Foundation expends all of its revenues for maintenance and operation of the projects. No monies are diverted to any outside activities.

8. The road repaving is a response to an already high volume of traffic on a presently unsafe and dangerous public road.[16]

In a discussion of the background of the project, the Ozarks Regional Commission report observed that "Eureka Springs is in a distressed area and desperately needs a sustaining industry," that the "entire Beaver Lake area relies on tourism and the Elna M. Smith Foundation projects form one of the central tourist attractions for the area." It added that "the justification offered for this project was that the road is a heavily traveled tourist route for visitors desiring to see the statue 'Christ of the Ozarks' and to attend the Passion Play."

As to the "Religious Activities of Gerald L. K. Smith," the Ozarks Regional Commission pleaded ignorance of Smith's connection with the project and with the Smith Foundation and claimed that "the federal staff had no reason to inquire into the background of the Foundation since the public road to be improved did not enter the property of that Foundation." Moreover, said the Commission, such an inquiry could only have dealt with "construction details" of the road project "since we are advised that the First Amendment to the Constitution prohibits a Federal agency from weighing the *religious affiliation* of any person in deciding whether to grant federal funds." [Italics added.] The Commission concluded:

> The overriding consideration . . . in declining to withdraw funds from the project on the grounds that Mr. Smith will enjoy some collateral benefit is the Commission's belief that such a withdrawal is contrary to the principles of the First Amendment. . . . Although

the Commission strongly condemns the intolerant views publicly
espoused by Mr. Smith, it does not feel that the objectionable nature
of these beliefs can serve as a basis for rejecting a needed public
project.

Much the same position—that the road would only incidentally
help the Smith projects, that economic aid to the area was para-
mount and that, in any event, the First Amendment precluded
withdrawal of the funds—was taken by Commerce Secretary Stans.
Responding to a letter that had asked him to rescind the grant,
Stans wrote:

> In reaching its initial decision to assist in funding this project, the
> Ozarks Regional Commission was concerned solely with benefitting
> the inhabitants of Eureka Springs in a manner calculated to enhance
> their economic life. . . . The fact that this project may also benefit
> a facility associated with Gerald L. K. Smith was not a factor in the
> original decision and cannot be a basis for a reversal of the grant.
> As was noted in the formal statement of the Ozarks Regional Com-
> mission, the First Amendment prohibits any other position.[17]

(On the First Amendment question alone, neither the Commission nor Secretary Stans paid heed to the authoritative and exactly
contrary position of the American Civil Liberties Union of
Arkansas. The ACLU, without even considering the question of
Smith's anti-Semitism and the propriety of government funds in
support of it, found the award of public funds in aid of the "sacred
projects" an unconstitutional violation on its face of the First
Amendment's prohibition against the establishment of religion.
In mid-December the Arkansas ACLU announced that if the
grants were not rescinded, it would file suit in federal court to
stop them and asserted:

> All of the available evidence indicates that the sole reason for paving
> the road is to improve access to the so-called "sacred projects" of
> Gerald L. K. Smith or the Elna M. Smith Foundation—the Christ
> of the Ozarks statue and the Passion play. Using public money for
> such a purpose violates the First Amendment prohibition against
> the establishment of religion and is contrary to the vital principle
> of separation of church and state. . . . The ACLU position is simply

that Smith has every right to run his projects without any governmental interference, but the public also has a right to see to it that public money is not used to support religious activities.[18]

For its part, the Bureau of Public Roads of the Transportation Department—supplying 50 percent of the road funds—sent out responses to its critics that avoided the whole issue of the use of government funds to aid an anti-Jewish bigot and dealt only with the Bureau's impeccable adherence to proper procedure in approving its share of the $182,000.[19]

To the indifference of the governor of Arkansas and numerous federal officials must be added the uninspiring performance of many members of the U.S. Senate and House when confronted with constituent complaints about the federal grant. Many congressmen routinely forwarded inquiries and protests to the federal agencies involved and then relayed back to their constituents the "fact sheets" and other self-serving justifications prepared by the bureaucracy. Covering letters usually stated that the elected official had no use for Gerald Smith or his views but that the government grants for the access road appeared to have been legally approved and allocated. Few members of Congress expressed any great outrage; the exceptions were five House members from Pennsylvania who co-signed a letter to Transportation Secretary Volpe objecting to the federal government's participation in the road project.[20]

Senator McClellan of Arkansas said "the road was approved on the basis of its potentially favorable economic impact and the general importance it will have to the overall development of tourism in the section of Arkansas, rather than a special interest project to benefit the Gerald L. K. Smith enterprises."[21] His colleague from Arkansas, Senator J. William Fulbright, wrote a constituent: "While I do not agree with the views expressed over the years by Gerald L. K. Smith, the need for improved roads in Carroll County exists without regard to the benefits which may accrue to those wishing to visit the Christ of the Ozarks statue."[22] Representative Hammerschmidt, representing the district involved—who had originally stated that he had "never met" Gerald Smith and disavowed any knowledge of Smith's activities[23]—replied to a letter writer:

> I can well understand your concern because I assume your impressions have largely been from one of the writers of a state newspaper as well as those of a national columnist, most likely inspired by the same source. However, in both instances they are commenting about a personality whose activities have been well known for a long time. I will also add that through the years this man's effort to peddle hate have been completely ineffective and it is unfortunate he is now receiving much undue publicity.[24]

It soon became clear that federal officials had been seriously misinformed about the basic facts surrounding the project. On March 8, 1970 the Arkansas *Gazette* published a long article, date-lined Eureka Springs, by reporter Ginger Shiras, who had conducted a detailed, on-the-spot investigation and found the road improvement project to be "not exactly what the public has been led to believe."

The project did not involve the mere repaving of "an existing county road"; the existing county road did not serve as a school bus route; Route 1226 was not, as claimed, a needed link between U.S. 62 and State Highway 23, because they intersected just two miles away; the existing road was not an entirely public thoroughfare, as claimed, but would be built across land belonging to the Elna M. Smith Foundation and one Mrs. Joyce Harvey, as well as on land owned by the city and the county. (This fact also cast serious doubt on the Commission's assertion, in its report, that "none of the federal money in question . . . will be used to improve property owned by the Foundation.") Finally, the traffic figures used in the application for federal funds—and cited by the Ozarks Regional Commission in its "Facts and Conclusions" —had been supplied by the Smith Foundation itself.

In short, the entire road project—using $182,000 in federal funds—was aimed at moving traffic swiftly and smoothly to and through Smith's "sacred projects" on two to three miles of paved road, some of it new construction. The road was to be rerouted to suit Smith's convenience and accommodate his Foundation and its projects.

As the winter of 1970 turned to spring, the sustained public protest by syndicated column writer Jack Anderson and the staff of the Arkansas *Gazette,* with its superb reporting and hard-hitting editorial campaign, began to have an effect. In a letter, Secretary Volpe declared:

> . . . No Federal funds have been released for, nor have I approved construction of, this project.
> We are obtaining additional information concerning traffic volumes presently using this roadway. In the meantime I have instructed my General Counsel to review the legality of using Federal funds for this project. . . .
> As soon as my General Counsel has submitted his views, I will render a decision in this matter.[25]

Not long thereafter several Arkansas newspapers that had been either sympathetic or not opposed to the road project began to take another view. The editor of the *Mountain Echo,* published in Yellville, Arkansas, asserted it was time the Eureka Springs road project was held up "until the whole thing is laid out in the open so it can honestly be evaluated." He added that "the existing road should be improved but with the public in mind—not Gerald L. K. Smith." The *Northwest Arkansas Times,* published at Fayetteville, observed that while tourists did flock to Smith's exhibits and the existing road was inadequate, there was "some doubt as to how vital the proposed route is to mail, school bus and normal commerce, which are reasons given in justification of the federal funding." The editorial went on: "There's additional doubt, too, that Gerald L. K. Smith's connection with the affair is savory for many Americans, to say nothing of Arkansans."[26]

But the clearest indication of change in the climate came from Gerald Smith, who on April 30 delivered himself of a shrill "open letter" to residents of Eureka Springs. He denounced attacks on the "sacred projects," blaming them on "the lethal enemies of Jesus Christ." He charged that "these Christ-hating enemies" were engaged in a "vicious attempt to destroy us" and that "a handful of people in Eureka Springs" had "joined with enemies from outside. . . ."[27] In a more subdued letter to the *Gazette* Smith falsely described his Passion play as "a perfect repetition of the account given in Matthew, Mark, Luke and John" and

clcsed with the kind of divisive tactic he has employed for decades
to pit Christian against Jew:

> In a nation where the overwhelming majority of the people are in
> the Christian tradition, why should people be denied normal trans-
> portation comforts who desire to view these magnificent tributes
> to our Lord Jesus Christ.[28]

Smith's letter to the *Gazette* was addressed from Los Angeles,
where he publishes his magazine and prepares his tracts and
pamphlets blaming Jews for all the world's ills.

Late in May 1970 reports began to circulate in Washington
that Secretary Volpe was about to cancel the grant of public funds
by the U.S. Bureau of Public Roads for the road project in Eureka
Springs. The word quickly reached Smith, who journeyed to
Little Rock, called one of his rare news conferences, announced
the death of the project himself and blamed it on a "conspiracy"
of "organized Jews." He told reporters he had retained counsel
to prepare a lawsuit and that a petition to the Department of
Justice would call for an investigation of the "conspiracy," which,
he charged, had deprived him of his individual civil rights.[29]
Smith's attorney filed such a petition on June 30; it was rejected
some weeks later by Assistant Attorney General Jerris Leonard,
who wrote Smith the Department's conclusion that "there are no
grounds for any action on the part of this department."[30]

Secretary Volpe's decision was made public on June 20, 1970.
A spokesman said that on the basis of a review conducted over a
period of months, it had been determined that the federal funding
should be withdrawn because the rebuilding of Route 1226 in
Arkansas was "a marginal project at best."[31]

The decision, however, ended neither the debate about Gerald
Smith and his road nor the episodes of his clear and present anti-
Semitism.

Dissatisfaction with Secretary Volpe's decision was aired on
the Arkansas political scene, where a primary contest for the
Democratic gubernatorial nomination was in full swing when the
decision was announced. One of the candidates, former Governor
Orval E. Faubus, paid a visit to Smith's projects in mid-June,

accompanied by his family and guests. Fulsome in his praise for the statue, the Passion play and the art gallery, Governor Faubus told the *Times-Echo:*

> No matter what happens, if that new road is not built before I am elected Governor, it will be built after I am elected Governor. These millions of people who come to see these sacred projects and who come to visit the beautiful Eureka Springs area deserve to be taken care of with proper highway construction. . . . The idea of cancelling the building of a highway because of the religion of one man who lives in the community is the most ridiculous violation of civil rights that I have ever seen.[32]

There is supreme irony in the statement by Governor Faubus, who more than a decade earlier barricaded the school doors and necessitated the entry of federal troops into Little Rock to enforce the Supreme Court's school desegregation order—complaining of a "violation of civil rights."

Nor did Secretary Volpe's decision put an end to efforts on behalf of the road project. Some months later Senator McClellan apparently indicated that he would confer with Volpe about reviewing the whole road project.[33] And in a letter to a constituent he wrote that he did not support the project for Smith's benefit, nor did he agree "with much of his philosophy," but because of "the favorable effect in terms of personal income to local residents and the safety factor of an improved highway which carries what appears to be an increasing volume of heavy traffic to tourist sites in and around Eureka Springs."[34]

About the same time, in October 1970, Judge Carter of Carroll County, who had filed the original application for the federal funding, wrote to Senator McClellan asking his assistance in securing approval of the road project. Apparently the county administrator thought his position still had enough viability among the citizens of Eureka Springs to be politically beneficial to him. His letter to Senator McClellan was printed as an advertisement for his reelection in the *Times-Echo* with the tag line: "—Pol. adv. paid for by Arthur Carter."[35]

The acceptance accorded Smith by Eureka Springs and the posture of most of the government figures involved in the road project helped to clothe the aging Jew-baiter in an aura of semi-respectability he had not enjoyed during his entire career as a rabble-rousing merchant of hate. And if he had suffered a defeat on the road project, Smith did not seem at all fazed by it. After a year had passed and the road controversy had blown over he announced a grandiose new "sacred project," a "Holy Land" replica that would reconstruct some of the places Jesus had lived in and visited, the project to cost "more than $100,000" and construction to take anywhere from five to ten years.[36]

Announcement during 1971 of the new project generated a number of feature articles in the respectable media—the Associated Press, for example, and such leading newspapers as the St. Louis *Post-Dispatch*, the Kansas City *Star*, the *New York Times* and other prominent dailies. In content and tone the articles tended to gloss over, ever so lightly, Smith's four decades as a vitriolic hate propagandist, painting him in a generally positive image, depicting the tourism he had attracted as having "saved" Eureka Springs and, on balance, enhancing—even while they reported it—the climate of acceptance Smith had built during the late sixties.

The Associated Press feature, written by John R. Starr, appeared in various newspapers during November 1971:

> EUREKA SPRINGS, Ark.—Across the nation Gerald L. K. Smith is described by some as a hate-mongering bigot and by others as a Christian patriot.
>
> In this Ozark mountain town of 2,000 he is known as the man whose "sacred projects" have put Eureka Springs back in the tourist business after 40 years of decline.[37]

Puffery for Smith's present and future projects and glossing over of Smith's anti-Semitic history characterized a long article on January 30, 1972 in the St. Louis *Post-Dispatch*, under the by-line of James E. Adams, the paper's religion editor. Buried in more than a column of complimentary description of the "sacred projects" old and new, date-lined Eureka Springs, were two short paragraphs:

Smith is the founder of the America First Party and the tireless publisher of "The Cross and the Flag," the monthly magazine of the
Christian Nationalist Crusade, which he founded in 1941. His winter
headquarters is in Los Angeles, but his summers are spent here close
to his projects.

Critics over the years have regarded Smith as an irresponsible
bigot. His life long campaign against what he calls the "international
Jewish conspiracy" has earned him a national reputation as an anti-
Semite.

Moreover, Adams followed these two paragraphs with a disclaimer from Smith:

But Smith says his critics are absolutely wrong when they read anti-
Semitism or other biases into his sacred projects here. All his "Christian patriotism" and anti-Communist propaganda have not—and
never will be—allowed on the projects, he says.

"To me these are as sacred as the church," said Smith. "I could no
more use them for political propaganda than you could pass out
political flyers at your grandmother's funeral."[38]

Five months later, the travel section of the *Post-Dispatch* Sunday "Everyday" magazine carried almost a full-page article on
Smith, his projects and Eureka Springs, adorned with large pho-
tos of the *Christ of the Ozarks* and the Smith home.[39] A breezily
written feature by a staff correspondent, it mixed the history and
lore of Eureka Springs' bygone days as a spa with travel promotion from the Eureka Springs Chamber of Commerce and self-
serving claims about Smith's projects by Charles Robertson,
Smith's long-time assistant in the business of hate. Ever the propagandist, Robertson had told the anonymous *Post-Dispatch* writer
that Smith conceived the "New Holy Land" project because, "the
original Holy Land in the Middle East is being destroyed. . . .
The holy shrines of Christ are controlled, possessed and cor-
rupted by the enemies of our Lord." The correspondent identified Robertson as "long the editor of 'The Cross and the Flag'"
and as spokesman "for Smith, who maintains that 'racial self-re-
spect is not bigotry.'"

Shortly after the St. Louis *Post-Dispatch* plug for Smith's "New

Holy Land" project a similar article appeared, also on a Sunday, in the Kansas City *Star* under the by-line of staff reporter Mike Zakoura, who had apparently been granted a five-hour interview with the Smiths in their Eureka Springs home. The layout included a four-column photo of the elderly couple ensconced among their Victoriana.[40] Zakoura wrote that in his long visit "conversation with the friendly, hospitable couple focused on old and new politics, religion and foundation projects." Zakoura identified Smith merely as "a source of political and religious controversy [for] nearly four decades, a man described by his enemies as a bigot and an anti-Semite" and printed without challenge Smith's lie that "because of my views on the Middle East, I have been branded an anti-Semite." In the article Smith described *The Cross and the Flag* as "Christianity and patriotism for conservative leaders'"—and said of the Christian Nationalist Crusade that it was "a committee that has lobbied for such things as keeping Communist China out of the UN and for prayer in schools." Had Smith hired the most skillful and expensive Madison Avenue public relations firm, he could not have hoped for any more positive image-building than was afforded readers of a respectable, responsible middle-American newspaper in the year 1972.

Zakoura made no reference to an article on Smith and Eureka Springs published in the *Star* on January 18, 1970—during the height of the road controversy—under the by-line of Harry Jones, Jr. Jones, an authority on right-wing extremist groups and author of a book on the Minutemen,[41] took pains to quote from Smith's writings and *The Cross and the Flag* to illustrate Smith's continuing bigotry against Jews and blacks. He pointed out that despite the claimed separation between Smith's anti-Jewish activities in the Christian Nationalist Crusade and the magazine on the one hand and his so-called "sacred projects" on the other, Smith, in an advertisement in the *Times-Echo* designed to answer some of his critics, had actually offered free samples of *The Cross and the Flag* to anyone who wrote in for one.[42] Jones then quoted the anti-Jewish, anti-black items in the issue of the magazine that had been sent on request.

Sins of omission regarding Gerald Smith's anti-Semitism and racism were not, however, confined to the journalistic output west of the Hudson. Perhaps because it is the nation's leading newspaper and more is expected by way of journalistic accuracy, the most offensive piece of puffery was printed by the *New York Times*.

On July 27, 1972 there appeared a rosy-toned feature under the headline "Hippies and Gerald L. K. Smith Make Ozark Resort Town a Model of Coexistence." The feature, date-lined Eureka Springs but bearing no by-line—not even the anonymous "Special to The New York Times"—read like a publicity handout from the offices of the Eureka Springs Chamber of Commerce. It told of how Smith's arrival had saved the town's economy and how the "sacred projects" had become "the town's largest economic asset." "The Chamber of Commerce says tourism has increased 42 percent over last year's rate," the encomium to Smith as the savior of Eureka Springs continued, adding that "deposits in the bank have doubled in four years [and] real estate values have risen sharply," with virtually no vacant commercial buildings and with "almost every old Victorian house in town" boasting "a new coat of paint and a fresh window box of petunias."

The *Times* article told how other entrepreneurs had followed the Smiths into Eureka, among them "200 or 300 young people who call themselves 'freaks' or longhairs." They had overcome initial hostility and suspicion, developed a "work ethic," set up small businesses and an arts and crafts cooperative and achieved a measure of tolerance. According to the *Times,* the long-haired residents had developed an "intense loyalty to the town" and were prone to kid it a little—"I'm proud to be a freakey from Eurekey." Fifteen of the longhairs were among 426 town residents who attended a reception for Gerald and Elna Smith on their fiftieth wedding anniversary and the young people had "covered" the event in straight society fashion in *Down Home,* an underground newspaper they had launched. Gerald Smith was, the *Times* said, so pleased with the behavior of his guests and their reportage of the event that he wrote a letter of thanks to *Down Home,* of which the *Times* quoted the following: "As one who has been misunderstood and misrepresented down through the years, perhaps I am in a better position to understand the victims of misrepresentations better than might be expected."

In all forty-two column inches of the *New York Times* story, the anonymous reporter—who briefly characterized Smith as "the 74-year-old right-wing crusader"—wrote only the following about Smith's four decades as the country's most notorious anti-Semite: "The Smiths and their 'sacred projects' became targets of criticism from many who disapproved of Mr. Smith's long crusade against what he calls 'the international Jewish conspiracy.'"

In the autumn of 1972 Bob Lancaster, who writes "The Arkansas Traveler" column for the Arkansas *Gazette,* made the same journey to Eureka Springs. Lancaster had done his homework and was armed with clippings from relatively recent issues of *The Cross and the Flag.* Lancaster wrote:

> Smith writes virtually everything that appears in "The Cross and the Flag." . . . I asked him about some passages . . . I'd brought along.
>
> His endorsement of racial apartheid, for example. His denunciation of Women's Lib because of the prominence of lesbians and "Jewesses" in the leadership. . . .
>
> Mainly, though, I wanted to ask him if he still favored the establishment of concentration camps in America. He didn't remember ever having proposed such a thing. So I read him these passages:
>
> "America cannot be saved without concentration camps. At least a million of our people must be rounded up, isolated and put away or they will destroy our universities, burn our homes, ignite our forests and enslave our population." (December 1970)
>
> ". . . I favor repression. I believe a million people should be in concentration camps. I believe that all these soft, spongy university professors should be replaced by he-men—military officials if necessary." (October 1970)
>
> Although he didn't remember having written the passages, Smith said: "That sounds as good to me today as the day I wrote it."
>
> We discussed the proposal at some length. Which million persons should be confined to the camps, how the camps should be run, and other such entertaining diversions.
>
> Such are the pleasantries of an October afternoon on the slopes of Golgotha Hill.[45]

Columnist Lancaster's reminder of the Gerald Smith who continues to this day to spread hatred of Jews and Negroes and who hankers after concentration camps reminiscent of Hitler's Germany capped a sustained record, dating back more than five years, of outstanding investigative reporting conducted by the Arkansas *Gazette* on the subject of Gerald Smith, his projects and his road. It deserves special mention in this otherwise depressing account.

The following selection from the *Gazette's* fine editorials captures their quality:

In the Name of Jesus and Gerald Smith [July 14, 1968]

. . . We have always felt that if this country ever were to turn totalitarian, it would be in the name of something calling itself both "Christian" and "Nationalist."

Gerald L. K. Smith was not the man to lead us to that happy estate, clearly, but . . . he has always done what he could.

The evil that men do does live after them, and in this category will belong Gerald L. K. Smith's Eureka Springs Passion Play and his blasphemous (considering the sponsorship) "Christ of the Ozarks."

We were never surprised by Mr. Smith's having the nerve to try it, and suppose that, in the end, it was local boosterism that was largely responsible. It has occurred to us before that the local booster spirit in America is such that some Chambers of Commerce would jump at landing the annual reunion of Sepp Dietrich's old Waffen SS outfit if it meant a little something in the till.

On to Buchenwald! [December 19, 1969]

The latest issue of "The Cross and The Flag," Gerald L. K. Smith's official publication, is hot off the press and we recommend it to Governor Rockefeller and Congressman John Paul Hammerschmidt of Harrison as required reading. . . .

. . .Consider this item from the "Smith Missiles" column in the December issue —

"Even Communist Poland is fed up with Jewish control. A terrific reaction had developed in Poland against Jewish aggression. Jews, generally speaking, lack discrimination. They fail to interpret unfolding events. The reaction that wipes them out is usually closer to them than they can realize."

Shades of Buchenwald!

Are you listening Winthrop Rockefeller? Can you understand now why federal aid to promote a tourist project to the "sacred projects" has grossly offended so many people, Jews and Christians alike, both in Arkansas and elsewhere in the Land?

Gerald L. K. Smith: His Rights and His Roads [May 24, 1970]

The most wondrous event of the week in Arkansas—even in a week when Orval E. Faubus announced for governor—had to be the announcement by Gerald L. K. Smith that he will go to the Justice Department with a complaint of conspiracy to deprive him of his civil rights.

This is not to suggest that G. L. K. Smith is not as entitled as the next man to the full complement of the Constitution, no matter what the burden upon his record, not to mention the burden upon his soul. But it is nonetheless remarkable to find a charge of rights deprivation brought by the man whose virulent anti-Semitism and radically reactionary career have made his name a "household word" for more than 30 years. Mr. Smith is the granddaddy of American hatemongers and if there is a deadlier foe of the U.S. Bill of Rights alive in this country the chances are that Smith taught him the trade, at least by example. . . .

No one has suggested—certainly we have not—that Gerald L. K. Smith was not entitled to choose a second home and a burial ground (under the arms of the Christ-of-the-Ozarks) in Arkansas. This is his right no matter how much many of us might wish he had chosen some likelier spot, like Pocatello or Nome. It would seem elemental, however, that the national taxpayer should not have to help develop Smith's hobbies, religious or sacrilegious as they may happen to be. Let Gerald Smith build his own road to his monuments, and let the Ozarks Commission find proven—even conventional—places to put its development money in the spread of its four-state domain.[44]

During the summer of '72, the Humble Oil and Refining Company included Smith's anti-Semitic Passion play in its list of outdoor dramas made available on request to customers and readers of its *Happy Motoring News*. When the Anti-Defamation League complained to the giant company the editor of *Happy Motoring News,* Charles F. Riesen, responded that Humble's only reason for offering the list of outdoor dramas was "to perform a public service." He added:

I personally have seen several of the dramas, as my family and I are the outdoors type, and have enjoyed them. Included in the ones I have seen is "The Great Passion Play" in Eureka Springs, Arkansas, which your letter takes exception to.

I judge from your letter, however, that you are not indicting the play itself, and rightly so, for it seemed to this observer to be a faithful portrayal, as the Bible would have it, of a portion of Christ's ministry on earth.

You did point out, however, that "this production is sponsored and operated by Gerald L. K. Smith, who properly has been characterized as America's most notorious professional anti-Semite."

Since we made no mention of Mr. Smith's name, and were not even aware that he had anything to do with the sponsoring of this fine production, nor were we even aware of the activities which you attribute to him, we do not feel that we have prejudiced your cause.[45]

When ADL made the correspondence public many Humble customers returned or destroyed their company credit cards in protest. In a subsequent letter to one such customer Riesen wrote that his failure to find anti-Semitism in Smith's version of the Passion play was "strictly a personal observation," that he viewed the message of Christianity in a positive manner. He declared that "we are all children of God" and added:

When we offered to send interested motorists a list of the approximately 40 outdoor dramas being produced in the United States, neither I nor Humble was aware that charges of anti-Semitism had been made against "The Great Passion Play" at Eureka Springs, Arkansas. We were unaware of Gerald L. K. Smith's affiliation with the play. In fact, I personally had never heard of Mr. Smith.

Since neither I nor Humble condones anti-Semitism, you can readily understand our regret at having offended anyone of the Jewish faith. We have discontinued offering the list of outdoor dramas to show our good faith.[46]

Obviously neither Mr. Riesen nor his company, on the basis of this incident, could be regarded as anti-Semitic, and his apology and discontinuation of the outdoor drama list closed the matter as far as the Anti-Defamation League was concerned. But the episode shaped another piece in the disturbing and puzzling picture of unconcern about the continuing activities of Gerald Smith.

On January 21, 1973 the Mutual Broadcasting System carried

an interview with Gerald Smith. On the program Smith touted his Eureka Springs projects, including the anti-Jewish Passion play, and offered listeners packets of propaganda; the program moderator, Bill Bertenshaw, five times gave listeners the address from which the literature was available. Two or three days later, the program was picked up by the U.S. government's Armed Forces Radio and Television Service and broadcast over its own transmitters, and those of the Voice of America, to the Armed Forces Network of 492 stations serving some two million American military and civilian personnel throughout the world.

The promotion of Smith's activities on a program broadcast under government auspices came to the attention of the Anti-Defamation League on January 24 and was brought to public attention a few days later by the Jewish Telegraphic Agency and by Jack Anderson in his syndicated Washington column.[47] The ADL communicated its concern to Defense Secretary Melvin Laird. The letter of protest said, in part:

> Gerald L. K. Smith's record as a propagandist of religious and racial hatred goes back some forty years and has been extensively exposed and condemned in print and by all responsible public officials. We are deeply concerned with the use of the Armed Forces Network, a government facility, as a vehicle for presenting and promoting a notorious bigot in the guise of a responsible religious leader.[48]

The Smith broadcast interview was part of a "public service" series called "Suggested Solutions," taped and packaged by Bertenshaw, an independent radio and TV producer of Maplewood, N.J. It was not the first time Bertenshaw had promoted Smith's activities on one of his taped programs; he had taped a program with Mrs. Smith in September 1972 and she had, of course, promoted the Passion play. On the "Suggested Solutions" series, Bertenshaw had been including a tag line at the end of each program, saying that the New Jersey Council of Churches had cooperated in the production. The Council of Churches had in fact cooperated with Bertenshaw, a member of its Commission on Radio and TV, in producing the first four programs of the series several years earlier, but that was the extent of its association with him. Bertenshaw, however, continued to use the NJCC credit line on his shows, and the Mutual Broadcasting System's special events and public service department assumed that the Council of Churches unit was in support of the production. But the Council, spurred by protests relating to the September appearance of Elna Smith, instructed Bertenshaw in writing to stop using its name. Bertenshaw said he could not recall whether or not he had informed Mutual of the NJCC's request to be dissociated from the series, and accepted full responsibility for the interview. The moderator reportedly said that the he "personally knew nothing about the guy" when he taped the program. "But I know now. I would not have put on the show if I had the background I have now."[49]

As for the Armed Forces Radio network, officials did not screen programs picked up by them for broadcast acceptability. When the protests and inquiries descended on them, John Broger, the director of the Defense Department's Office of Information for the Armed Forces, and Hoyt Wertz, chief of the Armed Forces Radio and Television Service, pulled the broadcast from their repertoire and said it would not be aired again, although normally such programs were broadcast several times. They also undertook to review the "Suggested Solutions" series to see if it conformed to armed forces network standards of acceptability.[50]

We have dealt at length and in considerable detail with the events of the past few years surrounding Gerald L. K. Smith and his "sacred projects" because anti-Semites cannot succeed without the acquiescence, overt and tacit, of a larger public. And Jews, who came to fear above all in the Diaspora anti-Semitism sanctioned by government policy, have felt particularly safe in America because of the safeguards of human life and liberty written into the earliest laws of this Republic. The Jewish community must therefore ask itself why the best-known Jew-hater in the country should have come so close to government largesse, an act stopped only by the vigilance of Jews themselves and a handful of other concerned citizens.

For American Jews, Gerald L. K. Smith is not the issue; the

relevant factor is the apparent willingness of so many to disregard his anti-Semitism and his racism—the townspeople of Eureka Springs in behalf of the tourist dollar; county, state, and federal officials in their zeal both to promote economic growth and, undoubtedly, to win votes; some of the nation's newspapers in the interests of good copy and others for any permutation of reasons known only, perhaps, to themselves.

3

The Blackman's Development Center and the Government

In 1971 "Colonel" Hassan Jeru-Ahmed was head of the Blackman's Development Center in Washington, D.C. He was also a forty-seven-year-old extremist agitator whose anti-Jewish activities had come to public attention in 1966.[1] He had parroted anti-Semitic lies and canards familiar in the propaganda arsenal of professional bigots who talk of an international "Jewish-Communist" conspiracy. In 1966–67 he had distributed a number of anti-Jewish propaganda tracts, one of them alleging a Jewish plot to exploit and enslave black Americans; the headline on one issue of his *Blackman's Defender Newsletter* screamed that "Zionist Jews and American Communists Plan Death Trap for All Blacks." Hassan had described the National Association for the Advancement of Colored People and the National Urban League as tools of the "Jewish-Communist" conspiracy; he had maintained a close association with and had admitted receiving financial aid from Willis Carto, leader of the far right Liberty Lobby and one of the most notorious anti-Semites of America's Radical Right, a man who has extolled Hitler and who has long favored shipping America's black people to Africa. In addition Hassan had boasted of "heartening" support from the late neo-Nazi George Rockwell and from the Ku Klux Klan and had been the guest on more than one occasion at the microphone of Richard Cotten, a well-known anti-Semitic radio broadcaster and pamphleteer.

In addition to operating the Blackman's Development Center, Hassan presided over a variety of other business and political activities. They included a "Blackman's Volunteer Army of Liberation," whose members wore military uniforms, held military ranks and observed military discipline.[2] By 1971 Hassan maintained two rural Virginia "bases" for his "army,"[3] some of whom apparently possessed weapons. His chief of staff, one "Major" Jamal, received a thirty-day sentence early in the year for carrying a concealed pistol while distributing leaflets in Washington, D.C.[4] Hassan—born Albert Roy Osborne—had an extensive arrest record and had served time in prison for passing bad checks.[5]

On February 26, 1971, the Department of Health, Education & Welfare and the Department of Labor authorized grants totaling $523,000 to the Blackman's Development Center for a remedial education and occupational training program for the disadvantaged, specifically including a methadone drug detoxification program for addicts.[6] The funds started flowing to Hassan in March. The Center also received $169,000 from the Narcotics Treatment Administration of the District of Columbia and picked up substantial support from private foundations and other private sources.[7]

Responding to ADL's first complaint of February 3, 1971[8] (Hassan had applied for the grant in January), Richard Hobson, chief of HEW's Experimental and Utilization Section, confirmed that the grant would be made to Hassan's Blackman's Development Center but asserted that the HEW action did not imply endorsement "of other activities of the organization or members of its staff."[9] When ADL replied that it was counter to public policy for government to function through professional bigots,[10] Hobson offered the startling response that Hassan himself had assured HEW officials that he was no longer anti-Jewish and that his anti-Jewish activities had ended five years earlier.[11] (It later developed, of course, that Hassan had reassured the HEW officials only when questioned closely by them and only when warned that he would otherwise not get the federal funds.)[12] The Anti-Defamation League, in yet another communication to HEW, then submitted evidence showing that Hassan's anti-Jewish activities had been conducted much more recently;[13] "An Open Letter to Americans," a propaganda tract written in the 1966–67 period and signed by Hassan, had in fact been distributed as late as the spring of 1970 on various Washington streets and at a gas station operated by the Blackman's Development Center. It stated that "America is threatened with takeover from within by a people that are conspiring to destroy the American heritage," and added:

> America's deadly enemy, the people that are using blackmen and blackwomen to support themselves, is The International Jewish Conspiracy. A Conspiracy for Jews only. . . .
>
> In high offices of the federal govenment of the United States down to the newly arriving Jew who opens his grocery store in black ghettoes, there are Jews who are avidly working for the success of their many-tenacled [sic] organ.
>
> Black America has lived for years as a blind pawn in the fantastic and deadly game that this conspiracy of Jews is playing to control America. We have shielded this cancer from the healing power of understanding simply because we are forced to work for Jews, rent our apartments and houses from Jews, buy our food, clothing, furniture, automobile from Jews.

Countering Hassan's claim that he was no longer anti-Semitic, merely "anti-Zionist," the ADL told HEW that Hassan's anti-Jewish writings made it abundantly clear that in his thinking the words *Jew* and *Zionist* were synonymous.

In April 1971 various press accounts—including several by columnist Jack Anderson—reported the grant to the Blackman's Development Center and cited Hassan's history as a bigot.[14] The Anti-Defamation League publicly condemned the HEW grant,[15] and on April 21 wrote directly to Secretary Elliot Richardson urging him to "take appropriate action" in view of the "impropriety of the federal grant."[16] Meanwhile, the Washington *Evening Star* quoted Hassan as having claimed that "Zionists have completely taken over the United States Communist Party."[17]

Secretary Richardson did not respond until late June. In the meantime outraged citizens who had read the press accounts wrote to their congressmen and to HEW to protest the grant. Replying, HEW officials offered basically laudatory explanations of Hassan's program and swift dismissals of the charges that Hassan had been and remained an anti-Semite. Some of these HEW responses were signed by Howard A. Matthews, director of the Division of Manpower Development and Training of the Office of Education, who repeated the HEW explanation that Hassan had repudiated his earlier anti-Semitism.[18] Matthews added that the ADL had offered no tangible evidence of recent anti-Semitic activity on Hassan's part, this despite HEW's knowledge by this time that the "Open Letter to Americans" had been circulated the previous spring.

But something must have been troubling the Department of Health, Education & Welfare. On June 18, T. H. Bell, deputy commissioner for school systems of HEW's Office of Education, wrote to Hassan reminding him of "several in-depth conversations with you concerning the seriousness of allegations that you and the Blackman's Development Center have been engaging in anti-Jewish activities in furtherance of the views reflected in a widely circulated tract entitled 'An Open Letter to Americans.'" Bell recalled that "in discussions prior to the awarding of the grant" Hassan had acknowledged authorship but repudiated the contents of the "Open Letter." The HEW official concluded:

> In light of recent complaints we must repeat that we cannot fund any project involving the use of funds, directly or indirectly, to support any such ideologies no matter whether they be characterized as "anti-Jewish" or "anti-Zionist."

The Bell letter, of course, made it clear that HEW officials did not blunder blindly into approving the grant to Hassan's Blackman's Development Center, that they knew they were dealing with an anti-Semite and had discussed the matter with him.

Replying on June 24 to ADL's letter urging his intervention, Secretary Richardson countered the League's charges with the same explanation offered by his subordinates—that Hassan had "repudiated the contents" of the "Open Letter," that he had "publicly denied allegations of anti-Semitism."[19] The Secretary added that HEW was "of course, very concerned about any introduction into the training project of bigotry or other antisocial views" and had "warned Col. Hassan that we are monitoring his program for evidence of such activities." Mr. Richardson did not, however, address himself to the main issue: whether any government grant should have been awarded to Hassan in the first place in view of his demonstrable record of professional anti-Jewish bigotry. That issue—whether anti-Semitism is to be rewarded by the respectable, responsible community—is at the heart of the matter.

The last section of Secretary Richardson's letter to the Anti-Defamation League nevertheless made news headlines in the Washington press when HEW released the story. Mr. Richardson wrote:

> The Department of Health, Education and Welfare, in cooperation with the Department of Justice and the District of Columbia, is also presently conducting an administrative audit to guarantee that the Blackman's Development Center is financially capable of conducting this vocational training project, and to ensure that the project is conducted in such a manner that all Federal funds will be used for vocational training purposes only. During the period that this audit is in progress, no HEW funds will be disbursed to the grantee. As soon as this audit is completed, we will be in a better position to evaluate the future course of this project.

In the wake of the fund cutoff and pending audit, on July 6, 1971, Hassan filed a $24,000,000 libel and conspiracy suit against the Anti-Defamation League, claiming that ADL had falsely accused him of anti-Semitism and that it had pressured HEW to suspend the grant funds for the Blackman's Development Center pending the audit.[20]

In November 1971 U.S. District Court Judge John Pratt dismissed Hassan's suit against the ADL, ruling that its charges about Hassan's anti-Semitism "are in fact true as is evident" from Hassan's "own utterances." Judge Pratt declared that ADL's statements "were not made with knowledge of falsity or with reckless disregard of truth or falsity," but rather "after careful and diligent research" pursuant "to its legal and moral duty prescribed" by its charter.[21]

Nor did Hassan fare better with the HEW audit of the use of

funds for his drug rehabilitation and detoxification program. Released early in January 1972 by HEW's Office of Education, the audit disclosed extensive irregularities in the expenditure of the funds, with some $27,000 of the first $39,000 spent for nongrant purposes, including auto repairs, food, catering and wine, as well as payments on a nongovernment loan. The remaining funds, the audit found, "were not accounted for adequately."[22]

On June 17 Representative Robert N. Giaimo of Connecticut in a public speech condemned the HEW grant to Hassan as "support of an anti-Semitic manipulator . . . whose record of anti-Jewish utterances and hatred of Jews has been well documented. . . ."[23] (Hassan also filed a multimillion-dollar libel and slander suit against Representative Giaimo,[24] which was subsequently dismissed.)[25] Of more substantive concern to Hassan, however, was undoubtedly the fact that Congressman Giaimo called for an audit by the General Accounting Office of Hassan's operation. The results of that audit were made public in May 1972 and reported in both the Washington *Post* and the' Washington *Star*.[26] According to the news accounts, the General Accounting Office had charged that more than $170,000 in federal drug treatment funds had either been misused by Hassan and his organization for relatives, friends, automobiles, real estate, food and wine or were not able to be accounted for. The auditors also charged that because the funds had been so spent, "the center often ran out of methadone to treat former heroin addicts enrolled in the organization's program."[27]

Hassan moved to Columbus, Ohio, to set up another drug rehabilitation center after the cutoff of HEW funds to his Washington operation. In December 1971 the ADL learned that the Ohio State Bureau of Community Services had granted the Columbus Blackman's Development Center some $25,000 in public funds; an additional $8,334 was made available by Franklin County's Mental Health and Retardation Bureau.[28]

On January 20, 1972 the Anti-Defamation League addressed a protest letter to Governor John J. Gilligan of Ohio similar to those it had sent repeatedly to the Department of Health, Education & Welfare. The letter made it clear that the League was keenly aware of the need for antidrug programs in Ohio but seriously questioned the propriety of the state's support of Hassan. On January 25 Governor Gilligan confirmed the funding for the Blackman's Development Center:

> . . . you have stated that the ADL's concern with the activities of the BDC is limited to the involvement of Hassan Jeru-Ahmed in anti-Jewish and extremist activities. *Let me say that the State's concern is limited to the support of BDC's drug treatment efforts.* [Italics added.] Thus far we have seen no evidence to indicate that there is a conflict between our two concerns. I can assure you that there has been and will continue to be full and accurate accounting of state funds to guarantee that they are employed only in support of the drug treatment program.
>
> The drug problem is of such serious proportions that I could not in good conscience withhold State support of the BDC Columbus treatment operation on the basis of evidence which is available at this time. I suspect that, regardless of your feeling toward Hassan, you would be reluctant to make such a direct request of me.[29]

ADL had no such reluctance. In a second letter, ADL inquired into the necessity of using a professional anti-Semite to combat drug addiction. A meeting with Governor Gilligan was requested to explore the problem. The meeting was never granted.

The Washington *Post* is one of the great newspapers in the United States. Emanating as it does from the nation's capital, and providing articles to other papers across the country through an extensive news and feature syndicate, it may well be the most influential. In 1973 it won a coveted and well-deserved Pulitzer Prize for its fearless investigative reporting of the Watergate scandal. Editorially it regards itself—and is generally regarded by friends and critics alike—as a strong champion of liberal causes.

Hassan Jeru-Ahmed's anti-Semitism, his right-wing anti-Semitic associations and his criminal record were not new to the Washington *Post*'s reporters and news columns when the ADL brought them to the attention of the Department of Health, Education & Welfare in 1971. Indeed, in 1966 *Post* reporter Michael Drosnin, in a story on Hassan's "army," had written pointedly about them,[30] as had a journalistic colleague on the

Washington *Star*, who in 1967, had described Hassan as "bitterly anti-Semitic."[31] Further, the ADL staff had responded to requests from various *Post* reporters over the years for background information from ADL's library on anti-Semitic and extremist groups and individuals, including Hassan and his supporter Willis Carto, the latter the subject of two long investigative pieces by *Post* reporter Paul Valentine in 1969 and 1970.[32] Late in 1970, however, the *Post* covered Hassan in a news story that reported his intention to mobilize his "army" for a "massive voter registration and informative drive" but omitted any details on his anti-Semitic background or his criminal record.[33]

In January, 1971—at just about the time Hassan's application for federal funds was under sympathetic consideration at HEW— Robert Williams wrote an illustrated *Post* feature article on Hassan, his operations, his family and his residence in the well-read Sunday "Living in Style" section. The feature was headlined "Col. Hassan's House of Liberation." Headlines on the "jump" pages depicted his entourage as "A Family of Islam" and "A Provisional Government and a Family as Well."

Mr. Williams made no reference to Hassan's anti-Semitism or his relationships with Carto or Rockwell. It was a warm story of the home and family life of Hassan at the "embassy" of the "Provisional Government of the United Moorish Republic." It referred to the Blackman's Liberation Army and the Blackman's Development Center drug treatment program. Williams noted Hassan's criminal record, reporting that he "went to prison for 13 months for mugging a poor soul on Christmas Eve of 1948" and that he had served time at the Western State Penitentiary in Pittsburgh for passing bad checks. Said Williams ". . . Now he is straight and you can accept his check, and he has it pretty much altogether, this former Albert R. Osborne. It may be that when he gets his hands on Africa you will find it a comfortable place to be, with many rooms."

On April 14, 1971, as the controversy about the HEW grant to Hassan's Blackman's Development Center was breaking into print, Hassan was the subject of a midweek newsfeature by *Post* staff writer Paul Valentine. The headline read "Hassan Turns Drug Program Into Black Empire." The article depicted Hassan's mushrooming activities. Valentine did not mention Hassan's anti-

Semitism or his relationship with Carto (about whom Valentine had earlier reported extensively). No reference was made to a *Post* 1966 article concerning support for Hassan from Carto and Rockwell, nor did Valentine mention Hassan's criminal past, reported three months earlier in the *Post* by Robert Williams.

On July 3, 1971, the *Post* carried a lead editorial, headlined "Col. Hassan, HEW and the ADL," sharply challenging ADL's view that it was improper for the U.S. government to fund a drug program operated by a professional bigot. The *Post* took the government's view, asserting that Hassan's anti-Semitism would be relevant only if it showed up in the drug program itself, only if Hassan had "translated any personal anti-Semitic attitudes into concrete actions on other fronts."

It was clear that in the first six months of 1971, the Washington *Post*'s proper concern with combating the drug problem had temporarily dulled its usual sensitivity with regard to anti-Semitism. Both the failure of its reporters during this period to mark Hassan's anti-Semitic statements and associations and the paper's editorial posture were deeply disappointing to the Jewish community. That community, both before and since the Hassan episode, has looked to the *Post* for leadership on civil liberties questions and support of Israel. In these it has not been disappointed.

On July 4, the day after the *Post* editorial, Hassan was interviewed on WTOP-TV and WTOP Radio.[34] He made statements that clearly indicated he was continuing to promulgate anti-Jewish ideology and that his current sentiments with respect to Jews were hardly different from his earlier anti-Jewish declarations of 1966 and 1967. He admitted appearing, during 1970, on several "Conservative Viewpoint" broadcasts conducted by Richard Cotten, the far rightist anti-Semite. He admitted his cooperative relationship with Willis Carto; with Schuyler Ferris, a former member of Rockwell's Nazi Party; with Jesse Stephens, identified in Washington *Post* articles as a leader of the Minutemen, and with Louis Byers, a one-time associate of Carto who was later allied with remnants of the National Socialist White People's Party, Rockwell's group renamed. Hassan explained that he hobnobbed with these extremists, racists.and anti-Semites in order to "find out what kind of people they really are."

On February 19, 1973 Hassan Jeru-Ahmed—now referred to in the press as "General" Hassan—was arrested in Washington, D.C., apparently because the car he was driving did not display the proper inspection sticker. He was found to be carrying a concealed .45 pistol without a permit and to be driving without a valid D.C. driver's permit, according to the account in the Washington *Post*.[35] At this writing, Hassan has pleaded guilty to the gun charge but has not yet been sentenced.

The sun has indeed apparently set on Hassan's "empire." His Columbus, Ohio, operation, after receiving early support from state and private sources, was affected by the federal audits on the Washington Blackman's Development Center and by legal difficulties encountered by Hassan's lieutenant in charge of the Columbus project, "Major" (later "Colonel") Danyil Sulieman.[36] The Center's source of funds dried up. On June 15, 1972 the U.S. Department of Health, Education & Welfare told Franklin County, Ohio, to eliminate the Blackman's Development Center from a proposal the county had made to the National Institute of Mental Health in Washington for a grant of $6.7 million for a drug abuse control program for the entire Columbus area. The Blackman's Development Center was slated for $2.4 million during the eight-year program. The connection between the Columbus operation and the fiscally irresponsible Washington Blackman's Development Center was reportedly the major reason for HEW's decision.[37] In December 1972 the Columbus Center was facing eviction from its headquarters for nonpayment of rent,[38] and by the start of 1973 the Columbus operation was, for all intents and purposes, defunct.

4

A Teachers' Association

The African-American Teachers Association (ATA), head-quartered in Brooklyn had been organized in 1964 as the Negro Teachers Association. Its name had been changed in 1967, shortly after the winds of "black power" began to blow from Stokely Carmichael and H. Rap Brown and from a "black power" conference held in Newark in the summer of 1967. Once the teachers' group adopted a militant black nationalist posture, only in part signaled by its name change, it began to pour forth a stream of anti-Semitism directed at Jews in general and Jewish public school teachers in particular. The Association's publication, *Forum*, was its official vehicle for anti-Jewish messages, but *Black News*, closely linked to ATA and targeted particularly to black youth, was also packed, issue after issue, with anti-Jewish invective.

In the November–December 1967 issue of *Forum*, the ATA published an article by John F. Hatchett, a public school teacher, that bore the title "The Phenomenon of the Anti-Black Jews and the Black Anglo-Saxon: A Study in Educational Perfidy." The Hatchett article said in part:

> We are witnessing today in New York City a phenomenon that spells death for the minds and souls of our Black children. It is the systematic coming of age of the Jews who dominate and control the educational bureaucracy of the New York Public School system, and their

> power-starved imitators, the Black Anglo-Saxons. . . . In short, our children are being mentally poisoned by a group of educators who are actively and persistently bringing a certain self-fulfulling prophecy to its logical conclusion.

The author added:

> Arise you Black teachers and cast off the chains of fear and frustration, the fight will be bloody and long, but we will win. Black Power to you all.

The Hatchett piece in *Forum* was an early example of the charge that "mental genocide" was being practiced against black children in the public schools of New York and that the prime perpetrators of that "genocide" were Jewish teachers and supervisors. It was to be echoed in some of the extremist propaganda circulated in and around the New York City school system in the late sixties and it was to have repercussions in the long and bitter school strike of 1968. Such bigotry to this day saturates the pages of *Forum* and the statements of ATA officials.

In November 1968, during the school strike, the *Forum* carried an editorial entitled "Needed: A Responsible Jewish Voice." It charged that the "Jewish-dominated United Federation of Teachers" had destroyed efforts to rescue black and Puerto Rican children from "incompetent teachers whose only goal . . . is stifling our children's intellectual growth." The editorial added:

> . . . the Jew, our great liberal friend of yesterday, whose cries of anguish still resound from the steppes of Russia to the tennis courts of Forest Hills, is now our exploiter! He keeps our men and women from becoming teachers and principals and keeps our children ignorant.

In December 1968, Leslie Campbell, Brooklyn coordinator for the African-American Teachers Association—who had written a racist article for the same issue of *Forum* headlined "The Devil Can Never Educate Us"—appeared on a discussion program over WBAI-FM in New York and read a poem he said had been written by a fifteen-year-old girl.[1] Dedicated to President Albert Shanker of the United Federation of Teachers and entitled "Anti-Semitism," it went this way:

Hey, Jew boy, with that yarmulke on your head
You pale-faced Jew boy—I wish you were dead;
I can see you Jew boy—no you can't hide,
I got a scoop on you—yeh, you gonna die.
I'm sick of your stuff; every time I run 'round,
You pushin' my head deeper into the ground;
I'm sick of hearing about your suffering in Germany,
I'm sick about your escape from tyranny,
I'm sick of seeing in everything I do
About the murder of six million Jews;
Hitler's reign lasted for only fifteen years—
For that period of time you shed crocodile tears.
My suffering lasted for over 400 years, Jew boy,
And the white man only let me play with his toys.
Jew boy, you took my religion and adopted it for you,
But you know that Black people were the original Hebrews.
When the UN made Israel a free independent state
Little 4- and 5-year old boys threw hand grenades.
They hated the black Arabs with all their might,
And you, Jew boy, said it was all right.
Then you came to America, land of the free,
And took over the school system to perpetuate white supremacy.
Guess you know, Jew boy, there's only one reason you made it—
You had a clean white face, colorless and faded.
I hated you Jew boy, because your hang-up was the Torah,
And my only hang-up was my color.

Campbell described the poem as "beautiful" and "true." The episode triggered a storm of protest in New York that led Mayor John Lindsay to call for an investigation of Campbell and his status as a public school teacher.[2]

Responding to the mayor at a news conference on January 19, 1969, Albert Vann, president of the African-American Teachers Association, declared, according to the *Times* account, that the mayor "in his hurry to appease the powerful Jewish financiers of the city," had "played fast and loose" with Campbell's rights. Vann contended that the poem read by Campbell had "no anti-Semitic overtones" but conceded that it was "critical of Jews." He asserted that "any people who persecute black people will be criticized by blacks."[3]

While the storm over Campbell's reading of the poem was still raging, another ATA spokesman, Tyrone Woods, went on WBAI-FM and in the course of his appearance said of Jews: "As far as I'm concerned, more power to Hitler. He didn't make enough lampshades out of them. He didn't make enough belts out of them."[4]

The end of the 1968 New York school strike did not end the anti-Semitism issuing from the Brooklyn-based African-American Teachers Association. In the years that followed, *Black News* published scores of anti-Jewish items (many of them written by Leslie Campbell under the by-line of "Big Black"). "The Unholy Sons of Shylock"—April 10, 1970—will be sufficient to capture the flavor of these *Black News* pieces. It said, in part:

> . . . today the despicable Jew boys are still perpetrating their crimes here in the U.S.A. and abroad. The American Jew today spends a great deal of time financing the imperialistic war effort by Israel against the Arabs, when he is not ransacking the pockets of black people. . . .
>
> Our communities are sucked dry and exploited by a Jewish Mafia, which has its tentacles in our groceries, our dwellings, in our schools, indeed in every area of our lives. These shylocks are the principal instruments of suffering and privation in our black communities. . . . It stands to reason, therefore, that black people in our community will not throw off the shackles of poverty until they drive these Jewish parasites and vile money-changers from our community by any means necessary. Let these Jew-boys take their thievery into the white community where it belongs!

The Anti-Defamation League learned late in 1971, through the pages of *Forum* itself, that in 1969, 1970 and 1971 the United States Department of Health, Education & Welfare had funded ATA at "an average of $80,000 per annum" for an "Education Talent Search Program," aimed at aiding school drop outs under the direction of ATA's president, Albert Vann.[5] Subsequent investigation by the ADL disclosed that in those three years HEW had parceled out $258,740 to ATA. During the first year, funds had been channeled through the Bedford-Stuyvesant Restoration Corporation, while the Bethany Baptist Church in Brooklyn had been used in the succeeding two years.

The Association also noted that it had received grants totaling $100,000 over a two-year period from the New York Urban Coalition to finance a training and placement program for prospective minority group teachers, directed by Tyrone Woods.[6] When presented with the facts about the African-American Teachers Association, Woods and anti-Semitism, the New York Urban Coalition terminated its funding of the ATA project.[7] No such response was forthcoming, however, from the Department of Health, Education & Welfare.

On February 29, 1972 the Anti-Defamation League wrote to Secretary Richardson, urging him to "take prompt action to discontinue any present flow of HEW funds to ATA and to refuse any further grants which it may request."[8] "Whatever else its purpose may be, a substantial aspect of ATA's activity is deliberate anti-Semitism," the League wrote, adding that therefore "grants to it from HEW in effect constitute federal funding of anti-Semitism." Enclosed was documentation of the anti-Jewish propaganda emanating from ATA and its spokesmen. The ADL was advised during March that Secretary Richardson had asked U.S. Commissioner of Education Sidney P. Marland, Jr. to investigate the League's charges and submit a complete report.[9] Subsequently further evidence of ATA's continuing anti-Semitism and of the direct connection between the African-American Teachers Association and the virulently anti-Semitic *Black News* was forwarded to Commissioner Marland.[10]

The HEW answer was sent May 1 in a detailed letter from Acting U.S. Commissioner of Education Peter F. Muirhead. He said that the Office of Education had conducted a "review" of the project that had included "a visit to the project site and first-hand discussions with Mr. Albert Vann, the Talent Search Project Director and President of ATA, the Rev. William Jones, Pastor of the Bethany Baptist Church, and Mr. Tyrone Woods."[11] Commissioner Muirhead continued:

At the outset it is apparent that the ATA through its publication, "The Forum," has made, and provided a vehicle for others to make, deprecatory attacks on Jewish personnel employed in the New York City Public School System. In addition, as you have pointed out in your letter, some of the employees and officers of ATA have in the past made overt statements of an anti-Semitic nature. While Mr. Woods advises us that the statement to which you refer in your letter was made in the midst of a heated debate and does not accurately reflect his views, either then or now, it is not our purpose to defend that kind of rhetoric. *Our purpose is instead to attempt to determine whether anti-Semitism has been deliberately introduced into the conduct of the Federally supported Talent Search project.* [Italics added.]

Asserting that that was "an important distinction since our review indicates that the subject Talent Search project has maintained a superior average in assisting young people to secure a post-secondary education," Commissioner Muirhead said the HEW review also established that Tyrone Woods had not been employed in the Talent Search project for two years, although he was "engaged in other activities of the ATA"; that Leslie Campbell, although a member of the ATA Board, was never connected with the funded project, and that "no anti-Semitic slant, direction or program content has been found" in the project itself. He concluded:

While the foregoing leads us to the conclusion that discontinuance of the subject project is neither justified nor indicated at this time, we do not come to that view without some reservations. We believe, however, that Bethany Baptist Church and ATA understand that at some point it may become difficult to distinguish between invective of the type complained of by the Anti-Defamation League and the manner of conduct of the federally supported project. At such a point the effectiveness and utility of a Talent Search project would, of course, become questionable. Hopefully good sense will prevail, for in such a situation everyone loses.

On June 16 the ADL told Secretary Richardson that it had read Mr. Muirhead's letter with shock and disbelief. The League asked Mr. Richardson whether HEW would grant funds to the Ku Klux Klan or the American Nazi Party for special projects so long as they did not "deliberately introduce" racism and bigotry into the project.[12]

Health, Education & Welfare responded on July 19 in a letter from Education Commissioner Marland:

> Our objectives in these reviews have been to determine whether or not the Talent Search project has, in fact, engaged in anti-Semitic activities, or any other activities prohibited by law, and whether or not Federal funds have been used for any purposes other than support of the Talent Search program. Our negative findings were reported to you on May 1.
>
> If there is evidence that funds for the Talent Search program have been misdirected, we need to have those facts, since the Office of Education cannot and will not tolerate or condone the use of Federal funds for purposes other than those described in the approved work program.
>
> In all candor, I cannot believe that I or other individuals in the Office of Education have been insensitive to the feelings of all concerned in the issues raised by the Anti-Defamation League. At the same time, I have the uncomfortable feeling that the League and the African-American Teachers Association are talking to each other through the Office of Education. I would propose, therefore, that all parties meet together to discuss these concerns . . . [under regional OE auspices].
>
> I must strongly reiterate, in closing that the Office of Education does not condone or encourage expressions of antagonism or hatred, whatever their source. We will do all that we can to resolve and ameliorate such conflicts.[13]

Some six months later, by the end of 1972, ADL learned that federal funding of the African-American Teachers Association and its projects in Brooklyn would be terminated at the close of the fiscal year.

No reason was given for the decision.

5

The New York
Scene

The late sixties was a period of racial convulsion. Watts, Detroit, Newark—all had had major race riots. But not New York. The city's young and liberal mayor, who had taken office in 1966 after having served in the U.S. Congress, became famous for his shirt-sleeve walking tours of the ghetto. He was widely regarded as one of perhaps only two white politicians (the other being Robert F. Kennedy) who not only would be welcome in the black ghetto but who could calm the just passions he found there. A rapport developed between Mayor Lindsay's staff and many of the militants who wielded a certain amount of street-level influence in the seething blocks of the nation's largest ghettos, Harlem and Bedford-Stuyvesant. Together with the existence within these black ghettos of a large, stable, working-class black population that looked not to violence but to orderly change, and given the genuine commitment of the city administration to improving the lot of the poor, that rapport probably helped to stave off large-scale racial violence in New York, for which New Yorkers could only be grateful. But part of the price some city officials thought they had to pay for it was acquiescence in "anything goes" tactics on the part of extremists, and "anything," while it excluded a resort to violence for the most part, did not exclude targeting on Jews as the archvillains in ghetto poverty.

Two Board of Education presidents, for example, were among

those who failed to take cognizance of the anti-Semitism taking place around school issues throughout the city. As early as August 1966, Board President Lloyd K. Garrison had nothing to say at a public hearing of the Board when Melvin Pritchard, testifying for the "Concerned Parents of Brooklyn Public School 9," made these comments:

> ... One particular ethnic group of non-Christians are willfully, deliberately and intentionally depriving American citizens of their right to first-class education in the community public schools of this city, state and nation. ... This controlling group willfully, intentionally and deliberately administers inferior educational programs to the Christians in their community public schools. The programs of the Board of Education are deliberately demeaned and de-emphasized only in the Christian communities, the plan being to mentally murder all citizens not of their religious, racial or ethnic group. ... An investigation should be conducted regarding these destroyers and their acts of destruction. ... These individuals should be removed summarily from their positions and off the public payroll.[1]

Nor did one of Garrison's successors as Board president, John M. Doar—formerly head of the Civil Rights Division in Robert Kennedy's Justice Department and executive director of the Bedford-Stuyvesant Development and Services Corporation—display any greater concern at a public hearing of the Board in January 1969, even after a long and divisive school strike during which charges and countercharges of racism and anti-Semitism had been hurled about almost daily. When William O. Marley, chairman of the Brownsville Model Cities Committee, in a long anti-Semitic diatribe, repeatedly attacked Jews as dominant in the school system and as attempting "to perpetrate their greedy rape of the city under the guise of 'unionism' and teachers' rights," there was no challenge from President Doar or from two other members of the Board present, Hector Vazquez and Dr. Aaron Brown.[2] Prodded by a newsman present at the hearing, a Board spokesman later stated that the silence did not indicate assent.[3]

When Melvin Pritchard won appointment in 1968 as vice chairman of the Education Committee of the Council Against Poverty, the City's official and policy-making antipoverty agency, it did not help to allay Jewish fears.[4]

After serving as the investigative arm of a committee of New Yorkers formed by Mayor Lindsay to look into bigotry manifest during the September–November 1968 school strike,[5] the Anti-Defamation League released on January 22, 1969, a report of its findings on the anti-Semitic quotient of the bigotry that had surfaced in and around the schools before, during and immediately after the strike.[6] (The mayor's committee had called the anti-Semitism a "dangerous component" of the anti-white bigotry manifest during the strike.)[7] The ADL report made public some of the most virulent anti-Jewish propaganda that had been seen this side of the American Nazi Party. It included a description of a flyer circulated by a white neo-Nazi group which charged that a "Talmudic psychology" prevailed in the schools "due to the Jewish monopoly of the American educational system."[8] In the main, however, the ADL found that most of the raw, undisguised anti-Semitism in the simmering two-year controversy over the control and direction of New York's public schools derived from "black extremists" and that its growth had been "aided by the failure of city and state public officials to condemn it swiftly and strongly enough and to remove from positions of authority those who have utilized anti-Semitism," including the Council Against Poverty officials involved.

The ADL report showed, for example, that repeatedly during 1967 Robert (Sonny) Carson and other members of Brooklyn Independent CORE (Congress of Racial Equality) had attempted to pressure Brooklyn school administrators out of their jobs by entering schools and making anti-Semitic statements and thinly veiled threats ("the Germans in Germany killed you Jews because you tried to control the economy of Germany and that is what you are trying to do to the black man in the United States").[9] The question the Jewish community had to ask — Where were the city school and human rights authorities, not to mention the police? — went unanswered. Similarly, the ADL report showed that at least one leaflet disseminated in Harlem just after the school strike and likening the United Federation of Teachers to "Zionists" who "kill black people in their own land in the Middle East" had been printed for the Tenant Rights Party (Jesse Gray, chairman) by Harlem Back Street Youth, a year-round program funded by the Council Against Poverty. Where, it had to be asked, were the CAP

officials responsible for overseeing the use of antipoverty funds
when this anti-Semitism was being produced? That question, too,
went unanswered.

Luis Fuentes was principal of a school in Ocean Hill-Brownsville, focal point of the citywide debate over "community control"
of the schools. Fuentes was also the city's first school supervisor of
Puerto Rican background. ADL made public affidavits from two
assistant principals who had served under Fuentes following his
appointment in September 1967 as principal of P.S. 155. The
assistant principals, both Jewish, charged that Fuentes had not
only repeatedly made anti-Semitic remarks but had displayed
a racist hostility to other groups as well, even to Puerto Ricans.

In 1968 Mario Biaggi, then president of the Grand Council of
Columbia Associations in Civil Service, an Italian-American
group, had filed charges against Fuentes with the Board of Education, declaring that Fuentes had harassed Italian-American
children and had used anti-Italian epithets in addressing an
assistant principal;[10] Italian-American supervisors said Fuentes
referred to them as "The Mafia" and used such terms as "wop"
and "guinea."[11]

On May 7, 1970, after Fuentes' anti-Semitism had become a
matter of widespread public knowledge, he appeared before the
Board of Education to dispute his pending dismissal as principal
of P.S. 155. He had this to say:

> I charge that the Board of Examiners is being used to screen out
> certain ethnic groups under the thin veil of its being a legal way
> while at the same time it lends itself well, very well, to favoring one
> ethnic group. And I maintain that the greed of this elite group or this
> country club bunch of officers are performing a service for racists
> that are dedicated to keeping blacks and Puerto Ricans in their place.
> I face your axe June 30 because I'm untested, I'm uncircumcized.[12]

Fuentes faced dismissal because he did not possess New York
City Board of Examiners qualifications to be a principal but had
only state certification for the job. His appointment was valid by
law only so long as the Ocean Hill-Brownsville schools formed
one of the three experimental, or "demonstration," school dis-

tricts in the city. When the state legislature passed the School Decentralization Law in 1969, it mandated that the demonstration districts be absorbed into the new regular school districts and as such their principals had to come via the regular Board of Examiners route. Fuentes got a reprieve when a federal court suit—not however, involving Fuentes—was filed in the summer of 1970 challenging the constitutionality of the Board of Examiners testing procedures. On July 14, 1971 U.S. District Judge Walter R. Mansfield ruled that the examinations had a *de facto* discriminatory effect and issued a preliminary injunction barring their use and the use of eligibility lists drawn up from them in the selection of supervisory personnel.[13] Fuentes' state credentials therefore remained valid. On October 6, 1971, however—the same day the Board of Education, acting on Judge Mansfield's ruling, dispensed with the existing supervisory examinations—the local community school board in Brooklyn, elected under decentralization procedures, removed Fuentes from his post.[14]

Fuentes' anti-Semitic remarks before the Board led to an official reprimand by the acting chancellor of the city's schools.[15] (Fuentes was to claim some two and a half years later that he had been referring to all whites, not Jews, when he complained of favoritism for one ethnic group—and that he was unaware that circumcision was a specifically Jewish religious practice.[16]

In July 1972 Community School Board 1 on Manhattan's Lower East Side appointed Luis Fuentes to its $37,000-a-year top professional post of district superintendent. Neither Fuentes' demonstrated anti-Semitism and racism nor his rejection in 1969 for the superintendent's job by a predecessor District 1 school board on the ground that he had falsified a letter of recommendation served to deter the local school board from appointing him.[17]

Indeed the local board had other considerations, for which Luis Fuentes was supremely qualified: the Board, dominated by a coalition of black and Puerto Rican community control militants in an area that for several years had been wracked by ethnic conflict over school issues, was extremely eager to pursue a policy of hiring along racial and ethnic lines, and Fuentes for years had been agitating for such a policy in the city schools. As early as 1967, for example, he had told colleagues that Negro children should be taught by Negroes, Jewish children by Jews, and that only teachers of the same ethnic background could teach in ghetto schools.[18] And on July 8, 1972, Community School Board 1 adopted a regulation requiring the superintendent to hire teachers and supervisors in such a way as to develop "an ethnic distribution among the staff that is more nearly representative of the student population in the district."[19] (The public school population was roughly 68 percent Puerto Rican, 17 percent black, 8 percent Chinese and 7 percent white, including Jewish.) Informed by New York City Schools Chancellor Harvey B. Scribner—after the ADL and other Jewish organizations had raised the issue[20]— that such a policy violated laws against discrimination based on race, religion or ethnic origin, Community School Board 1 purportedly withdrew the controversial regulation.[21] But not before it had hired Luis Fuentes, a man virtually guaranteed to implement the discriminatory policy whether or not it existed on paper. It was a true marriage of minds.

The appointment of Fuentes set off a controversy in New York that continues at this writing. It pitted the legitimate concerns of the Jewish community—and other fair-minded New Yorkers— against the apparent unconcern of the highest education officials in the city and state on the issue of anti-Semitism and the impropriety of appointing a known bigot to a sensitive edutional post. It reflected a callousness about Fuentes' real potential for harming teachers and supervisors as professionals because they are Jews. It reflected an indifference to whether the climate the District 1 superintendent created in the already turmoil-ridden Lower East Side schools would encourage more division or help to heal the wounds. It revealed, in short, a total lack of concern with Fuentes' fitness as an educator. And it helped to perpetrate a hoax on those thousands of Lower East Side parents who aspire to an education for their children and who instead found themselves at the vortex of a dispute that had nothing to do with education and everything to do with a grab for power by a militant few.

Shortly after the appointment of Fuentes, the Anti-Defamation League, American Jewish Congress, American Jewish Committee and Jewish Labor Committee publicly protested the act and called for his removal. In letters to Chancellor Scribner and Commissioner Nyquist, as well as to City Human Rights Commission Chairman Eleanor Holmes Norton and State Human Rights Division Chairman Jack Sable, the Jewish organizations said they found it "totally inexplicable" that Fuentes' well-documented record of bigotry was not sufficient to have kept him from such a key professional appointment.[22] In letters to Mayor Lindsay, Chancellor Scribner and the city's Central Board of Education, Rabbi William Berkowitz, president of the New York Board of Rabbis, also called for Fuentes' removal. Adding his voice, as well, to the general outrage was the president of the Board of Education, Joseph Monserrat, for years a leader in the struggle for Puerto Rican rights and the first Puerto Rican to head the Board. In a dramatic and unprecedented move, Monserrat charged, in a signed guest editorial in *El Diario-La Prensa,* the city's Spanish language daily, that Fuentes was a "racist" and "an embarrassment to the Puerto Rican community" and that his record of racism raised "the most serious questions about his suitability as an educator." Monserrat said he had been present when Fuentes made one of his racist remarks, that the groups opposing Fuentes did so not because he was Puerto Rican "but because he is a racist" and that these groups had pointed out that there were "other qualified Puerto Rican candidates" for the job. The Board president wrote: "The time to speak up and speak out on those issues that affect us most is when they hit close to home. Too many Puerto Ricans have been victims of the disease of racism for any of us to do any less."[23]

Chancellor Scribner's office maintained, however, that there was as yet "no basis for an investigation" and that under the Decentralization Law, the community school boards alone had the power to hire and fire the district superintendents; the Chancellor, they asserted, had authority over the school boards only if noncompliance with the law could be proved.[24]

Assemblyman Albert H. Blumenthal, a prime figure in the drafting and passage of the Decentralization Law, felt that Scribner had the authority to hold an immediate hearing on the charges of racism against Fuentes; he urged Scribner to do so and to suspend Fuentes pending the outcome of such a hearing. He reminded the Chancellor that the Decentralization Law made the chancellor ultimately responsible for failure of community school boards to enforce bylaws of the Board of Education, one of which was a prohibition of conduct unbecoming to personnel of the Board of Education.[25]

Others who demanded investigation of Fuentes' appointment included Representatives Biaggi[26] and Assemblyman Antonio Olivieri, the *New York Times, Daily News* and the *Post.*[27] The *Times* declared:

> So extensive have been the complaints against Mr. Fuentes that local and state authorities in both education and human rights should have initiated their own investigation long ago without any need for outside prodding.

The *Times* concluded:

> The integrity and workability of decentralization has always de- pended on the capacity and willingness of the Central Board of Education to prevent the community boards from abusing their newly acquired powers. Unless the city's schools are to be abandoned to racial and ethnic power plays, Chancellor Harvey Scribner and the central board have an immediate obligation to investigate the charges against Mr. Fuentes and review the appropriateness of his appointment.

The issue was not quite as clear to Chancellor Scribner and his advisers. When a month had passed with no action from the Chancellor's office, three of the four organizations that had ini- tially protested the Fuentes appointment—the ADL, American Jewish Congress and Jewish Labor Committee—filed a formal petition with Scribner seeking an investigation. It charged Fuentes with anti-Semitism and racism and the local board with "dereliction of duty" in failing to investigate Fuentes' previous conduct and with discrimination on racial grounds against other applicants for the superintendent's post. It asked the Chancellor to remove both Fuentes and the local board if the charges were substantiated. Factual evidence was submitted with the organizations' allegations, and they asked Chancellor Scribner to investigate as well charges that had been made through the years that Fuentes had submitted a forged letter of recommendation from a previous employer in seeking the District 1 superintendency in 1969 and that he had earlier defaulted on a $2,000 loan in Miami and left the area, requiring colleagues who had co-signed his note to make it good.[28] In making public their petition, the organizations said that a careful examination of relevant laws and guidelines had convinced them that the Chancellor had both the authority and the responsibility to undertake the investigation and to act against the local school board itself if the investigation indicated that the board had been negligent in its duty.[29]

With continuing indifference to the issue, however, the Chancellor's office denied it had any responsibility or authority and told the Jewish organizations to take their petition to the very District 1 Board they had charged with negligence. Counsel to Scribner maintained that "the Chancellor cannot accept jurisdiction" because "such grievances . . . should first be brought to the attention of the Community School Board so that the Community Board may take appropriate action."[30]

The readiness of the local board to "take appropriate action" on a matter profoundly affecting its own conduct and its own tenure was, of course, open to serious question. Militants in the district had a long history of shouting down any opinions opposed to their own, and in fact one mid-August meeting of Community Board 1 had been turned into a rally to support Fuentes at which, it was reported, only those sympathetic to Fuentes were permitted to speak.[31] On September 7, therefore, the three Jewish organizations rejected as "absurd" the suggestion that they seek redress through the local board. In a letter to Chancellor Scribner they told him that the Board of Education's own "Rules and Regulations Governing Grievances Against Community School Boards or Members" authorized him to take action on a complaint such as theirs.[32]

Meantime, Chancellor Scribner had appointed a hearing officer to investigate the charges filed by Mrs. Antoinette DiMauro, a dissident member of Community School Board 1 who opposed the appointment of Fuentes. On September 28 the Chancellor accepted the recommendation of his hearing officer that the local board had not acted improperly in its appointment of Fuentes. On the matter of Fuentes' racism, however, the hearing officer had said the charges were serious enough to warrant investigation, and Scribner directed the local board—the same board that had earlier ignored these charges in appointing Fuentes—to investigate them and report back to him within thirty days.[33] On October 30 the local board issued its report, predictably clearing Fuentes of the charges of anti-Semitism and racism and upholding his character. The community school board also denied any impropriety in its appointment of Fuentes, claiming that it was unaware of the charges of anti-Semitism against him at the time of the appointment.[34] The Jewish organizations labeled the report clearing Fuentes a "farce" and said they could prove the local board had foreknowledge of the charges of anti-Semitism against Luis Fuentes.[35]

Some weeks earlier, Chancellor Scribner, finally impressed by the determination of the Jewish organizations to have their case aired in a legitimate forum and the widespread public opinion that such an investigation was warranted, had appointed former New York Police Commissioner Vincent L. Broderick, now a practicing attorney, as hearing examiner on the charges against Fuentes and the local board. The hearings conducted by Commissioner Broderick extended into early 1973. His report was made public April 5, less than a month before community school board elections which, in District 1, were to pit a pro-Fuentes slate against one opposed to the superintendent; the election campaign was already intense, with Fuentes the main issue. The headlines the following day told the story of Broderick's finding. "Report to Scribner Denies Fuentes Is Bigot," said the *Times;* "Fuentes Ruled Not a Bigot," reported the *Daily News;* "Fuentes No Bigot 'Now'—Report," declared the New York *Post,* somewhat more accurately in terms of what Broderick had actually ruled.

Asserting that the charges against Fuentes were "time-barred" under provisions of the Education Law, since most of the anti-Semitic incidents had occurred more than three years earlier, Broderick found that Fuentes was "at the present time, neither a bigot nor a racist."[36] Inconsistent with that ruling, however,

Broderick urged Scribner to have the local school board instruct Fuentes to "refrain, in the future, from comments, public or private, of a slurring nature toward, or about, any racial, ethnic or religious groups, and from comments which even have the appearance of such slurring nature." (It was not clear why, if Fuentes was in fact unbigoted, he would have to be instructed to refrain from bigoted remarks.) Broderick never dealt with the "time-barred" anti-Semitism and racism Fuentes had displayed; the charges, documented by sworn affidavits, were therefore never disproved. As to the statement of May 7, 1970 before the Board of Education, Broderick held that Fuentes' use of the word "uncircumcized" was "highly improper, since it bespoke anti-Semitic prejudice."

Broderick also cleared the local school board of acting improperly, apparently accepting the testimony of members of the board as to the manner in which they had chosen Fuentes. His confidence in the local board was made clear when he explained that in exonerating Fuentes, one of the factors in his decision was "the commitment of the school board for which he works . . . against prejudice, discrimination and racism."[37]

On April 26 the Anti-Defamation League, American Jewish Congress and Jewish Labor Committee appealed Mr. Broderick's ruling to the central New York City Board of Education. That appeal is, at this writing, still pending.

On May 18 State Education Commissioner Ewald Nyquist, investigating the Fuentes matter on an appeal brought to him by Mrs. DiMauro, announced that in view of the Broderick hearings, "a further hearing would serve no useful purpose since such a hearing would simply be an expensive, unproductive duplication of the proceedings before Mr. Broderick." Nyquist asserted that before becoming a superintendent, "Mr. Fuentes on occasion exercised deplorable judgment for one who now holds so sensitive a position," adding that "inflamed rhetoric is not a substitute for a carefully reasoned discussion of issues." Nevertheless, reported the *Times* the following day, the commissioner said he had not found sufficient grounds for revocation of Fuentes' state certification as a supervisor.

As a result of the May 1973 school board elections, six of the nine seats on Community School Board 1 were won by candidates opposed to Fuentes and only three by his incumbent supporters on the board. The new board took office on July 1 and on October 16 voted to suspend Fuentes. His supporters, who had earlier gone to federal court to challenge the school election, called for a boycott of the district schools and sought a court stay of the suspension. The court granted a temporary injunction because of the pending suit on the election; on December 26, Federal Judge Charles E. Potter indicated he would order a new election in the district.

More than two and a half million Jews, nearly half of all Jews in the United States, live in New York City and its immediate environs. Moreover, the city is a hub from which ideas, fashions and fads radiate across the country. American Jews, therefore, regard New York as a sensitive barometer of changes in public opinion and political thinking that affect their security. The insensitivity of major elements of the respectable New York public to the issue of anti-Semitism has played a prime role in creating the climate of worry in the Jewish community. Only a clear and unequivocal demonstration, whenever it is required and promptly, that anti-Semitism will not be tolerated from any quarter under any circumstances will help to allay these fears.

6

The
Clergy

On March 20, 1972, Dr. A. Roy Eckardt, a leading Protestant theologian and chairman of the Department of Religion at Lehigh University, addressed the Third Annual Scholars Conference on the German Church Struggle and the Holocaust at Wayne State University in Detroit. In part of his paper, Dr. Eckardt analyzed what he called "the highly pervasive, contemporaneous anti-Semitism of the theological left" and warned that it should not be underestimated by focusing exclusively on the anti-Semitism of "the biblicist and theological right." Dr. Eckardt wrote:

> Christian particularists denounce Jews for their universalism; but Christian universalists denounce Jews for their particularism. The rejection of Jewish particularity, including most especially today the right to political integrity, is one more manifestation of the Christian death-wish for Jews.
>
> Is it the case that Christians who cast off central dogmas that inspire anti-Judaism and nurture Christian imperialism will thereby develop a non-anti-Semitic viewpoint? If often happens. But it does not necessarily happen. Contemporary negativism toward Jews extends to so-called liberal Christians.[1]

As one example of liberal Christian antipathy toward Jewish particularity—i.e., toward Jews as Jews—Dr. Eckardt cited *The Crime of Christendom* by a Unitarian-Universalist scholar, Fred

Gladstone Bratton. In the book—ironically, written to combat anti-Semitism—Bratton contended that "ethnic and cultural anti-Semitism . . . was originally provoked and continuously nourished by the orthodox Jewish dogmas of uniqueness,"[2] thus making the victims basically responsible for their own victimization. Bratton's ideal was the "liberal Jew" who was "no longer obsessed with the idea of uniqueness" but willing to "emphasize broad principles of living rather than particularistic beliefs." In his analysis, Dr. Eckardt wrote:

> Not strangely, Bratton's attack upon Jewishness climaxes in an attack upon Zionism and Israel: The "fanatical leaders of political Zionism have forced upon Jews everywhere the idea that they are a part of an ethnic, racial and political entity. . . ." In sum, Bratton perpetuates the central Christian transgression: the perennial refusal to honor Jewish particularity, the right of the Jewish people simply to be themselves.

Dr. Eckardt's paper was to be strangely and disturbingly prophetic. For on March 26, Palm Sunday, a liberal Protestant clergyman of national stature was to deliver a religious sermon that approached the very edge of the line between insensitivity to Jewish feelings and anti-Semitism itself. Many indeed thought that the line had been crossed.

Few clergyman of any faith can match the credentials of the Very Rev. Francis B. Sayre, Jr. Born in the White House, the grandson of Woodrow Wilson, married to the daughter of a United States senator, he is dean of the National (Episcopal) Cathedral in Washington, D.C. He is also a bona fide liberal, his certification including, among other acts, that moment twenty years ago when he called Senator Joseph McCarthy a "malicious imposter" and helped to launch the demagogue's downfall.[3]

On the morning of Palm Sunday 1972, Dean Sayre addressed worshipers gathered in the cathedral for the beginning of Holy Week. The season, of course, has a long history of trauma for Jews, Palm Sunday often signaling outbursts of Christian hostility, including the pogroms Jews had learned to expect from anti-Semitic authorities in czarist Russia and Eastern Europe.

Dean Sayre chose the occasion not merely to focus on the religious significance of Jerusalem, which would have been very much in the tradition of Palm Sunday sermons, but to attack Israel for its alleged policies in East Jerusalem, and to link these alleged policies with the "fatal flaw" of mankind that resulted in the crucifixion of Jesus.

Detailing, in traditional Christian terms, the glories and sorrows of "Jerusalem the Golden" during Holy Week and making the point that "it is just when man proclaims his faithfulness that he is nearest to betraying the Holy One," Dean Sayre said:

> . . . So Jerusalem, in all the pain of her history, remains the sign of our utmost reproach: the zenith of our hope, undone by the wanton meanness of men who will not share it with their fellows but choose to kill, rather than to be overruled by God.
>
> This, the terrible ambivalence of the human race about truth, about himself, about God — is what the service this morning serves to dramatize. Yet we hardly need such pantomime to make it vivid, for we could look at contemporary Jerusalem, if we wished, and see the moral tragedy of mankind enacted there all over again in the politics of latter-day Israel.
>
> Surely one can sympathize with the loving hope of that little state, which aspires to be the symbol, nay more: the embodiment of a holy peoplehood. For her, Jerusalem is the ancient capital: the site of the Temple that housed the sacred Ark of the Covenant. To achieve a government there is to realize the restoration of a scattered remnant; it is the fulfillment of cherished prayer tempered in suffering, newly answered upon the prowess of her young men and the skill of her generals. Around the world Hosannah has echoed as Jewish armies surged across the open scar that used to divide Arab Jerusalem from the Israeli sector.
>
> Now the Jews have it all. But even as they praise their God for the smile of fortune, they begin almost simultaneously to put Him to death. As if Jerusalem could ever be altogether theirs — or anyone's! But now oppressed become oppressors: Arabs are deported; Arabs are imprisoned without charge; Arabs are deprived of the patrimony of their lands; and homes; their relatives may not come to settle in Jerusalem; they have neither voice nor happiness in the city that after all is the capital of their religious devotion too![4]

After quoting a dissident Hebrew University teacher as justification for his untruths about the Israeli administration of East Jerusalem, Dean Sayre continued:

> What a mirror, then, is modern Israel of that fatal flaw in the human
> breast that forever leaps to the acclaim of God, only to turn the next
> instant to the suborning of His will for us. Hosannah, Lord—as long
> as it's our way! . . .

Sayre's sermon provoked a controversy whose reverberations,
in the words of one columnist, "carried all the way to England,
where the London *Express* called it 'an extraordinary fracas.'"[5]
The Washington *Post* was among the first to denounce the sermon. In an editorial it said Dean Sayre's words, "even as they
praise their God . . . they begin almost simultaneously to put
Him to death," were "painfully close to a very old, very familiar
line of the worst bigotry." The *Post* added: "Undoubtedly Dean
Sayre did not intend to evoke this recollection. But it is profoundly dangerous all the same. The gun is loaded, whether the
dean acknowledges it or not."[6]

The *Post* declared that Dean Sayre's allegations of mistreatment of Israeli Arabs were "highly unjust" and that "freedom of
religion and open access to the shrines are better protected now,
by the Israeli state, than at any time in memory."

Many clergyman similarly dissociated themselves from Dean
Sayre's views. The Rev. Edward H. Flannery, executive secretary
of the Secretariat for Catholic-Jewish Relations of the U.S. Catholic Conference, and Msgr. George G. Higgins, director of the
Conference's Division for Urban Life, wrote that they had just
returned from Jerusalem and had "failed to find any evidence of
Israeli oppression in that city."[7] The Rev. Graydon E. McClellan
of the Presbytery Executive, National Capital Union Presbytery,
recalled recent statements by returning Christian clergy com-
mending Israel "for its care for human rights, its fairness in housing, its practices of religious liberty, and its respect for the holy
places."[8] The Rev. John G. Steinbruck, pastor of the Luther Place
Memorial Church in Washington, recounted his trips to Israel in
1969 and 1972 and said that "Israel can well serve as a model to
the nations of the world as a standard of restraint in use of power
and [of] sensitivity shown to the residents of occupied areas."[9] The
Rev. Lester Kinsolving inquired, in his syndicated column, why
Dean Sayre had had nothing to say about the real and "sordid

atrocities being visited upon Jews by the Syrian government" or why he had not protested "the wholesale desecration of synagogues and expulsion of Jews after the Trans-Jordan Arab Legion invaded Jerusalem and occupied it in 1947." Kinsolving pointed out that this was in violation of the United Nations' order—"as Dean Sayre must know, since his father was Chairman of the Trusteeship Council in Jerusalem in 1947." The columnist also noted that Abdul Aziz Zuabi was an Arab "who has somehow escaped the persecution described by Sayre, to become an Israeli cabinet minister."[10]

Dean Sayre did get some support, however, at a press conference held by two clergymen who are long-time disseminators of anti-Israel, anti-Semitic Arab propaganda and one of whom, the Rev. A. C. Forrest, editor of the *United Church Observer*, had been described by Dr. Eckardt as "Canada's most notorious and perhaps most denominationally protected Christian anti-Semite."[11] At the press conference Forrest congratulated Dean Sayre for his "courage, knowledge and insight."[12]

Dean Sayre, who would probably be mortified to learn of it, was also defended by another unlikely bedfellow. In the October 1972 issue of *The Cross and the Flag*, Gerald L. K. Smith complained that Sayre, as a result of his Palm Sunday sermon, was "on the liquidation list of the mindwashing propaganda machine and the Jewish smear apparatus." Smith said Sayre was being victimized with "epithets which are used on people like me." He took the opportunity to blast Israel for "genocide and other crimes against humanity" and to promote his new "Holy Land" project in Eureka Springs, being built, he said, "because complete desecration of the sacred shrines in the Middle East is threatened."[13]

The smoke from the controversy over Dean Sayre's sermon had barely cleared when Sayre was in the news again. The date was September 10, 1972 and the occasion a memorial service for "the victims of violence during the Olympiad," held in the National Cathedral. Dean Sayre made it clear that he was mourning not only the innocent Israeli athletes slain at Munich by "murderous guerrillas and ruthless revolutionaries," but also "those additional victims of the violence in Munich: those villagers in Lebanon and Syria whose lives have been extinguished by the Israeli Air Force even as the Twentieth Olympiad yet endures." He added:

> An eye for an eye, a tooth for a tooth is the rationale of that violence by which I am desolate to think the government of Israel has sacrificed any moral position of injured innocence.[14]

Rabbi Joshua O. Haberman of Washington's Hebrew Congregation, an old friend of Dean Sayre, had written an open letter to him after his Palm Sunday sermon, citing the errors in the sermon's text and urging Sayre to "join hands in the search for more accurate information and deeper understanding of the complexities of the issue." Rabbi Haberman had invited the Episcopal clergyman to accompany him on a fact-finding journey to Jerusalem, which Sayre had not visited in many years.[15] Sayre had tentatively accepted and the two were assured the cooperation of Israeli authorities, including Jerusalem Mayor Teddy Kollek. Early in December, however, it was reported that Rabbi Haberman had dropped his plans for the joint visit. He had concluded, after Sayre's remarks following the Olympic murders, that the dean had "hardened his views and his mind is closed." Such a trip, Rabbi Haberman told an interviewer, "would only offer him an opportunity to get additional publicity for them, since he would see only what he wanted to see."[16]

One of the more disturbing aspects of Dean Sayre's comments on the Munich massacre and the Israeli raids—and an aspect that again called into question, as had the language of his Palm Sunday sermon, his attitudes not only toward Israel but toward Jews and Judaism—was his use of the "eye for an eye, tooth for a tooth" biblical reference. The *lex talionis* is a standard reference of classical anti-Semites, who often are familiar with it only in the New Testament version (Matthew 5:38-40) in which Jesus, according to the simplistic interpretation virtually discarded in contemporary Christian scholarship, opposes Mosaic law and offers an apparently new concept, that of turning the other cheek. Many scholars have shown that the Old Testament references (Exodus 21:24-25, Leviticus 24:20 and Deuteronomy 19:21 (a) may never have been literally enforced, (b) even if they had been, had certainly ceased being enforced more than a century before Jesus' time and (c) in any event, were principally an injunction against *excessive* punishment and an admonition to "make the punishment fit the crime," so to speak. And surely Dean Sayre must know that capital punishment—in defense of which the "eye for an eye" reference is often used—does not exist in modern Israel, unlike the United States, whose Supreme Court has ruled unconstitutional only its varying and unequal application.

It was entirely possible that Dean Sayre may have been influenced in his thinking by a document published as a paperback in 1970 under the auspices of the American Friends Service Committee, widely circulated by both Friends and fellow Christian liberals, heavily promoted in the Christian press and debated over the educational television program, "The Advocates."

The Quakers have been long admired among American and Canadian liberals and others of good will for their arduous humanitarian efforts in behalf of refugees (including Jewish victims of the Holocaust) and world peace. And they had a long history of cooperation with Jewish groups in these and other undertakings. Nevertheless, after several years of study and more than a dozen drafts—which had been sharply criticized by scholars, whose criticisms were thereupon virtually ignored—the American Friends Service Committee brought out *Search for Peace in the Middle East.*[17]

A pro-Arab document masquerading under repeated claims of objectivity by its authors, the Quaker report, in a rewrite of history, distributed blame for the Six-Day War evenly among Arabs and Israelis and put the onus squarely on Israel to make the peace. So widespread was the acceptance (the Quaker credentials were very good indeed) of the arguments advanced—biased as much in what they did not say as in what they did—that two leading Jewish organizations found it necessary to publish a counter-report exposing the Quaker distortions. *Truth and Peace in the Middle East—A Critical Analysis of the Quaker Report,* written by several scholars in the Boston area, came out in August 1971.[18]

What had the Quaker group said that led the authors of the

counter-study to charge that the Friends had, disappointingly, "displayed a blatant bias, repressed facts, distorted history and presented a slanted and one-sided set of conclusions"?[19]

First, the Quaker group accepted—and furthered without question or quotation marks—the Arab propaganda view that Israel was imposed on the area by Western states guilty of anti-Semitism to solve, at Arab expense, a problem Arabs never created; omitted was the truth—that far from imposing Israel on the Arab world, the Western powers did much to block its establishment and little to advance it; omitted was any reference to the role played by the persecution of Jews in Arab countries or the fact that more than half of Israel's current population comes from Arab lands.

Second, in writing of the 1948 war, the Quaker account implied that the fighting erupted spontaneously on both sides when, in fact, it was launched by the Arabs. The Quaker report mentioned neither the invasion of Israel by surrounding Arab states nor Britain's important role in turning over key installations and equipment to the Arabs.

The Quaker report insisted that Egypt and Israel were equally guilty for the outbreak of the June 1967 war and insinuated that Israel moved "aggressively" in search of territorial expansion. It contained not a single word about the role of Jordan, which was repeatedly urged by Israel to stay out of the fray—and which today would probably still be in possession of the West Bank and East Jerusalem if it had.

Despite repeated expressions supporting "the just recognition of claims denied to the abused Palestinian people," the Quaker account avoided any significant Arab responsibility for the plight of the refugees. Overlooked was the fact that the failure to establish the Palestinian state called for in the UN Partition Resolution of 1947 was solely a result of political decisions by the Arab states, and that these states denied the Palestinians a voice in the armistice negotiations of 1948–49.

Moreover, in 1970, at a time when diplomatic efforts were being undertaken by the UN and others in a campaign to get negotiations started toward peace, the Quaker report strongly advocated a "Big Four" solution, despite the fact that—given Soviet ambitions in the Middle East, Asia and Africa and the wooing of the oil-rich states by France and Great Britain—there was no reason to expect that the Big Four could or would guarantee a true peace. Or that anyone but the parties to the dispute themselves could do so.

Despite a history of broken Arab and Western pledges and agreements, and after three costly wars and unremitting Arab efforts to destroy her, Israel was required by the Quaker group to forego the possibility of negotiating a real peace, with secure and agreed borders, and rely instead on Arab "willingness" to live in peace. The Quakers insisted that Israel as a first step commit itself to withdraw from all the occupied territory—a strictly Arab reading of the UN Security Council's resolution of November 22, 1967.

But if the Jewish community found the dissemination of these and other views in the allegedly "objective" Quaker document disturbing, it was astonished at earlier drafts of the Quaker report, which apparently achieved some circulation. These stated, in part (italics added):

> We appeal to the leaders of the *powerful* American Jewish community, whose hard work and generous financial support have been so important to the building and sustaining of Israel, to reasses the *character of their support* and the *nature of their role in American politics.* Our impression . . . is that there is a tendency for the *American Jewish establishment* to identify themselves with the more *hard-line elements* inside the Israeli cabinet, "to *out-hawk the hawks,*" and to ignore or discount the dissident elements, in and out of the Israeli Government, that are searching for *more creative ways* to solve the Middle East problems.
>
> As free American citizens, members of the American Jewish community have every right to utilize all the instruments of a free society to register their convictions and desires, and to try to influence legislative and executive action. However, the *heavy-handed nature* of some of these pressures and their *extensiveness* have served to *inhibit calm and rational* public discussion of the issues in the Arab-Israeli conflict. It is not a new phenomenon in American politics, but it is nonetheless disturbing to have *Congressmen complain privately* that they have signed public statements giving unqualifed endorsement for Israel, even though they do not believe in those statements, or have agreed to sponsor resolutions concerning American policy toward Israel of which they secretly disapprove—simply

> because they are *intimidated* by *Jewish pressure groups.* In this
> situation are *clear dangers of an anti-Semitic backlash.* No one who
> is truly concerned about the *long-term fate of Israel* and the *long-
> term threats to interfaith harmony and brotherhood* can be indif-
> ferent to those dangers.[20]

This statement could only be read as indicating that unless American Jews cut back in their efforts in behalf of Israel, they might
face an "anti-Semitic" backlash.

In the published version, the more offensive wording in the
first paragraph became an appeal to "leaders of the American
Jewish community . . . to reassess the ways in which their support
can further the cause of peace and security for Israel and to re-
examine the *full implications of their role* with respect to Middle
East policies. . . . [Italics added.]

Continuing to allege that leaders of American Jewry (but now
only "some" of them) support Israeli hard-liners, the Quaker
report continued:

> As American Jews, most of whom have a strong sense of identity with
> Israel, search for ways to express their concern and support, we urge
> them to make special efforts to explore the variety of options avail-
> able for peace in the Middle East, to *reject simplistic military solu-
> tions,* and to encourage calm and deliberate examination of all the
> issues. The same admonitions, of course, apply to all other groups
> which attempt to influence public opinion and government action
> toward the Middle East. [Italics added.][21]

The language, though considerably modified, still implied
that American Jews had to be wary. (As for the "Congressmen"
who "complain privately" of intimidation "by Jewish pressure
groups," they turned out to be a lone congressman with virtually
no Jews as constituents; he was therefore omitted from the final
text.[22]

On January 13, 1971, the *Christian Century* magazine called
the Quakers' *Search for Peace* "an instructive and fair-minded
primer . . ."[23]

On October 19, 1973, in the midst of the Yom Kippur war, Father
Daniel Berrigan, the Jesuit priest admired by many for his anti-
Vietnam war activities, addressed the Association of Arab Uni-

versity Graduates in Washington, D.C. Father Berrigan castigated Israel for "domestic repression, deception, cruelty, militarism"; for having turned the "settler ethos" into "the imperial adventure"; for having failed "to create new forms of political life for her own citizens"; for having created "one and a half million refugees." Father Berrigan said that were he a "conscientious Jew in Israel I would have to live as I was living in America; that is, in resistance against the state"; in Israel as in the United States, he claimed, such a posture would result in his being "hunted by the police, or in prison." Father Berrigan accused "many American Jewish leaders"—and particularly the "Zionists in our midst"—of "ignoring the Asian holocaust in favor of economic and military aid to Israel."

The speech came to public attention when the text was printed in the October 29 issue of *American Report,* bi-weekly publication of Clergy and Laity Concerned. In the November 12 issue it was answered by Rabbi Arthur Hertzberg of Temple Emanu-El in Englewood, New Jersey, a committed Zionist and a founder of the anti-war Clergy and Laity Concerned. Rabbi Hertzberg said he had "reluctantly come to a sad conclusion":

> Underneath the language of the New Left, Daniel Berrigan has no patience with the Jewish community and judges it to be horribly sinful for living with some semblance of normalcy in the world. He wishes it would go away and leave to him the role of the true Jew. Let us call all this by its right name: old-fashioned theological anti-Semitism.

In the December 21 *Commonweal,* under the headline "The New Anti-Semitism," the Catholic writer Michael Novak also challenged Father Berrigan:

> . . . surely, the groundswell of American Jewish identification with Zion is overwhelming. Zion is home, Zion is roots, Zion is heritage, Zion is identity. To be a Zionist is now virtually identical with being Jewish—and the difference between the two is not for a Christian to adjudicate. There is a tone of voice, "the Zionists in our midst," which is as ominous as any tone the human voice can utter.

On December 21, the Rev. Donald S. Harrington, senior minister of the Community Church of New York, who was to have presented a peace award to Father Berrigan, withdrew from the presentation. He told a news conference (reported in the *Times* the next day) that Berrigan had "ceased to be a witness and an influence for peace and has become the opposite." Stating that Berrigan's remarks were "inflammatory," he said Father Berrigan's prescription for Israel would mean "a return to the role of 'suffering servant'" and asked: "What kind of prophecy is this that solemnly prescribes policies implying crucifixion for a whole people to an audience of their enemies?"

Certainly moral leadership on the question of Jews has not come from those who have the greatest access to the world's population, i.e. the purveyors of ideas and images via the mass media and the world of the arts. Time and again in the past several years, some of the best-read newspapers in the nation (as we have seen in previous sections and will see again), television, movies, literature—have shown a gross insensitivity to anti-Semitism and to the fears and aspirations of the Jewish community. Because of the vast influence of these media they have played no small part in helping to nourish the climate of Jewish anxiety about Jewish security.

Let us begin, then, in a very contemporary mode, by looking at a movie millions will see before this book is in print. As with everything else, apparently, when it comes to anti-Semitism, there's no business like show business.

7

The Media
and the Arts

Norman Jewison is the produce-director who brought to the
screen, with considerable sensitivity, the heartwarming story
of the trials and tribulations of Tevye the Milkman. If the Sholem
Aleichem tale, the enormously successful stage version that pre-
ceded the film, and the movie itself of *Fiddler on the Roof* said
anything, they spoke of the triumph of a faith, Judaism, and a
people. Epitomized by Tevye, his family and his neighbors, they
surmounted extreme adversity, perpetual poverty, harassment
and explusion. In the summer of 1973, again with powerful art-
istry, Mr. Jewison brought us the film version of the rock opera
Jesus Christ Superstar. But this time, Jewison helped to perpetuate the lie that pursued Tevye's people in (and out of) "Anatevka"
and all the "Anatevkas" of the world through two millenia, including Auschwitz: the charge that the Jews, collectively, killed
Christ. Mr. Jewison apparently failed to see what post-Holocaust
Christianity itself has confessed: the historical link between anti-
Semitism—the anti-Semitism of Czarist Russia or Nazi Germany,
for example—and the deicide myth that gave it birth. From an
anti-Semitic stage production he created an even more anti-Semitic film.

Jesus Chrisi Superstar is virtually Oberammergau and Gerald
Smith's "Great Passion Play" set to rock. In its initial run around
the world's movie houses, it must have been seen by more people
than have seen the Oberammergau presentation in three centuries.

To Christians the Crucifixion and Resurrection are at the heart of their faith; to Jews the Crucifixion is the event for which they have borne, through twenty centuries, an unjust and unconscionable burden of blame. No serious scholar today questions that the assignment to the Jews, as a people, of guilt in the death of Jesus, of deicide, is the root cause of anti-Semitism and the direct precursor to the murder of countless millions of people, including the genocide of the second quarter of the twentieth century.

It has not helped Jews to point out that Jesus himself was a Jew, that the Last Supper was a Passover seder, that Jesus entered Jerusalem on what is now called Palm Sunday so that he could be there to celebrate the Passover. It has not helped to note that the Disciples were all Jews and so were the early Christians. Neither has it helped to argue that, in fact, Jesus died at the hands of the Roman occupiers on the orders of a savage governor who was later recalled to Rome and tried for oppression, and not at the hands of the Jews; nor has it helped to advance the thesis, as has one distinguished Israeli jurist, that the Jewish Sanhedrin actually tried to save Jesus from certain death by Roman decree. Neither has it helped the Jewish people to appeal to Christians on the basis of that brotherly love which was the essence of Jesus' message; in the name of that love, although blaspheming it, Crusaders went forth to "rescue" Jerusalem from the "infidel," slaying as many of the "infidel" Jews as they could find along the way. Nothing has truly availed against the disease of anti-Semitism. partly because the death of Jesus is at the core of Christianity, but particularly because the blame for it was assigned to the Jews, including millions of Jews unborn at the time.

The Roman Catholic Church in 1965 declared that in the eyes of the Church, what happened "cannot be charged against all the Jews, without distinction, then alive nor against the Jews of today" and that "the Jews should not be presented as rejected by God or accursed as if this followed from Holy Scriptures." The Church condemned "displays of anti-Semitism." Similar declarations have been adopted in recent years by a number of Protestant denominations. The years since this "Statement on the Jews" emanating from Vatican II represent, of course, but a millesecond in the slow march of history; it is hoped that as the decades unfold, the message will truly take hold among Catholics and Protestants, clergy and laity. That day has not yet come.

It was with understandable concern, therefore, that many in the American Jewish community watched the progress of a single recording *Superstar,* launched in 1969 and purchased in the amount of one million copies, to a full-scale rock opera, *Jesus Christ Superstar,* dealing with Jesus' final days, that itself sold an estimated 3.5 million copies in album form, and thence to a Broadway stage production that opened in the fall of 1971 to one of the largest advance sales in theater history. A Passion play set to rock music is still, after all, a Passion play. Much depends on how the writers and producers of each version deal with the role of Jews in the events leading to the Crucifixion.

Broadway's *Jesus Christ Superstar* opened to mixed reviews among theater critics and theologians alike. One critic called it "decadent . . . cheap, shoddy, vulgar and worst of all, cynical."[1] A conservative Catholic group said it was "blasphemous," and similarly strong objections were heard from some Protestant quarters.[2] Yet a department of religion faculty member at a Catholic college thought the musical was especially valuable for young people because it presented Jesus "as a strong, radical leader, attempting to change the world and not merely from the standpoint of bourgeois religiosity."[3]

For Jews the rock opera was a disaster mitigated only by the facts that the lyrics were often unintelligible and that New York theater prices might well keep many people, even those who liked rock music, away. *Superstar* represented, after all, a very free adaptation of the New Testament story; Jesus himself, for example, was drawn to conform to the authors' picture of him, and other changes in emphasis and essential content were made to suit the tastes of the show's creators. Yet on the crucial issue of the role played by the Jews of the time, authors Andrew Lloyd Webber and Tim Rice chose to preserve the ancient lie of an evil conspiracy by scribes, Pharisees, high priests and others whom the audiences knew to be Jewish. The malevolent image of the street mobs of Jerusalem and of the priests was preserved intact

and once again they were assigned major blame for the Crucifixion. At the same time, the authors of *Superstar* chose to white-
wash the character of Pontius Pilate, exonerating Pilate of blame
in the condemnation and trial of Jesus and thereby heightening
the responsibility assigned to the Jewish priesthood.

A number in the show called "This Jesus Must Die" leaves
no doubt, for example, that the Jewish priests plotted Jesus'
death.
As a crowd of Jesus' followers sings its support outside, the following scene takes place:

PRIEST 1:	Good Caiaphas the council waits for you
	The Pharisees and priests are here for you
CAIAPHAS:	Ah gentlemen—you know why we are here
	We've not much time and quite a problem here
ANNAS:	Listen to that howling mob of blockheads in the street!
	A trick or two with lepers and the whole town's on
	its feet
ALL:	He is dangerous
PRIEST 2:	The man is in town right now to whip up some support
PRIEST 3:	A rabble rousing mission that I think we must abort
ALL:	He is dangerous!
	He is dangerous!
PRIEST 2:	Look Caiaphas—they're right outside our yard
PRIEST 3:	Quick Caiaphas—go call the Roman guard
CAIAPHAS:	No wait—we need a more permanent solution to our
	problem . . .
ANNAS:	What then to do about Jesus of Nazareth
	Miracle wonderman—hero of fools?
PRIEST 3:	No riots, no army, no fighting, no slogans
CAIAPHAS:	One thing I'll say for him—Jesus is cool
ANNAS:	We dare not leave him to his own devices
	His half-witted fans will get out of control
PRIEST 3:	But how can we stop him? His glamour increases
	By leaps every minute—he's top of the poll
CAIAPHAS:	I see bad things arising—the crowd crown him king
	Which the Romans would ban
	I see blood and destruction, our elimination because
	of one man
	Blood and destruction because of one man
ALL:	Because, because, because of one man
CAIAPHAS:	Our elimination because of one man
ALL:	Because, because, because of one, 'cause of one, 'cause
	of one man
PRIEST 3:	What then to do about this Jesusmania?

ANNAS: How do we deal with the carpenter king?
PRIEST 3: Where do we start with a man who is bigger
Than John was when John did his Baptism thing?
CAIAPHAS: Fools! You have no perception!
The stakes we are gambling are frighteningly high!
So like John before him, this Jesus must die
For the sake of the nation this Jesus must die
ALL: Must die, must die, this Jesus must die
CAIAPHAS: So like John before him, this Jesus must die
ALL: Must die, must die, this Jesus must, Jesus must, Jesus
must die![4]

Minutes later on stage, and apparently deliberately juxtaposed to the plotting of the priests, the authors have Pontius Pilate exonerating himself in advance and placing the blame on those "wild and angry men." Pilate sings "Pilate's Dream," for which, of course, there is no source in the Gospels:

I dreamed I met a Galilean
A most amazing man
He had that look you very rarely find
The haunting hunted kind

I asked him to say what had happened
How it all began
I asked again—he never said a word
As if he hadn't heard

And next the room was full of wild and angry men
They seemed to hate this man—they fell on him and then
They disappeared again
Then I saw thousands of millions
Crying for this man
And then I heard them mentioning my name
And leaving me the blame[5]

The penultimate scene, the "Trial Before Pilate," further reinforces the theme of Jewish guilt and Roman innocence. As the mob outside Pilate's house repeatedly screams "Crucify him!" and Caiaphas, the Jewish high priest, repeatedly urges Pilate: "We need him crucified—it's all you have to do/ We need him crucified—it's all you have to do," Pilate says: "He's done no wrong—no not the slightest thing," and adds:

I see no reason—I find no evil
This man is harmless so why does he upset you?
He's just misguided—thinks he's important
But to keep you *vultures* happy I shall flog him [Italics added.]

After the thirty-nine lashes are delivered, Jesus refuses to plead for his life and the mob continues to howl for his crucifixion; Pilate says:

Don't let me stop your great self-destruction
Die if you want to you misguided martyr
I wash my hands of your demolition
Die if you want to you innocent puppet.[6]

Other elements of the libretto added to the total depiction of Jewish guilt. Both Judas—whose role was expanded beyond anything hinted in the Gospels—and Pilate refer to savage beatings of Jesus by the Jewish high priests, totally without any foundation in the New Testament. The Jewish priest Annas thanks Judas for "the victim," Jesus, and invites Judas to "see it bleed"—"it," not "him." An exchange between Jesus and Caiaphas, again with no source in the New Testament, depicts the Jewish high priest as contemptuous of Jesus. A remorseful Judas, played on stage (and subsequently in the film) by a black man, is conceived as the unwilling dupe of the Jewish priests—who assure him that he "backed the right horse" inasmuch as the mob had turned against Jesus.

Thus in 1971, and for nearly two years thereafter on Broadway and longer on the road, was the death of Jesus portrayed for American theater audiences—Jesus as the victim solely of a Jewish conspiracy.

Jewish organizations, confronted with this and other anti-Jewish presentations of this type, always have to consider whether public protest will create more interest in the production and thus expose more people to its calumnies, or produce charges that they seek to "censor" the arts. In the case of the Broadway stage opening, an informal consensus held that the show was destined to be a hit but that its potential audiences were not so vast as to warrant making a *cause célèbre* of this new version of a Passion play. An effort *was* made by the American Jewish Committee, just prior to the Broadway opening, to sensitize theater critics to the potential harmfulness of the production to Jews and to its possible negative impact on slowly improving Christian-Jewish relations. The Committee circulated a scholarly analysis of the rock opera by a Presbyterian scholar, who pointed to the historical inaccuracies of the libretto and its perpetuation of the myth of Jewish guilt in the death of Jesus.[7] The reaction of several critics to this educational effort to shed light on the issues was surpassed for insensitivity only by the insensitivity of the rock opera's authors themselves. These critics, in effect, yelled Censorship!—although no effort had been made to stop the production, change its text, or prejudice artistic reviews.[8] For such critics, it appeared that *Superstar* was merely another stage production to be handled routinely and "objectively" despite the implications of 2,000 years of history—and suffering—on the subject matter itself. Queried by the *New York Times,* the Anti-Defamation League supported the Committee's analysis and said it regretted that the rock opera had ignored the new, ecumenical interpretation of the Crucifixion and had instead followed "the old, primitive formulation of the Passion play, the spirit of which was discarded by Vatican II."[9]

No such gentle condemnation, however, was to greet the newest of the many presentations of *Superstar.* In late June 1973, from its annual meeting in Washington, D.C., the National Jewish Community Relations Advisory Council—representing virtually all the major national and community Jewish organizations in the United States—publicly blasted the soon-to-open Universal Pictures presentation, *Jesus Christ Superstar,* as "a singularly damaging setback in the struggle against the religious sources of anti-Semitism."[10]

Why? And why did we begin this chapter not with reference to the recorded rock opera or its Broadway production, but instead to the film produced and directed by Norman Jewison?

Film, which many regard as the twentieth century's unique contribution to the range of art forms, has always had an advantage over stage presentations, and this advantage has been multiplied by modern filmmaking techniques. Depicting life but larger than life, a motion picture can bring every element of nature and artifice to bear in the dramatic presentation. The camera's eye can sweep the range of desert and mountain which makes a tremendous impact on mood and emotion. It can also magnify: facial expression invisible from the balcony of a legitimate theater becomes as clear as the image in a hand-held mirror when it is captured by a close-up shot. Lyrics that are inaudible in a Broadway house become, thanks to modern sound tracks, clear and unmistakable; such sound tracks carry background music scored after the filming that brings all the power of this art form to play in a given scene. Moreover, while a successful stage presentation may reach hundreds of thousands over the years—if, like the stage versions of *My Fair Lady* or *Fiddler*, productions are mounted in many languages throughout the world—a film may reach many millions in a week, the same film presenting the same images, making the same point simultaneously in hundreds of movie theaters.

All this was known to producer-director Jewison (who is not Jewish, although his name has led to some confusion) and his associates in the production of the movie version of *Jesus Christ Superstar*. It was spelled out, in fact, in the "Production Notes" distributed at previews of the film:

> The two-part album by Andrew Lloyd Webber and Tim Rice remains, three years after it was recorded, an unparalleled emotional experience and entertainment for millions of people. Concert and stage versions mounted throughout the world have electrified audiences and, on another level, quickened the faith of young and old, and changed countless lives.
>
> What its impact will be as a motion picture, given the immediacy and the power of the medium, taking into account the world audience commanded by films, cannot be predicted.[11]

Noting that Jewison had co-authored the screenplay and invested the film with his own "unique vision," the Production Notes observed that despite "fierce winds" that "whipped the flowing costumes of the high priests and scattered props," director Jewison "continued filming so that the gales became a movement in themselves, underscoring Jewison's dominant visual theme." Sunsets that were "invariably dramatic," eagles and cranes that "formed flight patterns against the sky" and other elements of nature cooperated, said the notes, adding:

> The emotional involvement of actors, and staff and crew members with the production deepened markedly during the filming of the Crucifixion. Tears were choked back even by non-Christians when Ted Neeley acted out Christ's death. An awestruck tension gripped the company as a black cloud blotted out the blue sky over the Negev when the cross was first raised.

The publicity copy made much of the fact that *Jesus Christ Superstar* was filmed in Israel, with the cooperation of many Israelis, and that in his effort to create a "timeless" motion picture, director Jewison blended the "old and new," depicting drug pushers, for example, in "The Temple" sequence and using Israeli army tanks and jets to pursue the fleeing Judas.

What neither producer nor publicists mentioned, however, was that despite Jewish concern over the stage version—which they knew about and which they were worried about to the extent of inviting Jewish community relations experts to preview the film, in an effort, perhaps, to blunt criticism—the movie version retains all the anti-Semitic impact of the rock opera album and the stage presentation. The libretto is virtually the same. Moreover, the insistence on Jewish guilt in the death of Jesus is heightened by the "dominant visual theme" director Jewison was said to have sought.

Thus the high priests described as "vultures" by Pilate appear several times standing on scaffolds, and looking for all the world like vultures. Thus they are garbed consistently in dark and sinister-looking costumes; the "blameless" Pilate wears an elegant maroon costume, topped by a wreath around his head. (Pilate speaks softly, reasonably; the chief priests shout menacingly.) The Temple courtyard, where foreign currency was exchanged in Jesus' time, is pictured as a haunt of pushers, whores and vendors of machine guns. In the most stereotyped manner possible, cash registers are enshrined and old clothes haggled over.

There are, moreover, several additions to the screenplay. For example, when the high priest Caiaphas tells Pilate, "We need him crucified," this line is repeated in the film by the mob. Further, when that mob chants, "Crucify him! Crucify him!," Pilate clearly identifies them in a line which appeared neither in the Broadway production nor, of course, anywhere in the New Testament. Pilate says: "You Jews produce messiahs by the sackful."

On July 13, 1973 Israel moved to dissociate itself from the film version of *Jesus Christ Superstar.* In a statement issued in Jerusalem, the Israeli government declared:

> The fact that the film was shot on location in Israel in no way constitutes any agreement whatsoever to it on the part of the Government of Israel. The creators and producers of the film are alone and exclusively responsible for its content.

The statement, reported in the *New York Times* by Jerusalem correspondent Terence Smith the following day, indicated that prior assurances had been received from Norman Jewison that the film would "contain no passages to offend the religious sensibilities of Jewish and other circles" and that Jewison had pledged "he would not associate himself with the production of a film in which there are anti-Semitic nuances." In light of these assurances, Israel said, "it would be very distressing and most disappointing if the film should include, after all, passages of a nature to offend the Jewish people."

One of the New york theaters where the movie first opened was the 86th Street East Theater in the heart of Manhattan's Yorkville. Yorkville was a German neighborhood that prior to and during World War II had a disturbing element of pro-Nazi feeling and activity. Today, although it retains much of its earlier German ethnic flavor and many old-time residents, it is very much a mixed neighborhood. The new high-rise apartment buildings hold many thousands of younger, middle-class professional people, including many Jews.

Just weeks prior to the opening of *Jesus Christ Superstar* on East 86th Street, a Jewish woman in her late thirties was standing in line at the express check-out counter of a supermarket a stone's throw away. An elderly but well-preserved woman approached her and asked, politely, whether she might precede her in the line, inasmuch as she had only a few items. The younger woman, who also only had a few items, responded, just as politely, that she too was in a hurry and would prefer it if the older woman would wait her turn. Whereupon the latter, grimacing and raising her volume, said to the Jewish woman:

"I know *your* kind—*you people* are the same everywhere."

Turning to a man behind her, the woman continued, raising her voice another decibel:

"That's what I get for being nice to *them*."

There was a moment of total silence. No one responded. Then the Jewish woman turned, white with anger, to the older woman and said, evenly but audibly to all in the vicinity:

"I know your kind, too. Your kind sent six million of my kind to their deaths. You were not so eager to be first in line for the gas chambers."

Into such a neighborhood, in mid-1973—and into similar neighborhoods all over America and the world—came *Jesus Christ Superstar,* proclaiming to all the oldest anti-Semitic canard in the world.

If the Jew as "Christ-killer" is the seminal stereotype and the most dangerous, its offspring have plagued the Jewish people through the centuries. From "Shylock" to "shyster," words and images have been used and invented to depict Jews as canny, crafty, usurious, power-mad, conspiratorial, unassimilable, pushy, clannish, aggressive, stubborn, weak, greedy. That these slurs often contradict each other and make no sense whatever is an old, familiar story to Jews. In many countries and many languages they have been attacked coming and going: "The trouble with the Jews is that they are so clannish—they stick together and keep to themselves and don't really fit in very well." But let a Jew try to "join the club" and he is zapped from the other side: "The trouble with the Jews is that they are so pushy and aggressive, always trying to horn in where they're not wanted."

At the end of World War II, many people began to realize that defamation led to discrimination and discrimination could lead to Dachau. In the late forties, fifties and early sixties, such gross stereotypes all but disappeared from American life—at least overtly.

But they are back—sometimes subtle, sometimes nearly as crude as the slurs of yesteryear; sensitivity, apparently, is a short-lived commodity. And the stereotypes are now being applied to Jews not alone by professional bigots but by their fellow Americans across the board, some of whom would probably find a less hackneyed way of asserting that some of their best friends are Jews.

JEWS CONTROL CRIME IN THE UNITED STATES blared the display type in a June 24, 1971 quarter-page New York *Times* advertisement for the book *Lansky* by Hank Messick. It was news to Jews, and startling to most readers who opened that morning's edition of the *Times,* for the advertisement reeked of the kind of appeal to anti-Jewish prejudice found in the pages of Gerald Smith's *The Cross and the Flag.* But on the book page of the *Times?* And under the aegis of a publishing house as old and as respected as G. P. Putnam's Sons?

Reinforcing the intended impression that this was indeed a reproduction of an actual headline from a real newspaper was the fact that it had a ragged edge, as if it had been torn off and pasted up for the ad. Moreover, the advertisement went on to describe *Lansky* as the "book that set off front-page headlines from New York to Tel Aviv!" (The publisher was later to claim that the FBI had "lost" Lansky and that the Messick book had "told" them he was in Israel.)[12] The advertisement was an obvious attempt to capitalize on current news stories dealing with Meyer Lansky, whose name had cropped up for years in press reports as a key figure in underworld activities and who was seeking sanctuary in Israel from a federal indictment in the United States. (After considerable debate and adjudication within Israel, he was denied permission to remain there.)

As to the book itself, it is not anti-Semitic, never charged that

"Jews control crime in the United States" or anywhere else, and indeed contained a statement by author Messick that "organized crime is not the province of any one ethnic group or secret society."[13] Messick himself contended he was appalled at the advertisement.[14] (It was also learned that the same "headline" was to be used for the cover of a paperback edition of *Lansky* scheduled for September 1971 publication by Berkley Publishing Corporation, a subsidiary of Putnam's.)

Within days after the advertisement appeared, the Anti-Defamation League wrote to Walter J. Minton, president of Putnam's, expressing its shock at the display with its fraudulent "headline" and ADL's conviction that since Putnam's had found the book worth publishing, it could have been advertised "without dipping into the murky waters of anti-Semitism." Copies of the protest were sent to Arthur Ochs Sulzberger as publisher of the *Times* and to the paper's advertising manager. Mr. Minton's response was prompt:

> I've got enough Jewish, Protestant and Catholic antecedents in my own immediate background so that when I observe a Jew, a Protestant or a Catholic doing something I believe he should not be doing, I judge that action without feeling I am falling prey to prejudice.
>
> I regret that your letter suggests that a man in your position is not capable of so doing. There are crooked Jews in America, and if you read Hank Messick's LANSKY you will learn something about some of them.[15]

After defending the advertisement on the ground that the headline had allegedly run in an Israeli paper and that many news stories had been carried about Lansky and Israel in the United States, the president of Putnam's told the ADL it was "wrong" and that he was "sorry" to see ADL "leaping to the defense of people such as Meyer Lansky."

Mr. Minton was told in a second letter from ADL that Lansky's religious background was no more relevant to his alleged criminal activities than was Minton's to his publishing career;[16] that to "judge" people in such terms was what prejudice was all about; that the protest was not a defense of Lansky but of Jews who had

been linked to Lansky in the insinuating ad, and that the allegation that Jews controlled crime was, in any event, an out and out
lie.

Mr. Minton was unpersuaded. He responded that the ADL
protest was "unfounded,"[17] and months later *Publishers' Weekly*
quoted "an angry Mr. Minton" as telling them he was "absolutely
appalled at both the position of the Anti-Defamation League and
at the reaction of those who blithely accept its handouts." The
matter, he said, was "with my attorneys for possible action."[18]

Confronted with Mr. Minton's disregard of its legitimate protests, ADL made public its correspondence with him and alerted
the Jewish community to the fact that the paperback of *Lansky*
was scheduled to carry the same slur against American Jews.[19]
Both Putnam's and Berkley were deluged with protests, to which
Berkley responded in late August and early September with a
form letter announcing its decision to change the paperback
cover. The letter said the company had reached "essentially the
same conclusion" as the protestors—that the line "Jews Control
Crime in the United States" could "serve to be divisive and/or
misinterpreted." It was therefore being dropped entirely and
"something relatively innocuous" substituted.[20]

From the *New York Times*, meantime, nothing had been heard
at all. Finally, in late August, Times Vice President Sydney
Gruson responded for the publisher, expressing sympathy with
the protest. Mr. Gruson said he was "trying to work out a policy
with the Advertising Acceptability Department to make sure that
even the barest chance of such an implication for any ethnic group
should not appear in the paper."[21]

In the motion picture *Portnoy's Complaint* Jews were demeaned
in a parade of anti-Semitic stereotypes emanating from Holly-
wood's film version of Philip Roth's novel, written, produced and
directed by Ernest Lehman.

Whatever the redeeming literary or social values of the Roth
book, the movie emerged as a cheap, vulgar, smutty, anti-Jewish
diatribe. Portnoy's mother and father became one-dimensional
Jewish parental clichés—and monstrous at that—no longer hu-

man beings, however broadly drawn, as they had been in the novel, but screaming anti-Jewish jokes. And so with Alexander Portnoy himself. Movie critic Vincent Canby of the *Times* said *Portnoy* should have remained a novel.[22] Critic Judith Crist, writing in *New York,* observed that "the Rabelasian wit and the humanity of the Roth work have been abandoned in the film version" and that Lehman's Portnoy was "the center of infantile dirty stories laced with anti-Semitic overtones." She described Portnoy's movie parents as "screeching impersonations of *Der Stuermer* cartoons," and added that "somebody up there (if not down here) must be laughing—and we suspect that it's Joseph Goebbels."[23] Former *Times* education editor Fred M. Hechinger, in a sober analysis of the anti-Semitism of the film, called it "an unfunny, vulgar anti-Jewish joke aimed at everything depicted as Jewish in the film." Hechinger added:

> The viewer's reaction is that if these people were "chosen" for any-thing, it could only have been by way of a bad example. That's no laughing matter. It is hard to overlook that Portnoy, despite his monumental vulgarity and selfishness, also serves as the Mayor's Human Rights Commissioner and thus supposedly guards the in-terests of the poor and downtrodden. This picture of the egomaniacal Jew as the establishment's protector of the "minorities" (are not the Jews a minority any longer?) can only seem like the brainchild of quintessential anti-Semitism. . . . It is as if the film's producers wanted to make sure that no Jewish participant in these proceedings emerged with dignity and humanity intact.[24]

Philip Roth's Alexander Portnoy, obsessed with sex, with other bodily functions, with some funny memories of an unfunny child-hood, had been regarded by many in the Jewish community as an anti-Semitic caricature; others saw him as the product of an anguished but very talented Jewish writer who had created a real, if highly neurotic and exaggerated, tragicomic figure that hap-pened to be Jewish and lived within a framework of self-debasing Jewish folklore, but who could have been just as easily the son of any other obsessive-repressive family of the given economic class. Whatever one's view of the sociological or literary merits of the book, however, it remained that the 1967 novel, a runaway best-seller, could readily have been used to reinforce anti-Semitic stereotypes in some minds and create them in others. It was neither the first nor, in all likelihood, sadly, the last time Portnoy was to serve as the model for an anti-Jewish caricature.

One classic method of slurring Jews is to generalize about all Jews from the alleged specific characteristics or acts of some Jews that may or may not have anything to do with their Jewishness—the myth of the Jews of Jesus' time and therefore all Jews of all time as guilty in Jesus' death being, of course, the prototype. Another form is to seize upon a prominent person of Jewish background and pillory him as a Jew. The often unstated object lesson is that this person's alleged unsavory characteristics are typically Jewish—shared by all Jews. It is very circular, of course, and often hard to distinguish where one type leaves off and the other begins. By 1971, in any event, it became clear that Henry Kissinger was to be a choice target not alone in the precincts of the hate-mongers but in more respectable circles, including the widely-read, nationally circulated *Village Voice,* a weekly pillar of the "radical chic" anti-Establishment "establishment" in New York and around the country. On March 11 and 18, 1972, the *Voice* devoted more than 300 column inches to a two-part character assassination of Kissinger, entitled "Portnoy in Tall Cotton or Making It on the Potomac," written by Noel E. Parmentel, Jr.

Kissinger, of course, had been choice grist for the Jew-baiting propaganda mills of the far right hate fringe. For such as Gerald Smith's *The Cross and the Flag,* Frank Capell's extremist *Herald of Freedom* and Willis Carto's Liberty Lobby front group, Americans for National Security, the mere fact of Kissinger's Jewish origins was sufficient to conjure up evil implications. His presence right there in the White House, at the president's elbow, was living "proof" of their own pet propaganda charges of a Jewish conspiracy controlling the American government. (Capell, who falsely identified Kissinger's father as a rabbi, was honored by having his attack twice inserted in the *Congressional Record* by Representative John Rarick of Louisiana, a prolific inserter of Radical Right and anti-Jewish propaganda.)

Kissinger was also, of course, the target of some precincts on the farther left, not for his Jewishness but for his membership in the Council on Foreign Relations, which some regarded as the wellspring of America's "guilty" role in the Cold War with the communist world since 1945, and for his role as President Nixon's foreign policy advisor. (Interestingly enough, elements of the Radical Right, including the John Birch Society, also denounced the Council on Foreign Relations as the "inner circle" of the "conspirary" destroying America.) For such persons and groups, Kissinger was seen as the architect of the first Nixon administration's prolongation of American involvement in the war in Southeast Asia.

Parmentel's attack on Kissinger in the *Voice*, however, had little to do with ideology, foreign policy or the direction of America's role in world affairs. It was a personal assault. The author ridiculed Kissinger's accent and his nose, devoted unseemly attention to his subject's alleged sexual tastes and behavior, and portrayed Kissinger as a fawning sycophant, coward, bully, flatterer, tyrant, social climber, evil manipulator, insecure snob, unprincipled seeker after power—and more. And underlying it all was a huge anti-Jewish put-down of Kissinger, in the guise of telling Kissinger, who allegedly shunned the company of "obvious Jews," that he was, after all, one of them. What came across, however, was an odious anti-Jewish stereotype whose net effect was to tell the reader that Kissinger was *just* one of *them* and would do well to remember it.

Parmentel compared Kissinger to Sammy Glick, the ruthless movie producer in the 1940s novel, *What Makes Sammy Run?*, and more pointedly to Alexander Portnoy, writing: "Kissinger has materialized into a fair likeness of our old friend Alexander Portnoy, alive and well and Making It big down on the Potomac." There were glancing blows at other Jews—*Commentary* editor Norman Podhoretz, author of *Making It*, and Philip Roth, described by Parmentel as two of Kissinger's "own." In the author's view, Dr. Kissinger was "a larger-than-life improvement on the original Roth model" of Portnoy and "he is Making It beyond Portnoy's (or Podhoretz's) wildest fantasies." But "Kissinger would *never* go for guys like Portnoy and Podhoretz," Parmentel wrote. "He remembers too many of their look-alikes at George Washington High School." And underscoring the Jewish "angle," the author added:

> There are certain *ethnic* factors at work here which are all too much for Kissinger. By the lights of any proper German Jew . . . Portnoy and Podhoretz, excellent fellows that they are, would have to be dropped. *Lumped with those awful Litvaks* who made life so miserable for an ungainly teenage Kissinger. How he hated them. . . .
>
> It is impossible to over-emphasize how ill at ease Kissinger is about being Jewish. How uncomfortable he is around obvious Jews. How studiously he avoids them. This factor is a key to the almost clinical insecurity which has molded the Kissinger character.
>
> Still and all, whether Kissinger likes it or not, there is something about him which reminds any fair-minded man of Portnoy, albeit a larger-gauged model. For Kissinger is Portnoy with power. . . .

Writing of the "apple-polishing" directed toward Kissinger by "everyone in Washington" who allegedly referred to him as " 'Doctor' Kissinger this and 'Doctor' Kissinger that," Parmentel said Kissinger "revels in this titled glory as much as any Great Neck dentist ever did." Again—with a nod to the conspiracy theorists, the Arab propagandists and, as we shall see, the New Left— Parmentel wrote that ". . . many people believe . . . that the invasion of Laos, the Cambodian adventure, the death of Biafra, and a hopefully unrealized plan to get American forces out of Vietnam and into Palestine can be laid squarely at his "door." The diatribe closed with a quotation from *Portnoy* that Parmentel termed "prophetic" with respect to Kissinger: " 'Yes, I was one happy Yiddel down there in Washington. . . .' "

Whether a negative image of Jews takes hold in the public mind—whether it becomes a new stereotype—has a direct relation, of course, to how frequently and insistently it is repeated and, sometimes more important, from whom it emanates.

> The truth of the matter about it is, the entire cultural press, publishing . . . criticism . . . television . . . theater . . . film industry . . . is almost 90% Jewish-oriented. I mean, I can't even count on one hand, five people of any importance—of real importance—in the media who aren't Jewish. I can't. . . .

If these people could have done me in, they would have done me in, like nobody's ever been done in. But they couldn't do me in. They would have done me in, because not only wasn't I Jewish and wasn't in the Jewish clique, but I *talked* about not being part of it. I've said for years: "Here's this god-damned Jewish Mafia working tooth and tong on the New York Review of Books, the New York Times, whether they're doing it consciously or not." And mostly they're doing it consciously. I'm not in the least bit frightened by them.[25]

The man who said that, as recently as the spring of 1973, has said it many times before, in the pages of some of the most-read magazines in the world and over national television to the millions of late-night viewers of Johnny Carson's "Tonight" show.[26] He has asserted, over and over again during the past five or six years, that there is a "Jewish Mafia in American letters." Charging that it consists of a "clique of New York-oriented writers and critics who control much of the literary scene through the influence of the quarterlies and intellectual magazines," he has stated:

. . . All these publications are Jewish-dominated and this particular coterie employs them to make or break writers by advancing or withholding attention . . . Bernard Malamud and Saul Bellow and Philip Roth and Isaac Bashevis Singer are all fine writers but they are not the *only* writers in the country as the Jewish Mafia would have us believe. I could give you a list of excellent writers . . . the odds are that you haven't heard of most of them for the simple reason that the Jewish Mafia has systemically frozen them out of the literary scene.[27]

Again, in another magazine interview shortly after this one, he talked about the "clique" of Jews in American letters:

Very talented, very powerful and very parochial. I call them the Jewish Mafia. They exclude too many good writers. They're afraid of me. I can manipulate beyond their reaches. I never would play the game. Styron [author William Styron] is accepted because if ever there was a goy Yid, it's Bill Styron.[28]

The charge that America's mass communication media as well as other sources that mold public opinion are "Jew-controlled"

is a propaganda lie that for half a century has oozed up from
the extremist elements of the United States. But Truman Capote
is not a professional anti-Semite; he is and has been for many
years a highly regarded member of the American literary world,
and justly so, for he is a talented and sensitive writer, a man
aware of the nuances of words and phrases; moreover, he knows
his way around the publishing industry. When he tells *Playboy,
New York* and *Rolling Stone* that there is a "Jewish Mafia," i.e.,
an organized, deliberate syndicate of Jews, engaged in a virtual
conspiracy to "make or break writers" and to "do in" the Truman
Capotes and other non-Jewish literary figures, he is playing a
very dangerous game, and it is difficult to believe that he doesn't
know it. He is reinforcing a very time-worn anti-Jewish stereotype for hundreds of readers of these magazines. And particularly
for the younger readers of *Rolling Stone,* he is planting the seed
of anti-Jewish prejudice where it may never have existed. When
Capote goes on nationwide television and reiterates the same
charge, he reaches an audience undreamed of by the professional
peddlers of hate, and his status gives his words an aura of truth
the hatemongers could never hope to achieve.

There are, of course, some demurrers from Mr. Capote. He
told *Playboy,* in 1968, that "anti-Semitism has nothing to do with"
his charges because he would be "just as opposed to a clique of
white Anglo-Saxon Protestant authors and critics exercising exclusive control over American letters and excluding talented
Jewish writers." And he noted that "almost as many Jewish writers as gentiles have suffered at their hands," adding that "this
Jewish Mafia is based more on a state of mind than on race; gentile writers such as Dwight MacDonald who toe the line are made
honorary members." (That is to say, you don't have to be Jewish
to be a member of the Jewish Mafia, just as you don't have to be
Jewish to be a "Jewish Princess".)

But even as he demurred, he alleged that Jews exercise "exclusive control" over American letters, and it was in 1973, not 1968,
that his charge of Jewish domination of the mass media was made
in *Rolling Stone.*

But Mr. Capote offered no substantiation of his charges because, of course, there is none. If, for example, Jews and Jewish

mafiosi control the mass media, how come Capote gets on the Johnny Carson show? How come three widely-read magazines interview him and print his allegations? How come Random House (Jason Epstein is one of its top executives and his wife helps edit *The New York Review of Books* that Mr. Capote so loathes) published *In Cold Blood?* How come Capote himself was on network TV early in 1973 with an excellent two-part prison documentary?[29] If the so-called Jewish Mafia is out to do him in and they are so all-powerful, why is it they haven't been successful? Perhaps it is because, as Capote himself suggested, he is not afraid of them and is smarter than they are; the premise is at least open to doubt. Mr. Capote has never spelled out just why this so-called Jewish Mafia is out to get him. He has not offered any reason for such persecution, other than his claimed refusal to "play the game"—whatever that means—and the fact that he is not Jewish. Mr. Capote has publicly exaggerated and distorted "Jewish power" in the field of letters and has conjured up an image of a "Jewish conspiracy" in the mass media. One can believe his denials of anti-Semitism, while experiencing profound regret at the consequences of his statements. There are better ways of getting attention—the kind of attention Mr. Capote has always achieved when he sits out there in eastern Long Island and writes, instead of talking nonsense.

In May 1972, the Bennington *Banner* of Vermont, a liberal newspaper, carried a column headlined "Decline and Fall" by Samuel R. Ogden who wrote about "WASP" decline resulting from the fact that "the news media, the recent books, the book reviews all speak the viewpoint of the Jews," that the doctorates and professorships are principally held by Jews, that as a result "the American culture is rapidly becoming Jewish in character," which may be its "manifest destiny" but which has contributed to a society that is "taking on the aspects of a dreadful nightmare." And finally, "anti-Christ is in the driver's seat and where it will all end up is not pleasant to contemplate."[30]

In May 1972, the Parkersburg (West Virginia) *News* carried a guest editorial column by Austin V. Wood, executive vice president and general manager of the Ogden Newspapers, Inc., which includes the *News Register and Intelligencer* in Wheeling. Mr. Wood wrote:

> Henry Kissinger is of German Jewish descent. He came over with a colony of German Jewish people who were fleeing Hitler. They established a colony in New York and there Kissinger was reared. He is answerable to no one in the Senate or any place else other than the President. What right the President has to place such reliance in a man who is not responsible to any other body in the United States is beyond my comprehension . . . . It may very well be that Mr. Kissinger is behind a great many of our troubles all over the world.[31]

In May 1972, the *NFO Family Farmer,* published in Wisconsin by the National Farmers Organization, ran a feature in part describing Mike Fribourg, wealthy grain dealer and chief owner of the Continental Grain Corporation, as having been born in Antwerp, Belgium "into a distinguished European Jewish family roughly comparable to the Rothschilds"; commenting on the description, which had been reprinted from a mass circulation publication, the *Family Farmer* editor writes: "Here is a gent that has made himself a billion dollars many times over dealing in a food product that hungry people had to have to stay alive. Of course, first he had to snare the production away from the 'Family Farmer' at a fraction of its value. I wonder," says the editor, "if that is how come those birds got themselves into so much trouble over in Europe back about World War II."[32]

The Cincinnati *Enquirer,* in November 1972, described TV star Lorne Greene as "a Jewish multimillionaire" who "has money invested in race horses, apartment buildings, real estate, stocks and a short company," although it would be hard to conceive of his being described as, say, a Congregationalist multimillionaire or a Methodist multimillionaire.[33]

The Houston *Chronicle* sports editor, in June 1972, interviewed a professional football "chaplain" and quoted him to the effect that "all denominations of Christians" are represented at pregame chapel meetings, but not Jews. Why? "Jews own the teams. This is for playing personnel."[34]

This is a limited sample of the hundreds of slurs published regularly across the country. None is, of course, anything but trivial in itself. Yet together they form part of the conditioning to which Americans are exposed in their daily reading. Over a period of time, exposure to stereotypes, slurs, put-downs and insults can and does have a cumulative and unhealthy impact on attitudes and thinking.

Bad taste, insensitivity to anti-Jewish stereotypes and the profit motive combined to produce a number of recordings ("When You're in Love the Whole World is Jewish," "The Jewish American Princess," "Have a Jewish Christmas" were just a few) in the late sixties and early seventies that brought negative images of Jews to millions of listeners of the nation's disc jockeys.

Cartoon books—"We Wish You a Kosher Christmas," "Diary of a Jewish Madam," "Fanny Hillman: Memoirs of a Jewish Madam," "How to Be a Jewish Madam," "My Son, the Santa Claus," "Loxfinger" and the noxious "It's Fun to Be Jewish!," which rehashed every anti-Jewish joke in existence and created some new ones—were printed by the score. "It's Fun to Be Jewish!" sired a greeting card, "Happy Birthday! It's Great to Be Jewish!!!," in 1968 about which complaints were still being received in 1970 and 1971.

Film cartoons—like the X-rated *Fritz the Cat*, which was translated to the screen from one of the new "comix" and which had a tasteless synagogue sequence, and *The Crunch Bird*, which used Jewish dialect and ethnic caricature for a vulgar joke and which won an Academy Award in 1972—contributed to the atmosphere of anti-Jewish denigration, along with anti-Jewish stereotyping found in such full-length 1972 feature films as Woody Allen's *Everything You've Always Wanted to Know About Sex*, *Such Good Friends* and *Made for Each Other* in addition, of course, to *Portnoy*.

Capping and capitalizing on the vogue for sick "ethnic" humor and dehumanization was a magazine that made its appearance as the seventies opened, *The National Lampoon*. Put together by some former editors of *The Harvard Lampoon*, it is published monthly, has a reported circulation of 300,000 and is a moneymaker. In the August 1971 issue, a little feature called "Children's Letters to the Gestapo" by contributing editor Michael O'Donoghue included the following:

> Dear Heinrich Himmler:
> How do you get all those people into your oven? We can hardly get a pot roast into ours.
>
> Dear Mr. Himmler:
> Please don't get rid of all the kikes because I like to fly them except when the string breaks or they get tangled in a tree.
>
> Dear Mister Himmler:
> I am Rolfe. I am 8. When I grow up I want to kill sheenys and wear big boots like the Fuehrer.

October 1972. A major item was a mock comic book entitled "The Ventures of Zimmerman," a put-down on folk singer Bob Dylan, drawn with Jewish features, blue yarmulke, and portrayed as a scheming, avaricious, money-hungry "superman" type who poses as a simple, idealistic folk singer. The mock cover of the mock comic depicted "Zimmerman" as an Israeli pilot, his plane bearing a bronze plaque reading "Gift of Mr. Robert Zimmerman, New York City, U.S.A." and adorned with Stars of David. The mock comic was ostensibly a production of "International Jewish Comics" and bore a "seal" reading "Approved by the Elders of Zion." The "story" was dreamed up by editor Tony Hendra and senior editor Sean Kelly.[35]

Are the editors of *Lampoon* anti-Semitic? Probably not. But they have made a signal contribution to the perpetuation of those destructive stereotypes—like the *Stuermer* cartoons—so intimately associated with the annihilation of European Jewry. All in the name of good, clean fun.

And it was in the spirit of good, clean fun—plus an apparent attempt to plunge television situation-comedy into social issues—that CBS brought us, in January 1971, Archie Bunker and "All in the Family." Producers Norman Lear, a member of the American Civil Liberties Union's California board, and Alan (Bud) Yorkin, both Jewish, were also apparently operating on the same premise as *The National Lampoon:* attack everyone equally and no one can be offended. Lear, who wrote most of the early "All in the Family" scripts and who is now the show's executive producer, recently said his inspiration for Archie and the show came from verbal battles he used to have with his late father, whom he never "forgave" for being a "bigot," but in whom he found "other things" to love.[36] He had never, however, "reached" his father on the subject of prejudice, and that is what he was trying to do in the show—to reach the Archie Bunkers in viewerland. Producer-writer Lear was also described as "constantly talking to bigots and bores" in search of "the Yiddish quality called *tahm*," which Lear translated as "the ability to be embraceable and human at your most villainous."[37]

So Lear created an "embraceable" bigot, Archie Bunker, a scared, working stiff baffled by a rapidly changing world around him, clinging for dear life to old ways and outmoded ideas. It remains a mystery, however, why Lear—an identifiable liberal who has no use for bigots and stereotypes—could have thought that by his making Archie lovable as well as bigoted, viewers would accept Archie while rejecting his bigotry, why Archie would be laughed at instead of with, why if the identification with Archie runs true, the viewer would not then be more accepting of his *own* bigoted self, since Archie is so acceptable.

The questions are answerable only by the producer himself. But what, in fact, happened was that Archie Bunker, the "lovable" bigot, quickly became a national hero. "Archie Bunker for President" sweatshirts and bumper stickers blossomed all over the country. Carroll O'Connor, the actor who plays Archie and is himself a concerned liberal, was repeatedly stopped on the street by people who congratulated him for his bigoted remarks. Mail to CBS made it clear that many viewers shared the prejudices articulated by Archie Bunker and were saying so. The show itself skyrocketed to the top of the Nielsen ratings in a matter of months and has stayed at or near the top. Some 100 million Americans of all ages—40 million families—are said to watch "All in the Family" every Saturday night, and every Saturday night for the past three years (in prime time) they have been exposed, invariably, to racial, religious and ethnic put-downs and such mindless slurs as "Hebe," "coon" and "spick." Laura Z. Hobson

noted in an article strongly critical of the show, and doubtful of
the producers' claim that they were trying to expose and counter
bigotry, that the use of "Hebe" was perhaps their attempt to sani-
tize the real language of prejudice and make it more acceptable;
"kike," said the author of *Gentlemen's Agreement,* was the usual
epithet.[38] They have been exposed as well, of course, to an image
of wives and mothers as "dingbats" who ought to "stifle" themselves.

The acceptance of Archie's bigotry was predictable from the
start to human relations groups working against prejudice over
many years. The Anti-Defamation League commented that "the
repetition of bigoted stereotypes and racial and religious canards
serves simply to reinforce the stereotypic images,"[39] and that it
was not possible "to combat bigotry by laughing at a central
bigoted figure who evokes the sympathy of the audience."[40]
A prominent American rabbi, in a widely-quoted article, wrote
that there was "no such thing as a harmless bigot any more than
there is such a thing as a friendly cancer or a benign drug-pusher
or a lovable murderer or rapist."[41]

Whether "All in the Family" created the "new freedom to be
offensive" or sought to profit from the widespread acceptance of
offensive "ethnic humor" that became a climate in the late sixties
and early seventies is open to argument; what is clear is the insensitivity of its producers to the awesome power of television
to imbed the stereotypes that have haunted most of America's minorities for many decades, and Jews for many centuries.

Insensitivity to anti-Semitic stereotypes and callousness with
respect to Jewish feelings, however, were apparently to continue
at CBS. In October 1972 the network weighed in again, this
time with a "Sandy Duncan Show" episode, "Play It Again
Samuelson," which was a heavy anti-Jewish stereotype from
beginning to end and which many Jewish viewers regarded as one
of the most offensive programs they had yet seen on television.[42]
It had no redeeming features, qualifying comments or statements
that might have put the plot in perspective. The episode was
built around a situation in which a couple—Mr. and Mrs. Samuelson—filed a phony lawsuit against Miss Duncan for alleged

personal injuries. The Samuelsons were portrayed as explicit Jewish stereotypes, with Jewish accents, intonations and modes of speech. The defendant, her lawyer and the judge were depicted as non-Jews. Every aspect of the Samuelson couple portrayed Jews as scheming and fraudulent connivers. Near the end, the Samuelsons, exposed as having a record of prior fraudulent lawsuits, offered to bargain on the amount of damages, indicating their willingness to settle cheap. (It was subsequently learned that the Duncan script originally called for the Samuelson couple to have an Italian name. It is not known whether the network's fear of complaint from an angry Italian-American community led it to conclude that it was far safer to caricature the Jews.)

Responding to protests, a top CBS official expressed deep regret and promised that the network would be more careful in the future.[43] But in the meantime, the damage had been done, coast-to-coast.

So far we have been dealing with the conduct of the mass media and other opinion-molding sectors of the American public in reinforcing old stereotypes and creating new negative images of Jews, largely through either insensitivity to anti-Semitism or unconcern about its continuing destructive power.

The respectable news media have helped to foster still another negative image in recent years: the false idea that Jews dominate American politics and manipulate U.S. policy in behalf of their special interests. It is an old canard in the hate press, part of the "conspiracy" the lunatic fringe imagines, but when similar intimations crop up in respected journals, Jews have reason to worry. Often such intimations are combined with a barely-disguised antipathy to Israel.

In March 1970, *Time* magazine, in an essay accompanying its news story on the visit and picketing of French President Georges Pompidou, asked bluntly: "Is There a Jewish Foreign Policy?"[44] While the question was never really answered, a few subtle digs at the American Jewish community made it clear that the *Time* writer thought there was.

Pompidou had come to the United States shortly after the French sale to Libya—one of Israel's most vitriolic enemies in the Arab world and the place where Arab murderers know they will get a cordial reception—of 108 Mirage jets. The Mirage had been the staple of Israel's air force until DeGaulle, piqued after Israel's victory in the Six-Day War, refused to sell any more to the Jewish state. The French government's hostility to Israel, manifest in the withholding of the jets and their subsequent sale to Libya, had angered American Jews, and, in an orderly though vocal manner, they had picketed Pompidou on his visits to Chicago and New York. The French president was offended, and President Nixon found it necessary to make a quick trip to New York to mollify his guest.

Time's news story referred to the "unconscionable" absences of New York's Governor Rockefeller and Mayor John Lindsay from a dinner in Pompidou's honor, and attributed it to their needing "the Jewish vote" and having "truckled to Jewish enmity for Pompidou." The accompanying essay, however, spelled out the implication when it noted that "booing Pompidou" was only "part of a larger question" and asked: "at what point does the emotional pull of Jerusalem distort the consideration of foreign policy in the U.S.? Is there what might be called a Jewish foreign policy?"

Time pointed out that "Israel is a democratic, modern, stabilizing force in a chaotic and brutally backward corner of the world" and noted that "if Israel were some day to fall, U.S. interests would suffer." *Time* also noted the "fierce emotional attachment" of most American Jews to Israel and traced this to the "interdependence" resulting from "two thousand years of Diaspora and persecution." The *Time* essay went on:

> The *vehemence* of the American Jewish community's support for Israel creates an impression in the minds of some that Washington is acting *not on the basis of national interest but out of fear of Jewish wrath.* When public officials of national stature, such as John Lindsay and Nelson Rockefeller, *abdicate* their ceremonial responsibilities toward a foreign leader, it is a sign that *pressure-bloc politics is taking precedence over common sense and public duty.* [Italics added.]

Acknowledging that "political pressure based on ethnic loyalty is a part of American democracy," and noting that Americans of Irish, Dutch, German and Slavic descent had used it, *Time* asserted:

> None of these groups, however, match 6,000,000 American Jews for economic and political support of *another country*. Since 1948, American Jews have raised more than a billion dollars for Israel, *all of it tax deductible*. At the same time, the U.S. Government allocated almost another billion in foreign aid to Israel. Jews account for only 3% of the U.S. population, but they are centered in such pivotal states as New York, Illinois, Pennsylvania, and California. More than most ethnic groups, they vote regularly and are heavy campaign contributors. Thus politicians are aware of the *potency of the Jewish vote*. When the Conference of Presidents of Major American Jewish Organizations held a recent rally in Washington, about 400 Congressmen and 70 Senators signed the conference petition urging continued military and economic aid to Israel. [Italics added.]

Time neglected to mention, of course, that it was a long-standing policy of the U.S. government to exempt charitable contributions from taxation, that private contributions to many other countries and many other peoples, including Palestinians and other Arabs, were similarly tax deductible; that foreign aid to Israel accounted for a tiny percentage of U.S. foreign aid to other countries; and that of the 400 congressmen and 70 senators who signed the petition, there were dozens with no Jewish constituency or campaign contributors to speak of.

Washington *Post* "Style" columnist Nicholas Von Hoffman commented on "oppressed people" in June 1972:

> For a brief few weeks last winter, the inhabitants of Bangladesh led the list of the most popular oppressed peoples. Since liberation and a fast slide into starvation, we've lost interest in them and the top spot on the charts has reverted to the Russian Jews, a group who never drop below second or third in the sympathy ratings.
>
> There is some doubt whether the Russian government treats its Jewish citizens worse than the Albanian government treats all of its citizens. Albania has *no organized claques,* however. Consequently, they're so far down they're off the top 30 Most Miserable list. Brazilians and Iranians do a little better by virtue of the work of a few of their students here.
>
> Still, if a people want to be oppressed and popular in the United

> States, they're best off being certifiably white with a *well-organized infrastructure beating gongs and calling attention to the victims.* The Free Soviet Jewry Movement is so successful at doing this that it continues with growing momentum even after a certain number of Soviet Jews are freed, allowed to go to Israel, and then, after they've gotten there, request deportation and re-enslavement back in Russia. [Italics added.][45]

Von Hoffman neglected to note that (1) the release of some Soviet Jews desiring to go to Israel did not solve the problem of freedom for tens of thousands still wishing to go; (2) those seeking to return to the USSR represent an infinitesimal percentage of those rejoining the Jewish people in Israel—usually immigrants who could not adjust to the change or those unhappy in a free society where the state did not automatically make decisions for them.

On June 6, 1972, the *New York Times* published a glaringly anti-Israel full-page advertisement purchased by Norman F. Dacey of Southbury, Connecticut, an Arab sympathizer, that was redolent with distortions, half-truths, exaggerations and outright factual error and that was not only anti-Israel and anti-Zionist but patently anti-Jewish. Ten days later, the Anti-Defamation League, reflecting the outrage of the Jewish community across the country, published a full-page advertisement refuting Dacey's outburst and branding it "defamatory."

In his advertisement, headed "A Letter to the President" (the 1972 election campaign was in full swing), Dacey made reference· to campaign contributions from so-called "Zionist sources" and added: "It is a sad measure of the degree of our fall from grace that our foreign policy can now be bought for a few shekels." At another point, the ad raised the old "dual loyalty" charge of the extremist hate fringe. Its author contended that the once-great United States has become

> ... a dancing bear, responding dumbly to the commands given it directly by the government of Israel and indirectly through a potent Fifth Column which operates here in America and which gives blind obedience to the Zionist credo that all Jews everywhere owe national loyalty to Israel.

In apologizing for the *Lansky* advertisement a year earlier, Times Vice President Sydney Gruson, it will be recalled, had told the ADL that he was "trying to work out a policy with the Advertising Acceptability Department to make sure that even the barest chance of such an implication for any ethnic group should not appear in the paper." Had such a policy been worked out? And, if so, did it include acceptance of the foregoing libel on the Jewish community?

In an unusual action the *Times* answered the question in an editorial entitled "Freedom to Advertise" appearing the same day, June 16, as the ADL advertisement rebutting the Dacey ad. Defending its right to keep its advertising columns open to "the widest possible latitude . . . to express what from our point of view may be even the most objectionable opinions," and reprinting a three-year-old editorial in which the *Times* said it would refuse ads "only on the grounds of fraud or deception, vulgarity or obscenity and incitement to lawbreaking or to racial or religious hatred," the editorial said:

> While The Times makes every effort to detect such violations and to eliminate them from the political advertising that it does accept, our screening process does fail us on occasion when, usually due to the pressures of time and deadlines, human error manages to nullify even the most carefully conceived administrative controls. Just such a regrettable lapse occured in connection with the Dacey advertisement; in any event, it was the general tenor of this diatribe, rather than any of its specific charges, that gave offense to so many of our readers.

The idea that Jews wield an enormous and disproportionate influence over the body politic, especially with respect to American policy in the Middle East, was furthered, too, by massive discussion in the print media of Jewish fund-raising, Jewish campaign contributions and Jewish voting patterns during the 1972 elections. The coverage ran from brief columns by syndicated journalists to full-dress "take out" stories spread over many pages in the nation's newspapers and magazines.

Typical of the intense 1972 interest in American Jewish political behavior was a front-page article in the Washington *Post* on February 20 by reporter Stephen Klaidman, headlined: "Jewish Appeal: The Power of Charity," with an overline that said: "Political Leverage Aids Israel." The "jump" page headline, spread over eight columns, was perhaps more to the point: "American Jews Influence Both Politics and Policy for Israel." Klaidman extensively analyzed Jewish fund-raising in behalf of Israel and traced the "not entirely coincidental" 1972 solicitousness of "leading American politicians" for Israel and Soviet Jewry to "the dimensions of the financial power of American Jewry." He asserted that "the influence of American Jews on American politics is quite disproportionate to their numbers in the electorate. . . . " In a key paragraph, for example, Klaidman also wrote:

> Jews vote Jewish issues and they support candidates whom they believe will advance Jewish causes. They lobby on Capitol Hill and often they have had direct access to the White House. This was certainly the case in the Johnson Administration, it is considerably less so under Mr. Nixon.

The fact is, however, that Jews do *not* vote solely on the basis of so-called Jewish issues; like all other groups, they take parochial concerns into consideration. But also like other Americans, they weigh a wide variety of non-Jewish issues as well — issues of war and peace and defense (and not only in the Middle East) and such domestic concerns as inflation, economic policies, urban deterioration, taxes, civil rights and civil liberties, everything that affects them and their families as Americans. It has often been pointed out, in fact, that unlike other Americans, Jews often do not vote their economic self-interest. If they did, many more would be Republicans and would tend to vote conservatively. Instead Jews are Democrats in overwhelming numbers and tend to vote for liberal Democrats espousing liberal causes. Even in 1972, when many complex issues were involved, only Jews and blacks gave majorities to George McGovern (Jews were 3-2 for McGovern over Richard Nixon) while other Americans voted exactly the other way (60 to 40 percent in favor of President Nixon).

The fact is that Jews have had no more, and often less, access to the White House than, say, businessmen, labor and civil rights leaders, and bankers. And if Jews "lobby on Capitol Hill," so do oil companies, farmers, labor unions, lumber interests, utilities, black people and, perhaps more to the point, church groups, among others. To single out the Jewish group for its efforts, in an age where it is easier to name those who do *not* "lobby on Capitol Hill" than to enumerate those who do, lends fodder to those who are too willing to accuse the Jewish community of undue influence in behalf of narrow concerns.

On March 7, 1973, in the wake of Israel's downing of a Libyan commercial jet that had strayed over occupied territory and ignored instructions to land, CBS White House correspondent Robert Pierpoint delivered a "First Line Report" that accused the United States of a "double standard" in regard to Middle East terror—and attributed it to Israel's "formidable political and propaganda force in this country in the form of six million Jews." Pierpoint complained that the U.S. had expressed "outrage" at the Munich slayings of Israeli athletes but "next to no outcry" at either Israeli raids against "Palestinian refugee camps" in Lebanon or the Libyan jet disaster.

The Jewish community objected strongly to Pierpoint's attribution of U.S. reaction to Jewish pressure—and it questioned the morality of equating the Olympic slaughter by terrorists with either Israel's protective raid against their strongholds or Israel's innocent, if tragic, downing of the jet. CBS News President Richard S. Salant, however, responded that Pierpoint's remarks had not crossed the "fine lines" between "permissible" news "analysis" and "impermissible" personal "editorializing," although he thought the reference to American Jews was "unfortunate."[46] (WCBS Radio in New York saw it differently. On March 16 and 17 it broadcast a local station editorial challenging the Pierpoint comments and distinguishing between the terrorism at Munich and the Israeli actions. The Pierpoint broadcast, however, had been aired nationally.)

The foregoing pages record merely the "tip of the iceberg" of stereotyping and anti-Jewish slurs to which the American public has been exposed in recent years. The media and the arts have nurtured current and too fashionable misperceptions of Jews as part of an affluent, problem-free segment of American society, that anti-Semitism and concomittant anti-Jewish discrimination are not realities today, that Jews "have it made," that Jews are themselves part of the "Establishment." These myths and misconceptions, many of them birthed and believed by some Jews themselves, are causing grave concern both within and beyond the Jewish community.

8

The
Radical Left

The Radical Left, comprising elements of the New and Old Left, poses a threat to the Jewish people. It is committed to the liquidation of Israel. And in attempting to fulfill that commitment it has turned its fire on those who support Israel's existence as a Jewish state—principally Jews—while it warmly acclaims and is virtually allied with those seeking Israel's demise—Arabs, their friends in the communist world and others espousing the cause of "Third World" peoples, defined by them as including the downtrodden of Asia, Africa, Latin America and the Middle East, and American blacks.

The Radical Left has indeed become a consistent and valued tool for the dissemination of Arab propaganda. The themes of both are identical. Israel and "Zionists" are viewed and portrayed as the handmaidens of "U.S. imperialism," sinister forces allied with all the other evil entities conceived in the radical demonology. Israel, a "colony" of American military, industrial, imperial interests, is itself militaristic and aggressive, a "colonial" barrier, say the left-wing extremists, to the national liberation of the Arab peoples, especially the Palestinians.

The Middle East wars of 1948, 1956 and 1967 were caused not by Arab armies massed on Israel's borders and prepared to drive Israeli Jews into the sea, but by Israeli "expansionism." Palestinian terrorism—Lod, Munich, Khartoum—is to be deplored, not

because the murder of innocents is inherently wrong and international terrorism a threat to world stability (indeed, in the Radical Left lexicon violence is a "necessary" component of "national
liberation" movements), but because insofar as it alienates world
opinion and delays the true "revolution" of the Arab masses, it
is a poor expedient. Such terrorism is, nonetheless, "justified"
because Israel is an "occupying power" (and not only since 1967),
preventing the return of the legitimate heirs to Palestine to their
native soil.

The "real" terrorism, Radical Leftists assert, lies in Israel's
retaliatory strikes into Lebanon and Syria, seen not as efforts to
stop terrorist attacks against Israeli citizens, but as continued
"demonstrations" of Israeli military superiority for the "educational" benefit of the Arab states; in this category, too, is placed
the erroneous and tragic downing of the Libyan civilian airliner.
Israel is a class-ridden, "racist" society, oppressing not only Arabs
but Jews from Arab lands; Israel must be "destroyed," to be replaced with a "democratic, secular" state.

And, finally, American support for Israel must "end," and it is
toward this goal that the Radical Left bends its major efforts.
"The fight against Zionism," declared writer Stephen Marks in
the Marxist paper, *Worker's Power,* is "a vital part of the world
revolutionary struggle."[1]

The Radical Left campaign against Israel has begun to escalate
its hostility to Israel and make U.S. support of Israel its chief
target in the years ahead. Dr. Hyman Lumer, a top spokesman of
the Communist Party-USA and editor of the official party ideological journal, *Political Affairs,* spelled it out in a recent issue:

> . . . the issue of peace in the Middle East has been kept out of the
> organized peace movement on the ground that it would be divisive
> in the fight against the war in Indochina. But with the ceasefire in
> Vietnam, attention will increasingly be focused on this issue and the
> peace forces will be impelled to take up the fight against present U.S.
> policy in the Middle East.
>
> A struggle must be developed for the abandonment of U.S. sup-
> port to the aggressive, expansionist policies of Israel's ruling clique,
> which U.S. imperialism is using as an instrument against the anti-
> imperialist forces in the Middle East. This is a difficult, uphill battle.

> But so was the fight against the aggression in Vietnam in its earlier stages. In the end, U.S. imperialism was forced to retreat in Vietnam, and this great victory for the people of the United States has demonstrated that it can be forced to retreat in the Middle East as well.[2]

Lumer has taken the same position more recently at meetings he has addressed in New York, Chicago and elsewhere. Moreover, a Radical Left international Conference for Peace and Justice held in Bologna, Italy, from May 11 to 13, 1973 (Lumer was one of the delegates) was reportedly a call for "peace and justice" in the Middle East based on a resolution blasting the Israeli government and the United States for "underwriting" its policies.[3] And early in 1973, the Moscow-dominated World Peace Council issued a call for a "World Congress of Peace Forces" to take place in Moscow from October 2 to 7, 1973, on the theme of "Liquidation of hotbeds of war, especially in the Middle East. . . ."[4] Where the Radical Left has mounted demonstrations, conducted teach-ins and sponsored rallies—New England, New York, Washington, D.C., the West Coast and elsewhere—a prime target has been Israel. And finally, while the Middle East was a subordinate issue in the Radical Left and New Left oriented underground press in the late sixties and early seventies, it has recently moved to the forefront.

Americans are war-weary. And the notion, highly unlikely, that the United States would actively intervene at some future date with American-flown planes and troops in the Middle East in Israel's behalf is being stimulated by the Radical Left.

Americans are also uneasy about the energy crisis, and the suggestion has come from several quarters, including at least three oil companies,[5] that perhaps American policy in the Middle East needs overhauling to comply with the *realpolitik* of the area, which is that the Arabs have the oil and Israel doesn't. There is the question of and, in this nuclear age, the legitimate need for détente with the Soviet Union; will that détente, fully supported by the Jewish community, ultimately involve an unfeasible solution imposed upon Israel against her will? And finally, there is, as we have seen in the preceding chapters, massive indifference to

Jewish concerns even among sophisticated people who understand the meaning of Israel to Jews and Judaism; for vastly
greater numbers of Americans, Israel is a tiny country in the
Middle East with no special significance; they can be counted on
to be apathetic at best.

Spearheading the Radical Left's anti-Israel, anti-Zionist campaign in America and lending its unflagging support to the Palestinian guerrillas is the Socialist Workers Party (SWP), the party
of the Trotskyist communists, together with its wide array of publications and affiliated organizations. The most important of the
latter is the Young Socialist Alliance (YSA), since 1969 probably
the fastest-growing Radical Left group aimed at students and
other youth. Support for the Palestinian revolutionaries and
opposition to Israel early received a higher priority in the activities of the Trotskyists than among most of the other parties and
organizations of the far left. Policy decisions adopted during 1971
indicated that the SWP apparatus was going to pay even more
attention to the Middle East in the ensuing period.

In the spring of 1971, the National Committee of the SWP met
in New York for four days and adopted several major resolutions
to be submitted to the party convention. *The Militant,* the SWP
newspaper, reported that at the meeting, "one important aspect
of the international situation, the struggle in the Middle East,
was singled out for a special resolution" which, the paper said,
"developed the SWP position in support of the Palestian people . . . against Zionism and the state of Israel, and in support of
the struggles of the Arab peoples against imperialism and its
Israeli beachhead.[6] At the SWP convention, held August 8 to 12,
1971 in Cleveland and attended by more than a thousand delegates and observers, the party resolution was introduced via a report emphasizing that

> . . . the major task confronting American revolutionists remains that
> of educating the radicalizing youth about the real history of the
> Zionist movement and the revolutionary character of the Palestinian
> and Arab struggle for *destruction of the state of Israel.*[7] (Italics added.)

The resolution adopted by the Trotskyists was a long document that set forth the basic political line of the party on the Middle East, purported to answer "the main Zionist arguments in defense of the present state of Israel" and outlined "the tasks the SWP has set itself in defense of the Arab revolution." The document pledged the SWP's "unconditional support" to "the struggles of the Arab peoples against the state of Israel."[8]

That Israel has no right of survival in the eyes of the Trotskyists was made clear in the following passage (italics added):

> The struggle of the Palestinian people against their oppression and for self-determination has taken the form of a struggle to *destroy the state of Israel.* The *currently expressed goal* of this struggle is the establishment of a *democratic, secular Palestine.* We give support to this struggle of the Palestinians. . . .

And the Trotskyists rejected as "false to the core" arguments that the Jewish people have a right to a state of their own or to self-determination of any kind. The party resolution stated:

> We explain to the Israeli Jews, as we have in the past, that their future lies only in aligning themselves with the Palestinian and general Arab liberation movements, wholeheartedly and without any reservation whatsoever. It will be to the extent that they do this that they can escape from the trap that Zionism and imperialism have set for them in the Mideast.

The anti-Semitic thrust of the SWP propaganda is seen again in its insistence that the Jewish people in Israel surrender their security and their entire future to the Arab guerrillas "without any reservation whatsoever."

With respect to the policy of the United States, the Trotskyist document charged that "the central role played by U.S. imperialism in continually attempting to contain and crush the Arab revolution" raised the possibility of a Middle East confrontation with the Soviet Union that could lead to war. It declared that "this places special obligations upon the SWP to educate the American people about, and mobilize opposition to, Washington's aims and actions in the Mideast."

In furthering this position, the Trotskyist press has fired off, with increasing frequency in the past year, a steady barrage of anti-Israel articles, including:

—Publication in two successive issues of *The Militant* (October 1970) of an official Al Fatah document calling for the dismantling of Israel and including a broad attack on the Jews of all countries. The manifesto, carried by the Trotskyist paper "for the information of our readers," said in part: "Jews contributed men, money and influence to make Israel a reality and to perpetuate the crimes committed against Palestinians. The people of the Book . . . changed roles from oppressed to oppressor."[9]

—A party pronouncement concerning "perspectives for world revolution" that appeared in the February 1971 issue of the *International Socialist Review*, another SWP publication, declaring that the Palestinians' fight would go forward "as long as the state of Israel continues to exist."[10]

—An article in *The Militant* by party Middle East specialist Robert Langston declaring that the Arab guerrillas would never "come to terms with the existence of the Zionist state" because even to accept the mere existence of Israel would be for them "national suicide."[11]

A *Militant* editorial following the murder of Israeli athletes by Arab terrorists at Munich during the 1972 Olympic Games said the "deaths of 11 Israeli participants" had produced "a hypocritical uproar of indignation from government officials and news media in capitalist countries around the world."[12] *The Militant* criticized the killing as being "ineffective" and a "diversion," that the purpose of the world's outcry had been "to make the criminal look like the victim". Thus *The Militant* placed the blame for the massacre on the murdered Jews while the Arab terrorists were slapped for a mistake in tactics.

The theme of condoning Palestinian terrorism while vilifying Israeli defense took up page after page of SWP publications during 1973. On March 5 the *Intercontinental Press*, another SWP journal, carried a long article by Jon Rothschild (one of several he has written for the publication) headed "Zionism and the Libyan Airliner," with an overline that proclaimed the author's attention to explain "Why Israeli State Commits Mass Murder."

Accusing the Israeli government of "a series of outright lies" in the aftermath of the incident. Rothschild said the answer was "to be sought in the nature of Zionism." He added:

> . . . As an inherently expansionist state founded on the denial of the rights of the Palestinian Arabs and implanted into a region that is socially and demographically Arab, the Zionist state must continually demonstrate its military superiority to the Arab states.
>
> It stands in permanent conflict with an evolving movement for revolutionary social change and depends for its existence on humiliating the entire Arab nation. The permanent demoralization of the people of the Arab East is a requirement for the Zionist state.

The commitment of the Trotskyists to the support of the Arab revolutionaries includes, in addition to the steady drumfire of these articles in SWP periodicals, a number of pamphlets and booklets produced and distributed by arms of the party publishing apparatus such as Pathfinder Press and Merit Publishers. It includes rallies, lectures, forums and teach-ins at which the Arab guerrillas are extolled and Israel vilified. It includes the formation of front groups and *ad hoc* committees for similar propaganda purposes. It includes active collaboration with Arab student groups and "third world" organizations in cities and on college campuses all over the country.

In short, the commitment is total and its threat to the deepest concerns of world Jewry is clear.

The Trotskyists in the late sixties opposed the injection of issues others than Vietnam into the programs of the National Peace Action Coalition (NPAC) and the Student Mobilization Committee to End the War in Vietnam (SMC), the two antiwar groups they dominated. They feared the inclusion of other issues would divide the hard-won coalition and lose them allies acquired by exploiting the widespread opposition to the Vietnam war. But even then they regarded the lessons, the techniques and the loyalties garnered in the antiwar movement as "transferrable" to other objectives when the time was right. With Vietnam a dead issue for the Radical Left, the time is ripe for a focus on the destruction of Israel, and, by logical extension, world Jewry.

The resolution adopted by the SWP at its August 1971 convention likened the Palestinian guerrillas to America's enemies in Vietnam. And it declared:

> The mass anti-war movement has sensitized large numbers of people to the role of U.S. imperialism and to solidarity with the colonial revolution. The expansion of these movements will be important factors in the increasing growth of sentiment in solidarity with the Arab revolution.

Even the slogans to be used in opposing U.S. support for Israel, said the SWP, would be "analogous to the slogans around the issue of Vietnam."

Some influential leaders on the far left long urged that the anti-war organizations be used as the nucleus of a mass movement opposing U.S. aid to Israel and rallying support for "Palestinian liberation." The rationale was spelled out in August 1971 by James Lafferty, a radical lawyer in Detroit who served as one of the national coordinators of NPAC. Lafferty's law partner, Abdeen Jabara, who was on NPAC's steering committee, has been the editor of *Free Palestine,* the leading pro-Fatah newspaper in the United States, and former president of the Association of Arab-American University Graduates, Inc., a fast-growing propaganda arm of the Arab cause in the United States. (While there is no evidence that Lafferty has ever been an SWP member, he has worked closely with the party's activists in NPAC and other causes.)

Lafferty, writing on "The Anti-War Movement and the Struggle for Palestine Liberation" in Jabara's publication, contended that the lessons learned in the peace coalition "are transferrable to the effort to build a movement to support Palestinian liberation."[13] Answering some leftist criticism that the antiwar forces had not done enough to "support other struggles," Lafferty argued that the supporters of the Arab guerrillas could learn much from the antiwar movement, which as far as "education" and tactics were concerned, already "provides the most effective possible support for Palestinian and other liberation struggles." Although "ostensibly" limited to the Vietnam war, he wrote, it had had a "beneficial impact" on the Arab effort to destroy the Jewish state.

Lafferty himself, while working in NPAC, was active in behalf of the Arab cause. In October 1971, his law partner, Jabara, filed suit in federal court in Washington on behalf of twelve plaintiffs, including Lafferty, against then-Defense Secretary Melvin Laird, Secretary of State William P. Rogers and presidential adviser Henry Kissinger, seeking to obtain public disclosure of alleged government "studies concerning the extent of American involvement and commitment in the Middle East."[14] The suit followed a letter from Jabara to the three officials which described his client, Lafferty, as being concerned that American policies in the Middle East were creating a situation "not unlike" that in Vietnam.[15]

Peter Buch of the Socialist Workers Party, writing in the September 1971 issue of Jabara's *Free Palestine,* was even more revealing of how the Trotskyists were planning to utilize the anti-ware movement for their own purposes with respect to the Middle East. Buch wrote of the "unparalleled opportunities for Palestine supporters to reach many people with their views during the massive demonstrations and community activities of the anti-war movement."

The SWP, wrote Buch, connects "the Vietnam and Palestine liberation struggles within the anti-war movement." He cited as an example his own six-month speaking tour "organized by the SWP in defense of the Palestinian revolution where I spoke to campus and anti-war audiences all over North America." (Buch toured the United States early in 1971 under the auspices of the SWP youth organization, the Young Socialist Alliance, covering more than sixty cities and college towns. At each stop he assailed Israel and "Zionism" and extolled Fatah and other Arab guerrillas. His speaking engagements continued in 1972 and 1973.)

In his 1971 *Free Palestine* article, Buch explained that "the leadership of the anti-war coalition, in which the SWP plays an important role," had not called out the masses in support of the Arab guerrillas because most of the people in the movement "don't yet understand that Zionism serves the same U.S. imperialist agressors who are destroying Vietnam." And yet, he declared, the Trotskyists were looking ahead to an improvement in that situation:

> There will surely come a time when the Palestine support movement will have a broader sweep than it does now, as U.S. intervention in the Middle East becomes more palpable and as our continued educational work around the issue becomes more effective. The lessons we have learned in building a massive anti-war movement surely will help us to build an effective opposition to American and Zionist aggression in Palestine, if we understand how to build a real united front on a principled basis, how to use defensive formulations that relate to the actual consciousness of the masses of people, and how to avoid the sectarian and self-isolating mistakes that doom such efforts from the start.
>
> Right now, we can make much progress in that direction with concerted educational efforts all around the country. The broadest based Palestine teach-ins, debates, lecture tours, *ad hoc* committees, literature distributions, etc., should be organized. The elementary civil liberties of Palestinian and Arab groups should be defended. Special efforts must be made to approach not only the anti-war movement, but also the women's liberation movement, the Black, Chicano and Native American movements, with the truth about Palestinian liberation. And those who approach these movements not only as revolutionary supporters of Palestine but also as builders and defenders of those movements will get the best hearing about Palestine too!

In short, tactics used in the anti-Vietnam war movement are to provide the basis for a groundswell to be engineered against Israel. And thus the domestic concerns of American minorities and women are to be supported at least in part because such Radical Left assistance will bring allies for the struggle against "imperialism," the new target of which is to be U.S. support of Israel in the Middle East.

Doing its best in the struggle to win allies to the anti-Israel cause is SWP's youth arm, the Young Socialist Alliance, the largest Radical Left youth movement in America since the splintering of the old Students for a Democratic Society (SDS) in 1969.

On its own or in cooperation with Arab student groups, YSA has organized Middle East rallies, teach-ins and "Palestine Support Weeks" to boost the Arab guerrilla cause on scores of campuses around the country. The YSA has collaborated with a number of Arab organizations which tag Israel and "Zionists" as their enemies. Members sold copies of *The Militant* to guests at the 1970 Convention of the Association of Arab-American University Graduates, held at the end of October. Earlier that month, at a meeting of the pro-Arab Middle East Institute in Washington, D.C., an Al Fatah display table was manned by YSA members. And at the YSA national convention in New York from December 27 to 31, 1970, a discussion panel on the Middle East included representatives of the guerrillas, the Organization of Arab Students (OAS) and Palestine House (Washington, D.C.). Of this convention *The Militant* reported: "All agreed on the necessity for closer collaboration and solidarity between American revolutionaries, Arab organizations in the U.S. and the revolutionary movements in Arab countries."[16]

The convention's decision was actually the climax of a Trotskyist pro-Arab campaign that had swung into high gear during the Middle East crisis period in the fall of 1970. At that time, the YSA, declaring that "the struggle of the Palestinians to regain their homeland usurped by Zionist Israel in a just struggle," issued a call for massive demonstrations on campuses throughout the country under the guidance of a Radical Left coalition. The YSA national office declared that the Middle East crises had "thrust the situation" there "before hundreds of thousands of students."[17]

The earliest manifestations of an intensive anti-Zionist cam--paign by YSA had taken place even before the national office published its call. Late in September 1970, a week of teach-ins and rallies took place at George Washington University in Washington, D.C. and at the University of Maryland nearby, with speakers from YSA, the Organization of Arab Students and the Arab Information Center. The week's climax was an "emergency" rally staged by the "Fair Play for Palestine Committee," a coalition that included YSA and OAS, joined for the occasion by the SMC, which was dominated at the national level by the Trotskyists. That same week, hundreds of students attended rallies at the Massachusetts Institute of Technology and in downtown San Francisco, both addressed by Arab students and SWP officials.

The call issued from the YSA convention in December 1970 resulted in increased Trotskyist youth activity in behalf of the Arab guerrilla cause, beginning in the early months of 1971. Teach-ins and "Palestine Weeks" were held on a number of campuses. There were anti-Israel demonstrations before the United Nations in New York and on the streets of other cities. During the April 1971 demonstrations in Washington against the Vietnam war, the YSA chapter of George Washington University circulated flyers inviting the demonstrators to partake of a number of events, including speeches on "Zionism and the Palestinian Revolution" and "How to Make a Revolution in the United States."

The Trotskyist youth activity continued throughout 1972, especially on the campuses. Typical was a September 11 demonstration in opposition to Israel's protective raids against the Fatah camps in Lebanon and Syria. In cooperation with the OAS and the Communist Young Workers Liberation League at the University of Indiana, the three groups jointly formed a "Palestine Solidarity Coalition" on the Indiana campus.

At the YSA's national convention in Cleveland from November 23 to 26, 1972, the situation in the Middle East did not arise for discussion except insofar as one entire session was devoted to an alleged anti-Arab "witchhunt" in the United States. This was the YSA reaction to efforts by U.S. law enforcement agencies, in the wake of the Munich slayings and a series of letter-bombs sent to Jewish leaders, to prevent Arab terrorist activities against Jewish targets here. The speakers at the session included Abdeen Jabara and Mathema Al-Hoory, general secretary of the OAS in the United States and Canada.

It was announced at the convention that the YSA had members on some 200 campuses. Credit was claimed for the distribution of two and a half million pieces of literature in 1972. Approximately 1,200 young people were in attendance at the gathering from various parts of the country; YSA's hard-core membership was reported to be about 1,250 and growing.

The end of American involvement in Vietnam seemed to signal a new flurry of anti-Israel activity by YSA during 1973. At Harvard University on March 1, for example, YSA joined forces with something called "The May 15th Coalition" which included the

MIT Arab Club, Tufts Hillel Non-Zionist Caucus (which was subsequently prohibited by Tufts from using the name of the campus Hillel organization),[18] Israeli Revolutionary Action Committee Abroad and the Middle East Research and Information Project. These groups co-sponsored a panel discussion on "Israeli Zionist Terrorism in the Middle East."

On the weekend of May 4 to 6, a "Socialist Conference on International Revolutionary Struggles" sponsored by YSA at New York University and open to the public included a Saturday morning session on "Zionism and Anti-Semitism," addressed by Dave Frankel, *Militant* staff writer and member of the YSA National Executive, who was introduced as having spoken at more than forty schools on the subject of the Middle East. He spouted the by-now-familiar anti-Israel line of the SWP and YSA.[19]

The SWP and its youth group take umbrage when its anti-Israel, anti-Zionist extremism is called anti-Semitism. But evidence of the anti-Semitism is not restricted to its advocacy of the destruction of Israel. Its domestic political course has been clearly anti-Jewish. It has willingly collaborated with overt anti-Semites and shared some of their anti-Jewish purposes. Although its spokesmen have been careful to avoid the use of crude anti-Semitic phraseology, the SWP's program and activities, as they relate to American Jewry, have been totally hostile.

The rationale for this anti-Jewish policy was set forth in a February 1969 *Militant* article by George Novack, a long-time leader of the SWP. The article, which was later reprinted in pamphlet form, expressed the view that:

> . . . at the present time there is a deadly symmetry between the attitudes of the Israelis toward the Arabs and that of the American Jews toward the Afro-Americans and their liberation struggle . . . the upper and middle ranges of American Jewry, comfortably ensconced in bourgeois America, some of them bankers, landlords, big and little businessmen, participate in the system of *oppressing and exploiting* the black masses, just as the Zionists have become oppressors of the Palestinian Arabs. Jewish teachers in New York, reluctant to give up their small privileges, resist the Afro-American demand for the control of the schools in their own communities.[20]

Thus, oppression by Jews, in the view of the SWP, is not confined to Israeli Jews versus Arabs but includes American Jewish attitudes and actions toward American blacks. Given this viewpoint, it is small wonder that whenever Jews have been under attack from anti-Semites who happen to be black, the SWP has consistently joined the fray against the Jews. During the 1968 teachers' strike in New York City and its 1969 aftermath, when Jewish teachers were being singled out for anti-Semitic attack by black extremists, the SWP vigorously defended the anti-Semites. When Albert Vann and Leslie Campbell, leaders of the anti-Semitic African-American Teachers Association (ATA) were threatened with discharge from their public school positions, the SWP not only jumped to their defense but elevated them to the role of martyrs of the black community.[21] As for the rights of Jews to be protected from anti-Semitic bigotry, they had none; according to the SWP, the proper role of the Jewish school teacher, presumably, was meekly to accept the charge that he was a "brainwasher" of black children and an "unholy son of Shylock" and to abandon his job.

On other occasions the SWP has actively collaborated with anti-Semites. They tried to stimulate the formation of an all-black political party in the New York area in cooperation with leaders of the African-American Teachers Association. If they were not successful, it was not for lack of trying but because the ATA refused to accept them. Ironically, the ATA's attitude toward left-wing parties is that they are "jew-controlled."[22]

Earlier, in 1967, the SWP participated in a public Harlem rally billed as a meeting to present "the other side" of the Middle East crisis. Its chairman was Paul Boutelle, who in 1968 because the SWP's candidate for vice-president of the United States; another Trotskyist speaker was Clifton DeBerry. Apart from the totally anti-Israel views espoused by all of the speakers, one of them, Charles Kenyatta, delivered a blatantly anti-Semitic speech. Kenyatta, then leader of the Mau-Mau, a uniformed paramilitary black nationalist group, asserted, for example, that "the only flag the Jew knows is the dollar bill," adding that a careful examination of a dollar bill would reveal a Jewish star hidden in it.[23]

Kenyatta's rabble-rousing speech was the longest and best-received of the entire meeting.

More recently the SWP found a new anti-Semitic hero, Luis Fuentes, the District 1 school superintendent discussed in an earlier chapter. The SWP and YSA have been among Fuentes' most vigorous supporters, together sponsoring numerous rallies in his behalf throughout the New York area, with Fuentes himself as the main speaker. In May 1973 the *Young Socialist* reported that YSA at New York University and LUCHA, the NYU Puerto Rican student organization, were supporting each other's campaigns for the student government at the Washington Square campus. Their platforms included "support to the community control school board slate in District 1" and "defense of Luis Fuentes . . . who is currently facing a vicious slander campaign whipped up by Albert Shanker, the reactionary head of the N.Y. United Federation of Teachers." The story quoted Anne Verdon, one of the YSA candidates in the student election, as follows:

> The struggle in the Lower East Side demonstrates very clearly that the student government must reach beyond the campus and link up with the oppressed communities in their fight to gain control over their lives. The student government should help mobilize student support for Luis Fuentes and the community control slate.
>
> It's time that we stopped looking to our enemy to run our university and our community. Just like the Black, Puerto Rican and Chinese people of the Lower East Side [but not the Jews, many of them poverty-stricken, who are a sizeable element of the Lower East Side population] are doing, we must organize ourselves to act directly against the problems we face.[24]

Similarly, the May 1973 issue of the *Young Socialist* sprang to the defense of a black student newspaper on the campus of Queens College of the City University, *The Last Word*. The paper several months earlier had published an article referring to "racist Jewish fascists" and had called on blacks to "Smash Jewish fascism."[25] The campus Council of Jewish Organizations brought charges against the paper's anti-Semitic diatribe before the Faculty-Student Disciplinary Committee. The *Young Socialist*, noting that it and the campus YSA chapter were supporting *The Last Word*, said that the charges had been brought by "Zionist students."[26]

Thus, although the SWP claims to be offended by the charge that it is anti-Semitic, its record of animosity toward Jews—in America no less than in Israel—is clear. To be sure, neither the Trotskyists nor any of the other Radical Left groupings voice classical Jew-hating views. For one thing, overt racism is out of tune with Marxist theory, which favors a class rather than a racial analysis of history. But because the SWP and other Radical Left groups seek to exploit racial and national antagonisms, they are prepared to forego a strictly class analysis. To advance their goal of seizing political power in the United States, they have developed an analysis which places nationalism and racism at the service of the "proletarian" revolution. According to the rules devised by the SWP for the playing of this revolutionary game, to be black, brown, or yellow is to be "objectively" on the side of the revolution. To be a Jew, however, is automatically to be an obstacle in the path of revolutionary "progress," unless one is prepared totally to abnegate all Jewish identity and consciousness, i.e., to become a "non-Jewish Jew." In this respect, the Trotskyists offer salvation to individual "revolutionary" Jews in the same way that bygone reactionary clerical regimes in Europe offered immunity to "their" Jews, by allowing them to convert to Catholicism.

It is unlikely the Socialist Workers Party will ever achieve any real political power in the United States, but in the effort thereto, in the use of an anti-Israel campaign to attack the U.S. government and in the wooing of racial minorities by villainizing American Jews, they cause concern among Jews everywhere.

As has long been the practice of other groups on the Radical Left and Right, the SWP supervises the formation of other organizations designed for specific propaganda purposes and/or to appeal to specific audiences. Sometimes the SWP participation is masked, sometimes not.

One such activity was the formation of an *ad hoc* group called the "Committee of Black Americans for Truth About the Middle East" (COBATAME). Its sole apparent purpose was to offer an imprimatur for a half-page advertisement in the November 1, 1970 issue of the *New York Times* which harshly attacked Israel and Zionism. Funds for the *Times* ad were solicited in advance via an announcement published in the SWP's *Militant.*[27] The COBATAME chairman was Paul Boutelle, who had just returned from the Middle East, where he and five other members of his "Committee" had been guests of the Al Fatah terrorists. Boutelle subsequently addressed college audiences under the sponsorship of YSA.

Several other Trotskyists were signers of the *Times* ad, along with a number of black nationalists, most of whom had little or no prominence in the black community or in the community at large. Their declaration that "imperialism and Zionism must and will get out of the Middle East" was in marked contrast to another advertisement, published the preceding June in the *Times,* which called for firm U.S. support for Israel and which was signed by sixty-four leaders of the black community across the country, among them Roy Wilkins, Bayard Rustin, Richard Hatcher, Shirley Chisholm and the late Whitney Young, Jr.[28] And in October, just months before his tragic death by drowning off the African coast, Whitney Young responded to a reader who had criticized his signing of the pro-Israel ad with an eloquent defense of Israel and its policies in the occupied territories; he delivered a scathing attack on the Arab nations for having done nothing to improve the lives of their people and a plea for "reason and common sense" in finding a solution to the Middle East conflict. The executive director of the Urban League added:

> In any event, I cannot believe that the criterion for relevance in the black struggle for liberation here in the United States is dependent upon adopting slogans and ill-informed opinions about issues of foreign policy. Black people have a duty to free themselves from other people's propaganda and to work together for justice and complete equality in our own country.[29]

Another SWP front group, the "Committee for New Alternatives in the Middle East"—founded by Berta Langston, who headed it, and her husband, *Militant* writer Robert Langston— was apparently wrested from Trotskyist control in January 1971 by members who proposed that it develop a less openly one-sided approach in seeking Middle East "alternatives." In resigning from the slightly reconstituted committee, Mrs. Langston declared that she could not "support an organization that is not clearly and unambiguously opposed to Zionism."[30] The Trotskyists' stand has always been clear and unambiguous.

Given the political commitment of Russia to the Arab cause in the Middle East and the traditionally slavish adherence of the American Communist Party to the line set in Moscow, the pro-Arab–anti-Israel posture of the Communist Party-USA is utterly predictable. The withdrawal from Egypt of the major part of the Soviet expeditionary force, at the request of Egypt's Sadat, did not change the political relationship, and Sadat and his emissaries soon made conciliatory moves in the direction of the USSR, moves that paid off handsomely in Russian arms for Egypt and its willingness to replenish Sadat's losses in the first week of the October 1973 war.

While the CP-USA has (in its 1972 platform) affirmed the right of Israel to "exist," the party—in common with other voices on the far left in the United States and in line with the declarations from Moscow—continually assails "Zionism," which party leader Henry Winston has dubbed "the nationalism of the Jewish bourgeoisie."[31] Party theoreticians fill many a page of their ideological journal, *Political Affairs,* with attacks on Israel and harsh criticism of the pro-Israel views and activities of American Jews.

One of the more important attacks of this kind was a long two-part diatribe entitled "The Reactionary Role of Zionism" that appeared during the summer of 1971 under the by-line of editor Hyman Lumer, the main CP theoretician on the Middle East.[32] Lumer attacked the American Jewish community, its major organizations, "Zionist and non-Zionist alike," and its "synagogues and temples" for their support of Israel, but in decrying American contributions to Israel and investments in that country (those of non-Jews as well as Jews), the Communist spokesman denounced the alleged role of "Jewish bankers," specifically naming the "Morgenthaus, Rosenwalds and Warburgs ... Kuhn-Loeb and Lehman Brothers"—the very same "Jewish bankers" who for five decades have been the whipping boys of the anti-Jewish lunatic hate fringe, including the Gerald Smiths and the late home-grown George Rockwells.

Lumer echoed the theme used by Arab propagandist and classical anti-Semite alike—that Jewish organizations and large blocs of Jewish voters in big cities and politically crucial states wield undue influence in domestic American politics and in American foreign policy on the Middle East. "Accompanying these mammoth fund-raising drives," Lumer wrote,

> is an uninterrupted flood of political activity, aimed at winning support for the Israeli government and its foreign policy. In the major centers of Jewish population, and especially in New York City, the big Jewish organizations wield not a little influence in the political arena [not Zionist organizations, it should be noted, but "big Jewish organizations"].

He went on to talk of the "well-organized pro-Israel lobby" which he said had been described as including "scores of Jewish organizations which have large amounts of manpower, money and zeal."

The Communist ideologue asserted that the "heightened influence of Zionist ideology" had led to, among other things, "an alarming growth of racism and chauvinism within the Jewish community." This, he charged, had aligned "the Jewish people with the forces of racism" and had produced "a campaign of vilification and slander" against the Soviet Union "based on the Big Lie of official 'Soviet anti-Semitism' and persecution of Soviet Jews, which has been built since 1967 to frenetic proportions."

Setting the line for the CP-USA, Lumer declared that "in this country, the heartland of U.S. imperialism and the home of the largest Jewish community in the world, the fight against Zionism takes on exceptional importance. It is here above all," he wrote, "that the battle must be waged against the machinations of U.S. imperialism in the Middle East and for the liberation of the Arab peoples."

The Communist line on the Middle East had been re-enunciated earlier, of course, at the 24th Congress of the Communist Party of the Soviet Union held in Moscow during the spring of 1971. The Soviet Party's resolution declared that the "representatives of the 14-million-strong army of Soviet communists sharply denounce Israel's imperialist aggression against the Arab states,

conducted with support from American imperialism. . . ." It also
denounced "the expansionist designs of the Israeli ruling clique
and the Zionist circles," and praised "the constructive position of
the Arab countries." It asserted that "the legitimate rights and
interests of all the Arab peoples, including the Arab people of
Palestine, will triumph" and called on the "fraternal parties" (the
Communist Party in all countries) to "strengthen solidarity with
the peoples of the Arab countries and to give them active support
in their struggle."[33]

The CP-USA responded with expectable obedience. Its 20th
National Convention, held in New York in February 1972,
adopted a resolution similar in tone and content to that adopted
in Moscow. It read:

> End the alliance of U.S. imperialism and Israeli expansionism
> directed against the peoples of the Arab countries and Africa. We
> call for complete withdrawal from all Arab territories in accordance
> with the 1967 resolution as a prerequisite to a political settlement.
> This includes the right to Palestinian self-determination and the
> continued existence of Israel.[34]

The issues to be acted on by the CP-USA convention were set
forth in a series of "Draft Theses" summarized over a period of
weeks in the *Daily World,* the party-oriented newspaper published in New York. One of the theses, dealing with "anti-Semitism and Zionism," told the party faithful that "Zionism . . . has
become a weapon of imperialism" and that "the state of Israel,
tying itself to the imperialist warmakers of the U.S., has become
the oppressor of the Middle East." Turning to American Jews, the
thesis declared:

> To carry out the aggressive policies of Israel, its Zionist supporters
> in the U.S. have sold themselves to the U.S. State Department. They
> support the Vietnam War and spread State Department slanders
> about "Soviet anti-Semitism."[35]

More recently, in its May Day 1973 Declaration, the CP-USA
asserted:

We greet the peoples of the Middle East in struggle against Israeli aggression backed by U.S. imperialism. Immediate withdrawal of Israel from lands occupied by their aggression, and restoration of Palestinian refugees to their rightful homes, can strengthen peace and end Israel's reckless war policy.[36]

Tom Foley, whose articles appear regularly in the *Daily World,* attended the Third Congress of the Communist Party of Lebanon in January 1972 as a fraternal delegate representing the CP-USA. He subsequently told readers of the *World* that the meeting in Beirut "was one of the most important political events to occur in the Arab world in the last decade" and that it might "well mark a turning-point in the history of the Middle East." The job of the CP-USA, Foley declared, "is to mobilize American public opinion against the U.S. government's support of Israeli aggression, so that the peoples of the Middle East will no longer be forced to live in an atmosphere of terror. . . ."[37]

The Communist Party is also the major defender in the United States of the Soviet Union's policies toward its Jewish citizens. The American Communists engage in a steady drumbeat of propaganda denying the existence of Soviet anti-Semitism and proclaiming that the Jews of Soviet Russia are the freest in the world. As far as the CP-USA is concerned, the denial of religious and national equality for Soviet Jews, the suppression of Jewish culture in the USSR, the virtual barring of Jews from the top ranks of government and the diplomatic corps and the publication of anti-Jewish books and pamphlets are mere figments of the imagination of "Zionist agents of U.S. imperialism."

The CP line on Soviet anti-Semitism was expressed succinctly in the December 1972 issue of *Political Affairs.* Soviet Jews, it claimed, "are free of all discrimination, and if instances of anti-Semitism are to be found, they occur as isolated remnants of the past." Protests on behalf of the rights of Soviet Jews were depicted in the article as "a part of the never-ending effort of monopolist reaction to paint a false picture of the Soviet Union."[38]

In February 1971, a "World Conference of Jewish Communities on Soviet Jewry" took place in Brussels, aimed at examining the plight of Soviet Jews and rallying public opinion in their behalf. Some 750 delegates from around the world attended, among them distinguished figures in government, academia, literature and the arts and several Nobel laureates. After hearing personal testimony from Soviet Jewish émigrés and carefully examining all the facts, the conference issued a declaration of "solidarity with our Jewish brothers in the Soviet Union," calling on Soviet leaders to respect the rights of Jews to practice their religion and culture and to emigrate to Israel if they so desired.[39]

Predictably, the American Communists responded with expressions of outrage that Jews should come to the aid of their oppressed brethren. The *Daily World* ran two full pages of polemics under a headline which read: "The Truth About The Lies at Brussels." The article, by Hyman Lumer, included a reply to the conference's charge that Soviet Jews are denied the right to conduct classes in the Hebrew language; this, claimed Lumer, was "an outright lie." As "proof," he cited a Soviet publication which claimed that in Leningrad University a certain Professor Vinnikov, an expert in "the Hebrew, Aramaic, Syrian, Phoenician, Ungaritic and Arabic languages," taught a course in spoken Hebrew. For Lumer, incredibly, this constituted proof that Soviet Jews, who number some three million, are permitted to study Hebrew. To the overall charge that the Soviets are guilty of anti-Jewish discrimination, Lumer replied that it was "a fraud . . . a Big Lie," that originated in "circles of right-wing reaction and in the State Department."[40]

On December 10, 1972, Hyman Lumer was honored by his fellow Communists at a testimonial dinner in New York City. Lumer made the major speech of the evening on "The 50th Anniversary of the USSR and the Jewish People." In it he set forth the official CP view on the question of Soviet Jewry and Soviet anti-Semitism:

> . . . Today Soviet Jews live on a plane of full equality with all other Soviet citizens, an equality which is not enjoyed by Jews in any capitalist country. They may live where they please and are free to enter any occupation or profession. Anti-Semitism in word and deed are outlawed.

> ... In a word, in the socialist Soviet Union the Jewish question has been fully solved—a fact which it is most important for us to shout from the rooftops on this 50th anniversary of the U.S.S.R.[41]

There was no mention of why Soviet Jews even today languish in Soviet prisons for merely asserting the right to live Jewish lives, why many have been deprived of work and thus livelihood for merely requesting exit visas, why still others risk that deprivation by continuing to apply; in short, if life for Jews is so wonderful in the USSR socialist paradise, why they ache to get out. But the answers to these questions would not have fit in with Lumer's view of the Soviet "solution" to the "Jewish question."

On the question of the State of Israel and Zionism, Lumer had thoughts to offer that would warm the heart of every Jew-baiter:

> Zionism is not only anti-Soviet; it is in its very essence a racist ideology. It sets the Jewish people apart as a special people, a "chosen" people—if you will, a superior people. In Israel the Zionist rulers have created a racist state.

In the thirties and forties, when millions of Russians were murdered or perished in labor camps at the hands of the Stalin regime, the CP-USA responded to the public protests then in precisely the same way that it now defends the Soviet government against charges of anti-Semitism. They simply denied that it had happened. This pattern of behavior makes the American Communist Party an accomplice in anti-Semitism. To the Jew, the parrot of my enemy is my enemy.

The Progressive Labor Party (PL) is a revolutionary left-wing sect founded in April 1965. It traces its origins to a split within the Communist Party. The leaders of PL for many years looked toward Peking rather than Moscow as the true center of world communism. However, when China began to engage in "ping pong diplomacy" toward a détente with the United States, PL decided that Mao had abandoned the course of revolutionary struggle and began to travel an independent Radical Left path. Perhaps the major accomplishment of PL in recent years was to capture control of Students for a Democratic Society (SDS) in 1967 from its "Weatherman" rivals within the organization — possibly because Weatherman leaders are wanted by federal authorities for a series of political bombings and other acts of violence and have gone underground or to Algeria.[42] Today SDS is simply a well-controlled front for PL.

The Progressive Labor Party is a self-avowed enemy of Zionism and of Israel, which it regards as a racist cat's-paw of American imperialism. The only thing that keeps Israel intact, according to PL's organ, *Challenge,* is "the 'security' issue (which involves whipping up racism against Arabs, national chauvinism to suppress the social conflicts, and anti-communism). . . ."[43] To drive home the point, the January 1973 article was illustrated with a photo of Golda Meir retouched by PL's artist to make her look like Hitler, complete with Hitler-type mustache, hair and swastika armband. The charges of fascism against Israel were repeated in a defense of the *Challenge* article (and the touched-up photo of Golda Meir reprinted) in *SDS* in response to outrage expressed by Jewish students at Lehman College of New York's City University at the circulation of the *Challenge* article by SDS members on the Bronx campus.[44] The *SDS* piece against Israel was written by Lehman student Robert Steinhorn.

The major point of the two anti-Jewish articles was to express support for Dan Vered, one of a group of four Jews and thirty-six Arabs arrested in Israel in December 1972 on charges of engaging in espionage for Syria and conspiring to assassinate Israeli leaders. Vered had been a member of PL's SDS chapter in Chicago while he was studying in the United States several years ago. When he returned to Israel he was active in Matzpen, a tiny anti-Zionist revolutionary party. Eventually Vered split from Matzpen and helped to form a "revolutionary Communist alliance," which has maintained fraternal relations with PL. His arrest was vigorously protested by PL, which charged that he was being punished for his revolutionary views by "the fascist Israeli rulers."[45]

On December 13, 1972, a PL-SDS group in Boston picketed El Al airlines and the Israeli Consulate to protest the arrest of Vered and his accused fellow spies. In a leaflet distributed by the pickets, it was charged that "Dan, like the others in the group, were [sic] arrested because they are active in the growing movement against the vicious racism of the Israeli Gov't."[46]

The informal debate between pro- and anti-Israel students at Lehman College apparently was formalized in April 1973 in what the *Challenge* reported as a "debate attended by over 175 people," although *Challenge*—its biases showing perhaps—slipped or slurred and said in its lead that the confrontation had taken place at "*Lebanon* College here" (italics added). Disputants were the Progressive Labor Party and the Jewish Students Union, and the PL paper accused the Jewish debaters of being "unable to argue in a factual manner" and of ignoring PL's charges, including "the long history of Zionist collaboration with Nazis, and the rampant racial discrimination in Israel."[47]

Robert Steinhorn and Jerry Schacter, another SDS student at Lehman College, led a discussion on "Zionism, a Racist Ideology," during a workshop at an SDS Conference on Racism held April 28 and 29, 1973 at the City College of New York and attended by some 300 persons. Observers reported that at the workshop, Steinhorn and other Jewish SDS members seemed eager to demonstrate "racism" among American Jews against Arabs; that some SDS members from around the country agreed that the Israeli government could fairly be compared with the Nazis while others, joined by radical participants in the workshop who were not, however, SDS members, thought this was going too far.

Whatever the dissent within SDS about the characterization of Israel's leaders as Nazis, PL was obviously holding fast to this idea. In July 1973, *Challenge* cited a spurious story in a French leftist newsletter to the effect that Israel's Superior Rabbinate was looking for those with "Jewish blood" in the occupied West Bank and seeking "to force them to return to their ancestral religion." The PL paper compared these alleged actions to those of the German occupiers of Eastern Europe during World War II. Its headline read: "Nazi Master-Race Trash Is Alive, Well, and Kicking—In Israel."[48]

There are other arms of Radical Left's anti-Israel, anti-Zionist propaganda apparatus, other purveyors of pro-Arab pamphlets, leaflets, reprints, posters, stickers and buttons—and films.

One of the more recent and active of these propaganda mills is the Middle East Research and Information Project (MERIP), formed in the spring of 1971 by a small group of New Left activists, some of them Jewish; several had visited Arab guerrilla training centers as guests of Al Fatah in September 1970. There are two MERIP units, one in Washington, D.C., and the other in Cambridge, Massachusetts.

MERIP states that it "provides literature, speakers, films, posters, slides and research material about political, economic and social conditions in Middle Eastern countries and the role of the United States in the political economy of the area."[49] In fact, however, MERIP is an unabashed propaganda outlet in the United States for the Palestinian revolutionary movement. A packet of some thirty items mailed out by MERIP in the summer of 1971 included materials issued by Al Fatah, the General Union of Palestinian Students and such Beirut-based organizations as the Fifth of June Society, the Research Center of the Palestine Liberation Organization, the Institute for Palestine Studies, the Arab Women's Information Committee and Americans for Justice in the Middle East. Some of these groups will be examined in the next chapter.

Another similar propaganda operation promoted by MERIP was the *Palestine Resistance Bulletin,* published monthly by a small group of Arab student activists and New Left radicals at the State University of New York at Buffalo who express "solidarity with the Democratic Popular Front for the Liberation of Palestine"[50]—one of the most extreme of the various guerrilla groupings. The Buffalo activists offer their own list of propaganda items issued by the DPFLP, including a pamphlet entitled *On Terrorism, Role of Party, Leninism vs. Zionism.*

Low-cost printing and reprinting has been provided for various arms of the New Left apparatus by The New England Free Press in Boston. This propaganda factory has offered a lengthy list of materials on various topics of interest to the movement, including several on the Middle East, all of them bitterly anti-Israel. One of these is *Zionism—A Political Critique,* by Tabitha Petran, a long-time far left journalist, published by the SDS before its collapse in 1969 and subsequently promoted by MERIP.

A New Left film collective called Newsreel is another purveyor of anti-Israel propaganda. Newsreel distributes three "documentary" films devoted to the cause of the Arab terrorist war against Israel: *Revolution Until Victory, Al Fatah Palestinians* and *Palestine Will Win.* The films are shown at churches, campus rallies and Radical Left gatherings. Newsreel's San Francisco office (there are also offices in Detroit, Milwaukee, Los Angeles and Lawrence, Kansas, in addition to the New York headquarters) claims that it alone is responsible for more than 200 showings of Newsreel films each month.

Revolution Until Victory is a 52-minute "documentary" produced and distributed by Newsreel, which described its background in a November 1972 letter:

> A short time ago, San Francisco Newsreel was invited to the Middle East by representatives of the Palestinian Liberation Movement to make a film about the people of Palestine, and their fight to regain their country.
>
> It soon became apparent that a film only about the Palestinian people would be inadequate to build support for a liberated Palestine in the United States. Zionism, with its racist policies toward all non-Western, non-white peoples, Palestinians and Jews alike, HAD TO BE EXPOSED! Israel had to be exposed as a bastion of U.S. imperialism in the Middle East. . . .[51]

With such an approach it was inevitable that the film would depict Zionists as the "real" enemy, Israel as closely aligned with American imperialism, Zionist leaders as having sold out the Jews of Europe during World War II (film sequences of Nazi parades and Zionist marches merge imperceptibly; Ben Gurion at a microphone is followed by Hitler at the *Sportspalast*), the 1967 war as having been triggered by Israel's declining economy and a lust for the Sinai oil reserves (none of the precipitating Arab actions are mentioned), the 1948 war as similarly the product of Israeli aggression (not Arab invasion). It was also predictable, given the thrust of Radical Left thinking, that the film should make a pitch to the U.S. peace movement by depicting the Arab-Israel conflict as having an exact parallel to the U.S. involvement in Vietnam.

The two other anti-Israel films distributed by Newsreel—*Al*

Fatah Palestinians, made in Rome by Unitele Film, and *Palestine Will Win,* a French production—similarly glorify the Arab terrorists and emphasize their role as part of the third world revolutionary front against the West.

Newsreel, a "film collective," was incorporated in New York State in 1968 under the name of Camera News, Inc. It has distributed a letter seeking contributions which states that tax-exempt gifts may be made payable to a New York nonprofit foundation also incorporated in September 1968.[52]

The unabashed support given by radicals of the far left to Arab regimes that have waged war against Israel, or to revolutionary terrorists sworn to Israel's liquidation, is a grim and unrelenting war against the security of the Jewish community. At stake of course—and it is too often forgotten—are the very lives of the Israeli Jews. And in a world that still harbors anti-Semitism, a world in which for Jews, at least, the memory of the Holocaust cannot fade, Jewish security in the Diaspora is inextricably intertwined with the survival of Israel as a sovereign state; Jews will neither feel nor *be* safe in a world which acquiesces in the destruction of the Jewish state, either all at once or piece by piece. In its assault on Israel's right to exist, the Radical Left engages in what is perhaps the ultimate anti-Semitism.

In this as in previous chapters we have come across the phenomenon of anti-Jewish Jews. Within the Radical Left are some who do not think of themselves as such; they may regard themselves as assimilated, universalist, "non-Jewish Jews" or even as Jews in some "higher" sense. Many even celebrate their Jewishness, publicly, and become anywhere from uncomfortable to enraged at the suggestion they are anti-Semitic. Jews within the "movement" become tools for those who are truly anti-Jewish to hide their hostility, much as the Soviet Union occasionally parades its "house" Jews to disprove charges of anti-Semitism, or trots out issues of an "official" Yiddish publication, which of course spouts the Soviet line that there are no Jewish problems in the USSR. But among some Jews in the Radical Left, here and abroad, there is an interesting psychological phenomenon at work. It is best illustrated, perhaps, in the opening paragraphs of an article that appeared in both the *Intercontinental Press* and *The Militant* of the SWP, under the by-line of Nathan Weinstock (it was described in the former publication as having first appeared in *La Gauche,* weekly newspaper of the Revolutionary Workers League, Belgian section of the Fourth International, and as having been translated from the French by the *Intercontinental Press*):

> This year, within the space of a few weeks, two great events in the contemporary history of the Jewish people will be commemorated—the thirtieth anniversary of the Warsaw ghetto uprising and the twenty-fifth anniversary of the proclamation of the state of Israel. The coincidence is not accidental, for the two historic dates are intimately related. One symbolizes the way in which the fate of the Jews came to represent the human condition under Nazi barbarism. The other is explainable by these sufferings: it took Auschwitz to push the Jewish masses—and with them Western public opinion—into the Zionist camp.
>
> But at the same time, what a contrast! In the Warsaw ghetto the survivors of the genocide against Polish Jewry embodied the dignity of humanity, resisting oppression, even without immediate hope of success; a revolt that ennobled all humanity, a tragic epic that prefigured the victories of the Indochinese revolution which, under different and more favorable circumstances, was able to triumph over bestial imperialism.
>
> But the creation of the state of Israel, on the other hand, symbolizes the spiritual degeneration of this same Jewish community, which has become the colonial oppressor in Arab lands, reducing a whole people, the Palestinians, to exile, poverty and powerlessness.[53]

The Warsaw Ghetto Uprising, the thirtieth anniversary of which was commemorated by Jewish communities the world over in April of 1973, was indeed a noble chapter in Jewish history; it will be remembered as long as there are Jews, both as a reminder of what Weinstock accurately called the "genocide against Polish Jewry," and as an example of Jewish will to resist against overwhelming odds. But the point that Weinstock and the Radical Left overlook is that the odds *were* overwhelming; the Warsaw Ghetto resisters died—and knew they were going to—brave martyrs of their people, crushed under the Nazi regime. The State of Israel came into being, at least in part, to make certain that it could never happen again. It represents Jewish life, not Jewish death. When Weinstock and his colleagues in the Radical Left celebrate the doomed ghetto uprising in one breath and vilify Israel in the next, they are in fact celebrating death over life; when they advocate the destruction of the Jewish state, as they so clearly have, they are asking for new Jewish martyrs; they are joining that element of the non-Jewish world which in its heart of hearts believes that the best kind of Jew is a dead Jew.

9

Arabs and
Pro-Arabs

Arab anti-Semitism is not a new phenomenon. Arab spokesmen who deny Arab hostility to Jews *as Jews*—they are *only* anti-Zionist, they allege—say with accuracy that historically Jews fared better as a minority in Arab countries than they did in the Christian West. Largely, they say, because the deicide charge was absent from Moslem culture. But the Koran is harsh on the Jews, who were no more willing to accept Mohammed than they were to agree that Jesus was the Messiah. And while Moslems did not for the most part impose their creed upon Jews by force or expel them, as Christian countries did, the position of Jews in Arab countries was never quite so ideal as has been portrayed by Arabs. The acceptance Jews found was discriminatory tolerance as alleged inferiors, predicated in part on verses in the Koran which described Jews as stamped with "humiliation and wretchedness" and "visited with wrath from Allah,"[1] not only in Moses' time but broadly thereafter, a divine decree fulfilled by a lack of political integrity and a position of subjugation.[2] Moslem theologians and historians explained that the dispersion of the Jews and their continued exile was the will of God, a punishment against a debased and degraded people.

The return of great numbers of Jews to the Middle East in modern times and the re-establishment of Israel as a political entity, achieved finally in an unwanted military struggle and secured in repeated Israeli repulsion of Arab attack, was seen by many Arabs as a triumph of Judaism over Islam. And this was at odds with every traditional interpretation of Moslem scripture and history. Widespread Arab disbelief after the 1967 war that Israel had won it alone, without American military intervention, had deep roots in Moslem tradition.

It does not take delving into ancient history to document Arab mistreatment of Jews *as Jews*. While undoubtedly stimulated by the modern Arab-Israel conflict, religiously-based discrimination, harassment and murder have afflicted centuries-old Jewish communities in Moslem lands so severely in recent years that approximately 800,000 Jews from Arab lands have fled mostly to Israel, the lesser number elsewhere. It is a matter of concern to Jews throughout the world that the plight of *these* refugees— casualties not so much of war but of state-ordered persecution— has attracted nowhere near the sympathy and support from the non-Jewish world as have the grievances, of the refugee Palestinians.

Many of the Jewish communities that have been dissolved by the Arab states since the establishment of the State of Israel had lived there for 2,000 years, under varying degrees of acceptance and rejection. Yemen, for example, where Jews were not allowed to ride a horse, to build houses higher than the houses of Moslems, where Jewish testimony was not accepted in the courts and Jewish authors were forcibly converted, was totally evacuated of all Jews after 1948.

Syria—where Jews were not allowed to occupy positions of public trust, to travel freely, to deal in real estate, where Jewish shops were officially boycotted, where pogroms were modern-day occurrences—today has a population of 3,000 Jews as compared to 40,000 in 1948, and those who remain, desperately seeking freedom, are still subject to harassment, torture and arrest.

Egypt, which held some 80,000 Jews in 1948, imprisoned thousands in 1948, 1956 and 1967. Today Egypt is finally *Judenrein*, as is Libya. The latter once had a population of 30,000 Jews, against whom, in Tripoli and Bengazi in 1945 and 1967, pogroms were perpetrated. In 1967, all of Libya's remaining Jews were imprisoned; later they were permitted to leave.

The 350,000 Jews of Morocco had scarcely broken out of the

confines of the *mellah*, the oriental ghetto, by 1948. Today there are approximately 50,000 Jews remaining there; on numerous occasions they have required the protection of King Hassan and his troops against anti-Jewish riots and boycotts. Attempted coups against Hassan in recent years sent shock waves through the Moroccan Jewish community.

Iraq had a Jewish community of some 150,000, whose history went back 2,500 years in the country. In 1941, anti-Jewish riots took place in Baghdad, instigated by the pro-Nazi Grand Mufti of Jerusalem, and by 1949, Iraqi Jews began to be attacked in the streets; their places of business were broken into and many were murdered. Jews were dismissed from all branches of public and civil service, their movements were restricted, hospitals were closed to them, their children were barred from public schools. In December 1949 an official reign of terror began, with thousands of Jews imprisoned on charges of "Zionism." The leader of the Jewish community of Basra was hanged in his own backyard and a public holiday declared to celebrate the event. At this stage, emigration became mass flight and by mid-July 1950, more than 110,000 Iraqi Jews had left the country. A ban was put on all Jewish cultural, social and communal organizations, apart from strictly religious gatherings. The community status accorded the Jews in 1931 was canceled in 1958, and control of communal property was transferred from a Jewish lay council to a government body. Regulations passed in 1963 decreed that all Jews who had left the country for whatever reason between January 1960 and March 1963 and had not returned within six months would lose their citizenship and have their property and funds frozen. Other special citizenship restrictions were placed upon the Jewish community.

In 1967 there were about 3,000 Jews left in Iraq, a tiny handful of the once-flourishing Jewish community. After the Six Day War, Jews were arrested by the score and released only on the payment of heavy ransoms. The situation worsened; an Iraqi newspaper declared:

> The Jewish cancer in Iraq constitutes a serious danger for our struggle to exist, for the future of our country. If interest, circumstances

and the law require that we do not hurt them at the present time, at
least it is incumbent on us to place them under strict surveillance
and freeze their activities.[3]

In 1968 new laws were promulgated, speeding up the process of
seizing Jewish property and designed to "establish that the Jews
living within Iraq shall be second-class citizens. . . ."[4] The anti-
Jewish campaign reached a nadir in "spy trials" during January
1969, when nine Iraqi Jews were condemned to death—the trials
were televised—and then hanged in the main square of Baghdad
to an appreciative populace brought in for the occasion by special
excursion trains.

At this writing the ancient Jewish community of Iraq consists
of approximately 400 persons, still persecuted, still imprisoned,
still subject to murder by the state.

There are more than half a million Arab citizens of the State of
Israel, enjoying full religious, social, cultural, political and economic rights and a standard of living higher than that of their
brethren anywhere in the Arab world.

Moslem Arab religious disdain of Jews as an inferior people and
persecution of remnant Jewish communities in Arab states have
their counterpart in contemporary Arab propaganda that draws
freely and fully on anti-Semitic tracts and themes in the Western
world. Scholars have debated the degree to which such originally
European propaganda finds a ready acceptance in the Arab mind
(and more sensitive Arab intellectuals have deplored its dissemination); but they concur that an ancient image of Jews as a degenerate people has been wedded to hostility to Israel as a non-
Arab entity in a sea of Arab countries. This dissemination has
become a useful tool, a political device representing neither the
lunatic hate fringe nor minuscule political parties but official
policy emanating from the highest Arab government circles and
carried out by government sponsored or government censored
newspapers, magazines and books.

Translated into Arabic as far back as the 1920s, the czarist forgery, *The Protocols of the Learned Elders of Zion*, for example, is today
a best-seller in the Arab world (the Lebanese newspaper *Al Anwar*

in March 1970, in fact, listed a new edition of the *Protocols* at the top of its non-fiction best-sellers).[5] There are more than a dozen complete translations by different authors under different auspices; hundreds of Arab periodicals regularly quote or summarize the *Protocols* or cite the fabrication as an "authority" on the alleged perfidy of the Jews. Organs of the Egyptian government have put out editions since the mid-fifties; the late President Gamal Abdel Nasser told an Indian editor it was "very important" that the editor read the *Protocols* because it "proves beyond a shadow of a doubt that three hundred Zionists, each of whom knows all the others, govern the fate of the European continent."[6] Nasser's brother published a new edition in Cairo in 1969;[7] in 1965, in fact, the UAR Information Services printed extracts in a pamphlet in English distributed throughout Africa, entitled "Israel, the Enemy of Africa."[8] A 1968 edition of the *Protocols,* published in Kuwait in English, French and Spanish, was distributed to hundreds of postmaster generals throughout the world by the State of Kuwait Ministry of Posts, Telegrams and Telephones, along with a letter urging its use in their postal libraries and a three-page "summary" informing them, in part, that the Christian world "has already been snared and lies prostrate at the mercy of this ruthless inhuman cabal."[9] In June 1970, Wasfi Tal, the Jordanian premier who was assassinated in November 1971 by Black September terrorists, devoted a major portion of a speech at the Jordanian University to "the world Jewish conspiracy," citing the *Protocols* as his principal documentation.[10] Reporters visiting Libya's Colonel Muammar el Qaddafi have noted that he keeps a pile of copies of the *Protocols* on his desk. One Western journalist, telling Qaddafi of his astonishment on seeing such long-discredited material, got the following retort from him: "You must read it; I always tell everyone it is a most important historical document."[11]

If the *Protocols* is the most popular anti-Semitic tract in the Arab world, Hitler's *Mein Kampf* probably runs a close second. After the Six-Day War in 1967, Israeli soldiers found that many Egyptian prisoners of war were equipped with small paperback editions of *Mein Kampf,* translated into Arabic by an official of the Arab Information Center in Cairo, one El Hadj (literally, the pilgrim), who had included his own commentaries about Hitler's thinking. "El Hadj" was well qualified to annotate *Mein Kampf;* he was Luis Heiden, a former Goebbels associate and high official in the Nazi Propaganda Ministry. Heiden had fled to Egypt in 1945 and had taken his new name several years later, after converting to Islam.[12] He was one of a number of former Nazi and SS leaders attracted to important posts in Egypt's ministries during the late forties and early fifties. There were also "retired" Nazi scientists who in the sixties volunteered to help Egypt develop the ultimate weapon for a new "final solution."[13]

The current leader of Egypt has a long history of pro-Nazi sympathies and anti-Semitic pronouncements. Anwar Sadat in his younger days was associated with the fanatical, anti-Semitic Moslem Brotherhood. He was a major conspirator in the clique surrounding Nasser, who had attempted to arraign Egypt on the side of Nazi Germany, and Sadat had acted as liaison with the Third Reich during the war.[14] In September 1953, several news agencies reported that Hitler was still alive; on the basis of this report, a Cairo weekly, *Al Mussawar,* asked a number of Egyptian personalities the following question: "If you wished to send Hitler a personal letter, what would you write to him?" And twenty years ago the man who is now president of Egypt offered this response:

My Dear Hitler:

I congratulate you from the bottom of my heart. Even if you appear to have been defeated, in reality you are the victor. You succeeded in creating dissensions between Churchill, the old man, and his allies, the Sons of Satan. Germany will win because her existence is necessary to preserve the world balance. Germany will be reborn in spite of the Western and Eastern powers. There will be no peace unless Germany once again becomes what she was. The West, as well as the East, will pay for her rehabilitation—whether they like it or not. Both sides will invest a great deal of money and effort in Germany, in order to have her on their side, which is of great benefit to Germany. So much for the present and the future.

As for the past, I think you made some mistakes, like too many battlefronts and the shortsightedness of Ribbentrop vis-a-vis the experienced British diplomacy. But your trust in your country and people will atone for those blunders. You may be proud of having become the immortal leader of Germany. We will not be surprised if you appear again in Germany or if a new Hitler rises up in your wake.

(signed) Anwar Sadat[15]

If it is unfair to hold a man's words against him two decades later, there is the following from Sadat, uttered in a nationwide address on April 25, 1972, celebrating the anniversary of Mohammed's birth:

We shall not only liberate the Arab lands in Jerusalem and break Israel's pride of victory, but we will return them [the Jews] to the state in which the Koran described them before: to be persecuted, suppressed and miserable.[16]

In a 1972 interview published in *Al Mussawar,* King Faisal of Saudi Arabia had this to say:

Two years ago when I was in Paris, the police discovered the bodies of five children who had been murdered and drained of blood. Afterwards it turned out that Jews had killed the children to mix their blood into their bread.[17]

He had said much the same thing earlier in the year to David Hirst of the *Manchester Guardian,* an interview reprinted in the Washington *Post.* Hirst reported that Faisal, "apparently carried away," had elaborated on the "blood libel"—the outrageous myth that Jews killed gentile children for ritual purposes in the preparation of Passover matzoth—"with an extraordinary outpouring of anti-Semitic prejudice."[18]

Sometimes "timeliness" dictates the theme of Arab propaganda. In the spring of 1973, the Palestine Arab Delegation, headquartered in New York City, registered with the U.S. Department of Justice as a foreign lobby and ostensibly representating the Lebanon-based Arab Higher Committee for Palestine, sent out a letter, received by U.S. officials, ordinary citizens and a number of newspapers, warning of "a very grave and serious crisis which will affect you and members of your family, and will endanger the national security and best interests of the United States." The letter, signed by PAD's chairman, Issa Nakhleh, declared:

> So-called "Israel" and the Zionist-Jew leaders in the United States have converted the Watergate incident, for which certain individuals are responsible, into a great "scandal" to blackmail the President of the United States and to force him into submitting to the will of so-called "Israel" and the Zionist-Jew leadership in the United States.
>
> The objective of "Israel" and the Zionist-Jew leadership is to dictate to the President the Middle East policy of the United States.[19]

The letter added that "having control of the legislative branch of the U.S. government," the "Zionist-Jew" leadership was "blackmailing" the Nixon administration to make it "subservient" to "their will and to their dictate." "Are you willing to sit back and helplessly watch Israel and the Zionist-Jew leaders in the United States complete their domination of the United States government?" Nakhleh asked, leaving little doubt why PAD propaganda is eagerly printed by virtually every anti-Semitic hate group in the United States.

In June 1973, King Faisal surpassed even the propagandists. He blamed not only the Watergate investigation but the Lambton sex scandals in England's Parliament on "Zionism." A United Press International dispatch out of Beirut quoted the Lebanese paper *Al Anwar* as reporting that Faisal saw the Watergage and Lambton affairs as "Zionist" plots to undermine the American and British governments because their policies were beginning to shift in favor of the Arabs.[20]

This is the Faisal who turned off the oil spigots all over the world in November 1973.

The examples abound of anti-Semitic books, pamphlets, press articles, speeches, radio broadcasts with which the Arab world is inundated daily. Such Arab anti-Semitism, from all indications, is part of official ideology; it stems not from the fringes of Arab society but from its center. It thus represents the views and tendencies among the political and cultural leadership of the Arab world.

If it reflects, in part, the thinking of an older generation of

Arab leadership, there is nevertheless little expectation that younger Arabs, indoctrinated in government-regulated schools and colleges—and especially those brought up in the Palestinian refugee camps and who today lay claim to leadership of the Palestinian people—will have escaped the absorption of Jew-hatred.

After the Six-Day War, the Israelis found classrooms in the refugee camps literally awash with anti-Semitic Arab propaganda; it preached the most violent hatred of Israel and Jews, glorifying slaughter and depicting as imperative a *jihad,* a holy war, to the finish against the Jewish people. An international commission of educators established under the authority of the director general of UNESCO to examine textbooks used by Arab children in refugee schools financed by the United Nations Relief and Works Agency (UNRWA) found 65 of the 127 books examined objectionable on grounds that they gave the students a distorted view of history, openly incited to violence or employed "the deplorable language of anti-Semitism."[21] The commission's initial report noted that "special mention should be made of students' exercises which are often inspired by a preoccupation with indoctrination against Jews rather than by strictly educational aims."[22]

In a letter to the UNESCO director general, Syrian Minister of Education Suleyman Al-Khash wrote: "The hatred which we indoctrinate into the minds of our children from their birth is sacred."[23]

The destruction of the Jewish state is itself the ultimate anti-Semitism. To the Arabs, the "de-Zionization" of Israel means the cessation of Jewish immigration, the termination of any link between Israel, Jews and Jewish communities throughout the world, and the dissolution, dismemberment or destruction of the state structure of Israel.

The attempt to deny the Jews the right of national self-determination and territorial independence accorded to all other peoples (and vigorously claimed by the Arabs for themselves) is in fact the new anti-Semitism of Arab Islam. It represents, just as it does when it emanates from the remainder of the non-Jewish world, or even from a handful of Jews, a callous denial of 6,000

years of Jewish peoplehood, more than a third of that time spent
in involuntary exile.

On November 8, 1969 a Dutch court ruled that "anti-Israel"
meant the same thing as "anti-Semitic." President U.W.H. Stheeman of the court found that "the situation of the Jews and their
common fate in the world" were intimately linked with the
existence and survival of Israel. The ruling came in an action
against the newspaper *De Volksrant,* the plaintiff alleging that the
paper was anti-Semitic, the paper responding that it was only
"anti-Israel." Judge Stheeman rejected the defendant's plea.[24]

Similarly, on April 24, 1973 a French court found a Frenchman,
the manager of the official Soviet Embassy newsletter in Paris,
guilty of defamation and "incitement to racial hatred and violence" for publishing an article the court determined to be anti-
Semitic. The defense had claimed the piece was merely "anti-
Israel," a "just and rightful reproach" against the "international
excesses" of a "colonialist state," meaning Israel. The suit was
brought under a newly-amended and tough French libel law
by the International League Against Racism and Anti-Semitism,
and Encounter, Christians and Jews. Among a score of witnesses
testifying for the prosecution was Nobel Prize winner René
Cassin.[25]

Just a week earlier in France there had been additional evidence of a long overdue but welcome acceptance of Jewish nationhood, a declaration by the French Bishops Committee for Relations with Judaism to the effect that—

> . . . universal conscience cannot deny the Jewish people, which has
> undergone so many vicissitudes in the course of history, the right
> to and the means for its own political existence among the nations.[26]

Arab terrorist activities are not the impulsive works of enraged
men and women. Arab terrorism is highly organized and could
not survive without the support, encouragement and material
aid of Arab governments. The largest terrorist organizations—
the roof unit, the Palestine Liberation Organization, and Fatah,
Saiqa and the Popular Front for the Liberation of Palestine—have
long histories of dependence upon the support of Egypt, Syria,

Libya, Iraq and Algeria. Terrorist organizations have been granted bases in almost all the Arab states. There are offices, recruitment centers and headquarters in Cairo, Beirut, Damascus, Baghdad and Tripoli; military bases in Lebanon and Syria; training bases in Syria, Lebanon, Egypt, Iraq and Libya, with training provided or permitted by the regular armies of those countries. Financial support is provided by oil states, chiefly Egypt, Libya, Iraq, Kuwait and Saudi Arabia; Fatah alone was recently reported to be receiving $85 million a year, plus a $5 million "bonus" in 1972 from Libya's Qaddafi for the Munich massacre by Fatah's Black Septembrists.[27] Weapons come from the Soviet Union and China through the courtesy of Egypt, Syria, Iraq, Algeria and Libya; the defense and intelligence establishments of these and other Arab states maintain close contact with the terrorist organizations. Several Arab governments have put their diplomatic facilities at the disposal of the terrorists—passports, both authentic and forged, diplomatic cover and the use of the diplomatic pouch for the transfer of documents and weapons.

Even more worrisome, however, are the Arab and pro-Arab organizations and individuals operating within the United States and disseminating Arab propaganda, often with the cooperation of the Radical Left and organized anti-Semites. Such propaganda ranges from the crude anti-Semitism of the PAD and total support of terrorist activities by the Palestine Liberation Organization (representing the PLO abroad) to the anti-Israel attacks of the Arab Information Center, the official propaganda arm of the fourteen-nation Arab League.

It includes the activities of a virtual army of Arab students represented by the 10,000-member Organization of Arab Students operating on some 125 American campuses, young people financed and primed for propaganda by their home governments before being sent to the United States. It includes the sophisticated legal, letter-writing and mass media activities of a six-year-old organization, the Association of Arab-American University Graduates, Inc., which has about 1,000 members and was headquartered in the law offices of its immediate past president, Abdeen Jabara of Detroit. (Its new president is Dr. Baha Abu-

Laban, professor of sociology at the University of Alberta in Edmonton, Canada, and its *Newsletter* now bears a North Dartmouth, Massachusetts, post office box number.)

And such propaganda includes the activity of some three dozen new pro-Arab organizations established since 1967 in the United States with names like Americans for Middle East Understanding (New York City), American Committee for Justice in the Middle East (Boulder, Colo.), Search for Justice and Equality in Palestine (Waverly, Mass.), Citizens Committee for Middle East Justice (Warren, Mich.) and Americans for United Nations Responsibility in the Middle East (Seattle), which wants to "disengage the United States from the conflict in the Middle East."[28] While the level and tone of the pronouncements of these groups vary, the theme is the same: Americans are not getting the full story on the Middle East; their thinking has been conditioned by "Zionist" influence; the "true facts" should be told so that American policy will change. The "true facts," somehow, are always anti-Israel.

And somehow the names of the same individuals who for many years have been spouting pro-Arab, anti-Israel, anti-Jewish propaganda turn up on the letterheads of these and similar organizations: the Rev. John Nicholls Booth, former pastor of the Unitarian Church of Long Beach, California, and now interim minister of the First Unitarian-Universalist Church in Detroit; the Rev. Humphrey Walz, Presbyterian minister long associated with the pro-Arab propagandizing of the now-defunct American Friends of the Middle East and more recently head of the New York-based Americans for Middle East Understanding; Alfred Lilienthal, a New York lawyer, author and prolific letter-writer to newspapers, and Rabbi Elmer Berger, formerly with the anti-Zionist American Council for Judaism, both paraded by the Arabs as examples of right-thinking Jews; and Norman F. Dacey of Southbury, Connecticut, who also writes letters and places anti-Semitic advertisements in the *New York Times* and elsewhere. There are others.

One other who is completely candid about his desire to win the propaganda war and shift American thinking on the Middle East is Mohammed T. Mehdi, "secretary general" of the Action Committee on American-Arab Relations. Mehdi, a long-time spokesman in the United States for the Arab cause, says his organization has 30,000 members; it is actually a one-man operation, but Mehdi is a whirlwind of activity, a skilled and able propagandist who lectures before various groups, appears as the "Arab expert" on local and national radio and television and even testified before the Republican National Convention Platform Committee in 1972. Mehdi is also the author of several books published by his own New World Press, headquartered at the same New York City address as his Action Committee; in *Kennedy and Sirhan: Why?*, Mehdi argued that the assassination of Senator Robert F. Kennedy was not murder but a political act.[29] *Action*, allegedly dedicated to "the establishment of a democratic non-sectarian state in Palestine," is the official publication of Mehdi's organization, a weekly that does not always appear every week but when it does is filled with all the current anti-Israel Arab propaganda.

Mehdi has organized a variety of front groups and has lately had some success in politicizing Americans of Arab ancestry; his press releases now appear in most of the publications of formerly cultural and social Arab-American organizations, and he has become a featured speaker at their meetings. One such Mehdi success is the Committee for Better American Relations in the Middle East, located in Birmingham, Alabama and headed by Salah el Dareer. It distributes literature, makes statements and has its own radio program. An April 1972 letter distributed by this Mehdi affiliate charged that the U.S. mass media had ignored the real issues in the Middle East because presidential and congressional candidates were vying for the "Jewish vote."[30]

An April 1973 story in the *Los Angeles Times*, headed "Arabs Set Out to Change U.S. Public Opinion," warned that the Arabs were "gradually awakening" to the fact that they had lost the "propaganda war" in the United States and were determined to carry on "information campaign directly to the American people to counteract Zionist influence in Washington." *Los Angeles Times* staff writer William J. Coughlin, writing that the "main thrust" of the campaign would be "toward those non-Jewish Americans who have no family, economic or emotional ties to Israel," added:

> It is believed that once the case of the Palestinians and of the Arab states who lost land to Israel is understood, the American sense of fair play will end the all-out governmental support of Israel.

Coughlin quoted Mehdi on a proposal that the Arabs and their supporters spend $50 million a year in America over five years "to influence the United States society and force the United States government to stop sending Phantoms and economic aid to Israel."

Mehdi told Coughlin that the financial support for such a campaign could come from growing oil revenues in the Arab world, and Coughlin wrote that "American oil interests" would be expected to play a role in the campaign "by bringing home to Congress and the White House the importance of Arab oil to the U.S. economy."

The *Los Angeles Times* story, date-lined Beirut, appeared on April 1, but by the midsummer of 1973 it did not sound like an April Fool's hoax. It was indeed time to take Mehdi and his cohorts seriously, for they had developed some very powerful allies.

Oil. By mid-1973 the very word had begun to ooze worry for American Jews and other supporters of Israel. For nearly a year, and especially in the first half of 1973, the American public has seen a deluge of articles, editorials and cartoons in the printed mass media and discussions over national radio and television linking the energy crisis to American policy in the Middle East, more pointedly to American friendship and support for Israel.

Arab leaders—who, apparently, had been "quietly" discussing the use of oil as a political weapon with representatives of American oil companies operating in the Middle East—publicly fueled the discussion in the United States.

In April, Saudi Arabia's minister of oil production, Sheik Zaki Yamani, told Secretary of State William P. Rogers during discussions in Washington that Saudi Arabia (according to the *New York Times* account) "would find it difficult to increase oil production if the United States did not help to bring about a political settlement in the Middle East satisfactory to the Arab States."[31]

On May 13 Libya's Colonel Qaddafi, during a five-and-a-half-hour news conference, stated that oil would be used as a "weapon of Arab self-defense,"[32] and two days later Libya and three other Arab countries—Iraq, Kuwait and Algeria—temporarily halted the flow of oil to the West, a demonstration that was supposed to have been timed to coincide with the celebration of Israel's twenty-fifth birthday on May 7.[33]

Egypt's Sadat called on the Arab states (according to the Associated Press account) "to use their oil to apply pressure on the United States to abandon support for Israel."[34] Sadat had been entertaining Faisal the previous weekend and announced he was also meeting with leaders of other oil-producing nations.

On July 6, the *Christian Science Monitor* published an interview obtained with Faisal by its staff correspondent, John K. Cooley, who quoted Faisal as declaring, "The United States gains nothing from support of Israel, which is a burden to it. The real interest of the United States in this region is to cooperate with the Arabs."

The campaign was on. Joining in its orchestration were three American oil companies, with others expected to follow suit. On June 21, 1973, Mobil took a quarter-page advertisement in the *New York Times* headed "The U.S. stake in Middle East Peace: 1" (it was allegedly the beginning of a series of such ads). Mobil explained the "energy crisis" to the million readers of the *Times:* "Our society cannot live without adequate oil supplies. . . . Like it or not, the United States is dependent on the Middle East even just to maintain our present living standards in the years immediately ahead." Having thus set a slightly hysterical tone, and pointing to Saudi Arabia and Iran as the principal suppliers of U.S. oil needs, the advertisement continued:

> We in the United States must learn to live with the peoples of these two countries and to understand that they look to us for policies that recognize their legitimate aspirations. If we want to continue to enjoy our present life style, or anything approaching it, then—no matter how much more efficient we may become in the use of energy—we will have to understand the changed and still-changing conditions in the Middle East.
>
> If our country's relations with the Arab world [Iran is not an Arab state] continue to deteriorate, Saudi Arabia may conclude it is not in its interest to look favorably on U.S. requests for increased petroleum supplies. The government of that country has the power to decide how much oil is produced within its borders. And to what countries that oil can be shipped.

> It is therefore time for the American people to begin adapting to
> a new energy age, to a vastly changed world situation, to the realities
> with which we will have to learn to live. Nothing less than clear
> thinking, a sense of urgency, and a grasp of what is at risk can lay
> the base for achieving a durable peace in the Middle East.

Of course, the Saudi Arabian oil minister had made it clear that
only a Middle East settlement favorable to the Arabs would dis-
pose his country to meet U.S. oil needs; thus the United States
must change its policy on Israel.

A letter was sent by O. N. Miller, chairman of the board of
Standard Oil Company of California (Chevron), to 262,000 stock-
holders in the company. The letter, sent from Standard Oil's San
Francisco headquarters and dated July 26, 1973, said in part:

> There is a growing feeling in much of the Arab world that the
> United States has turned its back on the Arab people. Many are said
> to feel that Americans do not hold in proper regard the national
> interests of the Arab states, their long history of important contri-
> butions to civilization, their efforts to achieve political stability and
> to develop sound and modern economic structures. . . .
> It is highly important at this time that the United States should
> work more closely with the Arab governments to build up and en-
> hance our relations with the Arab people. We as Americans have a
> long history of friendship and cooperation with Arabs. It goes back
> more than 100 years, long before the first oil operations, and involves
> cultural relationships which encompass education and religion, as
> well as commercial trading.
> During this time, much good will has been established which
> must be enhanced. There must be understanding on our part of the
> aspirations of the Arab people, and more positive support of their
> efforts toward peace in the Middle East.

Standard Oil did not mention exactly what "efforts" the Arab
states had made toward peace in the Middle East, nor did it tell
its stockholders that Arab "aspirations" included the destruction
of Israel.

On September 19, 1973, the chairman of the board and chief
executive officer of Texaco added his company's voice to the
growing chorus of oil lobbyists. Maurice Granville, in a public
address delivered in Scottsdale, Arizona, acknowledged he was

conveying a Saudi Arabian "appeal to the people of this country to review the actions of their government in regard to the Arab-Israeli dispute and to compare these actions with its stated position of support for peaceful settlement responsive to the concerns of all the countries involved." He urged Americans to "pause and examine" United States policy in the Middle East.

Withholding of crude oil by the oil exporting countries of the Middle East has less to do with politics in regard to Israel than with driving up prices; with having more dollars at present (and dollars worth a great deal less than they used to be) than the oil states can spend, and not particularly caring at the moment to have any more.

The truth is, as Washington *Post* reporter Jim Hoagland noted from the Persian Gulf state of Abu Dhabi, that the oil producers "are in fact laying plans for vast increases in both production and sales to the growing American market,"[35] and Abu Dhabi was willing to reserve half its oil for American consumers—provided, said the sheikdom's minister of oil, that we are willing to meet the new higher prices his country, for one, expects to get. (In the midst of the October 1973 war, Abu Dhabi proclaimed it was ending oil production for the United States until Israel withdrew to the pre-1967 borders. At the same time, news stories reported the tiny emirate as seeking loans from London banks, possibly to help finance the Arab war effort. Clearly, Abu Dhabi had no intention of a permanent U.S. boycott; like its fellow Arab oil producers—who announced the end of oil shipments to the United States—Abu Dhabi was participating in the Arab campaign to panic U.S. opinion and mobilize Americans against their government's support of Israel.)

The truth is that there is little likelihood of any permanent curtailment of oil supplies to the West. What are the Arabs going to do with all that oil—and what do they have to sell if they don't sell their liquid gold? As Leonard Mosley wrote on the question, "Not even the pleasure of seeing the United States squirm under a boycott is worth the destruction of a billion-dollar oil field."[36]

Moreover, as Senator Henry Jackson has pointed out, the geopolitical factors in the Middle East militate against ultimate withholding of oil for the West on purely political grounds. Senator Jackson, noting that the Saudis "understand . . . very well" that they would "not last long without a stable Jordan, a more or less calm Egypt and a contained Syria and Iraq" recently wrote:

> . . . Middle Eastern energy sources would be insecure even if Israel didn't exist. For it is inter-Arab rivalry, and the opportunistic exploitation of it by the Soviet Union, which threatens to disrupt the normal flow of oil. After all, it is not Israel which threatens Kuwait and its substantial oil reserves; rather, recent Iraqi military activity may have as its objective control of that oil-rich sheikdom. It is not Israel which threatens Saudi Arabia—but Yemen to the south, Soviet-supported Iraq and Syria to the north, and Egypt to the west.
>
> Whatever stability exists in the Middle East today, it is, in my view, largely the result of the strength and Western orientation of Israel on the Mediterranean and Iran on the Persian Gulf. These two countries, reliable friends of the United States, together with Saudi Arabia, have helped inhibit those radical Arab elements which pose a grave threat indeed to petroleum sources in the Persian Gulf. It is ironic that Saudi Arabia and the sheikdoms (which, along with Iran, will provide most of our imported oil in the years ahead) depend for regional stability on Israel's capacity to encourage an environment where moderate regimes in Lebanon and Jordan can survive and where Syria can be contained. Iran plays a similar and even more direct role in the Gulf itself.[37]

The nationally syndicated Evans and Novak column has since 1967 assumed a consistently hostile posture toward Israel. Seeking repeatedly to demonstrate why the United States must adopt a "more even-handed" Middle East policy, their columns have frequently echoed the main themes of pro-Arab propaganda, with a posture of alleged no-nonsense "realism" about Middle East and American politics. They have asserted that Israeli military achievements make additional U.S. arms sales to Israel unnecessary; that Israel is bent on territorial expansion to accommodate new immigrants and supplement its natural resources; that the negotiations deadlock has been brought about by Israeli—not Arab—instransigence; that the United States has been unable to exert sufficient leverage on the Israeli position because of the influence of Jewish pressure groups; that the Israelis have administered the occupied territories brutally and without regard for the rights of the Palestinians; that Israel has sought to change the "historic character" of Jerusalem by pursuing a discriminatory policy against non-Jews in the hope they will leave.

In February 1973, Evans and Novak published a column in which they alleged that "serious Administration efforts to liquidate the effects of the Six-Day War of 1967 ended in December 1971 when Nixon decided to open the weapons pipeline to Israel." They discussed Henry Kissinger's possible involvement in working out a Middle East settlement, declaring that the administration's "doing nothing" in the Middle East "assures growing hatred for the U.S. throughout the Arab world, which controls most of the world's oil reserves." In contemplating the Kissinger involvement, Evans and Novak noted that some Arab leaders privately sought it, and that the fact that they were "now looking to an American Jew for help is ironic evidence of a desperate dilemma."[38]

There were other prominent voices raised in the United States in 1973 in support of the Arab cause, but few more prestigious than the chairman of the Senate Foreign Relations Committee. Senator J. William Fulbright, admired by many for his stand on Vietnam, has a record of statements and Senate votes over many years that placed him squarely in opposition to Israel. On April 15, 1973 he told millions of Americans watching CBS' Sunday "Face the Nation" program that the administration was unable to exert pressure on Israel for a Middle East settlement because the United States Senate was "subservient" to Israel. He added that despite the fact that the U.S. provided Israel with "a major part of the wherewithal to finance or pay for everything Israel does," leverage could not be applied because "Israel controls the Senate." Linking a Middle East settlement to American oil interests in the Middle East, Fulbright declared: "We should be more concerned about the United States' interest rather than doing the bidding of Israel."[39] On May 30, at the opening of two-day hearings his Committee initiated on the energy situation, Fulbright charged that U.S. policy was to give Israel "unlimited support for unlimited expansion"; he urged U.S. cooperation with oil producing countries.[40]

Senator Fulbright receives front-page headlines in Cairo hailing him as a "courageous voice of truth."[41] Israeli and American Jews do not share that view.

Peace in the Middle East will come when Palestinian and other Arabs recognize that Jews are just as indigenous to the Middle East as Arabs; that it is right and just and inevitable that there should be a Jewish state in the ancient homeland of the Jewish people; that Israel is no artificial creation of Western imperialism imposed upon the Arab Middle East, but the Phoenix-like rebirth of a nation and a people from the ashes of destruction.

Peace will come when Palestinians and other Arabs recognize that there is plenty of room in the Arab Middle East for a Palestinian state alongside Israel—indeed, that one already exists in which Palestinians constitute a majority, and that it is called Jordan.

Jews and Arabs are indeed closer than cousins; they are linked by a common ancestor—Shem, the eldest of Noah's sons—by culture, land, language and custom. The hostility of the Arab world to the Jews of Israel is one of the great tragedies of mankind's history. It must not be allowed to continue; *salaam* and *shalom* must once again return to their identical meaning.

10

Anti-Semitism
in a Minority Community

While anti-Semitism has been demonstrably unrepresentative of the 22 million black Americans, pockets of prejudice against Jews have long existed in the black community. Such anti-Semitism always tended to be produced by professional Jew-baiters, who used bigotry and hatred in the same way as anti-Semites in the white community, to further their own extremist political ends and, in some instances, to line their own pockets.

Black nationalist Marcus Garvey and his Universal Negro Improvement Association reached a peak of influence in the twenties. With his "Back to Africa" movement, Garvey, a Jamaican, sought to induce blacks in America to join in an exodus to Africa, where they would set up a new society that could provide them he said, with status and integrity as black men. Garvey's followers never got to Africa. His messianic scheme was denounced by prominent leaders of the black community; he was barred from bringing his people to Liberia, and he was eventually sentenced to a jail term for using the mails to defraud by improperly selling shares of stock in his "Black Star Ship Line." The Universal Negro Improvement Association disintegrated when Garvey was deported in 1927 as an undesirable alien.

In promoting his enterprises in the United States in the 1920s, and in his writings and statements in later years abroad, Garvey did not hesitate to mix his own antipathy to Jews with propaganda

for his "Back to Africa" movement. Although Garvey's condemnation of Jews was sometimes clouded by his emulation of the Jews
quest for a *zion,* a homeland, which he sought for blacks in Africa,
his hostility was real. In commenting on the plight of Jews in
Germany under Hitler in the mid-thirties, for example, he wrote:

> [It] has been brought on by themselves in that their particular meth-
> od of living is inconsistent with the broader principles that go to
> make all people homogeneous. The Jews like money. They have
> always been after money. They want nothing else but money.[1]

Unhappily, some latter-day disciples of Garvey in the black
community found their mentor's scorn of Jews a useful weapon
in their propaganda arsenal. Arthur Reid, a one-time Garvey
lieutenant who was later a co-founder of the Harlem Labor
Union, Inc., attacked union leaders and ghetto merchants, among
others, on the basis of their religious affiliation, including in
his condemnation a host of anti-Jewish indictments. Similarly,
Carlos Cooks, a native of the Dominican Republic who for many
years headed the African Nationalist Pioneer Movement, a neo-
Garveyite group in New York, harangued a Harlem crowd in
1942 by stating of Hitler: "What he's trying to do, we're trying
to do." Yet another Jew-baiter in the black community in the
late thirties and early forties was Sufi Abdul Hamid, head of
the so-called Negro Industrial Clerical Alliance in Harlem. His
slogan was "down with the Jews" and he was labeled a professional
anti-Semite and a "black Hitler" by critics in the black community and elsewhere.[2]

Throughout, it should be made eminently clear, responsible
black leadership has always openly and publicly condemned
anti-Semitism and anti-Semites; and still does. By and large,
the anti-Semitism of an earlier day in the black community was
the trademark of the "con man," the manipulator, the professional bigot; by and large, it still is. It was certainly not representative of the black community as a whole, nor did it permeate
the community; it still has not.

But beginning in 1966 and continuing to the present time,
evidence of hostility in some parts of the black community to

Jews and Jewish concerns has increasingly come to public attention. Earlier chapters, focusing on "respectable" insensitivity and indifference to anti-Semitism and on such clear enemies of Jews as the Radical Left, have touched on anti-Semitism emanating from some blacks in the public eye: the right-wing black nationalist Hassan Jeru-Ahmed; the leaders of and publications linked to the African-American Teachers Association; self-styled "community spokesmen" like Robert (Sonny) Carson, Melvin Pritchard and William O. Marley, who fulminated against Jews during the New York school controversies of 1967–69; Radical Leftist Paul Boutelle of the Socialist Workers Party; Charles X Kenyatta, who delivered an anti-Semitic diatribe at a Radical Left Harlem rally; the teacher John Hatchett, who accused Jews of "mentally poisoning" black children, and others.

In each case, the relevance of being black to the anti-Semitism that emerged is that the individual claimed to be speaking for at least a segment of the black community (although the claims were often grandiose) and insisted on scapegoating Jews for its ills; in each case, the attempt to redress legitimate political, social and economic grievances of blacks involved the illegitimate tactic of Jew-baiting.

Many factors play a role in the current increase in frequency of anti-Semitic attacks by some blacks against Jews, not the least of which is the enormous influence of the media in giving broad exposure to extremists and their viewpoints. A street-corner haranguer in Harlem once had a limited audience. Today, via local and national radio and television and more comprehensive newspaper coverage of the black community, his audience can be vast, his imitators many; in the late sixties, if you were black and seeking some degree of instant celebrity, it paid to be anti-Jewish—the TV cameras were there in a flash.

The potential for damage against the Jewish community is significantly multiplied. And repeated public demonstrations of such anti-Jewish bigotry by blacks cannot fail to have an impact on the Jewish audience, and the natural tendency among Jews is to become defensive. Jewish support for the still unmet goals of the civil rights movement is thereby eroded. Social psychologists have long noted that prejudice is as injurious to its host as to its victim; in the arena of black-Jewish relationships, this psychological truth has substantive meaning. Black extremists who use and foment anti-Semitism may yet succeed in isolating the black community from its real and historic allies at a time when such allies are vital. Black and Jewish civil rights leaders know this, and they are worried.

But there is a more recent background, as well, to the anti-Semitism that has so marred black-Jewish relations, changes within the civil rights movement and the black community itself—and these are worth looking at.

By 1966, a dozen years had passed since the landmark U.S. Supreme Court decision on school desegregation. Yet integration of black children in the nation's public schools—and meaningful black integration into the nation's economic life—had been infinitesimal. Inevitably, optimism gave way to frustration. Coupled with a growing militancy, this frustration brought to the fore increased resentment of whites (including Jews) for the record of unkept promises. Accompanying the understandable frustration, anger and hopelessness was the development among some blacks of nationalist and separatist sentiments. These attitudes produced a change in goals, especially among some organizations in the black community that had previously espoused integration. The nationalists and separatists, in search of a new self-image and possessed of a new self-awareness, sought to develop their own black leadership and their own black organizations, exclusive of whites, and to make the institutions that controlled their lives responsive to their needs. In short, they sought black control over black community institutions. In so doing, they challenged the old pattern of white—and particularly Jewish—influence on the civil rights movement.

Complementing the rise of nationalist and separatist feeling in a segment of the black community—although overwhelmingly rejected by a vast majority of black Americans, who clung and still cling to integrationist beliefs and support mainstream organizations like the NAACP—was the advocacy of violent "black power" by some of the more militant and extreme individuals and groups. The rallying cry and the anti-white, anti-Jewish hostility behind it were first expressed in the summer of 1966 at a march through Mississippi taken up by a coalition of civil rights and other groups after the shooting of James Meredith. While the Rev. Martin Luther King, Jr. and his Southern Christian Leadership Conference (SCLC) emphasized nonviolence and expressed gratitude for white participation, militant Stokely Carmichael and other Student Non-Violent Coordinating Committee (SNCC) members repeatedly called for black power. They made eminently clear their antipathy toward white participants in the march and toward the white community in general. The advocacy of violent black power (it was later to include the slogan, "Burn, baby, burn!") provided a means for militants to strike out at whites, especially those supporting integration and civil rights, among whom Jews were prominent, and gave black extremists an excuse to engage in reverse racism and violence.

In an era marked by political unrest and turmoil in the United States and around the world—exacerbated by the clash of ideologies between the communist world and the West, the Vietnam war and the growth of the New Left—the rise of black left-oriented revolutionary groups in America was perhaps inevitable. The revolutionary stance of such groups was the product of an ideology that in large measure amalgamated the doctrines of Marx and Lenin, Mao Tse Tung, Che Guevara, Premier Kim II Sung of North Korea, Robert F. Williams (a black revolutionary who had preached the message of urban guerrilla warfare in America while in self-exile in Castro's Cuba and later in Communist China), and Frantz Fanon, the Martinique-born psychiatrist who had taken part in the Algerian revolution and advocated violence for "colonized" peoples, as outlined in *The Wretched of the Earth.*[3] These revolutionaries viewed blacks in America in Fanonite terms, as an exploited "colony" class in an oppressive, white-controlled "mother country," and believed that freedom and equality could only be achieved by destroying the capitalist system through revolutionary class warfare. In their eyes, Jews and the "imperialist" State of Israel became ready targets of hatred as enemies of the "third world."

In the late fifties and early sixties, another significant source of anti-white and anti-Jewish rhetoric in the black community was the racist propaganda of the Nation of Islam and its New York minister, Malcolm X, the chief lieutenant of Black Muslim leader Elijah Muhammad. Malcolm X's hatred for non-blacks pervaded segments of the black community in New York and elsewhere and echoed throughout the white community as well, as a result of the exposure provided him in the mass media. While the Black Muslim movement represents a minority of the black community in America—it has some 100,000 adherents—its hate-"whitey" and hate-Jews propaganda has been widely circulated. "In America," Malcolm X once fulminated, "the Jews sap the very life-blood of the so-called Negroes to maintain the state of Israel, its armies and its continued aggression against our brothers in the East."[4] Malcolm X was assassinated early in 1965 after having split away from the Black Muslims to found his own Organization for Afro-American Unity. But his thoughts continued to reverberate in the black community with the posthumous publication of *The Autobiography of Malcolm X.*[5]

Black-Jewish tensions also were exacerbated by the series of confrontations from 1966 to 1969 in and around New York City's public school system over the subject of decentralization and community control of the schools. The major dispute in 1967 and 1968 swirled around a demonstration school district, predominantly black, and the local teachers' union, predominantly white and largely Jewish. Some black extremists attempted to turn the controversy into an ethnic and religious conflict. They sought ethnic and religious scapegoats against whom they could channel the black community's frustrations over the shortcomings of the educational system, and they openly resorted to anti-Semitic propaganda. Although the school conflict was basically local in nature, its quotient of anti-Semitism and racism and the black-Jewish confrontation it engendered were nevertheless spread by the mass media beyond the confines of New York.

Undoubtedly, too, part of the school confrontation in New York between blacks and Jews was economic in nature, as blacks sought to obtain positions heretofore held by whites and, with some prominence in the schools, by Jews. The conflict between blacks and Jews over jobs, mainly in civil service areas of employment, has seen blacks increasingly come out in favor of the institution of preferential treatment and quotas.

It is clear in retrospect that 1966 marked a crucial turning point in some black attitudes toward Jews and Jewish concerns and the beginning of the modern use of anti-Semitism by black nationalists, black leftist revolutionaries and some black intellectuals to promote alleged political, social and economic objectives of the black community.

Open black hostility to Jews began to manifest itself almost from the beginning of the year. One prominent source of such anti-Jewish animus was a low-circulation (15,000) but significant publication aimed at ghetto residents, the *Liberator*. Published by the so-called Afro-American Research Institute in New York, the monthly dubbed itself "the voice of the African-American." Its editor was Daniel H. Watts, an articulate former architect out of Columbia University who was associated with one of the leading architectural firms until he became convinced that he "would never be judged as an architect, but only as a Negro architect."[6] Watts entered journalism in 1960, and his publication did not hesitate to print the extremist outpourings of, among others, LeRoi Jones. *Time* magazine noted in 1967: "Ever since it was founded in 1960, *Liberator* has been building up to anti-Semitism. From white-baiting, it passed to the baiting of moderate Negroes and finally to Jew-baiting."[7]

In its January, February and April 1966 issues, *Liberator* published a series of virulently anti-Jewish articles by Eddie Ellis, entitled "Semitism in the Black Ghetto," that represented virtually a handbook for black extremists on how to vilify and affront American Jews. Ellis charged that blacks in Harlem were being exploited by merchants and landlords, most of whom, he alleged, were Jewish. "What the brothers know, is what they see: the landlord, the corner butcher, the grocer, and the 'cat' from the credit or collection agency. In most cases these 'cats' are Jewish," he asserted, adding: "It follows that the first line of resentment against slum housing, inferior grades of meat, spoiled food and vegetables is directed against the *living person* who perpetuates these conditions. In general it is that segment of the Jewish population which has grown *rich* exploiting Black Americans for decades."[8]

Ellis also charged that the mass media and New York's school system were directly or indirectly controlled by Jews, that "Zionists"—a word which the black nationalist used interchangeably with "Jews"—had dominated black colleges and black organizations and had manipulated the civil rights movement. He asserted, for example, that, "More than any other, the Rosenwald Foundation, established by Julius Rosenwald, contributed in great measure to the almost absolute dominance of negro colleges and organizations by Zionists."[9] Black people had "for years been ruthlessly exploited by the Jewish community," Ellis declared, alleging that fear of being labeled anti-Semitic, coupled with "the realization of the political, economic and social tyranny induced by Zionist influence," had in the past stilled many black voices of dissent. "But nevermore," he said. "If this then is anti-semitic," Ellis concluded, "so be it . . ."[10]

Liberator editor Watts denied that Ellis' articles on "Semitism in the Black Ghetto" were anti-Semitic. He asserted that his aim in publishing the series was to start a "dialogue" between Jewish leaders and the black community. Watts argued that the articles were "valid" and declared: "The chief exploiters in the black ghetto are the Jewish merchants and landlords."[11] If Watts' own sentiments were not suspect in this charge, made clearer by his publication of the Ellis pieces, additonal evidence of the *Liberator's* anti-Semitism was its publication, in the same issue that contained the initial installment of Ellis' articles, of LeRoi Jones' notoriously anti-Semitic poem, "Black Art."

The *Liberator's* descent into anti-Semitism did not go unanswered in the black community. Two prominent contributors to the publication, author James Baldwin and actor-playwright Ossie Davis, publicly resigned from the advisory board of the *Liberator* and vigorously condemned its publication of Ellis' anti-Jewish tirades. Both men later explained their action in letters published in the black quarterly, *Freedomways.* Baldwin challenged the *Liberator* for taking "refuge in the most ancient and barbaric of the European myths" and concluded: "I think it is most distinctly unhelpful, and I think it is immoral, to blame

Harlem on the Jew." Davis denounced the Ellis diatribe for its "wild and unsupported contentions." Terming it "racist," he added: "In a war against all exploiters whomsoever, I am an ally. But Mr. Ellis seems to be calling for a war against Jews. If that is the case, I am an enemy."[12]

One month after the appearance of the first of the inflamatory anti-Jewish articles by Ellis in the *Liberator*, an anti-Semitic outburst occurred only a few miles away, in New York's Westchester County community of Mount Vernon. It was triggered by a controversy over racial imbalance in the Mount Vernon schools and involved a representative of one of the most responsible civil rights groups, the Congress of Racial Equality. The incident had far-reaching repercussions.

CORE's roots in the civil rights struggle go back thirty years. In 1942, James Farmer, then race relations secretary of the Fellowship of Reconciliation, suggested the establishment of an organization which would be devoted to the fight for racial equality, through use of "relentless non-cooperation, economic boycotts [and] civil disobedience." That same year, a sit-in at a Chicago restaurant led to the founding of the Chicago Committee on Racial Equality; out of that organization was born the Congress of Racial Equality. Under Farmer, CORE achieved a record of accomplishment in race relations; it became the second largest of the black civil rights organizations in the United States. In the mid-1960s, however, CORE began moving in the direction of militant black nationalism and racial separatism, eventually to emerge in the camp of the black power advocates who appealed to black racial pride; there were ominous overtones of black racism and go-it-aloneness. Under Farmer's successor, Floyd McKissick, CORE discarded the basic concepts of the civil rights movement, including integration, for which it had so long fought, and moved toward becoming an organization exclusively of and for blacks. Proclaiming itself a black power movement, CORE spiritually substituted "separatism" for "equality" in its name. Currently under the leadership of Roy Innis, CORE's guiding philosophy is that of black separatism. While CORE is not an anti-Semitic organization and CORE's official spokesmen have disavowed anti-Semitism, some individuals and chapters of the group have on occasion stoked the fires of the hatemongers.

In February 1966, at a public meeting of the Mount Vernon Board of Education discussing local problems relating to school integration, CORE's Mount Vernon educational chairman, Clifford Brown, a thirty-two-year-old Westchester probation officer, shouted at a number of Jews among the participants in the session that "Hitler made one mistake—he didn't kill enough of you."[13] Somewhat later during the meeting, Brown issued "a public apology."

The Mount Vernon *Daily Argus* called the incident "shocking and disgraceful" and declared: "There is no place in Mount Vernon for this type of intemperance, this type of bias, this type of prejudice, this type of hate."[14] In a public statement, Mount Vernon Mayor Joseph P. Vaccarella proclaimed:

> For those who neither attended the Board of Education meeting on February 3 nor read the Daily Argus of the following day, Mr. Brown stated the following in a place of public assembly:
>
> 1. "You know, Hitler made one big mistake—he didn't kill enough of you Jews."
>
> 2. "I am a racist and proud of it. I hate all whites."
>
> 3. And called the members of the Board of Education and the Superintendent of Schools degenerate and inept.[15]

Mayor Vaccarella asserted that Brown was "no longer welcome in City Hall, as a spokesman for any group."

Brown's outburst resulted in a wave of protest from human rights officials and other concerned individuals. CORE officials disavowed the bigoted statement as "intolerable." However, instead of taking immediate action to suspend Brown (who resigned from CORE on his own five days after the outburst), CORE officials ordered an investigation to determine "the context" in which Brown made his remark.[16] Three months later, following its "investigation" of the incident, CORE at last officially condemned the anti-Jewish utterance of its Westchester representative and expelled him and the CORE Mount Vernon chapter from the national organization.[17]

CORE's delay in severing its association with Brown resulted in the public resignation of one prominent Jewish leader, active for more than twenty years in the civil rights movement, from its national advisory board. Protesting the organization's "tepid and ambiguous response" to the incident, he asked whether CORE could "conceive of any context . . . any situation that would justify the kind of tirade that calls for more acts of genocide."[18]

Despite the rantings over the years of some among CORE's leadership, the national organization, although moving in a racially separatist path, long expressed opposition to anti-Semitism. A position paper of CORE during the 1967–68 period, stated in part:

> There is no room in CORE for persons with anti-Semitic sentiments. By word, by letter, by other educational means, and by deed CORE will continue to demonstrate it's abhorrence of anti-Semitic attitudes and will continue to initiate measures to abolish this social evil.[19]

The paper bore the name of CORE's then-national director, Floyd B. McKissick.

In 1970, Roy Innis, the current national director of CORE, strongly criticized Arab terrorist skyjackers for holding American Jews hostage near Amman. In an editorial headlined "The Jews Must Not Stand Alone," published in the *Manhattan Tribune*, a New York City weekly of which Innis has been a co-publisher, Innis declared that

> . . . the taking of Jewish hostages . . . the holding of innocent men, women and children merely because they worship in a synagogue . . . is a symbolic and frightening reminder of a disease which too many people ignored in Germany and a reminder of the days when slave families were similarly separated.[20]

More recently, however, Innis has shown a disturbing erosion in his erstwhile sensitivity to the twin issues of racism and anti-Semitism. In March 1973, Innis and three of his aides visited Uganda at the invitation of President Idi Amin. The *New York Times* reported that Uganda's government-controlled radio had made public a letter from Innis praising Amin;[21] a week earlier, Amin had bestowed Ugandan citizenship on Innis and his companions;[22] somewhat later, Amin revealed that Innis had made him a life member of CORE.[23]

Apparently, Innis did not view Amin's cruel expulsion of some 50,000 Asian Ugandans from the country as a matter of concern. Nor, apparently, was he distressed by Amin's widely-publicized message to United Nations Secretary-General Kurt Waldheim in September 1972, in which the Ugandan leader made the shocking assertion that:

> Germany is the right place where when Hitler was the Prime Minister and supreme commander, he burned over six million Jews. This is because Hitler and all German people knew that Israelis are not people who are working in the interest of the people of the world and that is why they burned the Israelis alive with gas in the soil of Germany.[24]

Nor, if Innis was aware of it, was he apparently concerned by a report in March in the Uganda government-controlled newspaper, the *Voice of Uganda,* that Amin intended to reproduce the *Protocols of the Elders of Zion* and to "translate it in all languages for the people of Uganda and Africa to understand the danger of Zionism in the world."[25] It would seem unlikely, however, that Innis was not at least aware of a more widely-known 1972 article in the *New York Times Magazine* under the headline: "If Idi Amin of Uganda is a madman, he's a ruthless and cunning one." It made clear Amin's anti-Semitism, stating that Amin would "foam at the mouth" whenever Jews were mentioned.[26]

In fact, Roy Innis was perfectly cognizant of Amin's anti-Semitism and racism. In an interview in an early 1973 issue of *Africa Report,* the CORE leader was pointedly asked by a Liberian journalist in New York: "What do you think of the action of Uganda's General Amin in expelling over 50,000 Asians from Uganda and his alleged endorsement of Hitler's persecution of the Jews?" Innis replied:

> General Amin took a bold step in a very explosive way. But foreigners need not capitalize on that action. As black people, we have no records to prove if Hitler was a friend or an enemy of black people.

> A country's economy is too important to be left in the hands of foreigners. It is proper to expel non-East Africans from Uganda. I hope West African states will do the same—perhaps more diplomatically, but it must be done. Black people must refuse to allow other people to dominate their economy.[27]

Innis had nothing to say, of course, about the virtual purchase of Uganda by Libya's anti-Semitic Colonel Qaddafi or the influence on General Amin of that old slave-trader, Faisal of Saudi Arabia. But, then, in the lexicon of the third world, such non-blacks are not "foreigners"; after centuries of persecution of African blacks by Arabs—including in recent years the annihilation of perhaps a million black Sudanese—these are their new friends.

The watershed year of 1966 also saw, as we have said, the beginnings of black-Jewish confrontation in the New York public schools—a confrontation at times rife with anti-Semitism. Properly disappointed in the failure of efforts to integrate the schools of the ghetto community, and incited by ambitious extremists, ghetto parents and others in East Harlem staged demonstrations around the demand to "control" the schools. They sought black principals and teachers for black children and began to scapegoat Jewish administrators and other personnel *as Jews.*

By October, anti-Semitism emanating from extremist elements in the black community contained a sufficient amount of sensationalism for TV host David Susskind to air a ninety-minute program on "Negroes and Anti-Semitism." Susskind offered a panel consisting of three black power advocates from Harlem, who asserted, among their scatter-gun charges against Jews, that blacks were exploited by Jewish landlords, retailers and other tradesmen.[28] The program brought a deluge of complaints from viewers protesting the use of the popular Susskind show, syndicated nationwide by Metromedia, as a forum for the dissemination of "crude anti-Semitism."[29] Susskind, however, denied the charge, stating that it was "important to spotlight this infection."[30]

On the West Coast, black hostility to Jews and to Jewish organizations was stirred by Mrs. Pat Alexander, the editor of the Los Angeles-based black weekly, the *Herald-Dispatch.* In a number of issues, for example, Mrs. Alexander scored the Anti-Defamation League as "the most dangerous organization existing in the United States today." While denying anti-Semitic prejudice, she nevertheless stated: "I do not hate anyone, and especially the Ethiopians, and Arab people who are the real semites. the ADL represents European white people who are the architects of HATE. Despite their hatred of my people, I do not hate them."[31]

Another black nationalist agitator on the West Coast during this period was Maulana Ron Karenga, the founder and chairman of a militant black nationalist group called US, based in Los Angeles. In an early 1967 booklet distributed by US, entitled "The Quotable Karenga," its leader's thoughts on a number of subjects were presented. In one chapter on religion, Karenga attacked the "dead Jew" Jesus. He charged: "Jesus said, 'My blood will wash you white as snow.' Who wants to be white but sick 'Negroes,' or worse yet—washed that way by the blood of a dead Jew. You know if Nadinola bleaching cream couldn't do it, no dead Jew's blood is going to do it."[32]

Sporadic attacks against Jews continued into 1967. In Washington, D.C. in early January, an anti-Semitic flyer bearing the imprimatur of black nationalist Charles X. Kenyatta and his New York-based black extremist Mau Mau organization was circulated at a rally in support of Congressman Adam Clayton Powell (now deceased). The leaflet blamed Jews for the "downfall" of Congressman Powell and the killings of Malcolm X, President John F. Kennedy, and Jesus. The flyer also proclaimed in bold lettering: "The slaves of Black Afro America thank Hitler for destroying six-million Jews. Hoping that he will appear again in America!!"[33] Some months later, a Salute to Israel Rally held in New York City's upper-Manhattan area was picketed by some ten steel-helmeted blacks identified as members of the Mau Mau organization. The contingent carried a blatantly anti-Semitic placard stating that Jews had no right to Israel and that Hitler had had the right idea in his genocidal policies.[34]

But the depths to which some black nationalists had sunk in their attacks on Jews *qua* Jews became startlingly apparent when *The New Patriot,* a white racist and anti-Semitic quarterly (now defunct) out of Jackson, Mississippi published in its March issue an anti-Semitic article by black nationalist poet and writer Lawrence P. Neal. It was entitled "White Liberals versus the Black

Community" and its author was described by the racist publication as "a distinguished Negro writer" who "explains the educated and informed Negro's attitude towards the Jewish community." Neal assailed what he viewed as the domination of blacks by Jews —especially in the merchant-consumer relationships in ghetto areas. He rejected any attempt by Jews to identify with blacks and concluded:

> We do not need pathological love-hate relationships. We want to be free from cultural oppression and political and economic domination by outside forces. We refuse to pretend that we are not suffering at the hands of Jewish landlords and merchants. We refuse to sit idly by and watch our culture being continually exploited by money hungry leeches . . .[35]

The article had orginally appeared in the *Liberator*.[36]

The black anti-Semites' charge that Jews exploited American blacks, widely disseminated by the extremists during 1966 and early 1967, was joined by mid-1967 to anti-Israel, anti-Jewish rhetoric identical with that we have earlier explored among Radical Leftists and Arabs, emanating now from black revolutionaries and other black extremists: the Student Non-Violent Coordinating Committee (SNCC), the Black Muslims and the Black Panther Party, among other groups, and from Stokely Carmichael and Eldridge Cleaver, among other individuals. The potential for anti-Israel propaganda had always been latent among Jew-baiting blacks, and the Six-Day War of June 1967 brought it out.

In the rhetoric of the black extremist and left revolutionary organizations, "anti-Zionism" became a vehicle for anti-Semitism; Israel was labeled an "imperialist aggressor"; Arabs and the third world were proclaimed brothers in oppression inflicted by world Jewry. The most extreme example of this distorted and disturbed thinking appeared in a midsummer 1967 publication of the Student Non-Violent Coordinating Committee and, together with SNCC's exhortations to violence, signaled the organization's rejection by the serious civil rights community and its subsequent disintegration.

SNCC was organized in 1960 by black and white Southern stu-

dents at the urging of Martin Luther King, as part of his effort
to keep civil rights demonstrations nonviolent. In those early
days, SNCC too had the dream of integration and believed integration could be achieved through brotherly love, conscience
and morality, if followers were willing to risk their lives in non-
violent protest. The outlook and goals of SNCC began to change,
however, in May of 1966, when Stokely Carmichael was elected
chairman. Within a few weeks, he began to popularize the black
power slogan and to attract widespread attention to himself and
SNCC by his violent and extreme statements, including calls
for racist guerrilla warfare by blacks in the United States.

H. Rap Brown succeeded Carmichael in May 1967, and within
a few months he likewise began to attract nationwide headlines
by urging Negroes to get guns, to "burn this town down," and
by voicing approval of rioting and looting. In this period, SNCC
showed clear signs of ideological orientation toward Havana,
Peking and Hanoi. It had evolved, in short, from an organization
that had the improvement of domestic race relations as its major
purpose into one that looked upon itself as part of an "international liberation movement" that preached violent revolution.

It was in this context that SNCC issued its June-July 1967 *Newsletter* containing a widely-reported attack on Israel, Zionism
and Jews in a centerfold article entitled "The Palestine Problem:
Test Your Knowledge." As part of the article, SNCC offered readers a series of "do you know"-type, anti-Israel and anti-Zionist
statements, such as:

> THAT under the Charter of the United Nations, the U.N. General
> Assembly had no legal right to recommend the 1947 Partition Plan
> which created the "Jewish State?"

> THAT the original 1947 Partition Plan was approved, at the first
> vote, only by white European, American and Australasian states,
> that every African and Asian stated voted against it? And that, in
> the second vote, urgent United States pressures (which a member
> of the Truman cabinet called "bordering onto scandal") had suc-
> ceeded in forcing only one Asian country (the Phillipines) [sic] and
> one African country (Liberia) both controlled by "Uncle Sam," to
> abandon their opposition. IN OTHER WORDS, ISRAEL WAS
> PLANTED AT THE CROSS-ROADS OF ASIA AND AFRICA

WITHOUT THE FREE APPROVAL OF ANY MIDDLE-EAST-
ERN, ASIAN OR AFRICAN COUNTRY![37]

And so it went. Further examination of SNCC's propaganda outburst showed, in addition, the heavy hand of traditional anti-Semitism. For example, one cartoon, apparently drawn by an artist for SNCC, showed a hand marked with the Star of David and a dollar sign, tightening a rope fastened around the necks of Gamal Nasser and Muhammed Ali, the controversial heavy-weight boxer. The SNCC *Newsletter* also charged that "the famous European Jews, the Rothschilds, who have long controlled the wealth of many European nations, were involved in the original conspiracy with the British to create the 'state of Israel' and are still among Israel's chief supporters." (Reference to the Roth-schilds and the Rothschild banking house has been a recurrent theme, of course, of anti-Jewish propaganda by anti-Semitic bigots in the United States and elsewhere.) In addition to the gratuitous anti-Jewish references to the Rothschilds, SNCC's *Newsletter* used large sections of at least one Palestine Liberation Organiza-tion pamphlet almost verbatim, in effect placing itself at the dis-posal of Arab propagandists.[38]

SNCC officials freely admitted that the anti-Jewish material in their *Newsletter* had come from Arab propaganda sources. Ralph Featherstone, SNCC's program director, said SNCC had requested and received propaganda documents from Arab or-ganizations. SNCC was drawn to the Arab cause, he said, because the Arabs were working toward a "third world alliance of op-pressed people all over the world." Featherstone added that SNCC was not interested in indicting all Jews but "only Jewish oppressors," a term he applied to Israel and to "those Jews in the little Jew shops in the ghettos."[39]

As with the CORE Mount Vernon incident, SNCC's outburst brought resignations from some of its most prominent long-time supporters. In a bitter "open letter" to the organization, Theodore Bikel, now president of Actors Equity and one of SNCC's earliest activists, wrote:

> I am an American. I am a Jew. Thus I have a commitment doubly reinforced by historical and moral commandment. I am determined

to make equality and freedom a reality in this country, no matter what the setbacks. I am equally determined to honor the bonds to my ethnic and religious background. . . . You have this day attempted to violate both my commitments. The violation of one alone would have been enough.[40]

After a point by point answer to SNCC's pro-Arab statements— "How do you think a cry of black power would be met in Riyadh or Mecca? How would poor power sound in Baghdad?"—Bikel added, prophetically:

What you have wrought in this latest of a long line of missteps will be with us for a long time to come. It will not deter those among us who are secure in the knowledge that the [civil rights] Movement is bigger than your pronouncements and that it speaks responsibly and with reason. But many thousands not so secure will in bewilderment withdraw support from all civil rights causes because of your incontinence and folly. Thus once again you will have harmed no one but the Negro himself.

The *Newsletter* was not the first time that SNCC or its spokesmen had been anti-Semitic in their public statements. In a 1966 article in *The New York Review of Books,* Stokeley Carmichael, then SNCC national chairman, wrote:

Black people do not want to "take over" this country. They don't want to "get whitey"; they just want to get him off their backs as the saying goes. It was, for example, the exploitation by Jewish landlords and merchants which first created black resentment towards Jews— not Judaism.[41]

In a subsequent issue of the same publication, historian-critic Irving Howe called Carmichael's statement "appalling" and said:

Exploitative landlords who happen to be. Jewish should be condemned as landlords, not Jews. They exploit in their social—not religious—capacity, and the same holds true for Christian or Buddhist or Black Muslim landlords. No fair-minded person objects, for example, to demonstrations against such landlords. What is at stake—and what Mr. Carmichael himself indulges in—is the *identification* of social oppressors by their religious origin. What is troubling is that the justifiable resentment against slumlords should be diverted, as it sometimes seems to have been, into Jew-baiting.

That a depressed and ill-educated Negro should indulge in this may be understandable. But that Mr. Carmichael, who sets himself up as an authority on the nature of freedom, should write so unnerving a sentence is unforgivable.[42]

In September 1967, Carmichael visited several Arab countries in an apparent show of black revolutionary solidarity with the Arabs against Israel. According to a broadcast on Damascus radio, he assailed "Zionist aggression," accused American officials of being in league with Zionism and pledged military aid by blacks to the Arab cause. Reuters reported that at a press conference at the end of his three-day visit to Syria, Carmichael declared, "Our support to Arabs and their legitimate right in Palestine is complete and absolute."[43]

Carmichael left the United States and became a naturalized citizen of Guinea, West Africa, where he has been a university lecturer in Conakry. There he has sought to promote his philosophy of Pan-Africanism. But his "anti-Zionist" biases remain, and for someone who was recently described as "anachronistic" in the contemporary black struggle in America, he gets a great deal of attention and media coverage on visits here. In mid-March 1971, Carmichael spoke before packed audiences at San Francisco and San Jose State Colleges. He drew vigorous applause from black students, according to the San Francisco *Examiner*, when he charged that European Jews were "subjugating Palestinian Arabs" and termed Israel an "unjust state" which had attacked Egypt, "cradle of civilization in our homeland."[44] On October 17, 1972, Carmichael told an audience of more than 2,000 students and visitors at Howard University that the State of Israel was "immoral, illegal and unjust" and that he personally would "fight it with every breath in my body."[45]

At an early 1973 speaking engagement at the University of California in Los Angeles, Carmichael denounced "Zionism" and the "illegal, immoral, imperialistic" State of Israel to an audience of 1,500 which "sat mesmerized for nearly an hour and a half as they listened to Carmichael's speech," according to the UCLA *Daily Bruin*.[46]

Carmichael and his wife, singer Miriam Makeba, were February 1973 guests on a WABC-TV program called "Like It Is" in New York. In the course of the interview, Carmichael asserted that blacks must control black culture because "it is a strategic weapon, especially in a revolutionary struggle." He went on to charge that culture in the black community "is controlled by an alien ethnic group" and "not only a competing ethnic group but an enemy ethnic group." He said: "The culture in our community is controlled by Zionist agents."[47]

Those "Zionist agents" in the Middle East were the targets of black nationalist-revolutionary coalitions at a series of meetings from 1967 to 1972. Among the earliest was a well-attended National Conference on Black Power in Newark in late July 1967. Held shortly after the racial riots in Newark during that long, hot summer, the gathering drew some 906 delegates representing 36 states, 42 cities and 197 organizations. According to the New Jersey *Afro-American*, the conference recommended, among other things, condemnation of "Israeli oppression against the Arabs."[48] While sessions of the conference's workshops were closed to the white press, one reporter, Saul Friedman of the Chicago Daily News Service, was able to pierce some of the secrecy. In a widely-syndicated article on the general theme of black antipathy to Jews, Friedman reported: "Black nationalist sources who attended . . . have told this reporter that anti-Semitism and anti-Zionism were prevalent at some of the private sessions."[49]

Further indication of the anti-Jewish and anti-Israel animus on the part of some delegates to the National Conference on Black Power was evident at a follow-up meeting in 1968 in Philadelphia. According to the New York *Post*, there was some disposition at the gathering to blame the Nigeria-Biafra war on Israel. As some delegates viewed it, the war was part of an Israeli "plot" to take over Africa. Such sentiments, the conference's vice-chairman noted, indicated growing anti-Semitism in the black community.[50]

A more pronounced example of black nationalist antipathy to Jews and to Jewish concerns occurred in early September 1967 at a convention in Chicago of the National Conference for New Politics (NCNP), an *ad hoc* organization aimed at creating a possible third party ticket in the 1968 presidential elections. Delegates to the Chicago convention represented much of the Old and New Left in the United States as well as a host of individuals and local organizations engaged in peace, antipoverty and civil rights activities. Among the organizations represented were SNCC, CORE, SDS, and the Communist Party.

The NCNP convention was billed as a united front for "peace and freedom." However, the meeting very rapidly found itself split along racial lines—a split which was to dominate it. No sooner had the conference convened than the black delegates formed a Black Caucus which presented several unusual demands to the convention. Although constituting no more than 600 of the 2,100 delegates present, the Black Caucus demanded fully 50 percent of the votes in the convention itself and on all convention committees. Beyond that, however, was a series of thirteen resolutions which the Black Caucus introduced with the demand that they be adopted in their entirety, without deletion or amendment. The Caucus warned that if its demands were not adopted, the entire black delegation would walk out.

Among the resolutions demanded by the black nationalist-dominated Black Caucus was one which urged condemnation of "the imperialistic Zionist war," and went on to declare that "this condemnation does not imply anti-Semitism."[51] Although some opposition to the resolutions was expressed, apparently the convention's white majority was so eager for the participation of the black delegates that it voted two-to-one in favor of all the demands presented by the Black Caucus.[52]

At the conclusion of the NCNP convention, and with the consent of the Black Caucus, the wording of the convention's statement on the Middle East was changed to reflect condemnation not of "Zionist imperialism" but of "the Israeli government."[53] Moreover, a foreign policy resolution adopted by the convention reaffirmed the Black Caucus's Middle East plank and went on to state: "We feel that it would be entirely possible for the peoples of the Middle East to solve their own problems in a just and reasonable manner if United States imperialism ceased interfering in the Middle East." The statement then asked the Arabs to recognize the "reality of Israel" and called upon Israel to "give reparations to Arab refugees, pay for damage inflicted in the last invastion and return to borders existing before June of '67."[54]

One knowledgeable observer of the political scene character- ized the goings on at the NCNP convention as a travesty of radical politics at work.[55] The *New York Times,* in an editorial headed "Appeasing Negro Extremists," said the convention's concessions to the resolutions of the Black Caucus were morally inexcusable and concluded: "The Negro extremists are using the old Stalinist tactics, and their victims will find—as did the Stalinists' victims earlier—that they have paid a high price for very little or noth- ing."[56] Dr. King denounced the anti-Semitism as "immoral," stated that Israel's right to exist was "incontestable," and declared that SCLC people who attended the NCNP convention "were the most vigorous and articulate opponents of the simplistic reso- lution on the Middle East question."[57]

But despite such almost universal condemnation of the con- ference, black extremist rhetoric against Israel and Jews and for the Arabs had clearly made some inroads in the black com- munity.

It was equally clear that as the black community sought to find a politics which would express its aspirations and achieve its aims, it would be hampered by some of the same divisive forces that dominated the Black Caucus of the NCNP Convention. Per- haps even more shocking to Jews than that convention's capitula- tion to an anti-Israel minority was the anti-Israel action taken five years later, in March 1972, by the first National Black Politi- cal Convention, held in Gary, Indiana and attended by some 3,300 voting delegates and 5,000 observers.[58] The convention, which witnessed an inconclusive tug of war between politicians who favored working within the traditional two-party system and black nationalists favoring separatist action, was co-chaired by Imamu Amiri Baraka (LeRoi Jones), Gary Mayor Richard Hatcher, and U.S. Congressman Charles C. Diggs of Michigan. Delegates included a wide spectrum of black representatives, among them elected office holders, persons chosen at local con- ventions, spokesmen for organizations ranging from black nation- alists to civil rights groups, labor leaders and businessmen— including members of the Nixon administration.

The resolution on Israel, offered by delegates from the District of Columbia in the closing minutes of the convention, after many participants had already left, was introduced by the Rev. Douglas Moore, who has been chairman of the militant black nationalist Black United Front in Washington, D.C. (Interestingly, on July 8, 1971, in a letter to the Anti-Defamation League, the Black United Front protested ADL's efforts to halt federal funding of anti-Semite Hassan Jeru-Ahmed's activities. The letter was anti-Israel and contained anti-Semitic innuendo.)[59]

The resolution by the Rev. Moore and the District of Columbia delegation declared:

> Whereas, the establishment of the Jewish State of Israel constituted a clear violation of the Palistinians' [sic] traditional right to live in their own home land,
>
> Whereas, thousands of Palistinians have been killed, and thousands made homeless by the illegal establishment,
>
> Whereas, Jews ruling Israel have demonstrated fascist desire through their occupation of other Palistinian and Arab land,
>
> Whereas, Israeli agents are working hand-in-hand with other imperialistic interests in Africa, for example, South Africa,
>
> Be it therefore resolved, that the United States Government should end immediately its economic and military support to the Israeli regime; that the United States Government should withdraw its military forces from the Middle East area; that the Arab peoples' land holdings be returned to Palistinians; and that negotiations be ended in the freedom of the representatives of Palistinians to establish a second state based on the historical right of the Palistinian people for self-government in their own land.[60]

Condemnation of the anti-Israel resolution came from many responsible black leaders. A statement released immediately thereafter by Representative Louis Stokes, chairman of the Congressional Black Caucus (not to be confused with the NCNP), consisting of the thirteen black members (it now has fifteen) of the United States Congress, reaffirmed the Caucus' friendship for and support of Israel. The statement asserted: "As the Black elected representatives to the U.S. Congress, we reaffirm our position that we fully respect the right of the Jewish people to have their own state in their historic National Homeland." It went on to detail Israel's "cordial relationships" with the developing black nations in Africa and concluded: "We pledge our continued support to the concept that Israel has the right to exist in peace as a nation."[61]

At the same time, Samuel Jackson of the Department of Housing and Urban Development, the highest ranking black man in the Nixon administration, who had participated in the Gary convention, expressed his "deep personal distress" at the anti-Israel resolution. "I must assure you," Jackson said, "that the views expressed in that resolution are not those held by the great majority of blacks in this country. We are both aware and appreciative of the role which Israel has played in the economic development of many of the African nations."[62]

On May 16, 1972, the NAACP announced its withdrawal from the National Black Political Convention "because of a difference in ideology as to how to win equality for the Negro minority in the United States." Roy Wilkins, executive director of the NAACP, singled out for special condemnation the anti-Israel resolution as a "one-sided condemnation."[63]

Several days later, the National Black Political Convention's Continuations Committee, which had been empowered to determine and shape the final convention pronouncements, released the group's "black agenda," including a "clarification" of the anti-Israel resolution. In it, the NBPC's condemnation of Israel was retained in a modified form, as an endorsement of Middle East resolutions made by the Organization of African Unity and the United Nations Commission on Human Rights. It read, in part:

> Be it resolved that the convention go on record as being in agreement with the OAU positions that call for:
> 1. The Israeli government to be condemned for her expansionist policy and forceful occupation of the soverign territory of another state.
> 2. Measures be taken to alleviate the suffering and improve the position of the Palestinian people in Israel.

3. The NBPC should also resolve to support the struggle of Palestine for self-determination.

4. The NBPC concurs also with the UN Position that Israel rescind and desist from all practice affecting the demographic structure or physical character of occupied Arab territories and the rights of their inhabitants.[64]

Two of the NBPC's three co-chairmen, Congressman Diggs and Mayor Hatcher, promptly disassociated themselves from the "clarified" anti-Israel resolution.[65] The third, Imamu Amiri Baraka (LeRoi Jones) did not. Baraka has had a long history of hostility to Jews and Jewish concerns. He has become one of the most influential leaders of the black nationalist movement in the United States today.

Baraka's influence has been second to none in the black nationalist Congress of African People, which has chapters throughout the country and has enjoyed the support of some black politicians and community leaders. In September 1972, Baraka was elected its chairman.[66] In October 1972, at a meeting in Chicago of the National Black Assembly, established to continue the activities of the National Black Political Convention, Baraka was elected secretary-general of the group; as a result, the Chicago *Defender* commented, Baraka had emerged as the strongest office holder in the Black Assembly.[67]

An indication of Baraka's respectability in the eyes of some religious and civic leaders, despite his anti-white and anti-Jewish stance, was evident when the Interreligious Foundation for Community Organization (IFCO), a coordinating body set up to distribute church monies to minority groups, provided Baraka's Committee for a United Newark with grants of $79,000 over a three-year period beginning in 1970.[68]

On March 8, 1973, Baraka opened a "symposium on culture and the black struggle" at Queens College in New York. The director of the school's African Studies and Research Institute, which sponsored the symposium, said that Baraka had been selected because "he personifies the application of intellectual theory in the black movement to real-life situations."

The eminence and prestige achieved by the black nationalist poet-playwright seems to support the evaluation of the school director. But it also provides additional and disturbing evidence of insensitivity and indifference to anti-Semitism. Baraka's extensive record of anti-Semitic writings goes back a number of years.

Jones' poem "Black Art," published in 1966 and widely disseminated by black nationalist publications, including New York's *Liberator* magazine and Detroit's *Inner City Voice,* called for poems to achieve a "Black World." With respect to Jews he wrote, in part:

> . . . We want poems
> like fists beating niggers out of Jocks
> or dagger poems in the slimy bellies
> of the owner-jews . . .
>
> . . . Setting fire and death to
> whities ass. Look at the Liberal
> Spokesman for the jews clutch his throat
> & puke himself into eternity . . .
>
> Put it on him poem. Strip him naked
> to the world! Another bad poem cracking
> steel knuckles in a jewlady's mouth . . .[69]

In December 1967, *Evergreen Review* published "Three Poems by Leroi Jones"—all of which were anti-white and two of which were anti-Semitic. "Black People," for example, told of the merchandise available in "Sears, Bambergers, Klein's, Hahnes', Chase and the smaller joosh enterprises" and how it could be obtained by blacks. The magic words, he said, were: "this is a stick up! Or: Smash the window at night . . . No money down. No time to pay. Just take what you want you need . . ."[70] Another poem, "The Black Man is Making New Gods," said:

> Atheist jews double crossers stole our secrets
> crossed the white desert white to spill them and
> turn into wops and bulgarians.
> The Fag's Death
> they give us on a cross. To Worship. Our dead selves
> in disguise. They give us
> to   worship

a dead jew
and not ourselves . . .

These robots drag a robot
in the image of themselves, to be
ourselves. Selling fried potatoes
and people, the little arty bastards
talking arithmetic they sucked from the arab's
head . . .[71]

In February 1968, at a memorial program for Malcolm X held at an East Harlem public school, those in attendance—primarily school children—heard "kill whitey" diatribes and an anti-white, anti-Jewish presentation put on by LeRoi Jones and his Spirit House Movers and Players. Among other slurs, the performers assailed "niggers" who were content to accept "slavery" and to go to "white, dirty Jewish-owned bars."[72] And in February 1972, Vintage Books published a collection of the essays of Baraka "since 1965." Entitled *Raise, Race, Rays, Raze,* it contained numerous derogatory references to Jews, most of which bore 1967 and 1968 dates. The author referred, for example, to a person being "jew-slick," to "jeworiented revolutionaries," to "cohen edited negro history" and to "new zionist conspiracies."[73]

The Black Panther Party was formed in the San Francisco Bay area during 1966 by Huey P. Newton and Bobby Seale. It expanded rapidly during the latter part of 1968 and reached its peak strength early in 1969, when it had a membership of 2,000 to 3,000 and a nationwide following not only among blacks but among the predominantly white organizations of the Radical Left. The Panthers were committed to the destruction and overthrow of existing American society through the tactics of guerrilla warfare, and their supporters also included white "radical chic" circles in New York and elsewhere—erstwhile liberals, many of them prominent in the social, intellectual and cultural life of the large cities.

As an armed revolutionary group, the BPP identified with similar regimes and movements overseas, both in the communist world and in the third world. The Panthers, for example, formed an alliance with Al Fatah in its terrorist war against Israel. By 1969, the Panthers had emerged as the leading supporter in the American black community of the Arab cause, and of Al Fatah in particular. The weekly newspaper of the party, *The Black Panther,* with a circulation of better than 100,000, regularly published Fatah communiques, interviews with Fatah spokesmen, and pro-Fatah declarations by Panther leaders that frequently contained denunciations of Israel and Zionism, often reflecting outright, transparent hostility to Jews as Jews. Like most of the Radical Left, the Panthers viewed Al Fatah as fighting a war of national liberation against Israel in the Middle East similar to their own against the United States. They regarded Israel as an oppressor nation and a tool of American capitalist imperialism, and they parroted the Arab propaganda line that the Jews in Israel had no right to a land which, they said, belonged to the Palestinians.

In December 1969, the Washington *Post* published a Reuters dispatch from Algiers reporting that Elridge Cleaver, the self-exiled (in an effort to avoid imprisonment in the United States) Panther "minister of information," and Al Fatah leader Yassir Arafat had embraced and kissed at the first International Congress of Committees of Support for Palestine, attended by some 200 delegates representing groups supporting Al Fatah in its terrorist warfare against Israel. Cleaver delivered a speech described as "a fierce attack on 'American Zionists,'" in which he declared: "We can no longer allow Zionists to point to the bones of the victims of Nazism and blind us [to] the piles of bones they are making of the Palestine people."[74] The Reuters dispatch added that Cleaver had stressed the activities of a number of prominent American Jews, including former U.S. ambassador to the UN, Arthur Goldberg, and Henry Kissinger: "Cleaver said Jewish intellectuals were helping Nixon formulate his domestic policies and added that Black Panther leaders Huey Newton and Bobby Seale were sent to prison by Zionist magistrates."

In an Algiers interview with a reporter for the Washington *Post,* Cleaver commented on an investigation that was being planned by an unofficial citizens "Commission of Inquiry" into clashes between police and Panthers in several American cities.

It was to be headed by Justice Goldberg, and Cleaver asserted: "The power structure is trying to take control of the situation by using a well-known Zionist and appointing Uncle Tom Congressmen. . . . Here comes Goldberg investigating a group that is a threat to both Uncle Toms and Zionists."[75] Also interviewing Cleaver in Algeria for an article which appeared in the May 1970 issue of *The Atlantic*, veteran writer Don Schanche, despite his own generally understanding attitude toward the Panthers, minced no words in describing Cleaver's anti-Semitism as "virulent" and "growing."[76] On April 3, 1973 the New York *Post* picked up a London *Observer* story that placed Cleaver in Paris, seeking political asylum in France. He had been forced by the authorities to leave Algeria.

Panther propaganda denouncing Israel often came from Arab sources; at other times, Arab propaganda themes were presented by the party's leaders in their own extremist vocabulary. For example, *The Black Panther* of August 30, 1969 devoted a full page to an article by Don Cox, then Panther "field marshall," which contained many of the basic Arab propaganda themes and was printed under a bold-faced scare headline:

"ZIONISM (KOSHER NATIONALISM) + IMPERIALISM = FASCISM."

The Zionist fascist state of Israel is a puppet and a lackey of the imperialist and must be smashed. Reparations must be made to all the displaced people, all the people who were forced to flee and abandon their homes and homeland by demagogy (lying and deceiving) and terror (fascism). All the property stolen by the Zionists with their fascist storm troopers headed by Moshe Dayan and the aid they received from the imperialist must be returned to the people of Palestine!

. . . what the Zionists and the state of Israel did and are doing to the Arabs can be and is equated to what the Nazis did to the Jews.

. . . Zionism is nothing more than negative, backward, reactionary nationalism—Jewish nationalism, Kosher nationalism. The philosophy of Zionism is reactionary nationalism . . .

Cox wished "Victory to the people's struggle of Palestine! Victory to Al-Fatah! Victory to Al-Assifa!"

Less than two years later, in mid-February 1971, "Field Marshall" Cox presented a "statement" of the party to a Palestinian Student Conference held in Kuwait:

> The Palestinian liberation struggle stands in the vanguard of the struggle against the Zionist menace that plagues the people of the entire Arab world in general, and has usurped the national rights and freedom of the Palestinian people in particular. Although Zionism itself is a vicious ideology of racial supremacy, fascist domination, and imperialist expansionism cloaked in the Jewish religion, it has been manipulated to serve the barbaric interests of the worldwide system of imperialism headed by U.S. Imperialism. Neither Zionism as an ideology nor Israel as a state could maintain its alien aggressive power in the Arab world without the powerful backing of the dominant imperialist powers, especially the United States. It is the resources of the U.S. ruling circles, war-mongering industrialists, and wealthy Zionist businessmen that finance and support the puppet state of Israel . . .
>
> The Black Panther Party unconditionally and firmly supports the just struggle of the Palestinian people and their war of national salvation against the lackey state of Israel and its imperialist backers.[77]

The anti-Israel thrust of Panther propaganda was often expounded through the cartoonist's brush wielded for *The Black Panther* by Emory Douglas, the party's "minister of culture." In the spring of 1970, several issues of the Panther paper devoted full pages to multicolor Douglas cartoons that singled out Israel, "World Zionism," and "American imperialism" as their chief targets—always depicted as pigs. The March 21 issue, for example, devoted almost the entire back page to a cartoon showing two pigs—"U.S. Imperialism" and "Zionism"—kissing, snout to snout. The pig labeled "Zionism" wore a black eye patch and held aloft in one arm a religious scepter crowned with a Star of David. The entire front page of the same issue was devoted to another multicolor Douglas cartoon—a massive pig labeled "U.S.A." suckling two piglets, one labeled "Israel," and the other "West Germany." A March 28 cartoon headlined, "If the Enemy Refuses to Get out Annihilate Him," showed two bullet-riddled pigs, again labeled "U.S. Imperialism" and "World Zionism." The April 11 issue of the Panther paper devoted its back page to a

Douglas cartoon featuring a group of pigs labeled "U.S. Imperialism," "Britain," "France," "West Germany" and "World Zionism." The latter was depicted sucking a baby's bottle filled with dollar signs and held by the pig labeled "U.S. Imperialism." The accompanying text carried derogatory material about each of the "pigs." With respect to France, for example, the text referred to French President Pompidou's connections with "the Rothschilds."

By mid-1971 an ideological conflict had split the Panthers. The schism developed between supporters of Huey Newton and Bobby Seale, co-founders of the party, and Eldridge Cleaver, leader of the Algiers-based international section of the BPP. In a pronounced shift in approach, the Newton-Seale group began to channel their efforts toward political ends and sought to gain control over institutions in the community. In June 1972, four Panthers were among nine directors elected at the time to the Berkeley, California antipoverty program's board.[78]

The Cleaver group, on the other hand, continued to espouse the original revolutionary concepts of the party. It branded the Oakland-based BPP as "Huey Newton's phony Panther Party." In late 1971, the Cleaver faction in the United States began publication of a newspaper similar in tone to older issues of *The Black Panther,* with emphasis on guns, violence and bloody revolution. Published in Harlem, the Cleaver-oriented Panther newspaper bore the name *Right On!* It sought in its own words, to serve as a "communications network . . . gathering information from revolutionary organizations nationally and internationally and getting it out to the people."[79]

American Jews and Israel have been regularly targeted for attack in *Right On!* An April 1972 issue charged that "the white man and Jews have become rich with their drugstores, grocery stores, liquor stores, and pawn shops in the Black community."[80] In May 1972, *Right On!* alluded to the purported activities of "Zionist forces" in the Forest Hills housing controversy.[81]

In a November-December 1972 *Right On!* editorial headlined "Israel: Lackey of US Imperialism," the Harlem-based Black Panther Party castigated "the so-called 'victims' of the recent Munich attack" and asserted that "the 'chosen people'" had declared war on the Palestinians, "one of terror, massacre and de-

struction sponsored and financed by western Jewish capitalists."
The editorial concluded:

> As the world now recoils in horror at the attacks on the "chosen
> people," one can readily see the paradox—the oppressed have be-
> come the oppressors, the people of the book, the men of light, the
> victims of Russian pogroms, of Nazi genocide, of Dachau and other
> Polish concentration camps have changed roles. . . . In the final
> analysis, Israel as a tool of imperialism, must be destroyed along
> with the other imperialist powers so that "man's inhumanity to man"
> will cease to be a philosophy among men.

The November-December issue also contained·an article by the
George Jackson Political Front of the Afro-American Liberation
Army which applauded the Black September murderers in
Munich. "Our hearts were enlightened immeasurably by the
courageous act of the Palestinian commandos," the article declared, adding: "We love you comrades. We hope to meet you
someday, somewhere on this international battle front." In addition, the newspaper's "International News" page featured a
propaganda statement by the anti-Semitic Palestine Arab Delegation on "the War Criminals Golda Meir and Moshe Dyan [sic]
and their cohorts, who refused to release the 200 Palestine Freedom Fighters illegally jailed under the most inhuman conditions
in so-called 'Israel.'"

Meanwhile, *The Black Panther,* despite the Oakland-based
Newton-Seale group's new emphasis on health centers, antipoverty programs and community needs, showed that it had
muted but not changed its anti-Jewish position with respect to the
Middle East conflict. A February 1973 article, for example, de-
cried the fact that King Hussein in his visit to the United States
made no mention "of the Palestinian people's struggle for return
to their homeland; for a dismantling of the Zionist, racist 'state'
of Israel; for the creation of a multi-cultural Palestinian state in
which Arabs, Jews and Christians live in equality and harmony as
one Palestinian people." The article also referred to Premier
Golda Meir as the "leader of the intruder, puppet 'state' of
Israel."[82] Similarly, a March 1973 editorial criticized the media in
the United States for its alleged "callous response" to the Libyan

airplane disaster "compared with the anti-Arab hysteria that swept over this country in response to the Munich Olympic event, in which 9 Israelis were killed and 5 Palestinian guerrillas were martyred." The editorial went on to refer to "the high degree of zionist and pro-Israeli ownership and control of the U.S. media (press, publication, radio, TV and screen)."[83]

The following month *The Black Panther* editorial entitled "Israeli Terrorism" characterized Israel as "the culprit in the Middle East" and charged that "the U.S. government shares grave responsibility by its diplomatic and material support to Tel Aviv." It also defended Arab terrorism, asserting that "death resulted from the refusal of the victims or the government of those victims to meet justifiable, human demands." The editorial added: "Israel must not be allowed to trigger another 'Vietnam' to endanger world peace."[84]

And in May 1973 *Playboy* magazine interview, Huey Newton, leader of the Black Panther Party, was asked about the terrorism engaged in by the Black September movement in Munich and elsewhere. "I can criticize it only in the context of how positive or negative an accomplishment it turns out to be for the freedom movement," he answered. He added that he would not make a "blanket condemnation" of terrorism. When pointedly asked, "So you would feel no hesitation about using violence as a tool, even to the point of killing people, provided it advanced your movement or your principles?" Newton replied: "That's right."[85]

The Black Panther Party—in Harlem or in Oakland—seems to have little support today among American blacks. Yet it continues to be a source of anti-Semitic infection within the black community.

Far less can the Jewish community afford to ignore the outspoken anti-Semitism of the Nation of Islam. The Black Muslims, spanning four decades in American life, are today at the peak of their influence, with seventy-five-year-old Elijah Muhammad presiding over a vast $75 to $95-million empire emcompassing real estate (more than 25,000 acres of farm land in eight states and a 43,000 acre farm in British Honduras), publishing (a multimillion dollar printing plant) and businesses (among them bakeries, barbershops, restaurants, clothing factories, air and highway transportation equipment, apartment buildings, schools and even a controlling interest in the former Guaranty Bank and Trust Company of Chicago). The Nation of Islam has a following estimated at up to 100,000, more than fifty mosques around the country, a weekly radio program broadcast over more than sixty stations and a weekly newspaper with a circulation in excess of 600,000 and a worldwide audience.[86] In short, the Nation of Islam has developed into one of the most influential of the left-oriented extremist groups in the black community throughout the United States.

A basic credo of the Muslims has long been hatred for all whites. However, Jews, "Zionists" and the State of Israel have been special targets of Black Muslim vitriol for many years—and the animus has intensified since the June 1967 war. The Muslims, paradoxically, view slave-trading and black-murdering Arabs as brothers in color and as co-religionists.

The present-day Black Muslim movement was founded in the early 1930s in Chicago by Elijah Muhammad, its prophet and self-proclaimed "Messenger of Allah," who was born Elijah Poole in Sandersville, Georgia in 1897. During World War II, the Muslims openly sympathized with the Japanese and many of their members were sent to jail for refusing to register for the draft. Elijah Muhammad spent several years in prison himself during that period.[87] By the 1950s, the Muslim movement began to expand rapidly, with many of its recruits coming from prisons as a result of the messianic efforts of Muhammad's second in command at the time, Malcolm X. In the sixties a rift developed between the two, and Malcolm X broke away from the Muslim movement headed by Elijah Muhammad. Malcolm X was assassinated in February 1965 as he addressed a meeting in Washington Heights; it was generally believed at the time that the murder was motivated by the split between Elijah Muhammad's Black Muslims and Malcolm X's black nationalist Organization for Afro-American Unity.[88]

In an article in an August 1972 issue of the Black Muslim organ, *Muhammad Speaks,* Leon Forrest, the publication's editor, summed up the Muslim's hostility to Jews and to Israel in an analysis of the candidates and issues in the 1972 presidential elections:

> McGovern—who carries himself as the new internationalist—is quite anti-progressive when it comes to backing Israel. He like Nixon is a lackey for the mythical state of Israel. Yet none of his Black colleagues and followers will call him on this question. He is simply timid when it comes to standing up to the Zionist media controlling, highly influential Jewish community.
>
> Yet the Arab-Israeli confrontation could well be the Viet Nam of the middle 1970s—during the period he (McGovern) claims the military budget will be levelled off, under his aegis. Already he is ready to go to war, like Nixon, against 100,000,000 Arabs in the name of Israel. This mythical state works hand-in-glove with white South Africa to keep the Black majority in chains.[89]

But perhaps the most telling indication of the overt anti-Semitism of the Nation of Islam was the fact that during most of 1972, and into 1973, the bookshop at the main mosque of the Black Muslims in New York City openly displayed and sold copies of the *Protocols of the Elders of Zion.* One edition being sold by the Muslims was published by Gerald L. K. Smith and bore the name of his Christian Nationalist Crusade. Other anti-Semitic literature from Smith was also on sale at the bookshop. So, too, were the edition of the *Protocols* published in English by the Social Reform Society of Kuwait and a virulent anti-Semitic book published in Pakistan entitled *A History of Jewish Crimes.* The latter, put out in 1969 by the Asian Book Centre in Karachi, bore a dedication to "the Gentiles of the World":

> Judaism enables and empowers the Jews to work great mischief and commit the crimes in all conditions, surroundings and circumstances. . . .
>
> The Jews always commit crimes because they are incapable of everything else. . . .
>
> Of course, crime is a casual, human activity but to the Jews it is an eternal and methodical activity of life. . . .
>
> The Jewish problem must not be regarded as a problem of any particular country, because it has become an universal problem. It must be solved at the expense of none but the Jews.[90]

Muhammad Speaks, a tabloid that runs to thirty-two pages weekly, has inundated its readers with outright traditional anti-Semitism as well as a barrage of attacks on "Zionism" and the State of Israel. Articles have borne such headlines as "When the blood flows, the money flows—Zionism is big business"; "Vatican-Zionist-racist conspiracy against Africa"; "Israeli professor says Zionism feeds on racism, ignorance, greed: 'The spirit of Hitler and Goebbels has eaten us up'"; and "Israel grants sanctuary to white Jewish crooks."[91] In a series of articles in January 1971, for example, headlined, "Oppenheimer of South Africa (and Israel)," the Black Muslim newspaper condemned South Africa diamond magnate Harry Oppenheimer for his "financial backing of Israel's Zionist government":

> Oppenheimer's friends ring like an exclusive roster of super-rich. They are all men of imponderable wealth—international monpolists such as the Rothschilds, the Sulzbergers, Charles Englehard, the Guggenheims, and the Rockefellers, to name a few.[92]

Louis Farrakhan, New York minister of the Black Muslims, wrote in an article in *Muhammad Speaks* in May 1972: "Since the Jews are in control of the mass media, newspaper, television, radio, we knew then that we could begin to look for a concerted attack on the Nation of Islam through the mass media."[93]

An article in the July 28, 1972 issue, headed "How Israel banks on U.S. Zionists," charged that it was the big monopolies and banks in the United States that were behind "international Zionism" and were financing and inspiring "Israeli aggression against Arab countries." The names of Jacob Blaustein, the Schiffs and the Lazarus family were prominent among such "Zionist millionaires" who had come "together by the common exploitative essence of capital, by their common hatred of progress and freedom of the peoples." Accompanying the article was a cartoon depicting a human scarecrow behind a barbed-wire fence with a Star of David on its breast pocket and a rifle labeled "U.S.A." under its arm.

In addition to its overt attacks on American and other Jews, *Muhammad Speaks* has bulged with attacks on Israel and praise of the Arabs. Appearing regularly are headlines like "Is Life Of An Arab In Israel Like a Black Man's In Alabama?"; "Modern Israel Rivals Ancient Pharoah in Brutality"; "'Israeli' Reporter Describes Nazi-like Blitzkrieg Against Arab Civilians"; "Israeli war planes, tanks massacre refugee innocents"; "Arabs describe Israeli torture"; and "Israel building new concentration camps."[94] The publication has also promoted the Fatah and Palestinian terrorist organizations with articles such as an "Interview with Palestine fighters" and another entitled "Growth of Palestinian resistance-liberation movement: What does Al Fatah want?"[95]

It was hardly surprising, therefore, to read in a 1972 issue of *Muhammad Speaks* that a number of Arab states had loaned or contributed more than $3 million to the Black Muslims. The Libyan Arab Republic, as we have seen, one of the most strident enemies of Israel in the Middle East, loaned the Black Muslims $2,978,406, interest free, to be repaid in three years, for the establishment of a national mosque. The loan was said to have been negotiated in Tripoli by Libyan President Qaddafi and boxer Muhammad Ali, a Muslim adherent. (In October 1972, *Muhammad Speaks* announced that repayment of the loan had been extended six years beyond the original terms, with final payment due in 1981.[96] In February of 1973, however, it was reported that Qaddafi had turned down a request by the Black Muslims for a second $3-million loan; he was reportedly responsive to arguments from orthodox Moslems that the Muslims' preaching of anti-white hatred violated Koranic precepts, and that Elijah Muhammed was a "false prophet."[97] Outright gifts of money to the Muslims came from Abu Dhabi, whose president contributed $125,000; from Qatar, whose ruler gave $100,000; from the Syrian Arab Republic, whose president gave $34,722; and from Bahrain, whose ruler contributed $20,000.[98]

One of the most notorious outlets for anti-Jewish, anti-Israel and pro-Arab propaganda in *Muhammad Speaks* has been a weekly column entitled "Middle East Report," written by Ali Baghdadi of Chicago, a former president of the Organization of Arab Students in the United States, who is himself a Palestinian. His propaganda has been variously headlined: "Why Zionists' Scheme to Conquer, Hold Arab Lands is Doomed To Failure";

"Israelis imitate their former oppressors"; "Israel, torture, theft cause hijackings"; and "Israel shares guilt for insane massacre."[99]
In May 1972 column Baghdadi wrote, in part:

> Today, the Nation of Islam is subjected to a war of propaganda and lies waged by the U.S. Zionist controlled news media. For supporting the just Arab cause and the Palestinian struggle for liberation, Muhammad Speaks, one of Mr. Muhammad's greatest accomplishments is branded as anti-semitic by Israel's loyal friends.[100]

In another article shortly thereafter, Baghdadi defended the murderous attack on innocent civilians at Israel's Lod Airport on May 30 by three Japanese gunmen. Baghdadi referred to the cold-blooded murderers as "three young Japanese who volunteered to give their lives for a just struggle" and went on to declare:

> The Palestinians, as well as the Vietnamese, and all oppressed colonized people are within their legitimate rights to use all means available in their struggle for liberation. Every dollar spent by a foreign tourist will only prolong the war and occupation. The tourist who visits the troubled region will enable Israel to buy destructive weapons and is as guilty as the Israelis.[101]

In yet another "Middle East Report" Baghdadi defended the murders of the Israeli Olympic team athletes in Munich: "Were the 11 Israeli hostages innocent? The society which denies the right of self-determination to people who are determined to live peaceably on the land which they cared for since time immemorial cannot be regarded as innocent."[102]
In 1973 Baghdadi called for increased Arab determination "to severely punish the Zionist war criminals and the destruction of the Israeli state in its racist political form."[103] And in the May 4 issue of *Muhammad Speaks,* the Arab propagandist told his readers: "In her declared war against so-called Palestinian terrorists, Israel does not hesitate to launch genocidal war—exceeding in its horror the one waged by Hitler and the Nazis."

Perhaps most disturbing of all to the Jewish community is the evidence of anti-Jewish attitudes (often, but not by any means exclusively, expressed in hostility to Israel) among young blacks on American campuses. These, after all, will be among the black leaders of tomorrow. Will they be Martin Luther Kings, Roy Wilkinses, Bayard Rustins, Whitney Youngs—or the Stokely Carmichaels, Eldridge Cleavers, LeRoi Joneses?

Anti-Jewish, anti-Israel propaganda has been disseminated in official or semi-official black student publications or by black student groups at the University of Oklahoma at Norman, Ohio State University, Queens and Brooklyn Colleges of the City University of New York and other colleges, and in Greensboro, North Carolina, where a local black youth group has mustered support for its publication on a number of school campuses.

One of the earliest, and perhaps typical, campus sources of anti-Israel, "anti-Zionist" propaganda was *The South End,* 16,000 copies of which were distributed free five days a week to students at Detroit's Wayne State University—the third largest college in Michigan. The publication took a blatantly pro-Arab and pro-Fatah position during 1968 and 1969 when it fell under the control of black radicals and was edited by black militant John Watson, who was quoted in the Detroit *News* as calling his paper a "revolutionary" publication. In one of its editorials, *The South End* described itself as a vehicle for "promoting the interests of the impoverished, oppressed, exploited, and powerless victims of white, racist, monopoly capitalism, and imperialism."[104] A number of news items and editorials published in this paper affirmed its support of the Al Fatah terrorists. In its May 15, 1969 issue, for example, it published a "Commemorative Issue on the Arab Struggle" that included pro-Fatah material, an attack by an Arab propagandist on "Zionist Colonialism," and similar anti-Zionist articles. Only months earlier, on February 10, 1969, William R. Keast, then president of Wayne State University, in a letter to Watson, had accused the newspaper of printing "attacks upon Jews, Poles and other ethnic groups that are disturbingly reminiscent of Hitler Germany."

Subsequently, *The South End,* under the control of an Association of Black Students at Wayne State, once again became a cause for concern and prolonged furor. From January 10 to 12, 1973, the paper, edited now by Gene Cunningham, published a series of anti-Jewish articles by the Rev. John Nicholls Booth, a long-time and notorious archfoe of Israel and supporter of the Arab cause. Booth questioned the need for a Jewish state and expressed doubt that six million Jews had been exterminated by the Nazis during World War II. Adding its own anti-Semitic touch, the paper "illustrated" the Booth pieces by superimposing a swastika over a Star of David.

George Gullen, Jr., the current president of Wayne State University, publicly charged *The South End's* editors with being anti-Semitic. In a published statement, Gullen and the eight members of the school's Board of Governors expressed their revulsion over "the anti-Semitic attitudes expressed throughout the articles."[105] In a January 29, 1973 reply to the charge, the newspaper's editors asserted:

> We respond to this false issue by stating that at no time have we consciously advocated any policy or position which would undermine the right to self-determination of the Jewish people. We admit that we made a grave error in our opposition to Zionism in all its forms when we unfortunately equated the legitimate national symbol of the Jewish people of the world with a swastika. It was a grave and tragic error and we apologized for that error.

However, in a self-serving statement, the editors of *The South End* added:

> Our editorial policy as stated many times is not in opposition to Jewish people. It is in opposition to the tragedy of Zionism as practiced in the Middle East. Under no circumstances will we ever attempt to undermine the integrity of the Jewish peoples of the world and we condemn all attempts to confuse our stand against Zionism with anti-Semitism.

On February 9, 1973, the Board of Governors of Wayne State University formally apologized for the anti-Jewish articles in *The South End.* They resolved that:

> . . . the actions of the Editor and staff of *The South End,* in their attacks on persons of Jewish faith, be and the same are hereby offi-

cially repudiated as actions of this University, and that all persons of Jewish faith together with all others offended by such attacks are hereby extended our sincere apology.

The Board's resolution went on to "officially censure the Editor of *The South End* together with such members of his staff responsible for such outrages" as the anti-Jewish articles previously mentioned, and requested their immediate resignations.

Yet another school-oriented source of hostility to Israel has been the National Association of Black Students, initially part of the National Student Association until the black student group's split from NSA in August 1969. At that time the National Student Association, funded in part by the Ford Foundation, voted to give the black separatist student group $50,000 in "reparations."

The National Association of Black Students' pro-Arab bias was apparent at its September 1971 convention in Chicago. One of the first resolutions passed by the convention was an "unconditional" statement of support of the Palestinian people.[106] Moreover, anti-Israel propaganda has appeared in *Struggle!*, the official organ of the National Association of Black Students. The March–April 1971 issue, for example, published an article entitled "Israel's role in Uganda coup" which was subheaded "Progress and democracy threatened US-Israeli profiteers." The article purported to be an expose of the alleged role of Israel in the 1970 military coup in Uganda.

The hostility expressed by some young black men and women on school campuses to Jews and Jewish concerns may in part result from heightened awareness to the works of some black writers who have been overtly anti-Semitic. We have already discussed LeRoi Jones/Baraka, but another literary personality casting aspersions on Jews for allegedly patronizing and exploiting black intellectuals has been black critic and writer Harold Cruse, author of a controversial 1967 book, *The Crisis of the Negro Intellectual*,[107] and a 1968 sequel, *Rebellion or Revolution?*[108]

In *The Crisis of the Negro Intellectual*, Cruse expressed the

belief that Jews were interlopers who had come between the
Anglo-Saxon Protestants and Negroes. He was particularly scorn-
ful of Jewish leftists, especially those who had been active in the
Communist Party in the 1920s, 1930s, and 1940s, for purportedly
placing black intellectuals, such as himself, in a position "wherein
representatives of another minority could dictate cultural standards to them." In Cruse's view, Jews, and especially Jewish Communists, were responsible for most of the major problems that
beset black intellectuals throughout the years.

Cruse also asserted that it was "no longer possible for Negro
intellectuals to deal with the Jewish question in America purely
on a basis of brotherhood, compassion, morality, and other subjective responses which rule out objective criticism and positive
appraisals." He went on to state that there was much evidence
to indicate that Negroes "truly have a Jewish problem, and the
Jew is not just a hatred symbol." According to him, there were
"far too many Jews from Jewish organizations into whose privy
councils Negroes are not admitted, who nevertheless are involved
in every civil rights and American-African organization, creating policy and otherwise analyzing the Negro from all possible
angles."

In addition, Cruse expressed great hostility toward the establishment of the Jewish state. He attributed the "international
machinations that brought about the State of Israel" to Jewish
"imperialism," and he questioned the loyalty of "a great proportion of American Jews" who, he intimated, function, "as an or-
ganic part of a distant nation-state."

Reviewing Cruse's book in *The Black Scholar* of November
1969, editor Robert Chrisman wrote:

> There is vicious anti-Semitism throughout the work. When faced
> with complexity, Cruse finds the nearest scapegoat and furiously
> lashes his way out of the jam. *The Crisis of the Negro Intellectual*
> is the crisis of Harold Cruse more than it is anything else.

In a review of the book in the *New York Times* of November 21,
1967, Thomas Lask commented:

Mr. Cruse finds them [Jews] wherever he turns: in left-wing and Communist activity, among liberal supporters of civil rights movements, as absentee landlords in Harlem. He even manages to say that Jews have fostered anti-Semitism among Negroes, though I think a statement that Negroes are responsible for anti-Negro prejudice would bring an angry demurrer from him.

Despite all that has occurred in the past half-dozen years in the arena of black-Jewish relations, and the obvious irrationality of blacks attacking Jews for the misdeeds of the Establishment, some black militants have continued to target on Jews rather than on the system for their troubles. For example, the September 23, 1972 issue of the Philadelphia *Tribune,* a newspaper serving Philadelphia's black community, published a lengthy attack on "Zionists" (that is, Jews) entitled "Zionist Attacks on Nationalism Are 'Hypocritical.'" It was written by Bill Mathis, described as chairman and director of Philadelphia CORE since 1965 and a co-chairman of the Congress of African People. Mathis' article was one of a series by him on black nationalism and its alleged enemies. In it, he attacked Zionism as "the political and economic nationalism of some Europeans called 'Jews' who have falsely claim[ed] the 'chosen people' mystique." He asserted that black ghetto dwellers had been oppressed for decades by Jewish businessmen. "We were tenants—they were landlords. We were consumers—they were merchants."

No one knows the extent to which such anti-Semitic sentiments emanating from black extremists have penetrated the black community generally.

Some years ago, as part of an ADL-sponsored study of anti-Semitism at the University of California at Berkeley, sociologists found, generally, that black Americans, to the degree that they distinguished between Jews and other whites, preferred Jews and were less anti-Semitic than non-Jewish whites.[109]

Updating of the original study confirmed most of the findings of the earlier one, but showed an interesting and important difference between blacks and whites on economically-oriented questions; when it came to these, while young whites were less anti-Semitic than older whites, young blacks were more so than their parents; on noneconomic questions, however, young blacks and whites scored roughly the same.[110]

A hopeful finding in the first study confirmed for the most part by still another updating was that violence and separatism were rejected as goals by the majority of the black community, and that the conventional civil rights groups and leaders—not the extremists—enjoyed overwhelming popularity.[111] Moreover, the latest research showed optimism in the black community about the possibilities for change; it revealed, as well, that much of the anger in the community remained directed toward inclusion in the system, not separatism.

Perhaps that is why in 1973 NAACP was able to boast, for the previous year, a 20,000 increase in its membership (now said to be around 412,000) and an income of approximately $4 million, making it "not only the oldest, but the largest and wealthiest of the civil-rights groups."[112] The NAACP and its director, Roy Wilkins, have been stanch foes of anti-Semitism from any source, long-time supporters of Israel; they have eschewed with vigor any other road to black equality than full integration and have opposed nondemocratic methods for black advancement.

But the data on which the University of California studies were based, even with the most recent updatings, are anywhere from half a dozen years to a decade old. A lot has happened in that time. If activists within the black community who happen to be anti-Semitic become true spokesmen, leaders of more than a tiny segment, there will be reason to worry about the effect of their anti-Jewish attitudes upon their followers. Morever, there is also suspicion about why such extremists seem to rely on Jew-baiting (as opposed, for example, to only slightly less noxious white-baiting) in the effort to attract followers. It is, of course, an old story among white extremist organizations that they have sought to tap the deep veins of anti-Semitism in the non-Jewish white community here and abroad.

A recent syndicated article noted that "today's blacks march to many drummers" and that no one leader, nor even several, could speak authoritatively for the nation's black community,[113] as diverse in its needs, feelings and behavior patterns as the Jewish community that black anti-Semites, in common with white anti-Semites, have sought so simplistically to scapegoat. It will be the task and the challenge of black and Jewish leaders to make sure the "drummers"—whoever they will be in the years ahead—remember, and continue to forge, the bonds that have long united these two peoples.

It will not be easy. There is ill feeling on both sides. But a heavy dose of truth, widely disseminated, should help. Within that truth the following observations must continue to be made, and made forcefully:

—That Israel, as has been indicated in this and earlier chapters, is a friend, not an enemy, and that only enormous self-delusion can alter the fact of long-time Arab enmity to African blacks and Israeli aid to emerging black nations; that American Jews regard attacks on the existence of Israel as the ultimate anti-Semitism.

—That the Radical Left, which pretends to support black causes, does so in the service of a revolution which would destroy the only institutions blacks and Jews have that are capable of addressing their needs.

—That Jewish exploitation of American blacks is a myth; that for every exploitative merchant or landlord who happens to be Jewish, there are fifty Jews demonstrably condemning such practices; that, moreover, a recent study of ghetto slumlordship, in New York at least, showed that:

> Contrary to popular belief that the slums are owned by large white property-holders ... black landlords own 52 per cent of the all-black buildings and 20 per cent of the buildings that are mostly black. Similarly, in Spanish-speaking areas, most of the buildings are owned by Spanish-speaking landlords.[114]

—That arguments that blacks who target on Jews are really "only" targeting on whites must be rejected by the Jewish community; such arguments defend quintessential, historic, political anti-Semitism, which consists most precisely in making Jews the villains for ills that are not of their doing.

—That Jews have been the oldest and most consistent friends of black people in the struggle to fulfill America's promise, and that their most broadly representative organizations continue in that commitment; that Jews, more than any other segment of the population save blacks themselves, are likely to vote for those candidates and support those policies designed to improve black status.

For their part, most Jews view anti-Semitism among blacks as a disheartening development. They believe it essential that black people develop a greater sensitivity to anti-Semitism—just as black people demand greater sensitivity on the part of Jews and other whites to racism.

Nevertheless, most Jews also know that they cannot and must not abdicate their role in the struggle for equality; that they cannot afford to allow the anti-Semitism they observe in the black community to sway them from continuing to fight for black justice; that extremists in the black community are largely the product of America's unresolved racial problems and that until American society—that is, the dominant white majority—moves meaningfully to confront the challenge of racial inequity, the entire nation will continue to be plagued by its extremist offspring.

The Baltimore *Afro-American* put it succinctly in a September 9, 1972 comment:

> We would like to suggest that blacks and Jews face no threat from one another that compares with the danger they invite by losing sight of the overriding necessity of their sticking together in an effective coalition.

The glue of that coalition has been seriously weakened in recent years by the evidence of anti-Semitism in the black community; it is time, indeed, to make repairs.

11

The USSR, Western Europe, Latin America

Nowhere in the world today is anti-Semitism masquerading under the guise of anti-Zionism more pervasively than in the Union of Soviet Socialist Republics.

Anti-Semitism has been endemic to Russia, of course, since czarist times, and while the Soviet state under Lenin would not tolerate official anti-Semitism, such was not the case under his successors. Anti-Semitism was revived as government policy under Stalin in the late thirties, forties and early fifties. William Korey's recent American scholarly study demonstrates that the Soviet brand of anti-Semitism long antedates Soviet enmity toward Israel, that deliberate policies and actions, including the decimation of Jewish cultural and religious institutions and the murder of Jews, were set and undertaken prior to May 1948 and continued well after the Soviet Union both aided Israel's efforts for statehood within the United Nations and was a friend during the 1948–49 War of Liberation.[1] The years 1949–53 saw the cold-blooded murder of the cream of Soviet Jewry's intellectuals. The Cold War had apparently intensified Soviet totalitarianism and chauvinism, the latter bordering on hatred of foreigners; Jews, those "cosmopolitans," were perceived on both the popular level and within Soviet officialdom itself as "unassimilable" and "counterrevolutionary," the prominence they had achieved in capitalist (and free) countries making them even more suspect to the xenophobic Russian mind.

In he wake of the Nazi Holocaust, however, traditional anti-Semitism—if useful at home to deflect attention from internal and foreign policy problems and not unfamiliar to the Russian masses—was not a readily exportable commodity. The exixtence of the State of Israel and Soviet ambitions in the Arab Middle East provided a camouflage. "Zionism" for Judaism and "Zionists" for Jews were substituted in a slander campaign that drew directly on the *Protocols of the Elders of Zion*—and still does. The distinction, it was expected, would enable the Kremlin to overcome the objectionable hate factors of Nazi themes and policies and, at the same time, to invest anti-Semitism with a "respectable" aura of political criticism that, it was hoped, would be accepted not only in the USSR and its satellites, but in many quarters of the world not allied with Soviet communism

But the veneer was often too thin, and often it was not there at all. In the early 1960s, world public opinion—not the least of it emanating from Western communist parties—forced Moscow to disown and withdraw from distribution a vicious anti-Semitic work, *Judaism without Embellishment* by Trofim Kichko, a Ukrainian journalist and former Nazi collaborator. Kichko's fall from grace was short-lived, however; he was reinstated in 1969 with the publication of *Judaism and Zionism,* hardly less odious than his earlier work, and in 1972 Kichko came out with *Zionism: Enemy of Youth,* in which he asserted, among other enormities, that "The killing of the young, not only of goyim but also of the Jewish young, is preached in the Torah and was long practiced by the believers of Judaism, forerunners of the Zionists."[2]

Beginning in the sixties, and continuing into the seventies, the Kremlin became what might well be called the central switchboard of "permissible," government approved anti-Semitism, exporting its views to the Arabs, of course, to its East European satellites, to Western Europe and to the United States—in the latter two instances under both its own auspices, including the Soviet embassies, missions and news agencies abroad, and those of its Radical Left adherents and Arab propagandists.

The "switchboard" was fully and energetically activated after the June 1967 defeat of the Arabs—probably induced at least in part by the exhuberance exhibited by Soviet Jews, no less than by

Jews everywhere in the world, at the Israeli victory and their pronounced disaffection with Soviet support of the Arab states. Moreover, by assailing Zionist "machinations" backed by "U.S. imperialism," the Kremlin could hope to divert domestic criticism for its having bet on the wrong horse in the Arab-Israel conflict.

At the same time, Kremlin policy sought to undermine the very survival of Israel by continuing to provide men, money and materiel—especially the last—to the Arab enemies of the Jewish state, including Arab countries and the terrorist groups. It was thus a two-pronged operation: dissemination at home and abroad of anti-Semitic propaganda under the guise of anti-Zionist criticism, and intended politicide of Israel through the agency of the Arab armies and guerrillas.

Accompanying this thrust was the periodic continuation or institution of domestic programs of anti-Semitism targeted on the allegedly unassimilable Jew and/or the so-called "Zionist"—ergo, traitor—at home. These programs have also been "cosmeticized" by an anti-Zionist theme, entirely transparent even to the uninitiated. They have ranged from subtle and blatant media campaigns, including publication of Nazi-like cartoons, to "show trials" that have ended in long prison terms for activist Jews seeking lawful emigration to Israel. Within that range have been intensification of discrimitory patterns against Jews, including restrictive unofficial quotas in university admissions, government service and other areas of Soviet life, as well as the unconscionable barriers placed in the path of those desiring to emigrate to Israel. The latter include harassment, arrest, psychiatric commitment, loss of jobs, the requirement of parental approval (even for those who may be parents or grandparents themselves!) and, for a period, the imposition of a stiff exit tax on educated Soviet Jews that amounted to a virtual ransom demand; the tax, inoperative while the USSR seeks U.S. Congressional approval of favored trading status with the United States, nevertheless has not been officially withdrawn from Soviet regulations.

The beginning of the contemporary, strident anti-Semitic campaign under the rubric of anti-Zionism came not long after the Six-Day War. It was signaled, in fact, during UN debates in the aftermath of the war by the Soviet representative and thereafter enunciated in the pages of official Soviet press: Israel was likened to Nazi Germany, alleged Israeli "atrocities" during the war were concocted (given the lie by the International Committee of the Red Cross, which reported on June 23, 1967 that Israel had indeed observed the Geneva Conventions)[3] and Israel was charged with genocide.

On June 15, with the fighting barely finished, *Izvestia* alleged that "Even the Western correspondents compare these crimes with what the Nazis did in the occupied countries during World War II";[4] *Izvestia* never named any such "Western correspondents" because what was important was not the truth, but that the charges be introduced in a major Communist organ and presented as if they had originated somewhere beyond the Kremlin walls.

Pravda bruited "This is Genocide!" in an article under that headline.[5] Soon after, the important magazine *Sovietskaya Rossiya* followed suit with an article likening the Israeli actions to "The Nazi crimes on the soil of France, Czechoslovakia, Poland and the Soviet Union."[6] *Pravda* again joined the chorus with a cartoon depicting a large-nosed, poorly shaven Israeli and Adolph Hitler, hands clasped; both figures were labeled "Expansionism" and the caption read: "Seeing eye to eye."[7] The cartoon was typical of others that were to follow in the weeks, months and years ahead, Soviet officials obviously stoking both anti-Semitism and the Russian people's abhorrence of Nazi deeds, themselves having been among the victims. The Arabs, despite the heavy postwar infiltration of ex-Nazi celebrities in their midst, were not displeased.

Broadcasting the accusations of Nazi-like tactics, genocide, aggression, imperialism and expansionism on the part of Israel was not assigned exclusively to reporters and essayists. On July 5, 1967, First Secretary of the Communist Party Leonid Brezhnev gave official sanction to the new anti-Semitic campaign in a speech before military graduates assembled in the Kremlin. "The Israeli aggressors are behaving like the worst of bandits. In their atrocities against the Arab population it seems they want to copy the crimes of the Hitler invaders," Brezhnev said, adding that "the aggression must not be allowed to go unpunished."[8] Around the same time Foreign Minister Andrei Gromyko added his own weighty voice to the campaign. The Israeli "aggressors," Gromyko observed, were "dizzy with military success" just as the Nazis had been at the beginning of World War II.[9]

Condemnation of Israeli actions soon became attacks on "Zionism" that ill concealed a raw anti-Semitism common to all purveyors of "Jewish conspiracy" charges. During the first week of August 1967, an article entitled "What is Zionism?" appeared simultaneously in the main provincial organs of the USSR. In the very first paragraph the theme was set forth: "A wide network of Zionist organizations with a common center, a common program, and funds exceeding by far the funds of the Mafia 'Cosa Nostra' is active behind the scenes of the international theatre." The article went on to describe a global "Zionist corporation" composed of "smart dealers in politics and finance, religion and trade" whose "well camouflaged aim" is the "enrichment by any means of the international Zionist network."[10]

Despite the Red Cross statement, reports from unbiased newsmen and other evidence, the Soviet Union persisted in disseminating the Zionist *qua* Nazi theme, the genocide slander and the "international conspiracy" myth. Why? Was it merely a face-saving device to camouflage the humiliation of the six-day defeat? Or did the roots go deeper?

Emanuel Litvinoff, the Russian-born English analyst of Soviet affairs, opted for the irrational workings of Soviet policy as regards the question of Jews:

> The inescapable conclusion must surely be that in regard to Israel, the Soviet authorities again succumbed to the irrational. As Judaism has been depicted as the most pernicious and corrupt of religions, as Zionism is represented as the most sinister and corrupt of contemporary ideologies, so Israel—the Jewish State—earns more obloquy, contempt and dislike in the Soviet press than any country ranging from Fascist Spain to Communist China. The charge of genocide, therefore, can be seen as Soviet overreaction to the mythical image of the Jew, its roots buried deep in the perversity of traditional anti-Semitism.[11]

It was indeed the perversity of traditional anti-Semitism that became apparent in Soviet propaganda from 1967 forward. In fact, Trofim Kichko's *Judaism and Zionism* and *Beware: Zionism!*, also a 1969 work by a probably pseudonymous pamphleteer named Yuri Ivanov, may be called, without serious contradiction, mere refurbished and updated versions of the *Protocols.*

Beware: Zionism! was issued by Moscow's Political Literature Publishing House; in short, it is an official Soviet government document. Ivanov twisted the "chosen people" concept into an obvious ethnic slur, fully utilizing the Zionism-Nazism campaign first evidenced in the immediate post-1967 war diatribes and cartoons. Ivanov made it quite clear that the enemy was not merely the political state of Israel, since in fact, the ruling circles of Israel "are junior partners in the International Jewish Concern [i.e., conspiracy]." The conspiracy theme of the *Protocols* is the major part of Ivanov's philosophy, and his heavy reliance upon it clearly reveals the interconnection between czarist propaganda and contemporary Kremlin cant. The "international Zionist conspiracy" was a favorite jumping-off point for Adolf Hitler as well. Speaking in May 1941 in Berlin, the Fuehrer declared that behind the Allies "stood the great international Jewish financial interests that control the banks and stock exchange, as well as the armament industry."[12] Ivanov put it this way: "The International Zionist Organization is economically connected by the closest of ties to the monopolies of the biggest imperialist powers, the U.S.A. first and foremost."[13]

The only difference between Hitler's viewpoint and that expressed by Ivanov, is that Hitler's word "Jewish" became "Zionist" in the official Soviet publication. Hitler never worried at all about charges of anti-Semitism, but apparently, the Kremlin in the last decade or so, is sensitive on this issue. In fact, the Kremlin propagandists have gone out of their way publicly to state what they regard as the difference between anti-Semitism and anti-Zionism. In a widely circulated pamphlet published by the USSR's Novosti Press Agency, *Soviet Jews: Fact and Fiction,* the distinction was supposedly made by condemning "bourgeois propaganda in the West" and the "spokesmen for Zionist organizations in the United States and Great Britain." These propagandists, said Novosti, had no real evidence of anti-Semitism in the Soviet Union and therefore resorted to "outright distortions and garbled facts." The pamphlet continued:

> To make their allegations ring true, bourgeois propagandists refer to articles in the Soviet press which expose the reactionary nature of Zionism, denounce the adventurous nature of the Israeli extremists, torpedoing efforts to arrive at a settlement of the acute military and political crisis in the Middle East. The bourgeois press bemoans the alleged growing anti-Semitism, persecution of Jews, etc. Attempts are made to draw a parallel between Zionist ideology and Israeli extremists on the one hand, and Soviet Jews on the other.[14]

By citing the alleged Western attempts to draw the parallel, Novosti tried although poorly, to indicate the distinction. Ivanov attempted the same distinction, for he clearly stated that the Zionist leaders not only aimed to take over huge areas of the Middle East and control international finance, but also sought the "establishment of control over the *Jewish* masses." Thus Jew and Zionist were "differentiated."

Clearly, however, the Kremlin propagandists intend to categorize all Jews as "Zionists," whether they officially consider themselves as such or not. Trofim Kichko, in his widely-read *Judaism and Zionism,* did not always employ the code word "Zionism" when he meant Judaism but tried to differentiate between the two terms in order more emphatically to deprecate both concepts. But the device soon failed. In an early chapter, Kichko stated:

> Judaism has always served the interests of the exploiting classes. In our times, its most reactionary expostulates have been taken up by the Zionists—the Jewish bourgeois nationalists.
> Judaism and Zionism have become the ideological foundations of the militaristic, semi-theocratic regime in Israel and its aggressive actions against the Arab people in the Near East.[15]

Kichko specifically attacked the Jewish religion and alleged "a direct connection between the morality of Judaism and what the Israeli Zionists are doing in practice." He repeated the *Protocol* bilge that the Jewish religion permits its adherents "to take away everything from *goyim,* peoples of other faiths," and that Judaism teachers "that the whole world belongs to the Jews." Kichko further insisted that in the absence of a personal disavowal one must consider that "every Jew is a Judaist [i.e., A Zionist], every Judaist an Israeli." Thus the cautious though clumsy inhibitions of Ivanov were thrown to the wind in the more dynamic propaganda of Kichko. His message was not merely that every Judaist is an Israeli but by extension that every Soviet Jew was potentially a traitor. The campaign of anti-Semitic propaganda has not abated.

A 1973 article by B. Antonov, one of the main political commentators of the Novosti Press Agency, charged that Klaus Barbie, the SS "butcher of Lyon," was an "old friend and partner in many crimes" of the "Zionist circles in Tel Aviv." Antonov wrote:

> The fact is that while living under a false identity, Barbie assumed the name of Klaus Altmann, and as Altmann he was engaged in the supply of arms to Israel. It was thanks to him that Israel received a number of missile boats from France, where they were purchased by Norway.[16]

The Soviet commentator added that Barbie "maintained close relations with Zionist leaders over a number of years" and during World War II, "acting with them, robbed over 100,000 French Jews and then dispatched them to the gas chambers."

In the spring of 1973, also, Soviet Jews were reported to be worried about a Soviet film "documentary" that had been screened privately but not yet released. Bearing the same title as the 1969 Ivanov work, *Beware: Zionism!* (there is apparently a paucity of imagination in Soviet circles when it comes to anti-Jewish titles), the ninety-minute film by the well-known director, Yuri Karpov, was said to describe the Czechoslovakian crisis of 1968 as "Zionist provocation" and to raise a number of other anti-Jewish themes. Indignation was said to be aroused in Moscow artistic circles even among non-Jews, one of whom was quoted as saying it would drive out of Russia even those Jews who wanted to remain.[17]

It is little wonder that life for the average Soviet Jew became, after 1967, an agonized ordeal. Not that the Jew had lived in paradise before. Post-Stalin regimes were hardly more friendly to Jews. In 1962 a so-called antistate "economic plot" was discovered by Krushchev's police in which Jews were alleged to be the chief conspirators. As a result of the so-called "economic trials," three Jews were executed for their "crimes," and many more imprisoned.

The anti-Semitic campaign, prompted in part by internal political considerations, subsided until the Six-Day War. As outlined above, it then became necessary for the Kremlin to initiate new aspects of its traditional anti-Semitic policy, aspects more in keeping with the times. Whereas in an earlier day traditional counterrevolution and economic malfeasance served as anti-Semitic alibis, now Zionist conspiracy—"treason"—was to be the theme. Kichko's references to the inherent "antagonism" of Judaism to normal society were among the essential conceits of the new campaign. But to give the movement teeth in terms of popular acceptance an anti-Soviet aspect had to be involved. The Soviet public—and it was hoped, Westerners as well—would have to be convinced that Jews in the USSR were an alien, unpatriotic source of dissent, taking their orders from Israel and the United States.

Unitl the Six-Day War the roughly three million Soviet Jews had remained largely silent. Statistically speaking, though they were worse off than their Ukrainian, Latvian or even Mongolian neighbors, the Soviet Jews managed to survive from day to day as they have done for centuries, largely by dint of a stoical pragmatism and a deep-rooted faith; the Six-Day War, however, provoked a new and rare phenomenon among them: a desire to be heard, to be silent no more.

But this new Jewish assertion naturally caused acute alarm in high places, especially when coupled by a demand for emigration to Israel under the provision of the United Nations Universal Declaration of Human Rights (Article XIII) which guarantees such emigration and which the USSR sanctioned. The Kremlin realized the disruptive dangers this outcry could provoke and obviously concluded that it required vigorous counteraction. It was quickly recognized that the Jewish outcry could be used to support government implications, imparted over the years, about Jewish infidelity to the motherland, about Jewish treason, the double allegiance, all the vices about which the propagandists had written. Clearly the time had come to functionalize the anti-Zionist theme, to crack down on the enemies and through them to mitigate all national dissidence. The confluence of Soviet anti-Israel, pro-Arab foreign policy and the renaissance of Jewish national self-assertion was ideal for Kremlin purposes.

The switchboard was therefore programmed to undertake massive counteraction against the new national (and international) enemy of all socialism, to wit the Zionist—never, of course, the Jew per se. Indeed "loyal" or house Jews, such as the writer Aron Vergelis and General V. E. Dymshits—as well as the (late) Chief Rabbi of Moscow, Yehuda L. Levin—were to be upgraded and praised for their patriotic resistance to Zionism. But the others, the great bulk of Soviet Jews, were to be kept under surveillance, discriminated against more than before, and when necessary, arrested and tried.

Oddly enough, at the same time, a small number of these very same "treasonable" Zionists were, in fact, allowed to fulfill their dream and emigrate to Israel. Perhaps this was undertaken in accordance with Premier Alexei Kosygin's declaration in December 1966 that "there will be no problem [concerning emigration]; the doors will be open."[18] Or it may have been done in the nature of a safety valve to let off dangerously accumulating steam and at the same time—perhaps it was hoped—expel Zionist instigators. Some even say the emigration policy was merely a threat against the Soviet's Arab clients; if they misbehaved, the emigration to Israel would increase as punishment. Whatever the motivation, the process once started could not be halted even by Kremlin intimidation. Oppressed as they were and continuously denied their civil rights, more and more Jews cried for relief and did so publicly. As the voices of Soviet Jews became more audible, reaching sympathetic ears in the West, so did the Soviet campaign to quiet them. From 1968 onward, utilizing the latest anti-Semitic disguises, the USSR began its systematic harassment of Jews. The charges were always the same: "Zionist betrayal and conspiracy."

The first Soviet trial to manifest patent anti-Semitism in the guise of anti-Zionism concerned a factory worker named Boris Kochubiyevsky, a young man awakened to his Jewish heritage as a result of the Six-Day War and the anti-Semitic campaign launched in its wake. Unwittingly, Kochubiyevsky provided the Kremlin leaders with their first full-blown "Zionist," a description which to them was synonymous with "traitor and conspirator." For Kochubiyevsky the word had a very different connotation. In a paper entitled "Why I Am A Zionist," he wrote (in 1967) that Zionism was "the only way out of the present situation [of discrimination]. Zionism for us means the gathering of the persecuted, the hope to return to Israel," and to escape anti-Semitism which "is again waiting for its hour to strike. What has changed is only the name—anti-Zionism—to adapt it to the new times. Anti-Zionism is nothing but anti-Semitism."[19]

Despite his perceptive analysis of the dangers, Kochubiyevsky was willing to confront his oppressors publicly. Shortly after the Six-Day War he spoke up at a meeting in the radio factory where he worked and challenged a speaker who had accused Israel of aggression in the war. He was later persuaded by factory officials to resign his position. In September 1968, he appeared at a memorial service held for the victims of Nazi slaughter at a desolate ravine called Babi Yar, near Kiev. Angered by official Soviet silence on the Jewish tragedy that had occurred at this site, Kochubiyevsky cried out: "Here lies a part of the Jewish people." His remarks did not go unnoticed.

The following November, Kochubiyevsky was informed after many delays that he and his wife had been granted visas to leave for Israel. But even as they waited in the visa office to collect their documents, the Kochubiyevsky apartment was searched and many papers confiscated. In early December he was finally arrested and charged with disseminating "anti-Soviet slander." In May 1969 he came before his accusers and judges in Kiev. The air was heavy with charges of Zionist "slander, contamination, propaganda . . ."

In his statement before the court Kochubiyevsky defended himself heroically, reminding his accusers of his loyalty to the Soviet State but repeating at the same time the indignation he and his fellow Jews had suffered for years at the hands of "covert anti-Semites." He ended his plea with a reaffirmation of his goal to emigrate to Israel.

His eloquence notwithstanding, Boris Kochubiyevsky was found guilty of anti-State slander and sentenced to three years of hard labor (he had already been in prison about six months). His trial and condemnation were hailed by the Soviet press, which emphasized the anti-Zionist theme by reminding readers that Kochubiyevsky had aroused other Jews "to leave their fatherland as traitors and as . . . class enemies." He was described as a Zionist provocateur "poisoned by Zionist propaganda" or "poisoned by Zionist ideology." Ivanov's favorite conceits were carefully woven into the stories as well: "Zionism . . . serves the interests of the most aggressive circles of the Jewish nationalistic bourgeoisie, whose banner is rabid anti-Communism."

Kochubiyevsky entered prison, reviled by Soviet officialdom, hailed in the West as a "hero for our time." His case was a dramatic one, a disturbing one for sensitive observers, but more important it was a germinal case. The pattern of Soviet anti-Jewish trials in the guise of anti-Zionism was now established.

Even as it tried Kochubiyevsky, the USSR continued to permit token emigration to Israel on the ground of "family reunion," although there was official protraction and the imposition of penalties, such as the loss of jobs or demotion, for those with courage enough to apply. The demands of Soviet Jews themselves, as well as growing clamor from Jewish communities in the West, seemed to insure continuance of this token amount of emigration. By 1970, however, Kremlin leaders apparently felt that even this token was too great a concession to what they called "world Zionist propaganda." They decided, so it seems, to balance their actions by stricter surveillance of dissident "Zionists" at home, and by stepped-up press reports and cartoons excoriating Zionist "imperialism" and "aggression" abroad.

On March 20, 1970, *Pravda* published a typical letter, allegedly written by eighteen Jewish workers in Moscow, under the headline, "We Brand with Shame the Zionist Provocateurs." In this piece, Israel was denounced as the perpetrator of "monstrous crimes" and the *Protocols* theme was reiterated by references to Tel Aviv's "ruling circles" acting with the help "of their Washington protectors." In the same month, the elderly rabbi of Moscow, Yehuda Levin, was obliged to denouce Zionism and declare in a radio interview that it "never had anything in common with honest Jews, no matter where they lived." The technique of employing "loyal" Soviet Jews to condemn the Zionist ilk became more and more evident in early 1970 and reached its peak at a large news conference in Moscow, dominated by well-known Soviet Jews who vociferously denounced Israel and Zionism at every turn.

Despite the prestigious nature of this "house" press conference and the dire warnings it broadcast about treason to the motherland, Soviet Jews continued to apply for emigration in increasing numbers and, more and, more, their demand for freedom was publicly heard. On March 11, less than a week after the elaborately staged press conference in Moscow, the *New York Times* reported that thirty-nine Soviet Jews—workers, housewives, young and old, from various Soviet cities—had declared that they were "ready to emigrate to Israel on foot, if necessary" in protest "against the current anti-Israel and anti-Zionist campaign."

The declaration of the thirty-nine was a blow to the Soviet propaganda machine which, in fairly hysterical fashion, immediately denounced the document as a fabrication and even accused Western journalists of conspiratorial activities at the behest of the Zionists simply because they had reported the story in the first place. From March until June, the Soviet press continued hammering the conspiratorial theme, while the Kremlin tightened its squeeze on emigration and undertook repression of the more or less *ad hoc* teaching of Hebrew among Soviet Jews. For good measure, a new item in the anti-Semitic bibliography made its appearance in April 1970. This was a so-called novel, *Love and Hate* by Ivan Schevtsov, which told the story of Nahum Holzer, a degenerate Jew who among other occupations was a dope peddler and a rapist, and who, in one detailed incident, murders his mother. *Sovietskaya Rossiya* praised Schevtsov's hideous book as a tool for "protecting the younger generation from the corrupting art of the bourgeois West."[20] It also published putative letters from happy readers, one of them a kindergarten teacher, who expatiated gratitude for this "realistic, fruitful book" which "teaches us how to fight against our enemies—the imperialists and their Zionist followers."

But words on paper, no matter how vivid, are pale beside events, and in June 1970 an event occurred that provided the Kremlin with its biggest weapon to date against the "Zionist conspiracy" and with its most perfect rationale for further trials and harassment. On June 15, nine Jews and two non-Jews arrived at an airport near Leningrad and, according to Soviet charges, attempted to hijack a small airplane allegedly in order to fly it to Scandinavia and then to Israel. The attempt of course was supposition, for the group was arrested even before it could reach the plane. Within hours, other so-called conspirators were picked up by the police in widely scattered places, some as far away as Riga and Odessa. Apartments were searched; documents, typewriters and Jewish books confiscated. By the end of the day nearly twenty persons—most of them Jews—had been arrested. Within a week, the total was in excess of thirty.

On December 18, Western news reports revealed that those arrested at the airport near Leningrad had been tried in secret, had pleaded guilty of attempting to hijack a plane and—most significant—had allegedly admitted working for "international Zionism." Then came the astonishing announcement of December 24: two of eleven "hijackers"—the so-called organizers—had been sentenced to death. Nine others received terms ranging from four to fifteen years in labor camps.

Only the outrage of Western governments, and even Western communists, held back the executions: In the wake of worldwide protests and demonstrations, the Soviets commuted the death sentences to fifteen-year terms in a maximum hard labor camp.

The Leningrad trial of December 1970—and, more specifically, the death sentences—focused world attention on the fundamental anti-Semitic nature of what the Soviet Union continued to call the "Zionist conspiracy." The French daily, *Le Monde,* saw the event as "a critical trial of Soviet anti-Semitism."[21] The London *Times* saw "suspicions of anti-Semitism" in the trial.[22] A Swedish newspaper, *Arbetet,* discovered that "the trials are really part of the anti-Semitic campaign in the Soviet Union.[23]

Despite the global denunciation of its techniques and despite the unmasking of its aim, the Soviet Union continued to blare the anti-Zionist theme in its posttrial propganda. *Izvestia,* after the conclusion of the trial, denounced international Zionists: "Zionism is the ideology, policy and practice of Jewish monopolies and bourgeoisie which are forever trying to poison the minds of the politically immature and gullible. . . ."[24]

Clearly the Kremlin, though probably embarrased to a degree by the outrage which the trial engendered, seemed determined, as 1971 dawned, to continue its restrictive anti-Semitic campaign in the guise of an anti-Zionist crusade. In fact, it announced a second series of trials connected with the airport incident. These took place in Leningrad and Riga in May 1971 and in Kishinev in June. At the end of these trials more than forty young Soviet Jews, both men and women, had been sentenced to harsh prison terms on charges stemming from the basic accusations of Zionist conspiracy, slander and disloyalty. Many of the defendants of 1971 were, in fact, charged with complicity in the airport incident; other were apparently condemned because they had known some of the Leningrad activists and shared their views about emigration to Israel.

The sentences were severe, the condemnation of Zionism and Israel widespread and vicious. Even so, Soviet Jews continue to apply for emigration and to demand their civil rights in letters, petitions and prayers to the West.

In the face of such conviction, the Kremlin seemed obliged to intensify—if possible—its anti-Semitic campaign by direct and indirect means, by propaganda both at home and abroad.

Throughout the period after the Six-Day War, the Soviet Union was confronted not only by Jewish activism but by the dissidence of what has been described as the "Democratic movement" of non-Jews in the USSR. Prominent scientists and scholars such as physicist Andrei Sakharov, writers such as Andre Almarik and Alexander Solzhenitsyn, as well as lesser known figures, began voicing temperate but urgent criticism of the regime and indicating a unity with nationalistic aspirations, including those of Soviet Jews. It was thus inevitable that Jewish activists

found themselves unwittingly part of the new Democratic movement. As a result the Kremlin was able, as never before, to charac-
terize "Zionism" as a dissident political rather than nationalistic
force, and thus impose punishments and harassments upon Jews
in line with the general counteraction against all dissidents.

The most startling of these counteractions involved psychiatric
commitment of those considered politically deranged. In this
new net of tyranny, the Soviet authorities snared Jew and non-
Jew alike on the theory that anyone who criticized the Soviet
paradise (or who opted to leave it) was at least hopelessly insane
or at best in need of a few weeks of mental rehabilitation in a
hospital. By the fall of 1971, an estimated 200 political prisoners
had been confined in mental institutions under this scheme.
Among them were prominent Jews such as Major Grisha Feigin,
the war hero who, disgusted with Soviet anti-Semitism and in
despair over the refusal of his visa to Israel, had returned his
war medals to the Kremlin. In February 1971, Feigin found himself in the Riga Psychiatric Institute. Similarly in 1973, Soviet war
hero Colonel Yefim Davidovich of Minsk found himself facing
psychiatric detention for having (a) demanded of Leonid Brezhnev the right to emigrate to his "national state," and (b) suggesting
that official Soviet anti-Semitic propagandists be tried in accordance with provisions of the Soviet Constitution.[25]

Solzhenitsyn, horrified by this latest Soviet harassment, spoke
out in his usual courageous and eloquent manner. In an open
letter published in the *samizdat* (underground) *Chronicle of Current Events,* the Nobel Prize winner denounced "the spiritual
murder" of such incarceration which he described as "a variation
of the gas chambers . . . even more cruel because the torture of
the people being killed there is more malicious and more prolonged."[26] Solzhenitsyn had not failed to comprehend the anti-
Semitic nature of such incarceration.

Again the question could be asked: What was the Soviet motive
in instituting this particularly sinister punishment? Though less
extensive than simple arrest, psychiatric commitment served
to enforce what Soviet propagandists had always implied about
Zionism, namely that it was alien, eccentric and perverse in
nature, driving its adherents not only to treason but to insanity.

Concurrent with the commitment policy, the Kremlin decided to refurbish the "parasite" or unemployment prohibitions of Khrushchev's day. In the early spring of 1972, a commission against "parasitism" was established in Moscow to find jobs for the unemployed. On the surface, this appeared to be nothing more than a typical welfare state maneuver for countering chronic unemployment, but in fact the Parasite Commission was basically an instrument for harassing Jews who had applied for visas to Israel and had consequently lost their jobs. Many of these Jews were scientists, doctors, educators. When they appeared by order before the Commission they were offered jobs such as street cleaners, latrine attendants and night watchmen.

Vladimir Slepak, a physicist of renown, who lost his position after applying for emigration, was offered the job of hauling gravel in a concrete factory. Failure to accept this assignment, he was told, would mean at least one year in a detention camp for unregenerated parasites. Because of a congenital weakness in his legs, Slepak could not accept the factory job and was ordered to trial, which, after two years, has failed to be held. Another scientist, Victor Yochut, facing a similar situation, accepted a job as a night watchman in a factory only to be told that the position was already filled. According to Yochut, he had been warned by the commission that failure to take one of the other jobs offered him would result in imprisonment.

Again Western outrage at the blatant discriminatory nature of "parasitism" apparently caused the USSR to ease up on the technique and revert instead of military conscription as punishment for attempted emigration to Israel. Indeed some of the same persons exposed to charges of "parasitism" would now find themselves facing the draft. In April 1972, thirteen young Jews—including Victor Yochut—were called up for immediate induction; one of them, a twenty-three-year-old medical technician, had previously been disqualified for service in peacetime because of poor eyesight. Clearly political, not military, requirements lay at the bottom of this new device. This became more evident when it was discovered that nine of the draftees had earlier sought permission for a public demonstration concerning exit visas, a demonstration timed to coincide with the

Moscow visit in May 1972 of President Nixon. Jewish sources
inside the Soviet Union reported a potential round-up of activists
in advance of Nixon's visit; the callup, they said, was but one
aspect of this stratagem.

Another aspect, touching upon military considerations, involved the "official secret" ploy. Jews seeking to leave for Israel
were refused permission for visas because, it was alleged, they
possessed highly-classified military information which they had
obtained in the course of their work or as members of the armed
forces. It is ironic to think that Kremlin officials, who regard
most Soviet Jews as potential traitors, i.e., Zionists, would ever
allow them any such proximity to "high state secrets." The
cynicism of this tactic was painfully self-evident no matter how
respectable and logical it may have seemed in Soviet eyes.

Apparently frustrated with the short-term tactics just described,
in the summer of 1972, the Kremlin think-tank devised a startling
device which would, if effective, gravely cut into the emigration
of scientists and educators; now, it was decreed, persons with
higher than elementary school educations would have to pay a
proportionate exit fee in order to compensate the government
for educating them. This exit fee concept soon became known as
the "ransom" or "head tax" of Soviet Jews.

Clearly the "brain-drain" aspects of emigration, as well as the
"Zionist" factors, had long troubled Soviet officials. According
to their own statistics—which are probably accurate on this
point—Soviet Jews "comprise the third greatest number of research workers [i.e., scientists]" in the USSR. In addition, "14%
of the total Jewish population in the country have a higher or
specialized secondary education."[27]

To keep these Jews from leaving, or to discourage them from
applying for visas in the first place, fees ranging from $10,000 to
$30,000 would be imposed depending upon the level of education
received. A man with Ph.D. status, for example, would have to
pay the equivalent of $26,000 for his lawful right of emigration.

Western reaction to the ransom of Soviet Jews was particularly
vociferous. Numerous editorials in the United States and Western
Europe denounced the tactic with such words as "slavery,"
"serfdom," and with comparisons to the Nazi ransom of intel-

lectuals and scientists, such as Sigmund Freud, in the 1930s. Leaders of both parties in the U.S. Congress were particularly incensed and initiated legislation that would limit Soviet trade benefits—including the "most favored nation" status—unless the ransom were withdrawn.

The threat of financial reprisal apparently was effective on this issue. In October 1972, leading American newspapers reported that Andrei Gromyko had conveyed word to President Nixon in Washington that the exorbitant exit fees would be—as phrased by the Chicago *Sun-Times*—"allowed to wither into disuse."[28]

The Soviet anti-Zionist switchboard, having worked efficiently and productively within the USSR and its major satellites, was activated around 1969 to connect its message to the West with an emphasis on France, Great Britain, Italy and, of course, the United States. Underlying this move was an obvious sense of respectable impunity on the part of the Kremlin propagandists; a justification of their effort based on the premise that this was no traditional racist, anti-Semitic campaign, but rather a purely analytical critique of a purely political entity: Zionism. The most perfect proof of the non-anti-Semitic basis of their campaign, asserted the Soviet propagandists, was the fact that the USSR was the foremost champion in the world of Jewish rights and that in reality Zionism "deliberately inflames anti-Semitism, while anti-Semitism stirs up Zionism."[29]

In Paris, toward the end of 1972, indignant French Jews and non-Jews alike began legal proceedings to prevent the Soviet Information Agency in that country from publishing its so-called anti-Zionist analyses which included obvious examples of pure Jew-baiting bias, such as: "Jewish scripture [teaches] that a Jew must rejoice when a non-Jew dies, and that it is better to throw a piece of meat to a dog than to a non-Jew . . ." As we have earlier observed, the French court, in a ruling with profound implications—not the least for the Soviet propaganda apparatus—was not deceived.

Soviet Jews themselves, in April 1972, spoke up at great personal peril to denounce a current anti-Zionist diatribe in an article *"Fascism Under the Blue Star"* by Y. Yevseyev—excerpts of which were carried in a West-oriented Soviet document entitled *Zionism: Instrument of Imperialist Reaction.*[30]

Yevseyev specified Hebrew Scripture as a blueprint for warring on other peoples by Jews throughout history. "Frequently in the Old Testament," he said, "extermination is advocated." He then quoted another "expert" named P. A. Holbach (an author whose works are published in Moscow) to remind us that the Hebrew God, as represented by Moses, always advised "violence and murder" as part of Jewish foreign policy. Jewish morality, based on the Jewish religion, continued Yevseyev, "has persuaded its followers that the Heavens themselves prescribe brigandry, murder, theft and that the Spirit of God conditions the ferocity of soldiers, inspires the rebellion of traitors and approves provocation and prostitution." Yevseyev, of course, disclaimed anti-Semitism, writing that "one of the favorite methods of the Zionist is to raise the hue and cry about any anti-Zionist action, calling it 'a foul act of anti-Semitism . . .'"

Having exposed the religion of Jews as the source of Zionist facism, Yevseyev—always protesting his innocence of anti-Semitism—then turned his guns on Jewish fraternal and community organizations, especially in the United States, which he described as "the more dangerous if less noisy Zionist elements . . ." One of his targets, and a favorite sorespot of Ivanov as well, is the B'nai B'rith, described by Yevseyev as both Zionist and fanatically anticommunist in character, carrying out "subversive activities" from its headquarters in Washington, composed of members who "most obey their superiors absolutely and pledge utmost secrecy." In addition, these benighted members employ "special signs and passwords as means of identification" and, of course, they have at their disposal "vast funds" and the guidance of something called "the intellectual elite." In short, they are the latter-day "elders of Zion."

Yevesyev was surpassed in 1972 by a new Soviet novel which appeared in the West, described by the London *Jewish Chronicle* as pushing "public anti-Semitism beyond the limits we have hitherto known."[31] *The Promised Land* by Yuri Kolesnikov, is merely hatemongering set into a fictionalized background concerning Zionism, the international conspiracy theme and the

Jewish "nazism" concept. One of the more lurid characters is a rabbi who operates a brothel, among other things, and is part of a "National Center" of "Jewish bankers and shopkeepers, factory owners and merchants from all ends of the earth," who believe that "if Adolf Hitler did not exist today, we Zionists-Beitarists would have to invent him."

One of the more eventful episodes in the novel relates how Adolf Eichmann, Hitler's chief executioner of Jews, comes to Palestine to make an arms deal with Zionist leaders and confesses to them "if I were a Jew without any doubt I'd be the most ardent Zionist." This idea elicits from one of the Jews the confirmation that "we and the Fascists have the same slogans!" Bringing Eichmann to Palestine enables the author to launch a turgid series of comparisons between Zionism and nazism; along the way, the alleged horrors of life in Israel are represented with vicious zeal.

The publication of this novel in the Soviet Union is disturbing enough, but it was also learned that *The Promised Land* had been serialized in one of the important literary monthlies of the USSR.[32]

The distribution in the West of materials such as these either in whole or as pamphleted excerpts is currently big business for the Soviet anti-Semitic operation. Most of this printed matter—usually well written in a variety of foreign languages—is published by Novosti, the overseas arm of Tass, which has offices on Riverside Drive in New York City. The propaganda takes many forms: pamphlets describing Jewish life in the USSR; anti-Zionist diatribes like the one in which Yevseyev's material appears; collections of alleged letters from ostensibly outraged Soviet Jews and reprints of articles that have appeared in leading Soviet papers and journals.

As the emigration of Soviet Jews to Israel became a focus of Western concern, such counteractive propaganda on this subject began arriving at the homes of American Jews and others who had signed petitions and protests in behalf of beleaguered Soviet Jews. The Soviet United Nations Mission in New York City became the headquarters for mailings of this nature. The method was fairly simple: Soviet personnel at the UN mission would cut the names and addresses of Americans from the petitions or letters received from them; adhere these snippets to an envelope with Scotch tape and stuff the envelope.

To what degree the Soviets have succeeded in affecting Western attitudes toward Israel and Jews remains to be seen. The notion of religiously motivated Jewish aggression may be tenable in certain quarters when offered in the right proportions; particularly receptive to such ideas are extremists of the left in Europe who regard Israel as part and parcel of a U.S. centered imperium, and who support the Arab cause ideologically and tactically. More surprising from a political standpoint are the right wing afficionados who—despite their denunciation of everything Soviet—have nevertheless, in many cases, chosen to espouse the Soviet anti-Zionist line. A particularly significant example of this appeared in the spring of 1971 in the pages of the *Deutsche Nachrichten,* the official party newspaper of West Germany's neo-Nazi NPD Party. In an article, "Is It Anti-Semitism or Anti-Zionism?" the following striking ideas were set forth: repression of Jews in the USSR is the result of government opposition to all religion and not the result of anti-Semitism; Zionism has organized a "fifth column" in the USSR, which threatens the present regime; the Soviet is justified in clamping down on Jews; since Israel is now under the protection of the United States, the Jews in Russia are suspect as tools of American imperialism. On top of this, says the right-wing NPD paper, Zionism opposes the "Leninist principles of a classless society." In adition,

> . . . the theory of the "chosen people" and the fact that all Jews consider themselves brothers also opposes the International Workers movement, and the international classless society as well. Zionists do not consider themselves citizens of their home country, but citizens of Jewish nationality whose major aim is to move to Israel.[33]

After spending several more paragraphs in apologia for the USSR, the neo-Nazi newspaper exonerates the Soviets of anti-Semitism once and for all by a piece of information—nonsense apparently originating with its own editors. Party Secretary Leonid Brezhnev, they say, is himself a Jew—ergo, how can the USSR be considered anti-Semitic!

The distressing irony of this particular article in the *Deutsche Nachrichten* points up a tragic truth: both right wing and left wing extremists choose to close their eyes to obvious persecutions of Jews whatever its source.

In the fall of 1971, Yakov Malik, the Soviet Union's ambassador to the United Nations, rose to address the Security Council in New York. All subtlety was cast to the winds as Malik launched into what was subsequently widely regarded as one of the worst statements of anti-Jewish bigotry ever heard in UN history. Speaking of Israeli concern for the plight of Soviet Jews, Malik asked: "Why did the Israeli representatives have to mention Soviet Jews again? That is not your business, Mr. Tekoah. Don't stick your long nose into our Soviet garden." Malik then turned to the Zionist-equals-Nazi theme:

> Mr. Tekoah was indignant at our parallel between Zionism and fascism. But why not? It's all very simple: both are racist ideologies. The facists advocated the superiority of the Aryan race as the highest among all the races and peoples of the world ... The fascist advocated hatred toward all peoples, and the Zionist does the same. The chosen people: is that not racism? What is the difference between Zionism and fascism? If the essence of its ideology is racism, hatred toward other peoples?
>
> ... Try to prove that you are the chosen people and the others are nobodies.
>
> ... I must only regret that some political leaders—including those in the city in which we find ourselves—under the influence and pressure of the Zionists, because of mercantile and electoral considerations, follow on the leash of the Zionists and support them by every means.[34]

Malik's reference to the stereotypic long-nosed Jew clearly placed his remarks in the ranks of the Nazi *Stuermer* magazine. Also reiterated was Kichko's "chosen people" canard and the myths about Zionist control of U.S. politics we have already observed from home-grown anti-Semites.

These clearly defined anti-Semitic sentiments could not be excused as the outbursts of an eccentric. Malik apparently weighed his words and went so far as to repeat them in the Security Council meeting, in what was described as a moment of calm contemplation: "Why do we all hate Zionism?" he said at that time. "Because of its racism. . . . As long as Zionism remains a racist ideology, as long as Zionist [sic] follows only one credo, one motto, the Chosen People, we shall hate it and we shall fight against it and its expansionist aim by all means."[35] Again, on October 21, Malik took pains to reiterate his "chosen people" theme, causing U.S. Ambassador George Bush to ask indignantly "that all of us put aside any temptation to use this hall to raise again the ancient plague of discrimination, anti-Semitism."[36]

One year after his "long nose" diatribe, Malik once more rose at the United Nations to offer an anti-Semitic slur, this time against the fact that the Israeli delegation was absent from a Security Council meeting owing to the observance of Rosh Hashanah, the Jewish New Year. "It's an artificial pretext," stated the Soviet ambassador, a pretext which would appeal "only to the naive." Again, U.S. Ambassador Bush was obliged to take the floor and denounce Malik's "trumped up charge against the representative of Israel for practicing his religion."[37]

Apparently the endemic nature of anti-Semitism in the USSR among many citizens and high officials, a majority of whom have come from peasant stock, makes subtlety an ordeal and requires Malik-like breakthroughs every once in a while. The West needs such reminders of the underlying malice, since the problem in the USSR runs very deep. A man who may be considered something of an expert on the subject wrote the following concerning the subject of Soviet anti-Semitism and its various disguises:

> Anti-Semitism was very much with us in the old (prerevolutionary) days and it's hard to get rid of. . . . After Stalin came to power instead of setting an example of how to liquidate anti-Semitism and its roots, he helped spread it. . . . Then after Stalin's death we arrested the spread a bit but only arrested it. Unfortunately the germs of anti-Semitism remain in our system and apparently there isn't the necessary discouragement of it and resistance to it.

The writer was Nikita Khrushchev setting forth his views in *Khrushchev Remembers.*[38]

The export to the West of anti-Semitism in the new Soviet disguises is at best a chancey operation for the Kremlin. The success of this campaign will likely be moderate so long as Western governments remain, even nominally, pro-Israel. On the other hand, the spread of what Khrushchev called "the germs of anti-Semitism" to the major satellite nations—Poland and Czechoslovakia—must be deemed an almost total triumph, serving not only Soviet requirements but also the scapegoat needs of the pro-Kremlin governments in Warsaw and Prague.

In the case of Poland, the export was readily received and easily integrated, given Poland's long history of anti-Semitism. Czechoslovakia was far less rooted in an anti-Semitic tradition, but the political crisis that ensued after 1968, with the co-called Dubcek revolution, demanded a scapegoat which the "Zionist Jew" easily became—despite the moderate historical tradition. Both satellites, of course, responded to Soviet manipulation in terms of style and technique. The updated *Protocols* for instance became commonplace reading material in both the Czech and Polish press. Indeed, Kichko's work was translated into Polish in 1969 at the height of the anti-Jewish witch hunts in that country.

Unlike the USSR, the two major satellites decided to solve conclusively their "Jewish problems" within a matter of a few short years. As a result, both countries by 1972 had become relatively *Judenrein,* and at the same time, each country had apparently overcome the crisis for which the Zionist scapegoat was mustered in the first place. Czechoslovakia, with the aid of Soviet tanks, had survived its brush with liberalism, and the student "revolts" of 1968 were largely memories in Poland.

The student revolts provided the excuse for a wave of rabid anti-Semitism which eventually reduced the Jewish community of Poland to a handful of infirm and aged pensioners. The crisis predictably began shortly after the Six-Day War with a warning from Communist Party boss Gomulka that "Polish citizens of Jewish nationality" refrain from celebrating Israwl's victory over the Arab states. Such celebrations on behalf of "aggressors," said Gomulka, were clearly unpatriotic and undoubtedly the result of subversive plots originated by "Zionists."[39] Competing with Gomulka for first place in naming the new scapegoat was a well-known Polish anti-Semite, General Mieczyslaw Moczar, head of the Secret Police, who was angling for Gomulka's job. The tension in Poland caused by economic depression, political rivalry and the reversal of anti-Stalinist liberalization was an ideal background for a bloodless but long-term "pogrom."

In June 1968, Polish students, some of whom were Jews, demonstrated publicly over the closing of a play which was regarded by the regime as anti-Soviet. Both Gomulka and Moczar immediately pounced on the "Zionists" as the instigators of this revolt, and the purge of Jews began in earnest that very week. Though only 25,000 Jews remained in Poland in 1967, these, according to party propaganda, were enough to be a serious threat to Poland's hard-won stability, especially under Zionist influence, for Zionism was to become synonymous with treason in the present campaign. Indeed treason was the "Protocolian" theme most played upon by party officialdom, including none other than Boleslaw Piasecki, a prewar Polish fascist, who warned the youth of his country to beware the Zionists whose foremost aim "was to influence intellectuals and young people to oppose the national interests of Peoples' Poland."[40]

Even as Piasecki spoke, the official Communist Party paper saw fit to vehemently reject charges that such "respectable" criticisms were anti-Semitic in nature. "We will not allow the Zionists to seek protection in accusing others of anti-Semitism," it said.[41] A similar theme was sounded by a member of the Politburo, later to succeed Gomulka, Edward Gierek, who denounced the suggestion that the party's policy was anti-Semitic as a "base lie."[42] Gomulka himself reiterated the familiar Soviet line regarding the alleged difference between anti-Semitism and anti-Zionism, stressing, as always, the "political nature of anti-Zionism":

> . . . regardless of what feelings Polish citizens of Jewish origin may have our party is decidedly against all manifestations having features of anti-Semitism. *We are combatting Zionism, as a political program,* as Jewish nationalism, and this is right. *This is something quite different from anti-Semitism.* It is anti-Semitism when someone comes out against Jews just because they are Jews. Zionism and anti-Semitism are two sides of the same nationistic medal. [Italics added][43]

Having thus invoked the disclaimer, Polish anti-Semites were now free to attack with impunity. Swastika daubings were blamed on Jews who, it was alleged, hoped to create evidence of anti-

Semitism by this action; Jewish loyalty was openly challenged in widely broadcast radio and TV speeches; collaboration between Nazis and Zionists was bruited via the airwaves; Zionists were linked with Stalinists plots. General Moczar went so far as to blame the Jews for causing Poland to fall under the Soviet sway after World War II and, in the end, the Polish Communist Party itself was criticized for its prewar "ethnic [that is, Jewish] makeup."[44]

Even the twenty-fifth anniversary celebration of the Warsaw Ghetto uprising—a distinctly Jewish episode in history—did not soften the official violent surge of anti-Semitism. Indeed the Jewish role in this heroic struggle was entirely minimized even as the Soviets had minimized the Jewish tragedy at Babi Yar. As the Warsaw celebration took place, the tragic observation of A. M. Rosenthal, which had appeared in the *New York Times* in 1965, seemed all too true in 1968. "Those Jews who died in the ghetto," wrote Rosenthal, "had lived their lives amidst the heavy stench of Polish anti-Semitism. That stench is lighter, now and again perfumed with guilt, but I believe it still hangs over Poland like a miasma."[45]

The miasma which Rosenthal had referred to began settling so thickly in 1969 that even Gomulka grew wary and advised his compatriots, via radio, that the anti-Zionist campaign should not create "an unfriendly attitude toward Jews in general." But the respectability of the campaign, now in its second year, and its scapegoating efficacy were too resonant, too successful to be reversed. The former Polish ambassador to Egypt, Kazimierz Sidor —who in 1972 became Poland's envoy to Rome—could not, for one, be deflected from his anti-Semitism. In his book, *Revolution Under the Pyramids* (1969), he alleged, among other notions, that the race of Jews had descended entirely from lepers. Moczar and Piasecki also could hardly be dissuaded from their *Protocols* themes, nor could the official press be persuaded to tone down the coupling of the inflammatory word "revisionism" with Zionism.

The year 1969 became one of decision for Polish Jewry, oppressively burdened as it was by the anti-Zionist campaign, which had now taken specific forms. Jewish students were expelled from universities; many were brought to trial on charges of subversion, revisionism, and even Zionism which, by now, was synonymous with treason in general. The newspapers kept up a barrage of propaganda that included blatant anti-Semitic cartoons and extensive quotation of *Protocols* verbiage—in short, all the time-tested Soviet techniques.

Faced with such harassment, economic and political reprisals, trials and imprisonments at the hands of the Warsaw regime, in the summer of 1969 many of Poland's 25,000 Jews sought the only alternative open to them—emigration. The government, intent on liquidating Polish Jewry, from the first it seems, eagerly compiled and issued short-term deadlines for Jews who sought to leave. September 1, 1969 was the first such deadline. Thousands poured out of Poland by that date to nearby Scandinavia, taking with them only what they could carry and paying, besides, exorbitant exit fees which reduced most of them to dire straits. By 1970 an estimated 15,000 Jews—even those of only one-quarter Jewish ancestry—were obliged to escape the Polish onslaught. An observer reported as early as November 1968 that "the dream of a 'Judenrein' Poland, long cherished by a wide range of Polish politicians of various ideological shades, is likely to materialize under the mounting brutal onslaught of aggressive Communist-style anti-Semitism."[46]

Yet though the Polish dream of a *Judenrein* Poland appeared to have been realized, the seemingly endemic Polish hatred of Jews, refurbished in Soviet style, remained insatiable. There began to develop in Poland, post-1970, a bizarre situation described by one writer as "anti-Semitism *without* Jews."[47] *Protocols*-style literature still found a respectable niche in Polish publications; the scapegoats of the post-1967 period, though safely emigrated, were still blamed for lingering social and economic problems under the new Gierek regime. Mr. Gierek himself, in the fall of 1972, added insult to injury. He publicly disclaimed an actual anti-Jewish campaign in the 1967–69 period. Gierek told reporters for *Le Monde* in Paris that "there is no Jewish problem in Poland" and implied that there never was:

> We have been, through the ages and right up to today, a tolerant people. The reason for this attitude is that history has never spoiled

us. It is not only the Communists, but the Polish people in its entirety, who have always condemned . . . the nationalistic initiatives
of certain Right Wing parties.

You are going to ask me then what happened in 1967–68? Something happened which we were least expecting. The decisions that
our government took following Israeli aggressions against Arab
countries were criticized by a large part of our population of Jewish
origin. This attitude was disapproved of by our people, including a
certain number of Poles of Jewish origin. One can therefore say
that in 1967–68, we were facing divergent political views concerning
the attitude over the Israeli aggression.[48]

Having thus insensitively whitewashed history with obvious
deceit, Gierek returned to his homeland whose government that
same week had eagerly accepted a cash award presented by West
Germany in memory of the Polish-Jewish writer and doctor,
Janusz Korczak, who was exterminated by the Nazis in the company of 200 orphans in his care at Treblinka in 1942. The $3,000
award was intended to support a Polish orphanage where, according to Israeli representatives of Korczak's estate, no Jewish children were accommodated as a result of the forced exodus of Jews
from Poland. The irony of this speaks volumes about the present
condition of Polish Jewry and the insensitive attitude of the
Polish regime. As the Central Council of Jews in West Germany
stated at the time of the presentation, "We cannot ignore that
while the memory of Janusz Korczak, who died in a Nazi concentration camp as a hero and martyr, is being honored [by the
award], living Polish Jews are still being discredited and facing
discrimination."[49]

By June 1967, the pro-Kremlin Czech regime of Antonin Novotny
was in very bad shape indeed. Civil disturbances, a poor economy, general disenchantment among the young, the intellectuals,
and those who still recalled the democratic traditions of Thomas
Masaryk, had caused Novotny to institute harsh strictures and
Draconian counteractions. As a matter of course, the Israeli victory was taken by the Novotny regime as proof that the Jews were
now bent on world domination and counter-communist revolution—and thus the source of all problems at home.

A wave of anti-Semitism spread through Czechoslovakia after
the June victory, endangering the country's approximately 15,000

Jews. Diplomatic relations with Israel were immediately severed; celebration of the 1,000th anniversary of the Prague Jewish community was abruptly curtailed; Jews were prohibited to meet with Israelis still in Czechoslovakia, even on religious occasions; names of Israelis of Czech origin were published, in the hope it would cast aspersions on their relatives at home; and throughout, the leading Czech papers shamefacedly announced that "there is no place whatsoever for anti-Semitism in Czechoslovakia and it will always be suppressed without compromise."[50]

As 1968 approached, the anti-Zionist campaign had become a national plague in Czechoslovakia, affecting Jew and non-Jew alike and especially intellectuals. Already writers such as Pavel Kohout—a non-Jew—had publicly denounced official anti-Zionism and Ladislaw Mnacko, whose books had sold over a million copies of Czechoslovakia, went so far as to abandon his homeland and settle in Israel, fearful, he said, of new anti-Jewish trials like the celebrated Slansky case in 1952.

Such events, along with the continuing deterioration of Czechoslovakian life, both morally and politically, finally brought the downfall of Novotny's regime. Many observers at the time believed his pro-Arab zeal was partially responsible for his demise and more so, its anti-Semitic quotient. There followed in the spring of 1968 what has been described as an "attempt for the first time in history to marry socialism with liberty," the so-called Prague Spring, or Dubcek's regime. With its ascendency, the anti-Israel campaign receded, and Mnacko—who had been stripped by Novotny of his Czechoslovakian citizenship—was rehabilitated. An Israeli flag even appeared in May Day demonstrations along with a banner reading "Let Israel Live" and plans were set under way to reestablish diplomatic relations with Israel. Once again prominent Jews reappeared in Czech life, in the arts, and above all in the Dubcek government.

These propensities were watched anxiously in Moscow and in nearby Warsaw, where the opposite attitude toward Jews was distinctly perceptible. Before long, dark clouds began to gather over Dubcek's Spring and consequently over the Jews of Czechoslovakia. Edward Goldstuecker, president of the Czechoslovakian Union of Writers and a deputy rector of Prague's Charles University, received an anonymous letter in June 1968, which crudely but prophetically signaled the theme that was to reappear with the fall of Dubcek. "As Zionists," it read, "you want to rule the whole world . . . we know for a fact that ringleaders of the latest events here in Poland are Zionists who are planning the final victory . . . your days are numbered, you loathsome Jew."[51]

The days of Czechoslovakia's attempt to marry socialism and liberty were numbered indeed. In August 1968, the Soviets invaded. As their tanks rolled through the streets of Prague, one could read in anonymously distributed pamphlets the ominous *Protocols* theme: "The words of the party's present leader [Dubcek] bear no relation to socialism. They employ . . . the tactics of international capitalism which in our country is represented by Jewry and its agents . . ."[52]

A month later *Izvestia* in Moscow launched the official scapegoat campaign denouncing Jiri Halek, the foreign minister under Dubcek, a Jew and, according to *Izvestia*, a Nazi collaborator who "wrote flattering articles for the Gestapo" during the German occupation.[53] Halek publicly refuted the accusation and the false information of the attack although he proudly acknowledged his Jewish origin. The newspaper countered by calling its original article an "innocent" mistake based on a faulty biography of Halek that somehow had come into its possession.

Soviet innocence was short-lived. Press attacks on Zionists as the instigators of the counterrevolution in Czechoslovakia flowed from Moscow. A political union between Israel and Dubcek was uncovered in these attacks and the blame squarely leveled at "many Jews residing in Czechoslovakia. . . . [who] occupy important political, scientific and cultural positions and favor the abolition of socialism in Czechoslovakia and the restoration of a capitalist regime which would favor Israeli interests."[54]

Leading Czech Jews, who needed no further warning, fled their country; others on duty abroad—like Ota Sik, the deputy premier, and Edward Goldstuecker—remained cautiously self-exiled. Dr. Frantisek Kriegel, however, a Jewish radiologist and a member of the Presidium was at home and remains to this day virtually under house arrest; even his patients are scrutinized.

The Soviet Union seems to have achieved in Czechoslovakia a

triumphant demonstration of its use of anti-Semitism disguised as anti-Zionism as "a calculated weapon to consolidate Soviet hegemony."[55] As a result, the ancient Jewish population of Czechoslovakia dwindled to but a few; religious and cultural institutions crumbled, and anti-Semitism became so rooted in the new orthodoxy that even with the dispersion of the Jewish population today' the press and media still continue to harass "Zionists" as the instigators of all domestic problems.

In November 1972, Prague Radio broadcast charges, once again, that Jews had collaborated with Nazis in war crimes committed in Czechoslovakia during World War II. There was "historical documentation," stated Prague Radio, that the "Jewish Council of Elders in Prague," during the German occupation "had its share in the genocide of persons of Czech and Slovak nationality." Once again, the cynical spectacle of "anti-Semitism without Jews" became apparent in a Soviet satellite; it seems destined to remain a political way of life in Czechoslovakia.

Soviet anti-Zionism was a welcome asset to the Arab nations intent upon the annihilation, political or otherwise, of the State of Israel. The unholy brotherhood that resulted from this situation placed the Kremlin in a dilemma. On the one hand, publicly, and especially in its West-oriented propaganda, the USSR proclaimed that it "has never been opposed to the State of Israel." On the other hand, it is *not* opposed to supplying aid (military) and comfort (technicians and finances) to those who specifically are opposed to the continuance of the State of Israel. Thus, the Soviet Union, which helped to bring Israel into being, now stands before the world as the chief supplier of the Arab drive to obliterate the Jewish state.

Soviet wrath at the time of the Six-Day War was almost immediately transformed into shipments of tanks, planes and bombs to resupply the "official" anti-Israel powers, such as Egypt and Syria. By October 1971, however, it was also clear to the West that the Kremlin had decided as well to sponsor Yassir Arafat, leader of the Al Fatah terrorist movement. Training in sabotage and terrorism was understaken directly by the Soviets, soon after, in Egypt, in Syria and in the satellite countries, particularly in Czechoslovakia and East Germany.

Analysts at this time attempted to explain this ostensible politicide campaign as the result of Soviet concern over China's competitive role in the Middle East; apparently the Kremlin felt it had to jump in before Mao took over as the world's chief expert in guerrilla warfare. Other explanations touched upon Soviet desire to bolster their orthodox Arab allies by deflecting Fatah terrorism from Cairo and Amman to Tel Aviv and Jerusalem. Overly benign observers even went so far to say that the USSR, by sponsoring acts of terrorism, was actually trying to bring about a Middle East détente on the theory that Israel would not be able to resist the attacks for long and thus would capitulate to an imposed peace.

Whatever the explanation, the USSR for more than a year, widened its role as the architect of Israel's obliteration by favoring both guerrilla and orthodox Arab military forces. But its efforts in Egypt particularly, and in Syria, were frustrating at best. By late 1972, the Soviet decided—with Egypt's apparent compliance—ostensibly to abandon its technical role as military advisor there. The "expulsion" from Egypt of Soviet technicians, however, did not lessen the Kremlin's military influence in the Arab states, nor in the guerrilla ranks. The extent of the Soviet arms commitment to Egypt and Syria—including the most up-to-date missiles, planes and tanks—was to become brutally clear in the Yom Kippur war of 1973.

At the United Nations, the Soviet ambassador continued to press the Arab and Palestinian or guerrilla cause against Israel. Palestinian extremists also found an opportunity, now and then, to stand at the United Nations podium and spew forth invective against Israel, much of which was in the pure Kichko-Kremlin line. In the fall of 1972, for example, Issa Nakhleh, chairman of the anti-Semitic Palestine Arab Delegation—the propagandists are an *ad hoc* nongovernmental observer group at the UN—sought recognition in order to condemn not only the State of Israel but the Secretary General of the United Nations and the President of the United States. Among his other vituperations, Nakhleh—who also found a Jewish plot in Watergate—reiterated the anti-Semitic slurs contained in the Soviet document later condemned by the French court. These slurs included the charge that Israel has set up "concentration camps for whole families in the

Sinai Desert," because—Nakhleh stated—"Talmudist war criminals . . . consider the Goy Palestinians as chattels—not human
beings." He went on to describe a fantastic world plot among Jews
to raise money for the destruction of the Al Aksa mosque in Jerusalem and the construction of a Jewish temple on its site. "The
Wailing Wall," he lied "was built by Moslems and is owned by
Moslems."[56]

Even in the face of terroristic acts by the Fatah's September
contingent, the Soviets remained committed to the Arab guerrilla
cause. When the Black September gang murdered eleven Israelis
at the Olympics in Munich, the huge Soviet team was ordered to
boycott the memorial services held at the Olympic stadium. It
was the only non-Arab team to do so.

This destructive attitude toward Israel must be regarded as the
chief threat to Israel's existence today, and as such is a major
source of grave anxiety for Jews throughout the world. The indifference of the Kremlin to Jewish anxiety on this score is best demonstrated by the fact that it continues to export anti-Israel materials to the West where Jews, like the ones in Paris, may see them
and agonize over them. Perhaps the Soviet thinks it can convince
neutral observers that its distinction between Israel (Zionism)
and the Jewish people—even the Jewish people of Israel—is justifiable. But anyone who has studied the Soviet's Nazi-like cartoons
or "Protocolian" propaganda knows that they are intended not
only as political criticism but above all as racial slurs. Indeed in
the Arab states, such material is widely distributed to give aid and
comfort to Israel's enemies, simply because it is so replete with
anti-Semitic caricature and innuendo. Thus the Kremlin conducts
its two-front campaign: worldwide slander of the Jewish people
and attempted politicide of the Jewish State.

The Jewish communities of Western Europe—unlike Soviet
Jewry—are not gravely jeopardized in the mid-seventies. Indeed,
virtually everywhere Jews are full and free and prospering citizens of Western European countries. Nevertheless, as in America,
there is a certain anxiety among Jews, a certain awareness that the
most basic of Jewish concerns are often no longer viewed by others
with sensitivity, understanding and moral firmness. More often,

in regard to the unresolved conflict between Arabs and Jews, for example, the attitude might well be described in Shakespeare's phrase, "a plague on both your houses." European Jews worry about a "neutrality" that includes a heavy dose of apparent unconcern with the continued existence of Israel—just three decades after the European Holocaust.

The "plague on both your houses" attitude was dramatically evident in the aftermath of the Olympic tragedy of September 1972. American Jews in Munich at the time of the Arab terrorist attack confessed a sense of alienation and frustration regarding public reaction to the crime. Of course there was outrage, and weeping was profuse during the memorial ceremonies in the Olympic Stadium. But these natural reactions were relatively short-lived; even as mourners left the stadium after the memorial, loudspeakers blared the announcement, in three languages, that the Olympic games would continue that very afternoon. The average European sports fan was largely unconvinced that the attack on the Israeli athletes demanded any meaningful response by the world at large; he saw it as purely a problem between Arab and Jew, part of their day-to-day hostility. Above all, he reasoned, other persons should not be penalized by losing out on their Olympic games.

While it is true that a man-in-the-street survey immediately after Munich would have produced overwhelming condemnation of Arab terrorism—indeed, the Arab/Palestinian image in Western Europe was probably at its lowest ebb since the Six-Day War—there was disturbing evidence at the same time of clear erosion over several years in popular support for Israel.

A Gallup Poll commissioned by the London *Jewish Chronicle* and published on November 3, 1972 found 60 percent of the more than 1,000 persons interviewed in the sample to lack measurable concern with Israel in the Middle East conflict. The 40 percent sympathizing with Israel was nineteen percentage points lower than in a similar poll taken after the Six-Day War. Twenty-seven percent said Israel should hold all or most of the territory it occupied in June 1967, as compared with 42 percent who thought so in the 1967 poll. The actual sympathy vote for the Arabs was a relatively low 5 percent, but far more significant was the clear majority of 60 percent showing marked disinterest—in a word, indifference—when it came to Israel. Such indifference is marked, as well, by the incidents of overt, traditional anti-Semitism that occur sporadically in Western Europe.

There is probably some endemic Jew-hating in the lack of interest expressed in the fate of Israel. More likely factors in Western Europe—on the official level, at least—include the often stated desire to improve and extend relations with the Arab world, especially with the oil exporting countries on whom much of Western Europe depends; the false belief of certain governments that by paying millions in blackmail to Black Septemberists they might buy immunity from skyjacking; and finally, a real insensitivity to the precarious situation in which the Jewish state finds itself—a peculiar unwillingness, much like that in responsible sectors of the American public, to take Arab threats and Arab policies and Arab behavior seriously when it concerns Israeli Jews.

The release of the three surviving Olympic murderers by the West German government to Arab terrorists who had skyjacked a German Lufthansa airliner was a case in point. This capitulation to terrorist blackmail, in light of the sorrow expressed by West German officials at the time of the murders, was viewed in Israel as a demonstration of almost cynical insensitivity. This same pattern was obvious not only in West Germany but elsewhere in Europe. In England, for example, the *Manchester Guardian*, the well-known liberal bastion, commented that "on balance it was right to yield to the Arab hijackers' demands."[57] West German public opinion polls at the same time, and a review of the German press, showed that most approved of the surrender to terrorism without apology to Israel. There was even evidence that the man in the street was becoming a bit impatient with "bending over backward" or the "special relationship" aspect of West German–Israel relations. For its part, the Bonn government officially described Israel's anger over the release of the Arab terrorists as a "passionate" reaction."[58] It is hard to believe that ten or even five years ago, West Germans would have responded as callously.

During a recent trial in Vienna of two former officers of the SS units at Auschwitz, public sentiment in Austria was perhaps expressed by a lawyer who said: "That [the Nazi holocaust] was a long time ago. It is time that we forgive and forget."[59] A Gallup Poll of Austrians around the same time showed that 58 percent of those questioned did not like Jews and 27 percent were unwilling to shake hands with a Jew.[60] One Viennese woman, speaking to a British diplomat's wife, stated: "It was never as bad as the Jews make out and many of them who were killed were really horrible people anyway."[61] The nadir of Austrian indifference came, of course, in the fall of 1973, when Chancellor Bruno Kreisky capitulated to Arab terrorists who had taken hostages from a trainload of Soviet Jewish refugees bound for a transit facility near Vienna. Kreisky gave his word to close the Schoenau Castle facility to Jewish emigrants en route from Russia to Israel. It was subsequently revealed that the suggestion to close Schoenau had not been a demand of the terrorists but had been offered to them by the Austrian government itself!

In France, in Amiens, certain newspapers and radio broadcasts reported the rumor that Jewish shopkeepers were engaged in kidnaping Frenchwomen off the streets for the purposes of selling them into a "white slave market." Soon after, in nearby Dijon, a hideous puppet with beaked nose and a devil's tail was offered for sale with impunity in the leading supermarkets of the area under the label "Jew." Business on this item was brisk until Jewish community leaders caused a stop to be put to it.

In Italy, defacements and, in some cases, arson of synagogues have been directly related to the Arab propaganda-terrorism campaign—and are largely ignored by the public. In Turin, late in October 1972, the defacement of a synagogue included a slogan reading "Viva Black September." Just weeks earlier in Padua, another synagogue was defaced with the slogan, "Freedom for Freda," a pro-Arab activist being held in Milan, and the synagogue was damaged by fire. In the spring of 1973, the Padua public prosecutor ordered the arrest of an official of the neofascist Italian Social Movement, Mussolini's refurbished party, and two other right-wing extremists on charges of criminal conspiracy and arson in connection with the synagogue incident.[62]

Anti-Jewish attitudes in Italy emanate from the Radical Left as well. Trotskyists and Maoists in Rome disseminate pro-Arab propaganda. Specific Soviet anti-Semitic material has also found its way into Italy—as it has into France—via far left groups, and in such quantity that even prominent Italian Communists have risen to protest what they described as the deliberate fostering of anti-Semitism.

Right-wing churchmen have also presented problems for Italian Jews. Early in 1973, for example, the Union of Italian-Jewish Communities was obliged to protest statements made to a TV audience by a Catholic priest named Father Pollano, the moderator of a program devoted to evangelical commentary, who had represented Judaism as a literal and materialistic observance and Christianity as the only true religion of the spirit.[63]

The Vatican often seems unwilling to take to task the purveyors of such sentiments, so clearly contrary to the specifics of ecumenism spelled out by Vatican II in the mid-sixties. It was perhaps not surprising, therefore, that during the same week of this broadcast, a report indicated that Professor Cornelius A. Rijk, the priest who had served commendably in the Vatican Secretariat for Christian-Jewish Relations, had been "quietly removed" from his office.[64] The report, which emanated from Amsterdam—Father Rijk's home base—indicated that the Vatican had been displeased by the Dutch priest's "too pro-Jewish views" during Prime Minister Golda Meir's trip to Italy in January 1973.[65]

In France, revolutionary left-wing elements hostile to Israel campaigned (parallel to agitation in the United States) to have the "imperialist" conflict in the Middle East replace the Vietnam war as a focus of agitation.

The theme of Israeli "torture, genocide and racism," was to become a resonant insinuation in the French Radical Left anti-Israel campaign for 1973, a charge that made itself felt even in non-leftist Gaullist circles—especially as the French national election of 1973 approached—and that obliged the president of the League Against Anti-Semitism and Racism, Jean Pierre-Bloch, to state at the annual meeting of the League in Paris, "We will never accept the accusation of being anti-Arab racists, simply because we defend the right of Israel to exist."[66]

The "new Vietnam" aspect of the Middle East conflict was fraught with dangerous implications for Jews and Israelis alike.

Israel was cast in the role of a U.S.-sponsored aggressor and imperialist, and the Palestinian revolutionaries in the role of the Viet Cong. The death in January of a Palestinian Liberation Organization official named Mahomed Hamchari in Paris, from wounds received when a bomb exploded in his home, was immediately denounced as the work of Israeli terrorists; the charge was made by far leftists, Arabs, and less blatantly, by a large part of the French press and electronic media. The revenge-bombing of the Jewish Agency building soon after in Paris, apparently by pro-Arab forces, went almost unnoticed in the local press. When Golda Meir arrived a few days after Hamchari's death, she had come, said the Radical Left posters, in time to witness the burial of "one of her victims."

By the spring of 1973, however, there were some encouraging signs in France. One was the ruling by the Paris court that the anti-Zionist propaganda disseminated by the French manager of an official Soviet newsletter was, in fact, anti-Semitic; another, the statement by the French bishops of the Jewish people's right to a nation of their own. Perhaps even more important was the defeat in France's March elections of several strong anti-Israel personalities, among them Foreign Minister Maurice Schumann. Also defeated in the French election was Jean Terrenoire, a leading pro-Arab candidate on the right.

Hopeful, too, for the future of France-Israel relations was that that Gaullist UDR party came out of the elections obliged to form a majority with other parties, specifically the Independents and Reformists, both favorable to Israel. French Jews were expressing cautious optimism, especially in view of the very minor vote accorded the extremist groups on the left and right who had demonstrated hostility to Israel. And buttressing their optimism was the announcement on June 28, 1973 that the French government had banned two extremist groups, one the neofascist New Order, whose anti-Semitism had long been overt in the pages of its publication, *Minute,* and the other, the (Trotskyist) Communist League.

Whether even such cautious optimism was truly warrented, however, was open to question when, in October 1973, in the middle of new Arab aggression against Israel, the French government dispatched yet further military hardware to Libya. The French Mirages that had earlier been provided to Libya by President Pompidou showed up—as Jews the world over had predicted they would—on the Egyptian side in the Yom Kippur War. It was unclear whether they were being flown by Egyptian, Libyan or even North Korean pilots.

In the summer of 1973 there appeared in *Stern,* West Germany's largest picture magazine with a circulation of 1.3 million, a series of articles whose publication would have been inconceivable a few short years ago.

In mid-June *Stern* unleashed what one observer described as a "violent anti-Israel campaign."[67] In the first of two articles on Israel written by Kai Hermann—a leading *Stern* reporter who had previously worked for *Der Spiegel* and filed an enthusiastic story about Al Fatah after spending two weeks with the Arab terrorists—the magazine asserted that "terror and force were used by the Jews in the compulsory founding of their state in 1948," adding that Israelis had "turned the Arab inhabitants of the country into serfs and appointed themselves as their leige-lords." Accompanying the text was a full-page picture of the bodies of two British soldiers allegedly executed by Jewish extremists in the late forties in retaliation for the hanging of a number of the extremists' comrades. The photo was captioned: "Fascism Had Many Admirers Among The Jewish Terrorists."[68]

In its second installment on "Israel—25 Years After Its Founding," *Stern* augmented the hostile view of the Jewish state set forth in the earlier piece. Hermann wrote that "Orthodox Jews find their state fascistic; Socialists find it a perversion of 'Prussianism' and nationalists consider themselves a master race." Describing the renaissance of the Hebrew language, the *Stern* writer added: "Only when they [the Jews] feel themselves threatened do they see themselves as one nation. Nothing but the tradition of the Bible united them and they had to converse in the language of the Old Testament, dead these 2,000 years."[69]

Such attitudes expressed in a magazine of *Stern's* mass circulation could be worrisome not only to the community of Jews who have returned to reside in West Germany but to Jews everywhere.

They bespeak an insensitivity to the Jewish state that is gross and callous just thirty years beyond the Holocaust; when they occur in Germany, they give rise, moreover, not only to Jewish anxiety, but to Jewish anger.

Equally troubling—and perhaps a root instigator of such attitudes expressed by the writer of the *Stern* piece—is the pattern of propaganda, agitation and terror instigated by some resident Arabs in West Germany in league with left revolutionary German forces, including such groups as the anarchist Meinhof-Baader Gang (now nonfunctional with the jailing of its leaders for crimes of violence) and the so-called Kommune I, a Berlin center of agitprop. In 1970, Kommune I had issued a detailed, thirty-six-page document by a young revolutionary leftist named Georg Von Rauch, outlining a plan for blowing up the 1972 Olympics in Munich. Von Rauch had called for "direct collaboration with the El Fatah and the Black Panthers . . ." in the scheme.[70]

In June 1973, in the latest of a series of reports by the Interior Ministry of West Germany, the number of members or active supporters of extremist Palestinian groups in Germany was estimated at 2,200, with the resident Palestinian population estimated at between 5,000 and 8,000. The official government report noted that "several [Arab] underground groups have expanded their local cells and auxiliary groups and created a net of contact points for units operating at the international level."[71] The report said that secret cells were maintained in West Germany by Fatah, the Popular Front for the Liberation of Palestine and the Popular Democratic Front for the Liberation of Palestine, among the most extreme of the Palestinian terrorist groups. Although the Bonn government, after the Munich massacre, banned both the General Union of Palestinian Students and its sister group, the Organization for Palestinian Workers, it is clear that Germany will continue to be the European center—perhaps the European "switchboard"—for Arab terrorism directed against Israeli and other Jews.

Will there always be an England profoundly ambivalent on the question of a Jewish national homeland? It would seem so, for nowhere in Europe is the propaganda battle between pro-Arab and pro-Israeli forces fought with more vigor than in England. Basic English fairness and decency mingle, on Middle East questions, with age-old resentments, paternalism and British financial and political interest in the Arab world. The latter, especially British petroleum interests in the Middle East, seem to have dictated in recent years a deliberate British policy of doing nothing that might offend the Arab states.

Thus Britain has joined several Western European nations, the Arabs and the Soviet bloc in clearly resisting effective civil aviation measures that would curtail terrorist skyjacking, at the same time voting with the Arabs on UN measures censuring Israel. In early September 1973, the *New York Times* reported that Britain had joined France and Italy, fellow oil consumers dependent on the Middle East, in pressuring the United States to alter its traditional support of Israel, this in the wake of reported political and economic agreements between Sadat of Egypt and Faisal of Saudi Arabia.[72] In October 1973, England was busy appeasing British oil interest in the Arab world by declaring an embargo on arms and repair supplies to the combatants. Since the only major combatant who would suffer was Israel—in need of parts for the British Centurions that are a staple of its tank corps—it was clear that British "balance" was tilted heavily in favor of the Arabs.

Typical of the so-called balanced English view was the *Spectator* editorial about the aftermath of the Munich murders, headlined "Cowboy Behaviour." Israel, asserted the paper, was:

> ... admired in the West for the courage and audacity of its army, and for the way that skill and hard work have begun restoring the wasted land of Palestine and enlivening the Biblical promise of a land flowing with milk and honey. Israel is also forgiven much, understandably, if illogically, because of the long and appalling history of Jewish persecution and in particular, because of the Hitlerian extermination. . . .
>
> But it is worth recalling that in the dispute between the Palestinians and the Israelis, it is the Palestinians who have been sinned against and not the Israelis: it is the Palestinians who have lost their land and their houses and their hope of a national home; it is the Palestinians who are the refugees, the victims. . . .
>
> If governments are to bring the present outbreak of guerilla or ter-

rorist activity to an end, then the governments themselves cannot behave like the guerillas or terrorists. This is recognized generally; but not, apparently, by the State of Israel. No other civilized state would respond to a Munich incident in the way that Israel did [with protective raids against terrorist training camps] and this is just as well, for if it became the rule of the states to behave like cowboys, the fragile international order which now subsists would be destroyed in the Middle East as elsewhere.[73]

Similarly, unfounded Soviet assertions of Jewish atrocities in the Six-Day War, of torture and mistreatment of Arab civilians and POWs, were echoed in a series of "Grim Reports" by Edward Hodgkins, foreign editor of the London *Times*, which appeared in that prestigious paper in 1969.[74] Hodgkins had gone to the Israeli-occupied territories in order to investigate conditions in the prison camps, and unearthed such "grim" findings as his preconceived pro-Arab bias led him to; during the Second World War, and from 1945–1947, Hodgkins had served as director of the Arab radio station, Sharq El Adna, in Great Britain.

Another prominent British journalist, Michael Adams, who wrote anti-Israel material for the Manchester *Guardian* soon after the Six-Day War, could scarcely have been more biased. Leaving the *Guardian*, Adams became in 1970 director of the Council for the Advancement of Arab-British Understanding (CAABU), the powerful pro-Arab lobby which, by means of such MPs as Christopher Mayhew, frequently attacks Israel from the floor of the House of Commons as well as from other respectable locations, the BBC included.

It was during a debate provoked by Mr. Mayhew in the Commons in 1972 that the anti-Israel pro-Arab line revealed its basic anti-Semitic nature. Picking up the CAABU line established by Mayhew, Andrew Faulds (Labour member from Smethwick), claimed that Palestinians under Israeli rule were subjected to systematic oppression. When Clinton Davis (a Labour member of Hackney Central) sought to intervene, Faulds told him, amid cries of protest, that "it is time some of our colleagues on both sides of the House forgot their dual loyalty to another country and another Parliament. They are representatives here and not in the Knesset!"[75]

Later, explaining his statement, Faulds compounded what he had proclaimed: "I did not suggest that there was any diminution of loyalty to this country, but it is undeniable that many MPs have what I can only term a dual loyalty, which is to another nation and another nation's interest." He then added that he found it difficult to avoid smiling at what he described as the campaign for Soviet Jewry, "organized and orchestrated by Israel and her friends."[76] Patrick Cormack (Conservative from Cannock) jumped to his feet at this point, condemning Mr. Faulds for "an entirely unworthy sneer," and added that the Soviet Jewry campaign had not been orchestrated by Israel or even by Jews, but that it was a humanitarian effort supported by many who might even agree with many of the things that Faulds had stated.[77]

But perhaps the clearest example of British ambivalence regarding Israel and Zionism is the liberally-oriented and prestigious Manchester *Guardian,* which has for years reflected a pro-Arab line that sometimes wavers into traditional anti-Semitic terrain.

One of the architects of the *Guardian's* current Israel policy is David Hirst, described by the paper as "our specialist on the Arab World," stationed in Beirut. Two 1972 articles on the subject of Jerusalem caused shock waves by charging Israeli "confiscations . . . and desecration" in Jerusalem after the Six-Day War, and "ignoble subterfuges" in obtaining more territory so it might fulfill what Hirst called its Zionist destiny, accomplished "by the classic Zionist method, staking a claim through the accumulation of *faits accomplis* and obliterating the rival Arab claim which is based on the abstract legality of immemorial possession of the land."[78]

Mayor Teddy Kollek of Jerusalem, in replying to Hirst's articles, noted that they were "outstanding for their one-sidedness as well as for a total disregard of the facts involved." This was not surprising, according to Kollek, since Hirst had spent only four days in the city he was writing about and was furthermore "armed with every argument and distortion available in the Arab world [and thus] unwilling to see anything which would not support his preconceived conclusions."[79]

Hirst responded to these criticisms by indicating that he had been in Jerusalem not four days but thirteen!—and that he had spent nearly three weeks there two years earlier. With his expertise thus extended by nine days, Hirst proceeded to report in the *Guardian* on the Black September terrorists at Munich in a way that clarified to all objective readers what Mayor Kollek had described as his "preconceived conclusions." Arab "terrorism," said Hirst, was insignificant compared to Israeli "crimes." He added:

> After the creation of the State of Israel, classical terrorism gave way to the outwardly more respectable terrorism, designed to cow and subjugate the Palestinians and their Arab sympathizers, which the state, with all its resources, can mount. Palestinian violence by contrast, is reactive, small scale, but easily branded as barbaric. We may, indeed some of us do, have misgivings about this kind of terrorism but we also condemn that of an Israel which was built on terrorism and continues to glorify its terrorists to this day.[80]

Reporter Peter Jenkins, stationed in Washington, D.C., added some of his well-known vitriol to the ongoing anti-Israel campaign of the *Guardian* in an August 1972 article headed: "The Zionist Lobby in the U.S.A." Jenkins's report criticized Israeli Ambassador Yitzhak Rabin's alleged endorsement of President Nixon. In ironic, even snide language, replete with implications of sinister Jewish political influence in Washington, Jenkins said 1972 "has to go down as the year of the Jews," regarding "racial and ethnic jockeying," and added:

> I gird myself . . . for the usual inpouring of abusive fan mail branding me as an anti-Semite. It happens every time I suggest Israel is less than blameless for the situation in the Middle East. Happily I shall be on vacation for the next three weeks, but that is not the reason I chose this moment to say that I find it distressing that so many American Jews, or at least their political leaders, are prepared to behave as a nation within a nation.[81]

The moment was chosen, Jenkins asserted, because it was an election year and ". . . nobody hopes policy to be rationally formulated when the Jewish question is involved." For this reason, both Richard Nixon and George McGovern "had to grovel for the Jewish vote."

The undercurrent of British ambivalence on Jewish questions came rushing to the surface in March 1973, after the tragic downing of a Libyan airliner over the Sinai by Israeli jet fighters who suspected the Libyan plane of terrorist potential. The *Guardian* published a cartoon reminiscent of the Soviet press after the Six-Day War; it depicted Moshe Dayan callously interviewing a corpse near the wreckage of the airliner and asking: "What is the purpose of your visit?"[82] The accompanying *Guardian* editorial, oddly enough, was less vitriolic than the cartoon. It called for an immediate settlement of the Middle East crisis to avoid similar disasters and hoped for reducing, "not ending," hostilities; for these hostilities "will not be ended in the lifetime of any Arab now rotting in his refugee camp."

The London *Times* viewed the event as a mere "incident" in the minds of the "defence establishment" who now control Israel, an Israel "that has been created not by idealism, but by war."[83] The Sunday *Times* went even further, calling for "a more fundamental review of how much Israeli aggression, at the cost of any prospect of a Middle East peace, the West would continue to underwrite."[84] Such a review was necessary, said the Sunday *Times* because of "a basic assumption of which Israel and Zionists around the world have long been possessed, namely that for her [Israel's] cause, the world must forgive everything . . . Arabs, in particular, must always be ferociously condemned . . . but whatever Israel does must be exonerated because Israel is fighting for survival."

In a much more sober analysis, the Sunday *Express* asked whether it was "really fair to put all the blame on the Israelis." The paper indicated that "it was the Arabs who began the campaign of terror against innocent men and women" and until the Arabs "abandon violence, until they concede Israel's right to exist, they must expect that violence will be turned on them."[85]

The *Guardian* reprinted letters from the public concerning the Libyan airliner crash. As the paper often does, it was able in this instance to reaffirm its own negative policies through the selected mouths of outspoken anti-Israel readers. One of them, a Mr. T. H. Fowke of Sussex, began his letter:

> I am writing in appreciation of the comparatively fair fashion in which you treat the Middle East conflict. Fair, that is, in comparison with most English organs of news and opinion. At least you give your readers some idea of the grievances of the Palestinians and the Arab States.

The writer deplored the frequent news stories about Soviet Jews and questioned why the public did not learn about other persons suffering around the world. "How about the Palestinians for a start?," he asked. The letter ended with what might be considered the theme of most anti-Israel opinion in Great Britain, especially as evidenced by the *Guardian:*

> Why is the central fact of the whole Middle East trouble so rarely pointed out? Israel stole Palestine and dispossessed its inhabitants. That is the core of the whole matter and it is being very successfully obscured by Zionist propaganda. The cause of peace and justice is not served by ignoring it.

The question one must ask of Mr. Fowke and many Britons of his persuasion is whether they grieve over the alleged theft of Palestine from the Arabs who lived there prior to 1948 or from the British who ruled there since 1918? And of journalists like David Hirst—who so correctly, as we have earlier noted, labeled King Faisal's repetition of the medieval "blood libel" as "an extraordinary outpouring of anti-Semitism"—the question must be asked: Is it any less anti-Semitic to tell lies about the contemporary Jewish state, canards based on nothing but pro-Arab bias, than it is to spread ancient myths about the Jewish people? Finally one must ask these Englishmen whether they seek, at this late date, to overturn the Balfour Declaration which gave the Jewish people a homeland.

World Jewry would indeed be distressed to discover that some British attitudes toward Israel reflect more than a yearning for the days of empire, that despite the current security of English Jewry and its representation in all areas of British life, including

Parliament, there are undercurrents of anti-Semitism in Great Britain not restricted to overt hostility to Israel.

Yet certainly an insensitivity to Jewish concerns, if not worse, was indicated by the midsummer 1973 decision of a London high court permitting the publisher of the *Oxford English Dictionary* to retain the definition of a Jew as an "unscrupulous usurer" or "a trader who drives a hard bargain and deals craftily." Rejecting the petition of a Romanian-born London businessman that the OED be barred from so defining Jews, Judge Sir Reginald Goff said the plaintiff had not proved he suffered personally from the definitions.[86]

It is an extraordinarily sad commentary on how far respectable opinion in England has receded from the postwar sympathy accorded Jews that a high judicial figure, certainly familiar with the Holocaust, could not concede the suffering over many centuries of individual Jews precisely because of such "definitions" as that put forth in this highly regarded dictionary.

While the immediate security of Western European Jewry has not been seriously challenged by the anti-Israel activities of most European nations and of Arab and pro-Arab forces on the Continent or in England, such is not the case for Latin American Jewry — some 850,000 persons comprising approximately 17 percent of world Jewry — which finds itself, in the mid-seventies, more than usually concerned with its present security and future viability.

Latin America, considered by the Arabs and their Radical Left supporters an integral part of the third world, has been the focus for nearly two decades of an intense campaign by the Arab states to develop stronger economic ties; to politicize the approximately three million Latin Americans of Arab descent toward a role in the Middle East conflict; to undercut the friendship Israel has long enjoyed in the Southern Hemisphere through its agricultural and technical assistance to Latin American countries; and to win away Latin American support for Israel in the United Nations. This campaign by the Arabs — carried out with increasing sophistication by Arab diplomats and propagandists in Latin American countries — threatens the entire Jewish people through its potential for harming Israel.

More immediately, however, it jeopardizes the Jews of Latin America through its deliberate stirring of anti-Jewish feelings in Christian countries where anti-Semitism has never disappeared and where unstable governments have not always been able or willing to protect their Jewish citizens.

The age-old phenomenon of scapegoating Jews for economic, social and political ills takes on an ominous dimension in Latin America, where more than elsewhere Arab troublemakers find ready allies on the extreme left and the extreme right. Latin America, with its vast disparities in the distribution of wealth and power, provides fertile climate for extremist movements. Jews, overwhelmingly middle class and largely committed to democratic reform, have become targets of the revolutionary left as an alleged part of the reactionary economic "haves," alleged agents of Yankee "imperialism" and its "puppet," Israel. And the revolutionary left, despite diminished organized influence in the United States and Europe, is a potent and growing force among workers, students, intellectuals and third world-oriented clergymen in Latin America. On the extreme right, long-time anti-Semitism in the military, the upper classes (and their children) and conservative Church circles has waxed and waned but never died. Starting with a more traditional, religiously-based anti-Semitism, extremists in these circles see Jews as agents of radical economic and political change, alleged representatives of "foreign" elements that foment revolution. Too often the Jewish community has seen such traditional anti-Semites play a role in government and has had to call repeatedly on the more respectable elements within government to adopt something other than a laissez-faire attitude toward the anti-Semitism of both the extremist groups and some of their own government colleagues.

In Latin America today, as elsewhere in the world, the anti-Semites on the right and left have largely converged; they often use the same themes—for example, a "dual loyalty" charge that can be effective among the profoundly nationalistic Latin Americans, rich or poor; and they have the same base of propaganda and financial support—the Arab states, operating through their embassies and missions, through the Arab League offices and, increasingly, through Latin Americans of Arab descent.

Worldwide Jewish concern for the safety of Latin American Jewry must inevitably be focused on Argentina, whose roughly 550,000 Jews have had to counter frequent outbursts of traditional anti-Semitism over many years. Today this history of endemic anti-Semitism must be taken into account in any assessment of the impact of anti-Israel propaganda by Arab and pro-Arab spokesmen.

Tacuara—more formally, the Movimiento Nacionalista Tacuara—and the Guardia Restauradora Nacionalista were pre-eminent among the right-wing, neo-Nazi groups that flourished in the Argentine in the early and mid-sixties, all of which had avowedly anti-Semitic platforms and most of which engaged in both anti-Jewish propagandizing and acts of violence against Jewish community institutions.

Both Tacuara and the Guardia were composed largely of upper-class teenagers; despite a period of relative quiet during the Onganía regime (which had little patience with them), they continued to concern the Jewish community well into the seventies. Many acts of sabotage and vandalism against Jewish institutions in 1969 and 1970 were traced to the Guardia, the perpetrators leaving behind leaflets claiming responsibility—and credit—for the attacks. Tacuara split into right, left and Peronist factions, demonstrating that its guiding principle was anti-Semitism, not politics; it continued to disseminate viciously anti-Jewish propaganda. A member of its student arm—the Union Nacional de Estudiantes Secundarios (UNES)—was following the movement's long-time reliance on the *Protocols* when he wrote in a student-edited publication:

> . . . At the Congress in Basel the fundamental motive was to obtain a site to reestablish a Jewish state as a point of departure for the subsequent completion of plans for a world government, ruled by the nauseating Code which is the Talmud.[87]

After the Six-Day War in 1967, Tacuara and its offshoots among the anti-Semitic youth groups discovered that they and the Arab propagandists were inevitable allies; after the attacks on Jewish communal instituions during 1969–70, in fact, the Argentine

Jewish community charged that Arab League agents were involved in the dangerous vandalism.[88] In 1971, representatives of various arms of Tacuara attended a meeting of the Sociedad Sirio Lebanesa in Córdoba, commemorating the Egyptian national revolution, a meeting subsequently described as "virulently anti-Semitic."[89] Among the public statements made was the following:

> Argentina and the Arab countries have a common enemy . . . international Judaism. The difference is that the Arabs have them localized, while the Argentines do not know where they are, because they hide.[90]

But Tacuara and the Guardia were by no means the only right-wing anti-Semitic groups operating in the Argentine. There was also the Legion Nacionalista Contrarrevolucionaria, an extremist reactionary and openly anti-Semitic group that emerged in the mid-sixties and apparently had some influence in the air force.[91] (The May 16, 1970 bombing of the La Plata Jewish community center, part of the wave of attacks on Jewish institutions, was ultimately traced to a right-wing extremist organization whose members were principally military personnel attached to the Seventh Infantry Regiment in La Plata; Argentine Jewry has reason to worry about anti-Semitic influences in the military.) There was also the Movimiento Nueva Argentina, an openly Nazi group, as well as the Alianza Libertadora Nacionalista, whose founder, Juan Queralto, announced in May 1973 that the infamous anti-Semitic group would resurface and continue operations.[92] Queralto, self-exiled in Paraguay for seventeen years, said he would return to Buenos Aires to lead the ALN, which teaches prospective members that communism is but one of the international movements seeking to "enslave" Argentina; the others, it says, include liberalism, masonry and Judaism.[93]

In addition to the traditional organizations, Argentina has had a heavy quotient of prominent individuals who have virtually made a career of fomenting anti-Semitism. Chief among them, perhaps, is Walter Beveraggi Allende, professor of political economics at the University of Buenos Aires Law School and a former legislator. Beveraggi Allende, well known both for his anti-Semitic activities and for his having been stripped of his Argentine citizenship by a legislative act that charged him with advocating foreign economic sanctions against Argentina, lived in exile for a time in the United States. There is increasing evidence, as we shall see, that Beveraggi Allende, an ardent Peronist, is back in favor with the advent of the Peronist government that took office in May 1973, and that he is playing a strong role in Argentine economic advances toward the Arab world.

Before this, however, Beveraggi Allende made a strenuous effort to exploit the issue of Argentine Jewry's alleged dual loyalties. In 1971 he sent a "public letter" to Jose Rucci, then general secretary of the country's large labor federation, charging that the union was in reality controlled by the "Zionists," who apparently exercised such enormous influence over "the economy, and the administrative power of the union, the judiciary, and the armed forces" that they were able to dictate the nation's policies, a situation leading to "total enslavement of Argentina by Zionism . . . a veritable genocide of our people."[94] The letter also alleged that Jews had arranged for the union's general strike, held earlier that year, to coincide with Yom Kippur to conceal the allegedly dominant role played by Jews in the nation's commerce and banking. Most outrageous of Beveraggi Allende's allegations, however, was the charge that "the world-wide Jewish-Zionist high command" was executing a plan to dismember the national territory of Argentina and to establish a "Jewish state" called "Andinia" that would include all of Patagonia, the southernmost province of Argentina.

The Jewish community of Argentina was inclined to dismiss the "Andinia plot" as another of Beveraggi Allende's mouthings until it learned that the charges in his letter were being widely distributed—they received front-page coverage by the Tucuman daily *Noticias* under a banner headline[95]—and were gaining credibility among factory workers, members of the armed forces and the national guard, all of whom were deluged with thousands of leaflets reproducing the letter.

Both as a mimeographed leaflet and subsequently in the bulletin of an Arab news agency, the Beveraggi Allende "big lie" made its way to all strata of Argentine society. Concern mounted in January 1972, when an attorney in Tucuman province, Exequiel Avila Gallo, filed suit in federal court demanding that the judge order an immediate investigation of the activities of the "Jewish-Zionist high command" as described by Beveraggi Allende. He urged that the investigation be pressed "with the aid of all security organs and intelligence organizations of the armed forces, federal and local police."[96]

Jewish anxiety did not diminish when the Tucuman judge ruled that his court did not have jurisdiction in the matter and referred it to the newly-created Special Federal Council, which was charged with jurisdiction over insurrectional and political crimes.[97] Nor did Jewish fears abate when, the same month, a new edition of the *Protocols* was brought out, incorporating the "Andinia plot." Beveraggi Allende was the self-admitted author of its lengthy introduction.[98]

There was some evidence who was behind the distribution of the notorious Beveraggi Allende letter. The weekly *Prensa Confidencial* reported that the wholesale distribution of the leaflet was financed by the cultural attache of an Arab embassy in Buenos Aires.[99]

Less openly anti-Semitic than the traditional right-wing groups, but far more worrisome to the Argentine Jewish community because of their enormous influence and potential in Argentina and elsewhere in the Southern Hemisphere, are the scores of left-wing groups active in university life, among the intellectuals and, increasingly, among the workers and the clergy—virtually all of them committed to third world politics, including support of the Arabs and enmity to Israel and its Jewish supporters. These encompass what was virtually the entire range of the Radical Left on and off American campuses during the heyday of the New Left in the late sixties and early seventies; but on and from the university campuses, the Latin American version has had far more influence, since student politics often control university life and it is often from university life that the nations' politics and policies spring. (Thus, for example, Chile's new ruling junta in September 1973 paid negative tribute to this power, announcing that it would replace all university rectors with military appointees;

previously, rectors had been elected by students, professors and other university staff members, and while elections saw bitter battles between leftists and anti-Marxists, the schools of economics and social sciences at the University of Chile had become what the *New York Times* described as "leftist strongholds."[100]

At about the same time, in Montevideo, Uruguay, despite elections restructured in an attempt to diminish left-wing influence, the controlling leftists won 80 percent of the ballots cast, choosing the General University Assembly and assemblies of each of the ten schools; these assemblies ultimately select the university rector and deans of the schools.[101])

The Radical Left in Argentina and throughout Latin America has become (as has its American counterpart) a virtual conduit of Arab propaganda. Thus Radical Left students and other groups, aided by the right-wing anti-Semites, have literally papered Buenos Aires with anti-Israel posters and placards (a feat duplicated as well in other Latin American cities). The magazine *Política Internacional,* published in Buenos Aires, has echoed the Arab left line that "Zionism, an agent of imperialism, is the principal propellant of anti-Semitism, which does not now exist."[102] The ultra-left publication *Propósitos* has frequently printed anti-Semitic materials put out by Arab propagandists, as has the left-wing weekly *Aquí y Ahora,* which as long ago as 1968 wrote with pleasure of the destruction by arsonists of Israel's Latin American Trade Fair site in Buenos Aires.

Of increasing worry, too, are the urban guerrilla groups spawned by Radical Left organizations. The Argentine parallel to the Uruguayan Tupamaros, who thrived several years ago and may again, is clearly the People's Revolutionary Army (ERP), armed wing of the (Trotskyist) Workers Revolutionary Party. In September 1973, Jose Rucci, the labor federation leader, was assassinated, the latest victim of a series of labor assassinations by urban guerrillas. Buenos Aires police said an anonymous caller, identifying himself as a member of an "Aug. 22" commando unit of the ERP, claimed his group had slain Rucci. (The ERP subsequently denied responsibility, however.) It was believed Rucci's death was in retaliation for a decree issued by the new Peronist government outlawing the Revolutionary Army.[103] The revolutionary left has apparently become disenchanted with the Peronist regime, which, after incorporating the revolutionaries in the coalition it used to win the election, spurned them in favor of a center and right-wing political grouping.) Several months earlier, hostility to Israel and devotion to the Palestinian revolutionary cause appeared in a flyer declaring all-out war on "International Zionism—the maximal expression in Argentina of strangulating capitalism."[104] The flyer bore the imprint of the ERP.

And finally, a severe blow to Argentine Jewry has been the disaffection of large numbers of its own young and their attraction to leftist groupings which espouse policies detrimental to Israel. A prime example of this took place at the September 1973 rally in the Luna Park stadium in Buenos Aires, the culmination of Argentine Jewry's celebrations of Israel's Twenty-fifth anniversary. Itzhak Navon, a deputy speaker of the Knesset, was delivering the main address when he was interrupted and booed by what the London *Jewish Chronicle* described as "5,000 young Left-wing members of the Zionist Youth Confederation." According to the *Chronicle,* a left-wing spokesmen

> . . . accused the local Jewish organisations of "communal bureaucracy" and said that he supported "a just peace [in the Middle East] based on the evacuation of all the occupied territories."
> During his speech, crowds of his supporters threw thousands of provocative leaflets into the stadium, proclaiming "the right of the Palestinians to self-determination."[105]

The March 1973 victory of the Peronist-dominated FREJULI (Frente Justicialista de Liberacion) coalition, the consequent election of Juan Peron's hand-picked candidate, Hector Cámpora, as president, and the subsequent election of Juan and Isabel. Peron as president and vice-president, respectively, brought a number of known "anti-Zionists" into the government, including Juan Carlos Cornejo Linares, who won election as a national senator for the province of Salta. Cornejo Linares is a long-time enemy of Israel and Argentine Jewry and a close ally of the Arabs; a decade ago, also serving as a senator, he introduced a bill aimed at "Zionist" activities in the country. In 1973 he was named vice-president of the Comité Argentino Continental por la Liberacion y Restauracion de Palestina (the former Argentine Movement for the Liberation of Palestine), which announced that in addition to having changed its name, it was extending its activities into.the interior of the country and to the rest of the continent.[106]

Moreover, the Peronist government has announced an "Operation Arab World," committed to improving economic ties with the Arab nations in the effort to develop new markets for Argentine beef, grain and manufactured products. Argentina also apparently desires to join the Arab states as a member of OPEC, the Organization of Petroleum Exporting Countries. Reportedly exercising a key role in the development of Operation Arab World—particularly in regard to the participation of some thirth-five financial groups within the Arab community in Argentina—is none other than Walter Beveraggi Allende, who is said to be working closely with Juan Gispert, secretary general of the Argentine airline pilots' union and Peron's "confidential envoy" to the Arab nationalists in Argentina. Beveraggi Allende visited various Arab countries to set the stage for Operation Arab World.

Somewhat later, a delegation headed by Faysal Noufouri, an Argentine Arab, undertook a six-week mission to Arab capitals on behalf of General Peron. Reporting directly to Peron on July 1, 1973, Noufouri at that time told reporters that various heads of Arab states would visit Argentina and many would soon appoint ambassadors to the country.[107]

But the Arab League states traditionally have attempted to barter their economic friendship for isolation of Israel by those who seek Arab ties (the oil squeeze being only the latest in a long line of Arab boycott attempts). Combined with the anti-Israel, anti-Jewish Arab propaganda onslaught in Argentina and elsewhere in Latin America, Jews have reason to worry about the repercussions for Israel of the new Argentine overtures to the Arabs.

They are worried, too, about the philosophic and social theory of the new government. President Peron has advocated—but at this writing, not yet defined—a *"socialismo nacional,"* which moved *La Prensa* to warn of eventual fascism and to forecast "very sad days for the nation."[108] The very term, of course, has special meaning for Argentine Jews and their fellow Jews around the world, many of whom lived—and many of whom died—under "national socialism." Its acronym was *Nazi.*

Thus far, the Peronist Justicialist Party has extended assurances to Argentine Jews that it will not tolerate anti-Semitism. Peron has expressed his friendship for Israel and Argentine Jewry and commented upon their important role in Argentina's development.[109] Earlier, Hector Cámpora had communicated similar sentiments in writing to the leadership of Argentine Jewry,[110] and there had been an editorial tribute to Israel in *Mayoría,* a Peronist newspaper, on the occasion of Israel's Twenty-fifth anniversary in May 1973.[111] Argentine Jews hope the words will be father to the deed. And with equal fervor they hope Argentine Arabs and Argentine Jews, who have lived side by side harmoniously for many decades, will not ultimately be sundered by the instrusion of Middle East politics into their country.

Such intrusion and such sundering are, however, the clear aim of Arab League diplomats and propagandists operating with apparent impunity and increasing success in Argentina and elsewhere in South America. Typical and prime among them is Colonel Jawdat Atassi, the Syrian ambassador to Argentina (and, since Arab ambassadors in Latin America are often accredited to more than one country, to several other nations). Atassi's outspoken anti-Jewish sentiments have brought protests from a number of quarters, including *La Prensa;* in 1969, commenting on Atassi's speaking tour of Bolivia, Paraguay and the Argentine interior, it said that at nearly every stop, the diplomat had˙

> . . . launched indiscriminate attacks against the Jewish collectivity as such, not against any determined attitude or person, but against "the Jew," which assumes a form of racism and can only bring as a consequence resentment and aggression among ethnic groups.[112]

The editorial in Argentina's most respected newspaper urged that diplomats limit themselves to their specific diplomatic functions.

One of the charges that the Syrian had leveled at Argentine Jews in 1969—and continues to make to this day—was that they were "financing Israel armaments with money stolen from the country in which they live."[113]

Thus in 1972, at a press conference in the wake of the Munich murders, Atassi attacked Zoinist organizations in Argentina for "poisoning the peaceful atmosphere of the country" and discussed the alleged distinctions between Argentine Arabs and Jews:

> The Argentine nation is solidly unified and the sector of the population of Arab origin is totally Argentine, integrated into the country. It has no political organizations except those of Argentina, it does not resist assimilation and the fraternal complementation of our noble Argentine people. It does not seek to influence the incidents of internal politics in ways that are foreign to the proper national interest to which it aspires and for which it works and fights.[114]

Atassi continued his public campaign against Israel and Argentine Jewry in July 1973, when he spoke to the Faculty of Philosophy of the National University of Rosario. Members öf the Peronist Justicialist Party attended, as did a delegation of key labor officials, Rosario city officials and staff and faculty of the university. Atassi resurrected Beveraggi Allende's "Andinia plot" in the course of his speech, and large quantities of anti-Zonist leaflets were distributed, some signed "Al Fatah."[115]

The campaign to impugn the loyalty of South American Jewry currently being waged by the Arab League has as perhaps its chief propagandist one Yusif Albandak, who was known as El-Bandak twenty years ago when he first started spreading anti-Semitic propaganda in the United States. Albandak's links to prominent anti-Semites in the United States were exposed by the Anti-Defamation League and the exposure led to his abandoning the country in 1950.[116] After holding various jobs, including work for the United Nations, the Egyptian government and the Popular Front for the Liberation of Palestine, he surfaced in Buenos Aires in late 1970 as director of the Arab League office for the southern part of South America. In 1971 he opened an office in Santiago, Chile—to which he transferred his base of operations prior to the military coup that overthrew the Allende government—and in 1972 he requested permission from the Peruvian government to open an Arab League headquarters in Lima. In Buenos Aires today, the Arab League office is directed by Albandak's former assistant, Abdel Wahab.

The Buenos Aires office publishes a Spanish-language monthly, *Causa Arabe,* that is often replete with anti-Semitism. Typical was the editorial that bluntly stated that the paper would continue to attack Zionism's "most formidable weapon," nonassimilation. The editorial charged that Jews' "refusal to assimilate wherever they live and their demand of loyalty toward Israel from the Diaspora" meant "disloyalty" toward the countries in which they live.[117] In addition, the Arab League publishes and disseminates a barrage of anti-Jewish leaflets and pamphlets targeted to specific groups within Argentine society that might be responsive to their canards. Thus a pamphlet entitled "The Tragedy of Christianity in Israel" allegedly "documented" assorted "atrocities" committed by Israel against Christian holy places.[118] Another piece included the wholly fabricated tale that the Israelis had "desecrated" the Church of the Holy Sepulchre.[119] (In addition to fomenting anti-Semitism among non-Arab elements of the Catholic population, the theme of alleged Israeli insensitivity or even hostility to Christian works and monuments is useful with the indigenous Arab population, which tends to be of Syrian and Lebanese origin and Christian rather than Moslem.)

The extent to which the Arabs have succeeded in this effort designed to appeal to the religious sensibilities of the predominantly Roman Catholic population is not clear. What is clear, however, is that the Arabs have occasionally succeeded in getting a hospitable reception from official church circles. Thus in October 1972, Arab officialdom—i.e., the ambassadors of Syria, Lebanon and Egypt and various Arab community leaders— arranged and attended a mass in Buenos Aires' cathedral, with Archbishop Antonio Caggiano giving the sermon. The mass was in behalf of "the victims of the [Israeli] attack in Lebanon"—the Israeli defensive strikes at terrorist camps in the wake of the Munich murders—and Archbishop Caggiano, much in the manner of Dean Francis Sayre of Washington's National (Episcopal) Cathedral, invoked the "eye for an eye" passage in condemning "this monstrous act of revenge." The *lex talionis,* he declared, had been denounced by Jesus, was not "valid in Argentina and should not prevail in any other part of the world." Archbishop Caggiano added, apparently with monumental indifference to the Arab terrorist murders of Israelis that had provoked the Israeli protect-tive raid, that "the Church rejects these acts . . . violative of hu-man rights and the laws of God."[120]

The Arab League organizes and assists front groups to carry out its campaign against Israel. In October 1971 the Buenos Aires· daily *Clarin* reported the formation of two groups of "free Pales-tine" supporters with Arab League connections,[121] and several days later it carried an advertisement headed: "Appeal in Favor of the Rights of the Palestinian People."[122] A similar advertise-ment was carried shortly thereafter by *La Razon,* another daily, which proclaimed that its signatories were "not against the Jewish race nor religion," but nevertheless asserted that they were "against Zionism incarnate by a usurping State that is racist, aggressive and expansionist" and opposed to "Zionist groups that operate in Argentina . . . utilizing the wealth and efforts of the Argentine people in order to sustain the aggression against the Arab people in general and in particular against the Palestinian people."[123]

The *Clarin* advertisement was signed by 600 well-known Argentine intellectuals, Peronist leaders and union officials; the signatories reflected the entire range of Argentina's political life, from the Rev. Carlos Mujica, a leader of the left-wing Third World Priests, to the well-known right-wing anti-Semite Sanchez Sorondo. After asserting that the "fight for national liberation of the Palestinian People is an integral part of the decolonization fight of the Third World," and that Zionism was being used by imperialism to achieve its objectives in the Middle East, the *Clarin* advertisement urged "Argentinians of the Jewish re-ligion" to join in resolving "this situation." It asked them to show their "solidarity with the just causes of the world" and "raise their voices in protest against the genocide of the Palestinian people."[124]

In addition to its inroads among other Argentines, the long campaign by the Arab League to involve Argentine Arabs in Middle East politics is beginning to bear fruit. (Its ultimate success, of course, would vitiate the propaganda arguments com-paring the assimilation and loyalty of local Arabs with the alleged "disloyalty" of local Jews.) Argentine newspapers gave wide coverage to the Third National Congress of the Federation of

Arab-Argentine Entities, which met in Mendoza June 23–25, 1973. Attending, among other Arab dignitaries, were Colonel Atassi, Arab League director Wahab and Imam Ahmed Abu Elila Kahlil, head of the Argentine Moslem community. The Imam called for the unity of all Arab peoples, asserting that such unity was necessary to "confront the enemy at whose head is international Judaism which intends to divide us"; his speech was warmly applauded.[125] A flyer bearing the imprint of the Consejo Federal Argentino-Arabe was widely distributed; among the causes it espoused was ". . . the battle which will liberate our country and the Arab nations from imperialism, cleverly managed by international Zionism."[126] Heartened by the Argentine meeting, the government of Syria convened a continental convention of Latin Americans of Arab descent, which met in Buenos Aires in October 1973. The First Pan American Arab Congress laid the basis for vastly expanded and coordinated Arab activity by proposing the creation of a parent organization called FEARAB-America to unite all national Arab federations on the continent. It also called for the creation in each country of an Arab cultural center; financial institutions which would stimulate trade with Arab nations; and a center of tourism and information.

The Argentine approach to the Arabs is paralleled in Brazil by the recent signing of favorable trade agreements between Braspetro, the international subsidiary of the state oil concern, Petrobras, and Egypt, Algeria and Iraq. Although Brazil has been a stanch friend of Israel—whose technical assistance has been much appreciated in the agricultural areas of the vast country—in recent months it has sought to maintain a studied neutrality in the Middle East conflict; its foreign minister, Gibson Barbosa, visiting both Egypt and Israel, reiterated on his return that Brazil wants to maintain "economic ties with Egypt and technological ties with Israel."[127]

Brazilian Jewry, long successfully integrated into virtually every area of the country's economic, political, social and intellectual life, is hopeful that this new "neutrality" will not come at the expense of Israel, and thus far, Brazil's ruling generals have shown no indication of abandoning the nation's friendship with the Jewish state.

There are, however, some signs that the Arab League propaganda effort—directed chiefly at Brazilians of Arab descent, who vastly outnumber the 160,000-member Jewish community in this nation of nearly 100 million—is making inroads. Articles geared toward a working-class readership have appeared in provincial newspapers; their apparent aim is to stimulate an ethnic consciousness among Brazilian Arabs, discussing, for example, the contributions of Arabs to the Brazilian economy and intellectual life. On the other hand, inexpensive pamphlets sold in bookstores deal with Palestinian aspirations, Arab liberation and other aspects of Middle East politics. They portray Israel and Zionists as oppressors and Nazi-like individuals. The Arab League recently published an edition of the *Protocols* in Portugese.[128]

Additionally, the two intellectual Rio de Janeiro news weeklies, *Pasquim* and *Opinão*, consistently take an anti-Israel, anti-Jewish posture on the Middle East and are a source of concern to Brazilian Jews, especially because a segment of the Brazilian press has begun to echo their line. Of concern, too, is the fact that the Arab TV program in São Paolo, which has traditionally limited itself to local issues, recently broadcast an Arab propaganda film; the change in programming was seen by informed observers as a prelude to new efforts by the Arab League to "awaken" Brazilian Arabs.

While much has been accomplished economically in the decade of military rule, the fact is that Brazil is today a military dictatorship in which those who have criticized, or who have been suspected of criticizing, the government have often simply "disappeared." Such repressive societies historically have not been good for Jews. Yet counterposed to this fact of Brazilian life is its much longer and much prized tradition of racial and religious tolerance, which would seem to militate against any imminent threat to the Jewish community. Whether Brazilian Jews, currently safe as Jews, are safe as Brazilians is another question.

For the Jewish community of Chile, at this writing, there are many unanswered questions, the most pressing of which is whether the military junta that toppled the Allende government in September 1973—assuming it retains power and is not itself overthrown by trade union and left-wing forces—will permit Jews to be made scapegoats for the economic, social and political ills that accompanied President Allende's ill-fated experiment in socialism. Despite the apparently normal functioning of Jewish community life at this time, the worry is a real one for Chilean Jews, more than a hundred of whom occupied key positions in the Allende regime.

Jewish community leaders had been ambivalent about the prominence of Jews in the government. On the one hand, the presence of Jews offered assurance that the Allende government would not permit anti-Semitism to flourish; on the other, Chilean Jewish leadership was concerned that right-wing elements might vent their anger on Jews, blaming them for the country's multiplying ills, particularly if Allende were to fall from power. One of them put it this way in the spring of 1973: "If things go well, everyone will say that is was very clever on the part of the government to have Jews in leading positions. If things go badly, it will be said that it was due to the undue influence of the Jews."[129]

Things went badly, and even before the coup, the right-wing attack had begun. *La Segunda*, a rightist paper in Santiago, in early August published two letters to the editor. One, patently defensive, termed Jews in the Allende government "renegades" who had been "expelled" from the Jewish community "a long time ago."[130] The other, more vicious and by a self-proclaimed (but anonymous) Jew, claimed that "those who caused the tragedy in Germany were exactly the class of Jews like" those who had been prominent in the government. The author recommended that 200 of "the criminals of my race" be hanged on the lampposts of Santiago.[131]

The anti-Semitic tirade was not limited to the right wing. On August 15, *La Prensa*, a paper identified with the Christian Democratic Party, carried a worse attack on Jews, headed: "Chile, Jewish Communism: Russia, Anti-Jewish Communism." The anonymous article blamed the nation's problems on "a communist cell of Jewish extraction" which had waged a "racial war" against the Arab colony. In the manner often used by those who seek to incite pogroms by portraying Jews as a foreign element, the author urged his readers to "fix in your memory against the day of final reckoning . . . that they have names which end in VIC, VICH, LEMY, BON and fifty more." The article was promptly denounced by Fernando Sanhueza, a Christian Democrat deputy and former president of the Chamber of Deputies, as "anti-Semitic phobia worthy of the best disciples of Hitler."[132]

Some 25,000 Jews remain in Chile, approximately 5,000, principally businessmen adversely affected by the economic policies of the Allende regime, having emigrated during the past three years. What is to be their future? So far, there is little indication that the junta itself will behave vindictively toward the Jewish community as an entity; in this regard, how it treats the Jewish former officials in the Allende government—i.e., whether it treats them differently from other former Allende political associates—will, in a measure, be a litmus test of its intentions toward Jews as Jews.

But in the long run, Chilean Jews would seem to be in a classic no-win situation. If they identify too strongly with the current military regime, they risk the wrath of those not now in power, particularly the revoltionary left; but in Chile, as elsewhere in Latin America, left-wing groupings comprise a formidable force, and insofar as they espouse third world politics, they are already antipathetic to Jews. On the other hand, if Chilean Jews fail to identify properly with the new regime, they risk further arousing the rightist fringe already demonstrably ready to blame the Jewish community for the failures of the Allende left. And if the junta does not itself scapegoat the Jews, it remains nevertheless that Jewish communities in Latin America have not always found governments ready to spring to their defense, whatever their frequent, and often sincere, denunciations of anti-Semitism.

Finally, as American and Jewish liberals, indeed as human beings, we cannot help but be appalled at the widespread reports of summary executions in Chile, apparently running into the hundreds, by the new regime and we cannot help but wonder how much confidence Chileans, Jewish and non-Jewish, can have in a government whose first acts have been so inimical to both the long tradition of Chilean democracy and the equally long tradition of noninvolvement by the Chilean military in political matters.

12

The
Radical Right

A decade ago, in the Preface to *Danger on The Right*, the authors drew a line between gutter-level bigots of the Smith and Rockwell type, on the one hand, and the political extremists of the Radical Right, on the other. Acknowledging that the Radical Rightists often had a "blind spot" about anti-Semitism within their ranks and failed to deal with it properly—and that professional hate-mongers were often drawn to far right political groups—we nevertheless wrote the following:

> The rabble-rousing gutter bigot, who combines political extremism with promoting racial and religious hatred, is often classified as part of the Radical Right. That is an easy error, for the peddlers of racial and religious bigotry who have sullied the national scene in the last thirty years have been, almost without exception, far to the Right in in their political thinking. These racists and anti-Semites, like the Radicals, believe the Republic has been and is being sold out from within by a sinister conspiracy, deeply entrenched in the national capital. But their view of recent American history differs again from the picture of the alleged conspiracy which is painted by the Radicals of the Right, who do not normally peddle race and religious hate. ... The bigots equate liberalism, socialism, and communism with Judaism. Often they chide the Radical Rightists for "pussyfooting" and for failing to brand Jews as the real culprits in American politi-cal life. ... The conspiratorial theory of the bigots is the same as that of the Radical Right, but with that extra noxious ingredient of racial and religious hatred.[1]

By 1967, with the publication of *The Radical Right: Report on the John Birch Society and Its Allies,*[2] while still focusing on the extremist danger these far right groups posed to all Americans, we reported a growing anti-Semitism within the Radical Right.

Today, the assessment of a decade ago is no longer true; the line between professional anti-Semitism and the tactics of the Radical Right has been blurred to the point of erasure. The Radical Right is no longer "pussyfooting" on the issue of a *Jewish* conspiracy, and the ingredient of racial and religious hatred is not something "extra" that professional anti-Semites incorporate into their predominantly far-right conspiratorial thinking, but rather something shared by both the lunatic and the right-wing fringe.

Differences do, however, remain. The professional hatemongers still give top priority to Jew- and Negro-baiting, using the issues of the day as a launching pad for their vitriol; for the far rightists, bigotry plays a secondary role to political action to thwart the "conspiracies" which dominate their interpretation of the daily headlines. But the difference in emphasis is diminishing, and in 1972 and 1973 the most influential of the Radical Right groups indeed used anti-Semitism for their own political purposes, and showed no reluctance to do so. Moreover, the Radical Right has a following in America in the seventies undreamed of by the hatemongers; it has elected candidates to public office, testified at congressional hearings and blocked progressive legislation. No such accomplishments can be claimed by the lunatic fringe.

Substantially ignored these days by the nation's news media, the sixteen-year-old John Birch Society, the largest and most active membership organization on the Radical Right, shows no substantial diminution in strength or in its determination to move America out of the twentieth century and into the nineteenth. In September 1972, Birch founder and president Robert Welch disclosed that the organization's overall expenses each month ran to $650,000, nearly $8 million annually, of which some 40 percent went to its payroll and 13 percent—about $1 million— for printing bills.[3] With a membership reliably estimated at roughly 60,000, served by some ninety paid area coordinators supervising 4,000 local chapters, the Birch Society claims to undertake 3,000 speaking engagements annually and to maintain 400 reading rooms (usually American Opinion Bookstores) that help distribute its flood of books, magazines, reprints, films, filmstrips, records and tapes.[4] The Birchers organized a "New Youth Beachhead" that began with a summer camp in 1970 attended by eighty students and grew, by 1973, to camps in six states attracting approximately 1,000 young people.[5] The Birch Society has claimed, probably correctly, that its efforts against the Equal Rights Amendment slowed—and may have halted—the drive toward ratification in a number of state legislatures. The foregoing is clearly not the record of a moribund organization.

Years ago, founder Welch was sensitive to charges the ADL made about anti-Semitism within Birch ranks—at least sensitive enough to remove from front-line positions within the organization several personalities who had been exposed as notorious anti-Jewish bigots. He had even written a pamphlet, *The Neutralizers,* calling anti-Semitism a diversion and arguing persuasively for some sixteen pages that communism was *not* a Jewish conspiracy.[6] But by 1972, Welch and others within the Birch leadership apparently made a decision to accept, even to endorse and propagate, some of the harmful slurs and canards that had been the stock in trade of professional hatemongers for half a century.

The focal point was a massive John Birch Society effort conducted during 1972 to distribute millions of copies of a paperback book, *None Dare Call It Conspiracy* by Gary Allen, geared for "a crucial election year"[7] and steeped in the blatant lies and half-truths that have characterized the recognized—and disproved—standards of anti-Semitica since the first publication of the *Protocols of the Learned Elders of Zion.*

For several years Welch has been promulgating the esoteric notion that a powerful, secret group, which he calls the "Insiders," actually plans the major policies and events that control the lives of individuals and of nations. Their alleged goal is the achievement of socialism or communism, country by country, until a dictatorial "world government" controlled by the "Insiders" finally takes over everything. In this vision, the communist conspiracy is merely a controlled part—perhaps even an unsuspecting part—of the larger, deeper conspiracy. So, too, are the fundamental political and financial institutions of the West.

Gary Allen's book is a 141-page polemic parading as "history" which seeks to substantiate the Welch theory. It revives outworn and discredited anti-Jewish themes—the "international bankers," most of them Jewish, are of course the true insiders among the "Insiders"—and cites a number of anti-Semitic sources, including czarist émigrés whose anti-Semitic diatribes had been put to profitable use by American hatemongers in the thirties. In labeling the alleged secret plotters as "Insiders," theorist Welch and author Allen employed a term that, in some places at least, is vague enough to allow devotees of the various conspiracy theories to supply their own casts of diabolical plotters. But there is enough "naming names" (Jewish names) and other anti-Semitic innuendo in Allen's book—despite a disclaimer he apparently felt necessary—to lead the unsure or the uninitiated down the deceitful paths of the hatemongers.

Robert Welch announced the Birch Society campaign for mass distribution of the book in the March 1972 issue of the *Bulletin,* the vehicle through which members receive their instructions for new activities. Welch wrote:

> You are about to see spreading over the American scene a gigantic flare from educational materials called forth by the emotions and events of a crucial election year. . . . And what has made this possible?

Welch supplied the answer:

> One pocketsize paperbound book, Gary Allen's *None Dare Call It Conspiracy,* will almost certainly reach a volume of over fifteen million copies. Hundreds of thousands of tabloids have already been distributed in New Hampshire, and that is only a beginning. . . .

By the beginning of 1973, sales were already well into the millions.

The crude anti-Semitic implications in Gary Allen's cry of "conspiracy" were not lost on *some* among the Birch Society's membership at least. When the conservative Manchester (N.H.) *Union Leader* published an editorial calling the book "anti-Semitic nonsense,"[8] the paper received a number of inflammatory responses from Birchites. One, for example, denied that the Birch Society was anti-Semitic but then declared that "to deny that the Conspiracy is being directed by international bankers—Jews mainly . . . is being naive in the extreme, as well as totally ignorant of the depth and extent of the REAL conspiracy."[9] Welch, incensed by criticism from conservatives such as William Loeb, publisher of the New Hampshire paper, in the August 1972 Birch *Bulletin* bitterly rebuked his critics on the right—Loeb, Major Edgar Bundy of the Church League of America, and the periodical *Human Events,* which had refused to accept advertising for Allen's book. Yet despite the criticism, Welch continued massive promotion of *None Dare Call It Conspiracy,* and the Society began to use the book—as it has used other books, lecture tours and various front-group activities through the years—as a mechanism for recruiting new members and as the opening wedge for the distribution of other propaganda. Two Birch chapters in California received the following advisory from a chapter leader:

> One member in Southern California has just recently donated $10,000 for the purchase of 40,000 copies of this book to be distributed throughout the thirteen western states. He purchased these books through The John Birch Society, rather than directly from the publisher, because he was assured every single person receiving one of these 40,000 books would have a follow-up contact from members.[10]

The John Birch Society was not the sole vehicle for promoting Allen's book or exploiting its anti-Jewish conspiracy theory. Designed as an election-year special, the book received wide distribution through the American Party, originally the party of Alabama Governor George Wallace but well before the election virtually under the total control of Birch Society activists. Gary Allen was himself the California co-chairman of the presidential campaign of Representative John Schmitz, the party's eventual candidate.

Schmitz had written the introduction to *None Dare Call It Conspiracy*. He later serialized it in the *Congressional Record*,[11] and now he used it as the chief propaganda weapon of his campaign. In June, before he had become the candidate, Schmitz was asked by the ADL "in the name of human decency and honest scholarship" to withdraw his endorsement of the anti-Semitic book and repudiate its contents.[12] Congressman Schmitz not only declined to repudiate the book but attacked the ADL for even approaching him, and he inserted both the request and his reply, which contained false statements about the ADL, into the *Congressional Record*.[13]

Schmitz and his running mate, columnist Thomas J. Anderson (who was to become chairman of the American Party in April 1973), were both members of the John Birch Society's ruling National Council. With this party leadership, with Birch members in key positions in its state and local structures, and with the party's three heaviest contributors being Birchites, Robert Welch's Society dominated the American Party campaign.

After accepting the nomination, Schmitz began advancing a conspiracy theory of history identical to that promulgated by the Birch apparatus. When questioned by reporters at the American Party convention about his theory that both the Republican and Democratic parties were part of a "conspiracy," Schmitz referred them to Allen's book.[14]

Listed on the ballot in thirty-two states, the American Party garnered 1,080,541 votes in November 1972. Unhappily, Americans accepted with almost total equanimity the phenomenon of the American Party and its election day achievement; nobody was "shook up" by it. There were few meaningful critical press editorials, no important adverse comment from church leaders, no real protest from any organized nonsectarian quarter. This kind of reaction or, rather, nonreaction, to such political bigotry is a new and disturbing phenomenon.

A major thrust of some of the more radical elements on the right, often as a direct consequence of broader anti-Semitic attitudes, is seen in the increasing attacks on the policies (or even the very existence) of the State of Israel, on U.S. sympathy for Israel, or particularly on the support of Israel by American Jews.

While some on America's right—notably the Buckley conservatives and some religious fundamentalists such as the Revs. Billy James Hargis and Carl McIntire—have been moderate and almost friendly on Middle East issues, other rightists have virtually carbon-copied the communists and other revolutionary leftists—allegedly their enemies—in denouncing Israel (while blinking Arab terrorism) and in blaming "Zionists" for the world's troubles. Even where opposition to Israel has been couched in broadly legitimate language, there has often been an undercurrent of seamy innuendo—charges, for example, that a "Zionist-controlled" news media or a Zionist-fearing U.S. Congress is anxious for American soldiers to "die for Israel" in order to further the objectives of an imagined conspiracy.

At its 1972 national convention in Louisville, the American Party adopted a plank for its platform demanding "that: America declare its neutrality in the Middle East and that it repudiate any commitment expressed or implied to send U.S. troops to participate in the Middle East conflict" (as if there had been any such commitment).[15]

An additional part of the plank of the American Party in California that was proposed for adoption by the national convention but was apparently later eliminated, called for the prohibition of "arms sales to belligerents, private loans by American banking interests to warring powers and sales by foreign governments of their bonds in the U.S." When a Connecticut delegate labeled the last "frankly anti-Semitic" during the platform debate, he was shouted down.[16]

On a radio talk show during the subsequent campaign, American Party presidential candidate Schmitz declared: "We are the only party that is neutral in the Middle East. The Democrats and Republicans are virtually committing American boys to fight for Israel."[17] Commenting that "I've got Jewish supporters" (perhaps some of his best friends), Schmitz added: "What's wrong with Saudi Arabia as an ally? What's wrong with Jordan and Lebanon as allies? . . . If arms to Israel meant losing Jordan, Lebanon and Saudi Arabia, I wouldn't think it would be worth it." At another time, Schmitz remarked, "The doves are angry because we are shooting Communists instead of Arabs."[18]

Schmitz's vice-presidential running mate, fellow Birchite Tom

Anderson, was even more vitriolic. Writing on the American Party's Middle East position, Anderson rambled: "Liberals are still obsessed with that maniac, Adolph Hitler, who exterminated six million Jews. Or was it really two million?"

In another column on the Middle East, Anderson wrote:

> Why are our politicians and press so overwhelmingly pro-Israel? Simple. How many American Arab voters are there? And how many Arabs own newspapers, magazines, or radio-TV stations in America? . . .
>
> The answer to the Arab-Israeli conflict is simple: the Israelis should give back to the Arabs the homes, the land, the businesses they have stolen from them.
>
> . . . It's hard for me to believe that the Bible means for the Jews— if the present Israelis are really the Jews described in the Bible— to steal Israel from the Arabs. Even our "Urban Renewal" or TVA are not quite that bad.[19]

Anderson echoed some of the country's most extreme professional anti-Semites, and perpetuated myths that have nothing to do with Middle East issues—namely, that Hitler did not really exterminate six million Jews; that Jews control America's media and its politicians; that the Jews of today are not the Jews of the Bible.

Another propagandist of the Radical Right who has broadened the attack on Israel to include world Jewry is Dan Smoot, the Dallas-based writer whose *Dan Smoot Report*, once issued as an independent weekly, is now a periodic feature of the John Birch Society publication, *Review of the News*. Smoot's assaults on "Zionism" began in four consecutive issues of his *Report* in 1969 devoted to a fevered history of the birth of the State of Israel, three Arab-Israeli wars, and underlying Middle East issues.[20] The articles reflected the general thrust of the Arab propaganda effort of three decades and an emphasis on alleged Jewish "power" in the United States.

Smoot blamed all the troubles of the Middle East on Zionism, which he called a political movement "whose purpose was to colonize Palestine with alien Jews" who were to steal the land from the Arabs. He assailed the "wealth, power and influence of world Jewry, especially in America," and he charged that "Jewish pressures" and "the powerful influence of Jews" had dominated the development of U.S. policy.

Smoot proposed the elimination of the State of Israel and the creation of "a new political state with dominion over the entire area," a state which would be "secular" and would be called Palestine. In the meantime he proposed American "neutrality" in Middle East conflicts and the termination of all aid to Israel, even in the face of massive Soviet support of the Arabs. Smoot's proposals were indistinguishable from those of the Arabs, the pro-Arab revolutionary left or the anti-Semitic hate fringe.

The twin Radical Right thrusts which contain anti-Semitism — the attacks on "Zionists" and the charges of "international banker" conspiracies — are boldly manifest in the propaganda and activities of Liberty Lobby, the Washington-based far right political pressure group which for about a decade has been one of the more significant of extremist organizations. (Since the mid-1960s its *Liberty Letter* has been able to boast the largest circulation of any Radical Right periodical in America.)

Liberty Lobby was founded in the late fifties by Willis A. Carto, who is still officially its treasurer and actually its behind-the-scenes boss. Carto, who had been a prime mover in *RIGHT*, a blatantly anti-Jewish newsletter published in San Francisco during the 1950s, brought to his new organization's Board of Policy a number of professional bigots, including Ned Touchstone, Joseph P. Kamp, W. Henry MacFarland, Richard Cotten and the late Kenneth Goff. But for years Liberty Lobby managed to parade under a banner of respectable radical "conservatism" and actually enlisted the support and cooperation of a number of U.S. congressmen and senators. Carto, a professed admirer of Adolph Hitler, remained a silent figure deep in the background of Liberty Lobby activities, leaving the front office and the rostrum to "Chairman" Curtis B. Dall, a retired Army colonel and former son-in-law of President Franklin D. Roosevelt.

In the meantime, Carto, a tireless organizer, built up a network of loosely affiliated publications and organizations dispensing openly anti-Jewish propaganda of varying degrees of virulence.

These have included the "new" *American Mercury,* the *Washington Observer Newsletter,* Noontide Press (a publisher of racist and anti-Semitic books), the Nordic-racist *Western Destiny* (now defunct), and the openly neo-Nazi National Youth Alliance and its successor, Youth Action.

Liberty Lobby continued to pursue its "conservative" political goals. It took a firm stand critical of Israel but one which avoided the outspoken anti-Jewish attitudes of those less savory groups in the Carto complex.

As the 1970s dawned, however, Liberty Lobby began to take off all the wraps. The significant event was the publication by the organization of an anti-Israel, allegedly "pro-American" booklet entitled *America First.*[21] Under the pretext that it is a plea for American "neutrality" in the Middle East, *America First* not only is admittedly "harsher against Israel" than against the Arabs, but is an anti-Semitic broadside that unhesitatingly defames all Jews of the past and the present.

The book details allegations of a "world Zionist conspiracy" in terms reminiscent of the *Protocols.* Israel, it asserts, is a "bastard-state," and "the product of the political machinations of one political group—the Zionists—made up largely of atheistic Jews." The "Zionists" control the U.S. Congress and the nation's radio and television broadcasting facilities. "In Washington today," says the book, "Capitol Hill simply reeks with Zionist lobbyists. We hear Congressmen and U.S. Senators mouthing statements written for them by Jewish propagandists."

But the Jews of all times have been equally guilty conspirators according to the Liberty Lobby view of history. Most Americans, the book asserts, are "unaware that Hitler's hostility toward the Jews originated in the Zionist leaders having pushed the United States into World War I on the side of the allies." And as for World War II, it complains that "those who singled out the Jews for their part in getting us into the war were scorned and ridiculed." And going back through history, "Almost all of the early Bolsheviks were Jewish." Finally, "The Jews rejected their Messiah, even had him crucified."

With the injection of raw anti-Semitism into its ideological line, Liberty Lobby has adopted a more radical pro-Arab position on the Middle East, a stance strikingly similar to that of groups on the far left—strange comrades indeed for the "anti-Communist" Lobbyites. In April 1973, the Lobby sponsored a two-week "fact-finding" tour of the Middle East. All the "facts" were to be found in Arab countries, the stops on the tour being Egypt, Jordan, Syria, Iraq, Lebanon, Bahrein and Saudi Arabia.

Liberty Lobby has been carrying on a scare campaign—almost identical to that undertaken by the Radical Left—suggesting that the world "conspirators" are planning to send American troops to the Middle East. "YOUR SON COULD BE DRAFTED TO FIGHT FOR ISRAEL ... and probably will be, unless some changes are made immediately!" wrote Chairman Curtis B. Dall in a recent undated letter to members. He continued with the charge that "some highly professional propagandists (many of them holding dual citizenship in both the United States and Israel) try to misrepresent and downgrade anyone who dares to speak up for America."

On his "Liberty Line" recorded telephone message of July 31, 1972, Dall assailed presidential candidates Nixon and McGovern for supporting the integrity of the State of Israel. "Just what does 'integrity' mean?" he asked, and continued: "Does this mean the two candidates favor ordering Christian soldiers to fight, perhaps die, in furthering the political objectives of the Zionists?"

Given Liberty Lobby's blatant anti-Semitic leanings, it was not surprising that the organization—along with an assortment of both Radical Right and Radical Left groups—should go after Henry Kissinger, their campaign swinging into high gear in September 1973 with Kissinger's nomination as secretary of state. The Lobby had earlier accused the then presidential advisor of acting "Svengali to Nixon's all-too-willing Trilby," and had repeatedly referred to Kissinger's "foreign" birth.[22] It pulled no punches, however, in a September flyer (accompanied by diatribes over its daily radio program, "This Is Liberty Lobby," heard by more than a million listeners on eighty-one stations in twenty-eight states) that accused the nominee of being "pro-world government" and claimed his designation was "a slap in the face of the oil rich Arabs who know where his loyalties really lie."[23]

By mid-September there were reports that a flood of hate mail opposing Kissinger was pouring into congressional offices, particularly those of the Senate Foreign Relations Committee, stimulated by Liberty Lobby and other extremist groups.[24] Nevertheless, Lobby Chairman Dall was permitted to testify at the confirmation hearing for Kissinger, calling for an investigation of Kissinger's alleged involvement with "secret" groups and complaining about the "widespread and extremely vocal concern for the 'human rights' of certain favored minorities in the Soviet Union."[25]

Also testifying was Nicholas C. Camerota, representing the formerly Willis Carto-affiliated National Youth Alliance. Camerota offered the senate hearing the wisdom that Dr. Kissinger "as a Jew cannot help but feel a personal stake in the fortunes of Israel" and testified that his confirmation would not meet "the best interests of the majority of white Americans."[26]

Astonishingly, none of the senators present thought it necessary to rebuke either Dall or Camerota for their injection of outright bigotry into the hearings; both, like other witnesses, were merely thanked for their testimony. Newspaper accounts said the three senators present—John J. Sparkman, George D. Aiken and George McGovern—seemed interested only in getting the hearings over.[27]

Liberty Lobby has some 25,000 members on its Board of Policy; it employs more than forty staff workers and mails its publications to 200,000 readers every month via computerized mailing lists; it has grossed at least $1 million annually in recent years. Yet it is virtually ignored by the general press; on those rare occasions when its activities make the news, it tends to be described as "rightist" or "ultra conservative," its anti-Semitic, racist posture either overlooked or played down.

This is, in fact, the continuing danger on the right, particularly to the Jewish community. There are functioning, viable and growing right-wing groups in existence with a demonstrated hostility to Jews and Jewish peoplehood. Very few Americans seem concerned about them.

13

The

Hatemongers

The most dangerous thing that a public man can utter is to remind the public that Jew-Zionism is the spearhead of the anti-Christ on this earth, dedicated to the evaporation of the Christian religion, the Christian population and the governmental authority of nations that are predominantly Christian.[1]

—March 20, 1973

The enemies of Christ are determined to capture the world—not through the United Nations, not through what people call a World Government, but through the manipulating political, financial and military power of World Zionism.[2]

—April 19, 1973

. . . *I weep* and *I groan* and *I pray* when I realize how ignorant the American people are concerning what is really going on and how close we are to annihilation, destruction and a revolutionary upheaval with the Jew-Zionist machine of the world hovering over us, determined to drain our blood and our purses in the establishment of their Imperial Empire in the counterfeit State of Israel.[3]

—May 7, 1973

The Watergate smokescreen is being used to so preoccupy the American public that the counterfeit State of Israel can carry on her campaign to enslave millions of Arabs, desecrate the shrines of Christ, and precipitate an incident designed to force us into a Middle Eastern war.[4]

—May 25, 1973

The beautiful City of Los Angeles, with a population of nearly three million, just elected a Negro as its Mayor. The Superintendent of all education in the State of California is a Negro. Both of these men belong to the McGovern clique. The Grand Jury in Washington, D.C., which temporarily, at least, holds the destination of our Nation in its hands, is all Negro. The chief investigator for the lynch-mob committee, known as the Ervin Committee, is a Jew. The prosecutor, working with the Grand Jury toward incarceration of men who risked their lives to uncover the treason secrets of the revolutionary political machine, is a Jew. . . . The Watergate noise is designed to preoccupy the American people while the Jews conspire to bring us toward the fulfillment of an international conspiracy. . . .[5]

—June 6, 1973

The foregoing are among the milder selections during the first six months of 1973 from the prolific hate pen of Gerald L. K. Smith, the grand old patriarch of Eureka Springs, Arkansas. In fund-raising solicitations to "friends," in the pages of *The Cross and the Flag* and other materials distributed by his Los Angeles-based Christian Nationalist Crusade, in occasional letters circulated to members of the U.S. Congress through a front group he launched twenty years ago, the dean of America's hatemongers does his best to undermine the safety and security of American Jews and destroy the State of Israel.

Does anyone listen to him?

The Christian Nationalist Crusade earns approximately $300,000 annually through contributions and literature peddling. Some 26,000 people receive *The Cross and the Flag* monthly. Many tens of thousands each year see the anti-Semitic Passion play at Eureka Springs, and their admissions enrich the Elna M. Smith Foundation, run, as we have earlier seen, by Smith and his wife.

In the spring of 1973, the Smith-organized and Smith-directed Citizens Congressional Committee (although its letterhead does not bear his name, *The Cross and the Flag* announced that its activities were "planned and executed" by Smith)[6] sent a mailing to members of Congress clearly aimed at destroying U.S. support for Israel.[7] More than fifty congressmen and senators sent written responses, which were promptly published by Smith in a sixteen-page pamphlet.[8]

The aura of respectability thus surrounding Smith led, in 1973, to yet another coup for him. The May/June issue of *The Motorist*, official publication of the American Automobile Association, received by probably millions of members of the AAA-affiliated automobile clubs throughout the nation, featured a front-page photo of the *Christ of the Ozarks* statue at Eureka Springs. It led to a glowing account of the "Elna M. Smith Foundation" projects, serviced of course by "numerous first-class motels and hotel accommodations, approved by the American Automobile Assn." According to the AAA account, the statue "has now become the most visited Christian shrine in America" and the Passion play often had "standing room only" during 1972. Said *The Motorist:* "The enterprise is non-sectarian and is being praised by every variety of Christian believer, from Pentecostal evangelists to Jesuit priests, and including representatives of all the major denominations."

Despite the fact that Gerald L. K. Smith himself was one of the two figures seen at the base of the *Christ of the Ozarks* in the AAA's cover photo, he was never mentioned in the article.

A protest to the president of one regional automobile club brought a response that he was ignorant of Gerald Smith's background—but no apology or offer to carry an explanatory note in the next edition of *The Motorist*.[9] Similar complaints to national AAA officials brought no response at all.[10]

If the organized hate groups that once flourished in the United States and the professional bigots like Gerald Smith represent not more than a tiny handful of the American people, they have not disappeared from the American scene. We do not share with some the view that they have no influence at all, or that their activities do not merit the closest scrutiny.

On the contrary, such scrutiny by concerned people is particularly necessary at a time when the American press, with few exceptions, is not covering the hate groups and individuals in a straightforward and responsible manner. It is, in fact, ignoring them as hatemongers—anti-black as well as anti-Jewish—and the result is that their activities continue apace, often under the protective screen that Gerald Smith, for example, has set up for himself with the help of those too easily gulled. (Earlier examples of

this media indifference have been given, of course, but many
readers were particularly incensed when, in January 1972, the
New York Times, publishing an "Op-Ed" article by the Rev.
Charles E. Coughlin, described him as "the 'radio priest' . . .
known for his controversial broadcasts in the nineteen-thirties."[11]
The *Times* neglected to tell its readers that Coughlin's name was
almost synonymous with the American Nazi-Fascist movement
and the virulent anti-Semitism of those years.)

One is forced to conclude that those who mold American community opinion could not care less about the hate-filled activities
of Gerald L. K. Smith. Our worry is that good people are not
concerned — at least not enough to speak out, protest or condemn.

Jesse Benjamin Stoner and Edward Fields cannot be considered
junior partners in the business of bigotry. They have been on the
scene as leaders of the white supremacist, viciously anti-black and
anti-Jewish National States Rights Party since its inception in the
late fifties as an organization committed not only to hate but to
violence as well. Stoner, an attorney, is chairman and general
counsel; Fields, the moving spirit behind the NSRP, is secretary
and editor of its monthly organ, *The Thunderbolt.* Both had had
earlier careers in the demiworld of professional bigotry.

Although federal agencies and informed observers estimate
the NSRP membership at no more than several hundred, principally in the South and its border states, circulation of *The Thunderbolt* has ranged from 12,000 to 16,000 over the past several
years and some local chapters have their own hate sheets, e.g.,
The White Marylander and *The American Nationalist* of Illinois.

Yet despite its small membership, NSRP is riding high today.
In October 1971, after spending its first decade and a half in locations which were "beneath the proper dignity needed to present
us in a highly professional light to the public,"[12] the NSRP moved
into a two-story brick building in Marietta, Georgia, which would,
Fields said, enable the organization to "put its best foot forward,
because new people who constantly visit the Party Office must be
impressed that here is an organization of permanency and
substance."[13]

Moreover, the NSRP ran chairman Stoner in the 1972 Democratic primary in Georgia for a U.S. Senate seat. As might be expected of a man who once founded a "Christian Anti-Jewish Party" with the goal of making "being a Jew a crime punishable by death,"[14] Stoner conducted a campaign based on racial and religious bigotry. In some 120 radio and TV broadcasts during the primary race, Stoner delivered a "message" that said, in part:

> I am J. B. Stoner. I am the only candidate for the United States Senate who is for the white people. I am the only candidate who is against integration. The main reason why the niggers want integration is because the niggers want our white women. . . . You cannot have law and order and niggers too. . . . Vote white.[15]

Interviewed by a TV newsman, Stoner described Atlanta's Mayor Sam Massell as a "Christ killer," "race mixer," and "Jewgangster."[16]

It was clear to both ADL and the NAACP that Stoner's radio and TV spots—appearing on an average of ten times a day—represented an abuse of free speech, endangering the physical and mental health of Georgia's citizens. Together with the Community Coalition for Broadcasting, the organizations petitioned the Federal Communications Commission to permit the stations "to withhold such announcements or advertisements . . . which pose an imminent threat to the safety and welfare of the public."[17] In August 1972 three FCC commissioners, "acting as a board," ruled in favor of Stoner's right to air his blatant bigotry,[18] a ruling that came as no surprise to anyone familiar with the FCC's consistent failure to protect the very public over whose airwaves it exercises a powerful guardianship. Stoner hailed the FCC ruling:

> I appreciate the FCC upholding my constitutional rights and the constitutional rights of all white Christians. As it is in general, Jews and niggers have freedom of speech, but not us white Christians. So this is a victory for freedom of speech for us white Christians.[19]

Stoner received 40,675 votes in the primary for U.S. Senator, more than doubling the 18,000 votes he had garnered in a 1970 race for the governorship of Georgia. The result prompted

Thunderbolt editor Fields to exult in a "Personal News Letter" to
NSRP members:

> The reason his new total is so sensational is that all the odds were
> against us. . . . Stoner spent only $10,000 for 40,675 votes . . . Every-
> one knew we could not win, that our main goal was to reach the pub-
> lic with our message. The Senate race was an ideal vehicle for the
> broadcasting of our views . . . It resulted in $1 million worth of
> publicity for this cause. . . .
>
> There were many positive accomplishments in this race which
> have brought many new converts into the National States Rights
> Party. Mr. Stoner traveled and spoke all over the state of Georgia.
> Tens of thousands of pieces of literature were distributed to the
> people. Then the Stoner campaign purchased T.V. time in the cities
> of Atlanta, Chattanooga, Macon, Augusta, Columbus, Savannah and
> Albany. . . . Millions of viewers were able to see and hear someone
> with the guts to stand up openly and tell the truth about what is
> going on in America. . . .
>
> As a result of this Senate race our presence on the national scene is
> well known and our future opportunities for building the NSRP into
> a powerful movement is [sic] greatly enhanced. . . .
>
> It should be noted that in Europe political parties are considered
> to have come into their own, in political recognition, as a growing
> force once they pass the 5 percent mark in the vote totals. We are
> around 6 percent and the number of votes we now influence assures
> us of the respect and recognition of other political figures who will
> seek our support in the future.[20]

Fields noted that the NSRP had "held to our open and clear cut
message of White Racism and Anti-Jewism," although it might
have "garnered more votes" with "a more moderate approach."
The trouble with such an approach, Fields said, is that once you
win, it is inhibiting. This way, if the NSRP ever came to power, it
would "have a mandate to sweep the nation clean of the subversive vermin eating away at the foundations of our race and
civilization."

What Fields meant by a "clean sweep" had been spelled out in
the July 1972 issue of *The Thunderbolt.* An article headed "The
Enemy Within" blamed Jews for every ill of American society—
past, present and future—and then asserted: "What is required?
Every Jew who holds a position of power or authority must be

removed from that position. If this does not work, then we must establish [the] Final Solution!!!"

Such are the people for whom more than 40,000 Georgians voted in the senate primary in 1972; such are the positions the FCC thinks suitable for airing over the public airwaves.

Too often these days, because their membership is small and their influence limited (6 percent of the vote is, after all, only distressing to those who share our view that Stoner should have had no votes at all), such groups are dismissed as of little significance to the Jewish or general communities. The measure employed to determine significance apparently is the size of the organization's national impact, and the National States Rights Party and similar groups have no national strength or viability. What is overlooked is the anxiety such hatemongers create for the Jewish and black communities on a local basis.

How do Jews in Georgia feel about the fact that somewhere out there, protected by the secrecy of the democratic ballot, are 40,000 of their fellow citizens who regard J. B. Stoner highly enough to give him their vote—who presumably share his antipathy to Jews and blacks and presumably endorse the NSRP "solutions"? In one Southern city, immediately after the Munich slaying of Israeli athletes by Palestinian terrorists in September 1972, announcements of a forthcoming NSRP rally featuring Stoner were made on local radio stations. Rage and sadness prevailed in the Jewish community. To this locality, the NSRP is not an insignificant group. Here Jews must live with it and its pronouncements daily; they must fear the violence it advocates and has occasionally perpetrated, its frequent incitement to riot and its admonition to "white people" to arm themselves to the teeth; they must worry that constant exposure to such rabid Jew-hatred will inevitably affect their well-intentioned fellow citizens.

The Jew-hatred of the NSRP and other gutter-level anti-Semites is not a new brand of anti-Semitism; what is new is the indifference manifest by so many to the continued existence of this ancient plague.

It was clear to informed observers in 1973 that the Ku Klux Klan bombings, shootings, beatings, arson, terror and intimidation that had marred the decade of the sixties was not over. There had been Klan-instigated violence in recent years in Pontiac, Michigan, scene of a raging controversy over school busing, and in Houston, Texas. In Wilmington, North Carolina, a Klan off-shoot called Rights of White People had engaged in so much violence that local police regarded it as more dangerous than the Klan itself; in May 1973, its leader, Leroy Gibson, an insurance agent and retired Marine Corps gunnery sergeant, was arrested and charged with the bombing of a local bookstore.[21]

Yet at the same time, at least one leader of the badly split KKK—James Venable, "Imperial Wizard" of the National Knights of the Ku Klux Klan—was soft-pedaling violence and telling interviewers: "There's only one answer—the ballot box and the boycott. You can't use violence. You can only use the ballot box."[22]

Where was the truth? What was the status of the Klan in the autumn of 1973? What were its aims and its strengths?

The "third" Ku Klux Klan, heir to more than a hundred years of KKK activity on the American scene, came into being after World War II, grew with the Supreme Court's school desegregation decision in 1954 and expanded rapidly thereafter during the civil rights movement of the early sixties under the leadership of Robert M. Shelton, Jr., an ex-rubber worker who brought togeth-er for a time many of the bickering and ineffectual Klans. Today this third Klan is not a single unit but many, each jealously guard-ing its individuality and each itself torn by personality disputes. The overall hard-core membership of the Klans has ranged from 10,000 down to 5,000 nationwide, but the "invisible empire" in-cludes some additional 25,000 to 35,000 like-minded racists who belong to an assortment of Klan-type organizations, including a number of "gun clubs." Organizing as "churches" or church groups is a new form of underground development by some KKKers who believe that if use of the Klan name should become untenable, many klaverns would still be able to operate under that front. The Mountain Church in Michigan, the National Christian Party in Oklahoma and The Southerners in Alabama are examples of this type of development.

Shelton heads the largest Klan grouping, the United Klans of

America, headquartered in Tuscaloosa with a membership estimated by informed observers at about 4,000 nationally and claimed by Shelton to exist in all fifty states. For the leader of a band of predominantly working-class bigots, Shelton does quite well. He lives in a $60,000 home; publishes the United Klans' official magazine, the *Fiery Cross* (50,000 copies are printed monthly from The Imperial Press, headquartered in an $80,000 building); rides around in a large black Cadillac with a two-way radio; wears expensive, well-tailored suits and a large diamond ring, and carries a handsome briefcase. In short, he looks like a well-heeled banker and has been trying of late to get his followers to shed the bedsheets, hoods and masks that have been the historical trademark of the Klan. Shelton also has a large camper—with its own power supply, a public address system, screen and projector and other facilities—that he uses to travel some 130,000 miles per year to confer with local Klan leadership, give lectures and appear on radio and television.

James Venable, with his National Knights of the Ku Klux Klan, is Shelton's main rival for Klan leadership. He claims a membership of 81,000 but somehow was only able to attract some eighty adherents to his 1973 convention (Shelton had 350 at his). Venable's principal strength is in Georgia, although he has picked up members recently in such northern states as Ohio and Michigan.

Despite attempts by both leaders to cosmetize the Klan, the rhetoric remains largely the same—issue after issue of the *Fiery Cross* contains the worst anti-Jewish, anti-black venom (with the emphasis these days on the former). The attempt to create a "new image" for the old saws was perhaps best exemplified in March 1973, when Indiana Grand Dragon William B. Chaney led twenty-five of his hooded and robed followers (no masks, though) on a walking tour near the courthouse square of Parke County, Indiana, handing out literature and greeting passers-by amiably. Explaining that the "new Klan" hoped to regain the political clout the Klan had had in the twenties by working lawfully through conventional political means, Chaney told reporters the Klan was trying "to preserve our racial integrity, our racial purity" and that "people are tired . . . of seeing our white women escorted on the street by nigger bucks." He added that American·institutions were being undermined by a "world Zionist conspir-acy of kike Jews."[23]

Will the Klan now go "semi-respectable"—that is, retain its simplistic, gutter-level anti-Semitism and racism but operate through the political processes? There are signs that it indeed is following that road. The Ohio Grand Dragon announced his candidacy for the governorship of his state,[24] and a Texas Klan leader is running for mayor of Houston at this writing.[25] In 1972, Florida Grand Dragon John Paul Rogers was a candidate for the Polk County School Board; he lost in a runoff, 12,000 to 7,000.[26]

Will it succeed? Most people believe that the KKK is today on the wane in American life. Yet it has shown for more than a cen-tury an astonishing ability to re-emerge in times of stress to create further divisiveness within America. Perhaps a warning was sounded by the Miami *Herald* which reported a South Dade Klan rally addressed by Robert Shelton in February 1973:

> Cars pulling into the field were greeted by rifle-toting deputies of the Klan who flash-lit the way to a podium where various Klan speakers divided sermons about "niggers, Jews, pornography, drugs and atheists."
>
> A film entitled "Revolution Underway" attributed black power movements in the United States to Communists' plots to overthrow American government.
>
> Jay Kulp, 47, a vacationer from Rochester, N.Y., was among the curious spectators.
>
> "This is very interesting . . . I really agree with these people and when I go back home, I may start attending meetings up there," he said.
>
> Approximately 50 Klansmen, dressed in the organization's histori-cal robes and peaked hoods, were interspersed throughout the crowd.
>
> When the rally was over the crowd gathered around a 30 foot high cross planted in the ground and watched as it was set afire.[27]

The Klan may be on the wane and may have little influence in the national life—indeed, recent Gallup polls have reported only a 2 or 3 percent "highly favorable" view of the KKK, while majorities of 75 and 80 percent said they had "highly unfavorable" views of it.[28] The trouble is that although they may regard Klansmen unfavorably, few Americans bother to speak out against them; a neighbor known to be a member of the hooded order is still bid good morning as if he were the community parson.

There are literally dozens of other professional hate groups, individuals and publications throughout the country, none of them with a large or active membership or audience, none with any national impact, all of them capable of fomenting trouble in local situations that often need only a spark to start a fire. They do not constitute by themselves an overwhelming danger to the Jewish community. The Jewish concern is rather that they have been so long on the scene that people are now inured to them—inured to the point of forgetting, as they have in the case of Gerald Smith, who they are and what they stand for. In addition, a new generation has come of age, people who never knew the overt hatemongers of yesterday and who do not recognize them or their descendants today. If the professional bigots mute their message, if they are permitted to camouflage it beneath a veneer of respectability, if their activities are ignored by the mass media—or if the media persist in giving them a forum—could this country one day elect a Klansman to major public office, even as it enshrined the dean of American hatemongers as a respectable promoter of Christian tourist attractions?

Epilogue

In retrospect, it was almost predictable. Not only had there been for the past decade, and especially since the Six-Day War of 1967, the palpable erosion in worldwide sympathy and friendship for Jews that has been the subject of this book, but events of the summer of 1973 themselves offered dangerous signs. They flashed to Israel's Arab neightbors—and, more important, to their Soviet patrons—the message that yet another attempt to annihilate the Jewish people would be greeted, in the mid-seventies, with massive indifference if not active support. Perhaps it did not do so deliberately or even consciously, but in the summer of '73 much of the world gave a green light to aggression against Israel.

On Friday, August 10, Israeli planes intercepted a Lebanese airliner bound from Beirut to Baghdad and required it to land in Israel. The pilot complied, the plane landed and the passengers were searched and detained for several hours before being permitted to continue their journey, inconvenienced but unharmed. The Israeli objective had been to capture four leaders of the Palestinian terrorist movement suspected of being aboard the plane—the men who had helped to plan and execute the murders at Lod and Munich and Khartoum, bombing attempts at busloads of Israeli schoolchildren and Israeli supermarket shoppers, arson against elderly Jews in West Germany, the mailing of letter-bombs to Jewish officials throughout the world, numberless airplane skyjackings and a spray of machine-gun fire at innocent passengers in the Athens airport.

Yet on August 15—after twenty-five years of failure even once to condemn armed attacks against Israel by Arab states or from the territory of Arab states as transgressions against the United Nations Charter and international law, after the clear refusal, over several years, by sovereign nations within the international community to take any effective measures against the threat of worldwide terrorism from the Palestinian guerrillas and their supporters—the United Nations Security Council voted unanimously to condemn Israel for "a serious interference with international civil aviation and a violation of the Charter of the United Nations." It warned Israel that "if such acts are repeated, the Council will consider taking steps or measures to enforce its resolutions."[1]

Reasonable men will deplore any interference with commercial avaiation, but it was clear that Israel was being condemned for doing what the world had left it no alternative *but* to do. Within the Security Council, Israel's permanent representative to the UN charged that the Council had "not even once brought itself to condemn the murder of Israeli children, men and women." He asserted that Israel would "continue to protect the lives of its citizens. It will give no quarter to the ruthless killers of the innocent."[2]

At the same moment the Security Council was taking its usual anti-Israel posture in New York, the UN Economic and Social Council in Geneva established an Economic Commission for Western Asia under ground rules excluding Israel from all participation. By a vote of 33 to 8, with 9 abstentions, the Council adopted a Lebanese resolution opening membership on the new Commission only to those nations now using the services of the UN economic office in Beirut—thus putting the UN imprimatur on the political isolation of Israel from its neighbors, in clear violation of the United Nations Charter provision guaranteeing "the principle of sovereign equality of all . . . members." An American resolution to postpone establishment of the Commission until a ruling could be obtained from the World Court on its legality was defeated.

While these events were taking place in New York and Geneva, Israeli athletes participating in the World University Games in Moscow were being vilified in what could only be described as official Soviet government-sponsored anti-Semitism. During the opening ceremonies, Soviet citizens attending the games—some 100,000—whistled and jeered in derision and Russian TV cameras turned the other way as the Israeli team paraded behind the Star of David; the speaker announcing the teams at the stadium perceptibly lowered his voice as he announced the Israeli participants; at a basketball game between Cuba and Israel, Soviet army cadets and soldiers packed the gymnasium and led the jeering of the Israeli players, shouting anti-Semitic epithets, while Soviet Jews who held tickets to the game were not permitted to enter the arena. Israeli newsmen scheduled to cover the World University Games at the last moment had been denied visas to go to Moscow.

Less than a year from the murder of Israeli athletes at the Olympic games in Munich, it was a frightening reminder of the climate that had made the Munich atrocity possible—that indifference to Jewish security and Jewish safety, that growing hostility to Israel, which both encourages the terrorists and dooms effective action against them. Jack Aizner, an American-born Tel Aviv University basketball player participating in the Moscow games, had been a member of the Israeli Olympic team; he had escaped the fate of his teammates only because part of the team had been playing a consolation game in Augsburg at the time of the massacre. One can only imagine his thoughts at the Moscow tournament.

Meantime, as we have seen, the "oil shortage" propaganda campaign had been escalated by the Arabs with an assist from American oil companies, and much of the world press gave credence in its coverage of the "energy crisis" to the Arab argument that Israel was at the root of the West's oil troubles. Allies of the United States—Great Britain, France and Italy among them—were urging a modification of U.S. policy, away from Israel and toward the Arabs. In West Germany, the Bonn Government was waffling on its "special relationship" with Israel, and in East Germany, a formal agreement was reached by Erich Honecker, the Communist Party chief, and Yassir Arafat for the opening of a Palestinian guerrilla office in East Berlin "to further mutual understanding between the people of the German Democratic Republic and the Arab Palestinian people and to increase solidarity in the joint struggle against imperialism and Zionism and for social progress."[3] The *New York Times* reported in August that the scheduled September opening of the Palestine Liberation Organization headquarters was "for the purpose of procuring arms, money and other support from East Germany and the rest of the Soviet bloc."[4] In Latin America, historic friendship for Israel was steadily being undermined by left-wing revolutionaries, by Arab propagandists and by governments engaged in the economic wooing of the Arab states.

In the United States, the Radical Left and the Radical Right alike were fulminating against U.S. support of Israel, attempting to steam up American public opinion with dire warnings of "another Vietnam." They were joined, with much more telling effect, by such prestigious voices as the *Christian Science Monitor.* On August 18, the *Monitor* continued its anti-Israel fusillade. It applauded the Security Council's censure of Israel over Israel's diversion of the Lebanese aircraft, telling its readers "The argument invoked by Israel that the end justifies the means when it comes to its secret war against Palestinian terrorists is totally unacceptable."[5] The *Monitor* had a much more "even-handed" approach to Arab terrorism, persistently tracing every Arab atrocity to its alleged "root causes" in Israeli actions; there was no comparable willingness to explore in this instance the root causes of what the Israelis had attempted.

There were other voices in the American media. The nationally syndicated columnists Evans and Novak alleged that "leaders of the powerful American Jewish community"—never specified—were annoyed with Israel over the Lebanese plane incident. They called this an "ominous warning to the country which controls by far the most powerful military might anywhere in the Arab Middle East" and cautioned against "the explosive ingredient of Israel's seeming contempt for the opinion of major U.S. allies, particularly in Western Europe, and the U.S. itself." They wrote of alleged Israeli plans to "build a city for 50,000 on the Israeli-occupied (but Syrian) Golan Heights and an 'urban center' in Israeli-occupied (but Egyptian) northern Sinai."[6]

On September 10, 1973 the Columbia Broadcasting System aired an anti-Semitic commentary by Jeffrey St. John over the radio network's "Spectrum" program. St. John, a self-described "conservative" and, in 1966, the Conservative Party candidate for the congressional seat vacated by John Lindsay, used the CBS microphones to spew forth the following:

> The reason, it seems to me, that we don't have an ongoing debate in this country as to whether we have been paying a high price to guarantee Israeli security, is that American public opinion is shaped largely by a pro-Israeli viewpoint. And whenever someone suggest we should begin changing our policy, as an American oil company executive did recently, *the pro-Israeli propaganda machine in America crucifies him in public.*
>
> What this lop-sided state of affairs suggests is an insecurity on the part of many American Jews to thrash out in the open the issue of Arab oil and U.S. support of Israel. In fact, ever since the founding of the State of Israel, the Arabs have had precious little opportunity to present their point of view in this country.
>
> Emotions, not reason, govern our policy toward Israel. This emotion translates itself into political support from American Jews. But I suggest that the Arab oil vs. Israel debate raises a touchy issue that American Jews don't like to talk about, especially those Jews who are devoted Zionists and support the State of Israel. *The issue is whether you are an American first and a Jew second and if forced to choose, which commands your loyalty first.* The Arab oil vs. U.S. support of Israel may be the first of many hard questions American Jews must face. [Italics added.][7]

St. John's use of the word *crucifies* in relation to the "pro-Israeli propaganda machine" was a clear appeal to the hardiest of the roots of anti-Semitism, the deicide charge. His raising of the dual loyalty canard was in much the same category. It bespeaks the mentality that has attempted to force on Jews everywhere, at all times, a choice between loyalty to the countries in which they have have been citizens—a loyalty vigorously demonstrated over and over again through Jewish contribution to those countries in every area of human endeavor—and deep attachments to fellow Jews throughout the world. It is a false choice, especially for

American Jews, who see their commitment to America and their commitment to Israel—indeed, their commitment as well to Soviet Jews—as part and parcel of a devotion to religious liberty, human freedom and other democratic principles which they assume they share with other Americans.

(Not long ago, Harry Golden answered the dual loyalty canard in typical Golden fashion. In a letter to the *Times,* this profoundly American patriot and profoundly Jewish author and humorist said that in the event of war between the United States and Israel, no one would have to worry about where his loyalties were: in response to the schizophrenia thus thrust upon him, Golden asserted, he would commit suicide.)[8]

CBS announces that the "diverse opinions expressed on 'Spectrum' are those of the commentators themselves and should not be attributed to CBS or any of its affiliates."[9] But the September 10 St. John commentary was neither the first nor the last CBS airing of opinions revealing an anti-Jewish bias.

There were two major events which, in combination with the factors we have already explored, were to have a profound effect, we believe, in the Arab decision to strike at Israel on the Day of Atonement.

On September 29, in what the *New York Times* was to headline a day later as "A Triumph of Terror Over Compassion,"[10] the Austrian government capitulated to two Arab terrorists who had boarded a train bearing Russian Jewish refugees from Moscow to Vienna and had taken hostage three Jews—including a couple in their sixties—and an Austrian guard. Chancellor Bruno Kreisky agreed to close the Schoenau transit facility to Israel-bound Soviet Jews. Many first thought it a prudent decision designed to save the lives of the hostages. But Kreisky stuck to it after the hostages had been released, despite strong criticism throughout the world and a personal appeal from Mrs. Meir.

When it became known soon thereafter that closing Schoenau had been a suggestion of the government itself—eagerly accepted, of course, by the Palestinian terrorists—the magnitude and implications of Austria's attitude were appallingly clear. Although Chancellor Kreisky and his government have prided themselves on Austria's post–World War II role as a way station for refugees, and particularly in the last several years, for Jews emigrating from the Soviet Union, the message was unmistakable that Austria now found Jewish refugees bound for Israel not only inconvenient, but also a perceived aid to Israel unlikely to create friendship and influence in the Arab world.

That Kreisky, born a Jew and politically a democratic socialist, should thus surrender to Arab terrorism at the expense of two of the deepest concerns of the Jewish people—Soviet Jewry and Israel—could not help but fan the fires of Arab *revanchism.*

In Washington, D.C. six days earlier, a ceremony had taken place in the White House fraught with implications for the Middle East, especially for those who for twenty-five years had rejected diplomatic solutions, arrived at through negotiation, that might bring normalcy to this troubled part of the world. Henry A. Kissinger was sworn in as Secretary of State of the United States, bringing the East Room audience to an ovation—and many to tears—when, referring to his past as a German Jewish refugee from nazism, Dr. Kissinger declared: "There is no country in the world where it is conceivable that a man of my origin could be standing here next to the President of the United States." An even more prolonged ovation greeted his concluding remarks:

> We will strive not just for a pragmatic solution for this or that difficulty, but to recognize that America has never been true to itself unless it meant something beyond itself. As we work for a world at peace with justice and compassion and humanity we know that America is fulfilling man's deepest aspirations.[11]

There had been mixed reaction in the Arab world to President Nixon's nomination of Kissinger as Secretary of State. The weight of publicly-expressed opinion was overwhelmingly toward the view that Kissinger, as a Jew, would be partial to Israel on *that* ground, in addition to his implementation of American foreign policy historically supportive of Israel. "Kissinger's accession to the State Department can be interpreted only as a declaration of unofficial war against the Arabs," screamed *Al Diyar* of Lebanon.[12] *Al Anwar* of Cairo termed the appointment an "Israeli victory over the Arabs, not only in America but in the Middle

East."[13] The Algerian Embassy in London stated that "as far as we are concerned, there is no difference between a Jew and an Israeli" (thus laying to rest the Arab propaganda myth that the Arabs were merely anti-Zionist, not anti-Jewish) and that Algeria would act as though an Israeli had been appointed U.S. Secretary of State.[14]

It was possible, of course, that the emergence of an American Jewish Secretary of State spurred conviction in the Arab world that American policy would harden against Arab interests, and that Arab leadership opted to strike while the thrust of world opinion was, in their view, at best openly anti-Israel and at worst "neutral" in favor of the Arabs.

But there were other opinions in the Arab world as well, expressed cautiously in public and less so in private. These speculated that Kissinger—as the architect of "détente" with the Soviet Union and China, the man whose face-to-face negotiations with the United States' North Vietnamese adversaries had proved fruitful (and were later to bring him the Nobel Peace Prize)— would bring some sort of impetus toward settlement in the Middle East. There was even talk that precisely because he was Jewish, Kissinger would face less "pressure" from the "pro-Zionist lobby" in the United States and would therefore be able to extract certain compromises from Israel. There were notes of optimism in such speculation.

But for Arab leaders, who had so long inculcated in their people the thirst for *jihad,* holy war, the same interpretation—that Kissinger would perhaps succeed in bringing about negotiations —was, we believe, a politically untenable prospect. It is not inconceivable that Egypt and Syria, encouraged by the Russians and with newly-cemented ties to the oil-producing states, opted for war instead of a chance for peace, opted for killing Israelis as an alternative to sitting down at a negotiating table with them, opted for sacrificing Arab lives in a fourth attempt at exterminating the Jews, precisely because the possibility of negotiation loomed large.

Whatever the reasoning in the Arab world, the fact is that on Saturday afternoon, October 6, Yom Kippur, the holiest day of the Jewish year, Egypt and Syria launched a massive coordinated attack against Israeli positions on the Golan Heights and the east bank of the Suez Canal, in an obvious attempt to overrun the Israeli army on the one day of the year it was least likely to respond effectively—not because Israel was napping but because Israelis, along with fellow Jews the world over, were at prayer. The fact alone is one that neither Israel nor any Jew anywhere is likely soon to forget. There are other facts to be remembered.

The first is that the Soviet Union, mouthing déten̄té with the United States, clearly armed its Arab clients with the most sophisticated weaponry available in the world and trained them well to aim it and use it against American interests in the Middle East. That the Soviet Union, if it did not deliberately goad Egypt and Syria into war with Israel, did nothing to stay their hands and, with advance knowledge of the attack, did nothing to warn its détente partner, the United States. That it re-armed Egypt and Syria in an emergency airlift as soon as their losses proved heavy, and only when the Syrian army had been pushed back to Damascus and the Egyptian army had been encircled by Israeli forces in a daring military maneuver did the USSR bring the mechanism of détente into play—lest the Arabs lose all—to bring about a cease-fire negotiated between Leonid Brezhnev and Henry Kissinger.

The second is that despite the claims of Arab diplomats in Washington and some European capitals that Egypt and Syria and their Arab allies were bent from the start on a "limited" war to regain parts of the occupied territories and, thus, a better bargaining position, no rational person can believe that the aim of the Arab states, with 58 million people, was not the liquidation of Israel and its 3 million Jews. Both the nature and scale of the invasion and the statements of Arab leaders and the Arab press in 1973 leave little to imagine about what would have happened to Israelis in Tel Aviv and Haifa and Jerusalem and the farms of the Galil had the Yom Kippur war been launched from the pre-1967 borders of Israel. The following represent but a sampling of such statements:

> Zionism is our first and only enemy. We must see things clearly. It is the enemy who occupied our land, settled it and wants to gain control over the Arab world. This will enable him to dominate the

Islamic world. We are duty bound to direct attention to the truth. We must realize that the Israelites are our enemies from the very beginning and that peace between us and them is impossible.

—Egyptian Vice President Hussein ash-Shafi in
Al-Gomhuria, Cairo, April 27, 1973

[The State of Israel] is doomed to extinction and has no future in the Middle East . . . Israel cannot continue to exist while it is ostracized from its neighbors and depends solely on its military strength . . . But this military superiority cannot resist the numerical superiority of the Arabs. The day will come and the Arabs will overtake Israel in the technological field.

—Mohammed Heykal in *Al Ahram,* Cairo, June 8, 1973

[The Jewish people] have no scruples. They respect no religion, other than their own, and are traitors to the countries that give them shelter . . . History has begun to vindicate the anti-Semitic policy of Hitler. The world now understands that Hitler was right and that there was a logical reason for constructing the cremation furnaces in order to punish those who show such scorn for the principles of humanity, the principles of man, and the faiths and rights of mankind.

—Amin Mansour in *Al Akhbar,* Cairo, August 19, 1973

Q. What specific changes would you like to see in America's Mideast policy?
A. If the U.S. tells Israel it has no right to occupy Arab land, it will be a major plus in our relations.
Q. You mean the territories occupied in the 1967 war?
A. The occupied territories don't interest me. I'm talking about Palestine.

—President Muammar Qaddafi of Libya, interviewed by *Newsweek*
senior editor Armand de Borchgrave,
September 24, 1973

Israel's withdrawal from all the occupied territories is a partial demand which the Arab states call for as part of a general liberation plan whose purpose is to bring an end to the racist colonial existence in Palestine.

—*Al Gomhuria,* Cairo, September 29, 1973

It is against such statements that Israel is asked to believe that Egyptian and Syrian soldiers were fighting only to liberate Egyptian and Syrian land occupied by Israel in 1967.

There is a final fact to remember: Israel chose not to strike pre-emptively at the Arab armor and personnel massed at the Suez and on the Golan Heights. Because the world found it convenient to forget that Nasser's dismissal of the UN Emergency Forces in the Sinai, his massing of the Egyptian army in the desert, his seizure of Sharm el-Sheik and his blockade against Israeli shipping through the Straits of Tiran were acts of war against which Israel was required to defend herself, this time Israel wanted to make it crystal clear to the entire world exactly who the aggressors were; she chose to absorb the first blow, and for this forbearance she has paid in human lives.

Can the world understand what the loss of thousands of lives means not only to Israeli Jews but to the Jewish people? Will the world mark that Israel supplied plasma and other medical supplies to be carried by the International Red Cross through its lines to the encircled Egyptian Third Army on the east bank of the Suez, and that it agreed to permit UN observers to drive a convoy of 100 trucks bearing food and water through its forces to the trapped Egyptians? And if the world can take cognizance of these humane gestures, will it also recall that in 1948, when five Arab armies invaded the State of Israel in defiance of the United Nations Partition Plan (which Israel accepted), the Arabs laid seige to Jerusalem, depriving the Israeli civilians therein of necessary food and water? Will it recall that in October 1973, Israeli soldiers retaking the Golan Heights found the mutilated bodies of their comrades, victims of Syrian atrocities in the first days of this allegedly "limited" war? Will the world remember that Egypt sought to barter wounded Israeli prisoners for sand dunes, in violation of the Geneva Conventions ascribed to by most of the civilized world?

We have no reason to believe that the world—beyond the United States government and a few moral voices here and there —is at all prepared to accept fact instead of fantasy or outright lies when it comes to the Middle East. The first noise heard as the sun set on Yom Kippur 1973 was the clamor of the Arabs and Soviets charging "Israeli aggression"—in total contradiction of UN observer reports unequivocally describing an unprovoked attack by Egypt and Syria on the Israeli forces. The Soviets and their Arab clients were immediately echoed with total fidelity

by their minions on the Radical Left everywhere. Within days, the
UN Security Council erupted into outright anti-Semitism, one
delegate reporting that it felt "like being in the middle of a
lynch mob."[15] England "embargoed" spare parts for Israel's
Centurion tanks; France shipped tons of new military hardware
from Marseilles to Libya. In the face of massive Russian resupply of the Arabs, allies of the United States—including
England, France, West Germany, Italy, Spain, Greece and Tur-
key—let it be known that the American decision to replace war
materiel Israel had lost, and needed to survive, could not be
implemented at U.S. bases on their soil or by U.S. flights over
their territory (only little Portugal was cooperative). The Bonn
government, striking a posture of alleged "neutrality," vigorously
protested the loading of an Israeli ship at a West German port
with arms from a U.S. military base in West Germany. The
Vatican, too, struck a posture of neutrality. On the second day
of the new war the Pope issued an even-handed plea to those
involved "not to turn a deaf ear to overtures of honorable compromise." And *Il Populo* of Rome, leaked a quote from uniden-
tified "Christian sources" in Jerusalem to the effect that "the
new tragic events confirm the validity of the proposal to interna-
tionalize the holy places."[16]

   Just thirty years after the Holocaust, a new chapter was being
written in the history of European anti-Semitism. It was being
written in Arab oil and Jewish blood. It was sickening.

   The United States held firm to its commitments in the Middle
East, using the carrot-and-stick tools of détente diplomacy to
bring about a cease-fire and even to win a Soviet promise to push
the reluctant Arabs at long last to the negotiating table with Israel.
The timetable of negotiation will take a while to set up (one re-
calls the endless debates about the shape of the table to be used
in Paris for the long-awaited Vietnam peace talks), and the road
to a just and durable peace will be strewn not with rocks but with
boulders. If it is genuine, however, the thrust toward peace can
have a life of its own and, once started, may be even more difficult to stop than war. That is a hope, not an expectation, but
the fact that Jews everywhere—in Israel as in the Diaspora—
can cling to it, even in this bitterest of moments as they bury their
dead, is a measure of eternal Jewish optimism.

For the American Jewish community, American reaction to the Yom Kippur War confirmed both the best of its hopes and the most gnawing of its fears. Heartened by the response of their government, American Jews were deeply troubled—although by this time not at all surprised—by the voices of callous dissent.

Senator J. William Fulbright took to the "Face the Nation" microphones on October 7 to reiterate his assertion that "the Israelis control the policy in the Congress and the Senate." When the program moderator called Fulbright's statement "a fairly serious charge," the Senate Foreign Relations Committee chairman countered: "The charge is a fact of life."[17]

Jeffrey St. John stated over CBS on October 15 that U.S. Middle East policy "has been, and continues to be, shaped in large measure by the financial and political power of American Jewry."[18] On the same date, WCBS-TV in New York broadcast a station editorial that was moderate in tone yet came squarely down against any American resupply of Israel, despite its acknowledgment of the Russian resupply of the Arabs.[19]

On October 13, *Christian Science Monitor* chief editorial writer Joseph C. Harsch stated that it was within the bounds of "responsibility" for Moscow to give the Egyptians and Syrians "the means to defend themselves and to try to regain their lost lands." Harsch asked: "Is it aggressive for the Egyptians and Syrians to attempt to recapture by force of arms their own lands taken from them as spoils of war in 1967?" His answer was no, and it was a clear echo of the Arab-Soviet posture, "balanced" only by the assertion that it was "not aggressive for Israel to repel an attack on its armed forces."[20] Three days later, the *Monitor*, in language paralleling the Harsch piece, again swallowed whole the Arab interpretations (for Western consumption only) of the Yom Kippur attack:

> A common assumption during the last week was that Egypt and Syria had attacked Israel. . . . That was a mistake. There was an Egyptian-Syrian offensive against Israeli armed forces. But those Israeli armed forces were in occupation of Egyptian and Syrian territories. . . . Last week's Arab attacks were attempts to reclaim Arab territories taken by armed force in 1967 and held in defiance of a UN resolution and, indeed, of the official policies of the United States. . . .
>
> This is a war over the spoils of another war which means negotiating positions for the future. The United States has no commitment

> to help Israel retain the spoils of the 1967 war, most of which Wash-
> ington officially thinks should be handed back to their Arab owners.
> . . . We urge those who favored America staying out of Vietnam,
> Cambodia and Bangladesh to follow suit in this instance. We urge
> all Americans to keep in mind the fact that the issue is not the sur-
> vival of Israel (which is not the question) but only the spoils of the
> 1967 war.[21]

In the highest ranks of the Catholic hierarchy, with few exceptions, there was only neutrality or silence. The Council of Bishops
issued no statement until weeks after the ceasefire, and then it was
carefully "balanced." It remained for simple priests and nuns to
issue their own statements, in a large number of cases vigorously
supporting Israel.

American Jews were angered, but not surprised, by continuing
equivocation on the matter of Israel by the National Council of
Churches. Many individual churchmen and church groups,
Catholic and Protestant alike, and many local councils of Protestant churches indeed dispatched messages of strong support. And
at an emergency convocation of the Jewish community in Washington, D.C. on October 9, the Rev. David Hunter, deputy
general secretary of the National Council, delivered in his own
name perhaps the most ardent and eloquent denunciation of the
Arab attack, calling the Yom Kippur assault "an offense before
God." "To desecrate Yom Kippur by armed aggression is an offense so great as to totally invalidate the religious sanctions of
those who were responsible for it," Rev. Hunter asserted, adding:

> These are the principal moral demands confronting us in this hour:
> The right of a nation to exist.
> The right of a whole nation to be in prayer before God without being
> violated and murdered in the midst of it.
> The right to forego being a pawn in a world of kings and queens
> and holy men who trade oil for blood.[22]

His remarks could not have been more forthright or more welcome in that lonely hour.

Yet a week later, the National Council of Churches, as a body,
continued to hem and haw, its Governing Board issuing an al-

legedly "balanced" statement which, however, completely failed morally to condemn Egypt and Syria for their aggression and, at the same time, put the onus squarely on the United States alone, not on Russia, "to effect a cessation of hostilities at the earliest possible moment."[23]

In its pretension of "even-handedness," the Council took refuge in a July 7, 1967 resolution of the Executive Committee of its Governing Board, which asserted: "Indispensable to peace in the Middle East is acceptance by the entire international community of the state of Israel. . . ."[24] Yet that resolution was never adopted as a policy statement by the Governing Board—which had come very close to adopting an anti-Israel resolution at its 1972 session —and thus never became official National Council policy.

What did become policy, however, was its call for "the recognition of the right of Palestinian Arabs to a 'home acceptable to them which must now be a matter of negotiation.'" And finally, despite the clear anti-Jewish hostility evident in the United Nations Security Council—and widely reported just days earlier in newspaper accounts—the National Council's October 15, 1973 statement repeatedly urged the United States to look to the UN "as the primary instrument for achieving and maintaining peace in the Middle East." It was clear that not even Israel's fourth struggle for survival in twenty-five years could budge the National Council.

We cannot pretend to know, or to predict with any accuracy, as we write at the end of 1973, the short-term or long-range effects of the newest Middle East crisis. It would be naive in the extreme to expect peace in the imminent future; it would be a disservice to all mankind to pray for anything less. Once again, Israel has militarily defeated Arab neighbors bent on her destruction; once again, irrationally and tragically, human lives on both sides have been grossly misspent; once again, a world short on memory and long on hostility to Jews may attempt to snatch an Israeli political defeat from the jaws of an Israeli military victory.

In that attempt, we hope the world will be required to contend vigorously with an American government firm in its commitment to the safety and security of Israel and forthright in its actions in fulfillment of that commitment. For whether Israel survives from this day forward is clearly dependent upon the courage and strength of its own people, the devotion of Jews the world over and the support of the United States. For all practical purposes, there is no one else.

That is a shattering conclusion; we reach it with extreme sadness and utmost reluctance, and, to be sure, many decent people here and abroad will rush to dispute it. The Jewish community will welcome such disclaimers.

But as the content of this book has demonstrated, there is abroad in our land a large measure of indifference to the most profound apprehensions of the Jewish people; a blandness and apathy in dealing with anti-Jewish behavior; a widespread incapacity or unwillingness to comprehend the necessity of the existence of Israel to Jewish safety and survival throughout the world.

This is the heart of the new anti-Semitism.

Notes

2. Gerald Smith's Road

1. *New York Times,* May 27, 1944.

2. *Herald Tribune,* August 22, 1956.

3. Calvin Trillin, "U.S. Journal: Eureka Springs, Ark.—The Sacred Projects." *The New Yorker,* July 26, 1969, pp. 69–79. This is an excellent report of the Smith's arrival in and acceptance by Eureka Springs. We are indebted to reporter Trillin for his on-the-spot detailed research.

4. *Ibid.,* p. 70, as quoted by Trillin.

5. April 1, 1965.

6. April 19, 1965.

7. Attributed to Gary Eagan of Eureka Springs in "Hippies and Gerald L. K. Smith Make Ozark Resort Town a Model of Coexistence," *New York Times,* July 27, 1972.

8. "God Bless Eureka Springs and Her People, Thank God for Eureka Springs and Her People," November 9, 1967.

9. Rev. Lester Kinsolving, "Ozark Atrocity—Or, Holy Summer Stock," Wichita, Kansas *Eagle,* August 6, 1972.

10. Trillin, "U.S. Journal," p. 77.

11. "Facts and Conclusions—Carroll County, Arkansas Public Road Project," report of the Ozarks Regional Commission, Department of Commerce, January 6, 1970.

12. ADL News Release, December 12, 1969.

13. Telegram from Dore Schary, National Chairman ADL, to President Nixon, January 17, 1970.

14. Arkansas *Gazette*, December 19, 1969.

15. Arkansas *Gazette*, December 26, 1969.

16. "Facts and Conclusions," Ozarks Regional Commission Report, January 6, 1970.

17. Letter to Jordan Band, Chairman, National Jewish Community Relations Advisory Council, March 6, 1970.

18. Arkansas *Gazette*, December 19, 1969.

19. Letter to Senator Philip A. Hart of Michigan who had forwarded a constituent complaint on the road to the Department of Transportation, from R. R. Bartelsmeyer, Director of Public Roads, January 14, 1970.

20. Representatives William A. Barrett, Robert N. C. Nix, James A. Byrne, Joshua Filberg and William J. Green, listed in Jewish Telegraphic Agency *Daily News Bulletin,* April 21, 1970.

21. Quoted in "Look at 'Smith's Road' Plans Raises Question by Some: Is it for Flatlanders," Arkansas *Gazette*, March 8, 1970.

22. Letter to Jordan Band, March 9, 1970.

23. Quoted in "J. P. Hammerschmidt: Meet G. L. K. Smith," Arkansas *Gazette*, December 9, 1969.

24. Quoted by the Arkansas *Gazette*, "Look at 'Smith's Road'", March 8, 1970.

25. Letter to Jordan Band, March 24, 1970.

26. Both reprinted in Arkansas *Gazette*, May 3, 1970.

27. *Times-Echo*, April 30, 1970.

28. Arkansas *Gazette*, April 25, 1970.

29. *Gazette*, May 22, 1970.

30. Letter from Jerris Leonard to Gerald Smith, quoted in "Senator McClellan to Press for Action on State Road," *Times-Echo*, September 24, 1970.

31. "Smith Orders Petitions Filed Accusing 65 of Conspiracy," Arkansas *Gazette*, June 23, 1970.

32. June 18, 1970.

33. *Times-Echo*, September 24, 1970. The story quoted Gerald L. K. Smith as saying he had a letter to that effect from Senator McClellan.

34. October 7, 1970. Recipient not identified.

35. October 29, 1970.

36. Smith announced the project in an "exclusive release" to the *Times-Echo* ("Plan Re-Creation of the Holy Land on the Smith Foundation Grounds," February 4, 1971). In subsequent press interviews, discussed below, he and his associates gave various estimates of its cost and construction time. According to John Starr in "The Controversial 'Christian Patriot'," Riverside *Press Enterprise,* November 11, 1971, Robert Hyde, the artist engaged to design the project, estimated that the Holy Land would take "10 to 20 years to complete and could cost over $100 million." The *Times-Echo,* October 26, 1972, reported, "It is estimated that it will take ten years to complete the Holy Land construction at a cost of between $10,000,000.00 and $20,000,000.00."

37. Riverside (California) *Press Enterprise,* November 7, 1971; Seattle *Times,* November 14, 1971.

38. On February 4, 1972, responding to protests, Adams finally published an interview with an ADL spokesman making clear that, in the ADL's view Smith's projects and "piety" were an attempt to buy respectability for a lifetime of hatemongering.

39. "The Town That Runs on Water," June 25, 1972.

40. July 16, 1972.

41. J. Harry Jones, Jr., *Minutemen,* Garden City, New York, 1968. The minutemen are a group of radical right extremists who in the 1960s felt that a communist takeover of the United States was so imminent that they armed themselves to prepare for guerrilla warfare against the communist regime in Washington which they anticipated.

42. September 11, 1969.

43. October 26, 1972.

44. Similar editorials appeared in the Arkansas *Gazette* on March 17, 1970, June 26, 1970, and September 25, 1970.

45. Letter to Justin J. Finger, National director, Department of Fact Finding, ADL, September 18, 1972.

46. Letter to Alfred A. Levingston, Cleveland, Mississippi, November 1, 1972.

47. JTA *Daily News Bulletin,* January 29, 1973; Jack Anderson, "Turning Out," New York *Post,* January 29, 1973.

48. Letter from Seymour Graubard, National Chairman, ADL, January 26, 1973.

49. Quoted in the JTA *Daily News Bulletin,* January 31, 1973.

50. JTA *Daily News Bulletin,* February 1, 1973 quotes a "memorandum for the record" sent to Senator Jacob K. Javits (R. NY) by John C. Broger dated January 26, 1973. Broger said in his memo that he gave instructions ". . . to review this show for conformance with AFRTS standards."

3. The Blackman's Development Center

1. For early exposes of Hassan's activities, see James Ridgeway, "Black Mischief," *The New Republic,* December 24, 1966, pp. 14–16; Michael Drosnin, "Blackman's Army Sets Africa Coups," the Washington *Post,* December 26, 1966, and note Washington *Star* article August 5, 1967.

2. Ridgeway, op. cit.

3. Paul Valentine, "Colonel Hassan and Anti-Semitism," Washington *Post,* August 8, 1971.

4. Jack Anderson, New York *Post,* April 14, 1971.

5. Federal Criminal Record #2 395 429 for Albert Roy Osborne shows repeated charges of "passing worthless checks."

6. Letter from Edward A. Matthews, director, Division of Manpower Development and Training, to Col. Hassan Jeru-Ahmed, March 1, 1971.

7. The Stern Foundation contributed approximately $8,000; the Strong Foundation also contributed $8,000. In a letter of June 7, 1971, to Benjamin Behr, Howard A. Matthews wrote that the Center "receives funds from a number of area agencies, foundations, unions (including AFL-CIO) business firms, churches, and individuals."

8. Letter from Jason R. Silverman, Washington, D.C. regional director, ADL, to Timothy Halnon, Program Advisor, Experimental and Utilization Section, HEW Division of Manpower Development and Training.

9. Letter to Jason Silverman, February 25, 1971.

10. Letter to Richard Hobson, Jr., from Jason Silverman, March 19, 1971.

11. Letter to Jason Silverman, March 24, 1971.

12. Letter to Hassan Jeru-Ahmed from T. H. Bell, deputy commissioner for School Systems, Department of HEW, June 18, 1971.

13. Letter to Richard Hobson, Jr., from Jason Silverman, March 29, 1971.

14. Jack Anderson, Washington *Post,* April 14, 1971; April 15, 1971; April 22, 1971.

15. "ADL Scores Government for Grant to Group Headed by 'Professional Anti-Semite,'" JTA *Daily News Bulletin,* April 15, 1971.

16. Letter from Seymour Graubard, national chairman, ADL.

17. Duncan Spencer, "Hassan Accused of Anti-Semitism, Fund Cutoff Asked," April 21, 1971.

18. Letter to Harvey Schechter of Sherman Oak, California, May 25, 1971; letter to Benjamin Behr of Rockford, Illinois, June 7, 1971.

19. Letter to Seymour Graubard.

20. Complaint, *Hassan* v. *ADL,* United States District Court for the District of Columbia, July 6, 1971.

21. Order Quashing Return of Service of Summons on Defendant Seymour Graubard, J. H. Pratt, Judge, November 9, 1971.

22. "Report on Review of Costs Claimed on Department of Health, Education, and Welfare Manpower Development Training Grant No. OEG 071 1926 (337) awarded to Blackman's Development Center Washington, D.C., for the Period March 15, 1971 through June 30, 1971," Philadelphia regional office, HEW Audit Agency, January, 1972.

23. Paul Valentine, "Drug Unit Probe is Sought," Washington *Post,* June 18, 1971.

24. Complaint, *Hassan* v. *Giaimo,* United States District Court for the District of Columbia, June 21, 1971.

25. Order dismissing plaintiff's complaint, Aubrey E. Robinson, Jr., United States District Judge, October 22, 1971.

26. Stephen Green and Paul Valentine, "Audit Shows Fund Misuse by Hassan," Washington *Post,* May 31, 1972; Jack Kneece, "Audit Challenges Blackman's Unit," Washington *Star,* May 31, 1972.

27. Washington *Star,* May 31, 1972.

28. "$25,000 to Help in Drug Battle," Columbus *Dispatch,* December 5, 1971; "Drug Cure Center Gets Needed Cash," Columbus *Citizen-Journal,* December 6, 1971.

29. Letter to Jack S. Resler.

30. "'Blackman's Army' Sets Africa Coups," December 26, 1966.

31. Ernest Holsendolph, "D.C. 'Black Army' Leader Denies Promoting Newark Riots," August 5, 1967.

32. "The Student Right: Racist, Martial, Insular," May 25, 1969; "Liberty Lobby Does All Right By Itself in 10 Years," November 15, 1970.

33 David R. Boldt and William L. Claiborne, "Hassan Rejects Race, Launches Voter Drive," October 14, 1970.

34. "Washington News Conference," George Allen, commentator.

35. "Hassan Arrested on Gun Charge," Washington *Post,* February 20, 1973.

36. "Drug Center May Lose License," Columbus *Citizen-Journal,* June 5, 1972. Danyil Sulieman was convicted in 1960 in Los Angeles for violating federal narcotics laws. On July 27, 1960 he was sentenced to five years in prison. His conviction had been concealed on the application for licensing of the BDC.

37. Charles Fair, "Drop Drug Center, U.S. Tells County," *Citizen-Journal,* June 15, 1972.

38. Charles Fair, "Blackman's Drug Facility is Evicted," *Citizen-Journal,* December 9, 1972.

4. A Teachers' Association

1. Discussion of "Great Proletarian Resolution," moderated by Julius Lester, December 26, 1968.

2. "Mayor Requests Inquiry In Racism," *New York Times,* January 19, 1969.

3. "Mayor Assailed On Disputed Poem," *New York Times,* January 20, 1969.

4. "Outcry Growing Against Bigotry," *New York Times,* January 25, 1969.

5. *Forum,* September 1971.

6. *Ibid.*

7. By vote of Executive Committee, New York Urban Coalition, December 9, 1971.

8. Letter from Seymour Graubard, National Chairman ADL.

9. Letter to Seymour Graubard from S. P. Marland, Jr., March 31, 1972.

10. Letter from Seymour Graubard, April 11, 1972.

11. Letter to Seymour Graubard.

12. Letter from Seymour Graubard, June 16, 1972.

13. Letter to Seymour Graubard.

5. The New York Scene

1. "Brief Presented by Melvin Pritchard . . . at a Public Hearing on Proposal on Use of Federal Funds and Aid to Private and Parochial Schools, August 17, 1966."

2. Transcript of comments made by William O. Marley at Prospect Heights High School, January 3, 1969.

3. Leonard Buder, "Speaker Ousted by Police in Brooklyn Debate on School Decentralization," *New York Times,* January 4, 1969.

4. Information supplied by telephone to ADL, January 1969, by Donald Mathis, Director of the Office of Review of Human Resources Administration.

5. Special Committee on Racial and Religious Prejudice: Justice Bernard Botein, Chairman; Robert L. Carter, Matilde P. de Silva, David Dubinsky,

Leo McLaughlin, S.J., David Salten, Whitney North Seymour, Sr., J. D. Weiler, Franklin Williams, Arnold Forster, Counsel, Leroy Clark, co-Counsel.

6. "Anti-Semitism in the New York City School Controversy," A Preliminary Report of the Anti-Defamation League of B'nai B'rith.

7. "Statement of the Special Committee on Racial and Religious Prejudice," January 17, 1969.

8. *National Renaissance Bulletin,* Spring 1969. The *National Renaissance Bulletin* is the official organ of the National Renaissance Party, a small neo-Nazi hate group led by James Madole which has operated for some years in New York City, particularly in the Yorkville area.

9. Letter signed by Stanley Seidman, principal, and Eugene S. Friedman, assistant principal, of P.S. 9 at 80 Underhill Avenue, Brooklyn, New York, September 14, 1967.

10. Letter to Board of Education from Mario Biaggi, April 23, 1968.

11. *Ibid.*

12. Brief submitted to Vincent L. Broderick by Victor Herwitz, special counsel to American Jewish Congress, ADL and Jewish Labor Committee, January 31, 1973.

13. Opinion, Judge Walter R. Mansfield in case of *Chance and Mercado* v. *The Board of Examiners et al.*

14. "Ocean Hill Ousts 2 As Principals," *New York Times,* October 7, 1971; "Ed Board Kills City Test for Supervisors," New York Daily *News,* October 7, 1971.

15. Letter from Irving Anker, acting chancellor, August 3, 1970.

16. Vincent L. Broderick's Report to the chancellor in the matter of the grievance submitted to the chancellor with respect to community School Board District 1 and Luis Fuentes, March 30, 1973.

17. "Lower East Side Board Hires Principal Ousted in Brooklyn," *New York Times,* July 21, 1972.

18. Affidavit of Berton Lax, January 21, 1969.

19. Leonard Buder, "School Unit Told to 'Clear' Hiring," *New York Times,* June 17, 1972.

20. ADL News Release, June 15, 1972.

21. Leonard Buder, loc cit.

22. News Release, American Jewish Committee, American Jewish Congress, ADL, Jewish Labor Committee, July 26, 1972.

23. "A Time to Speak Up," *El Diario,* August 4, 1972.

24. "Four Jewish Groups To Meet With NYC Chancellor Today On Appointment of School Head Charged With Bias," Jewish Telegraphic Agency *Daily Bulletin,* August 3, 1972.

25. Letter to Harvey Scribner from Albert H. Blumenthal, August 7, 1972.

26. "Fuentes Removal Pressed," *Jewish Week,* August 17–23, 1972.

27. "The Fuentes Case," *New York Times,* August 8, 1972; "Conduct Unbecoming?" *New York Post,* August 9, 1972; "Handling a Hot Potato," *Daily News,* August 11, 1972.

28. Petition sent to Harvey B. Scribner on behalf of ADL, American Jewish Congress and the Jewish Labor Committee submitted by Victor J. Herwitz, special counsel, and Arnold Forster, general counsel, ADL, August 29, 1972.

29. ADL News Release, August 31, 1972.

30. Letter to Victor J. Herwitz and Arnold Forster, August 30, 1972.

31. "The Fuentes Farce," *Jewish Press,* September 15, 1972.

32. Letter from Arnold Forster.

33. "Scribner Defends Board on Fuentes Appointment," *New York Times,* September 29, 1972.

34. Peter Kihss, "Community Board That Hired Fuentes Issues Report Clearing Him of Anti-Semitism," *New York Times,* November 19, 1972.

35. "Fuentes Ruling Called 'Farce' By Accusers." *American Examiner—Jewish Week,* November 23, 1972.

36. *New York Times,* April 6, 1973.

37. Peter Kihss, loc cit.

6. The Clergy

1. Roy Eckardt, "The Churches, Antisemitism, and the Holocaust," presented March 20, 1972.

2. Fred Gladstone Bratton, *The Crime of Christendom: The Theological Sources of Christian Anti-Semitism* (Boston, 1969).

3. Rev. Lester Kinsolving, "Dean Follows Familiar line of Bigotry," Waterville (Maine) *Sentinel,* June 24, 1972.

4. Sayre, text of sermon, National Cathedral, Washington, D.C., Palm Sunday, March 26, 1972.

5. Rev. Lester Kinsolving, loc cit.

6. Editorial, "Dean Sayre on Jerusalem," April 4, 1972.

7. "Letters to the Editor," Washington *Post,* April 4, 1972.

8. *Ibid.*

9. "Letters to the Editor," Washington *Star,* April 6, 1972.

10. Rev. Lester Kinsolving, loc cit.

11. Roy Eckart, "The Churches, Anti-Semitism and the Holocaust."

12. "Jesuit, Canadian Protestant Back Dean Sayre on Jerusalem Issue," Religious News Service, April 7, 1972.

13. "Dean Sayre Attacks Israel."

14. "Dean Sayre Condemns Israeli Retaliation to Olympics Slayings," Religious News Service, September 11, 1972.

15. "Rabbis denounce Sayre sermon as threat to decent relations between Christians and Jews," *American Examiner—Jewish Week,* April 13, 1972.

16. "Dean Sayre's Trip to Israel Dropped," *Jewish Post and Opinion,* December 8, 1972.

17. *Search for Peace in the Middle East* (Philadelphia, 1970).

18. Arnold M. Soloway with Edwin Weiss and Gerald Caplan, *Truth and Peace in the Middle East—A Critical Analyses of the Quaker Report* (New York, 1971).

19. Introduction, *Truth and Peace in the Middle East.*

20. Quoted in *Truth and Peace in the Middle East,* p. 66.

21. *Truth and Peace in the Middle East,* p. 68.

22. *Ibid.*

23. Editorial, "In Defense of Friends."

7. The Media and the Arts

1. Alan Rich, "The Selling of the Savior," *New York Magazine,* October 25, 1971.

2. George Gent, "'Superstar': The Cheers and Jeers Build," New York *Times,* October 14, 1971.

3. Rev. James Di Giacomo, Fordham University, Assistant Professor, quoted in "'Superstar': The Cheers and Jeers Build."

4. Libretto, *Jesus Christ Superstar,* Copyright Leeds Music Ltd. 1970.

5. *Ibid.*

6. *Ibid.*

7. Gerald S. Strober, "'Jesus Christ Superstar': The 'Rock Opera' and Christian-Jewish Relations," October 10, 1971.

8. Henry Hewes, *Saturday Review* critic, and George Oppenheimer, *Newsday* critic, quoted in Martin J. Flusser Jr., "Jewish Group Raps 'Superstar,'" *Newsday,* October 12, 1971.

9. Lawrence Van Gelder, "Two Jewish Organizations Are Critical of 'Superstar,'" New York *Times,* October 31, 1971.

10. Statement, National Jewish Community Relations Advisory Council, June 23, 1973.

11. *"Jesus Christ Superstar* (Production Notes)," Universal Pictures, 445 Park Avenue, New York.

12. Letter to Justin Finger, national director, Department of Fact Finding, ADL, from Walter J. Minton, July 19, 1971.

13. "Author's Note," *Lansky,* (New York, 1971).

14. Letter to Lynne Ianniello, editor, ADL *Bulletin,* from Hank Messick, November 14, 1971.

15. Letter from Justin J. Finger, June 28, 1971; letter to Justin J. Finger, June 30, 1971.

16. Letter from Justin J. Finger, July 14, 1971.

17. Letter to Justin J. Finger, July 19, 1971.

18. *Publisher's Weekly,* September 1, 1971.

19. "ADL Charges Publisher Used Biased Headline to Promote Sale of Book," Jewish Telegraphic Agency *Daily Bulletin,* August 17, 1971.

20. Form letter to Mr. Samuel S. King, Harrison, New York, from Larry Gershel, Vice President, Berkley Publishing Corporation, August 31, 1971.

21. Letter to Dr. Alvin M. Lashinsky, Queens Jewish Community Council, Inc., July 8, 1971.

22. "'Portnoy' Should Have Stayed a Novel," June 20, 1972.

23. "Grounds For Complaint," July 3, 1972.

24. "'Portnoy's Complaint': An Anti-Jewish Joke?" *New York Times,* July 16, 1972.

25. "Sunday with Mister C. An Audio-Documentary by Andy Warhol starring Truman Capote," *Rolling Stone,* April 12, 1973.

26. Truman Capote quoted in *Rolling Stone,* loc cit.

27. "Playboy Interview: Truman Capote," *Playboy Magazine,* March 1968.

28. C. Robert Jennings, "Truman Capote Talks, Talks, Talks," *New York Magazine,* May 13, 1968.

29. "Crime Watch," WABC-TV, Part I, May 8, 1973; Part II, June 21, 1973.

30. May 5, 1972.

31. May 7, 1972.

32. Charles Macleish, editor.

33. November 19, 1972.

34. June 29, 1972.

35. Cover of "The Ventures of Zimmerman," *National Lampoon*, p. 43.

36. Martin Kasendorf, "Archie and Maude and Fred and Norman and Alan," *New York Times Magazine*, June 24, 1973.

37. *Ibid.*

38. "As I Listened to Archie Say 'Hebe' . . .," *New York Times*, September 12, 1971.

39. Victor M. Bienstock, "Likeable bigot' on TV perturbs ethnic leaders," *American Examiner—Jewish Week*, February 25, 1971.

40. "Archie: Lovable or Lamentable?" letter to the editor of the *New York Times* from Benjamin R. Epstein, October 3, 1971.

41. Arthur Lelyveld, "The Archie Bunker Syndrome," *Congress Bi-Weekly*, April 28, 1972.

42. "Sandy Duncan Show." October 22, 1972.

43. Letter to Harvey Schechter, West Coast civil rights director, ADL from Franklin Barton, executive producer CBS, October 30, 1972.

44. March 16, 1972.

45. "The Most Oppressed Peoples," Long Island *Press*, June 27, 1972.

46. Letter to Jacob Stein, quoted in *American Examiner*, March 22, 1973.

8. The Radical Left

1. "Zionism, the Arabs and the Jews," October 23–November 5, 1970.

2. "The Fight for Peace in the Middle East," March 1973.

3. Statement adopted by the International Conference for Peace and Justice, Bologna, Italy, May 11–13, 1973, according to Hyman Lumer in a speech at Debs Auditorium on June 19, 1973.

4. "World peace congress set for October," *Daily World*, March 20, 1973.

5. "The U.S. stake in Middle East peace: I," Mobil Oil advertisement, *New York Times*, June 21, 1973; Letter to stockholders of Standard Oil Company of California, from O. N. Miller, Chairman of the Board, July 26, 1973. Quoted in "Texaco and Saudi Arabia Question Policy in Mideast," *New York Times*, September 19, 1973.

6. Barry Sheppard, "National SWP Convention is planned," April 30, 1971.

7. Jon Rothschild, "American Trotskyists Hold National Convention," *Intercontinental Press*, September 6, 1971.

8. *Ibid.*

9. "Al Fatah: Towards a Democratic State in Palestine," October 9, 1970.

10. "Perspectives on world revolution."

11. "The real facts about the Palestinian struggle," October 2, 1970.

12. "The Munich killings," September 15, 1972.

13. *Free Palestine*, August 1971.

14. Complaint, *James Lafferty et al* vs. *William Rogers et al* filed October 8, 1971.

15. Letter dated September 2, 1971.

16. "Convention had many int'l guests," January 15, 1971.

17. "National Campaign for Middle East Teach-Ins," *The Organizer*, October 14, 1970.

18. Copy of flyer calling attention to the March 1, 1973 panel discussion lists members of the May 15th coalition.

19. The ADL has traditionally viewed close monitoring of extremists activities as part of its obligation to the Jewish and American communities. Therefore, its representatives often attend open meetings, conventions and conferences of extremist groups (left wing and right wing) to keep abreast of what the groups are doing. Material in this chapter and others which is not otherwise documented stems from reports of reliable observers.

20. "Isaac Deutscher on the non-Jewish Jew," February 7, 1969.

21. Elizabeth Barnes, "Lindsay continues crusade against black community," *The Militant*, February 7, 1969.

22. "Mantan Moreland and the Houseniggers of Revolution," *Black News*, May 7, 1971.

23. ADL observer report of July 15, 1967, Harlem rally on Mid-East Crises. Sponsored by the Harlem Committee Against Imperialism, the meeting was billed in advertising leaflet as "The Other Side" of the Arab-Israeli Crisis.

24. Elizabeth Joyko, "YSA, LUCHA back Fuentes at New York U."

25. "Strongest Among Working Class," March 8, 1973.

26. Mack Satinoff, "Queens College, Zionists Attack Black Campus Paper," *Young Socialist*, May 1973.

27. "Black Americans slate pro-Arab-revolution ad," October 16, 1970.

28. "An Appeal by Black Americans for United States Support to Israel," June 28, 1970.

29. Letter, October 7, 1970, quoted in "A Black American Looks at Israel, the 'Arab Revolution,' Racism, Palestinians and Peace," pamphlet, American Jewish Congress.

30. Form letter from Berta Langston, February 5, 1971.

31. Henry M. Winston, "Black Americans and the Middle East," *Political Affairs,* September 1970.

32. July 1971; August 1971.

33. Congress Document, "For a Just And Lasting Peace In the Middle East," reprinted in *New World Review,* Summer 1971.

34. "CP Adopts Broad Election Platform," *Daily World,* February 24, 1972.

35. Mary Thomas, "The Fight Against Anti-Semitism and Zionism," *Daily World,* December 18, 1971.

36. May Day Declaration of Communist Party, U.S.A., reprinted in "A day of world workers' unity and struggle," *Daily World,* May 1, 1973.

37. "Lebanon CP congress marks a turning point," January 18; 1972.

38. Editorial comment, "USSR: A New Historical Community."

39. Declaration of World Conference of Jewish Communities on Soviet Jewry, quoted in Richard Cohen ed., *Let My People Go* (New York, 1971).

40. March 20, 1971.

41. Excerpted in *Daily World,* December 30, 1972.

42. Trudy Rubin, "Where Have All The Radicals Gone? I," *Christian Science Monitor,* February 23, 1973. According to Ms. Rubin, "The last three SDS presidents—Mark Rudd, Michael Klonsky and Bernardine Dohrn have all disappeared underground, with Miss Dohrn reputed to be in Algeria."

43. "Israeli Anti-Communist Frame-up Can't Defuse Exploding Strike Wave," January 11, 1973.

44. "Golda as Fascist," *SDS,* Lehman College, Bronx, N.Y., undated.

45. *Challenge,* January 11, 1973, loc cit.

46. Leaflet, "Israeli Government Frames Anti-Racist Organizers."

47. "PLP Debates Zionists at Lehman College," April 19, 1973.

48. July 12, 1973.

49. Imprint on MERIP reprint of an article, "From Refugees to Palestinians," *Liberated Guardian,* September 17, 1970.

50. Subheading on issues of *Palestine Resistance Bulletins.*

51. Form letter signed by Christopher Hilger, San Francisco Newsreel.

52. Form letter from Sara Shulman.

53. "On the Twenty-Fifth Anniversary of the Zionist State," *Intercontinental Press,* May 21, 1973.

9. Arabs and Pro-Arabs

1. Koran, Sura II, The Cow, V. 61; Sura III, The Family of Imran, V. 112.

2. Yehoshafat Harkabi, *Arab Attitudes Toward Israel* (New York, 1971), p. 220.

3. *Shawt al Arab,* June 17, 1967, quoted in Dafna Alon, *Arab Racialism* (Israel, 1969), p. 59.

4. Iraqi Government *Gazette,* March 3, 1968, quoted in *ibid.* p. 60.

5. March 8, 1970.

6. R. K. Karanjra, *Blitz,* October 4, 1958, quoted in M. S. Arnoni, "Rights and Wrongs in the Arab-Israeli Conflict," *The Minority of One,* September 1967.

7. *Al-Nahar,* September 5, 1968.

8. Harkabi, p. 235.

9. Copy of Ministry of Post letter, April 29, 1968.

10. Quoted in "The Assassination of Premier Wasfi Tal," *Intercontinental Press,* December 13, 1971.

11. "Gadaffi Praises 'Elders of Zion,'" *Jerusalem Post,* December 17, 1972.

12. Peter Lust, "Nasser's Nazis," pub. by Labour Friends of Israel, undated.

13. Wolfgang Lutz, *The Champagne Spy* (New York, 1972).

14. Gabriel Rey, "Semitic Anti-Semitism—Sadat's Past Catches Up With Him," *Analysis,* published by the Institute for Jewish Policy Planning and Research of the Synagogue Council of America, May 22, 1972. Reprinted from London *Jewish Chronicle,* May 12, 1972.

15. *Israelis reply,* Bulletin published by Israeli students of Middle East Affairs, December 1971.

16. "Sadat: Israel So Be 'Persecuted, Supressed and Miserable,'" *Brief* (Israeli fortnightly publication on Middle East affairs), April 16–30, 1972.

17. Al Mussawar, July 31, 1972, quoted in *Brief,* August 1–15, 1972.

18. "Faisal's Land of Faith and Oil," April 9, 1972.

19. May 14, 1973.

20. "Zionism blamed for Watergate, Lambton Affairs," *Jerusalem Post,* June 4, 1973.

21. Report of the UNESCO Commission.

22. Ibid.

23. May 3, 1968, quoted in *"Hatred is Sacred."* Extracts from Arab School Texts Compiled by E. Hess for Ministry for Foreign Affairs, Information Division, November 1968.

24. "Court says 'anti-Israel,' same as 'anti-Semitic,'" *Jerusalem Post,* November 9, 1969.

25. Nan Robertson, "Paris Court Says Reds Defamed Jews," *New York Times,* April 25, 1973, "Soviet Embassy Publication On Trial In Paris For Spreading Anti-Semitism," Jewish Telegraphic Agency *Daily News Bulletin,* March 27, 1973.

26. Paul Hofmann, "Arab Attacks on Jewish Issue Seem to Be Worrying Vatican," New York *Times,* April 25, 1973.

27. "Arab States Supply El Fatah With $85 Million A Year," JTA *Daily News Bulletin,* February 1, 1973.

28. News Release, Americans for United Nations Responsibility in the Middle East, 3500 West Howe Street, Seattle, Washington, undated.

29. Mohammed T. Mehdi, *Kennedy and Sirhan: Why?*

30. Letter signed by Salah El Dareer, April 17, 1972.

31. "Oil For U.S. Linked by Saudi To Peace," April 20, 1973.

32. Henry Tanner, "Libyan Sees Oil Becoming Arab Weapon," *New York Times,* May 14, 1973.

33. "4 Arab Nations Temporarily Halt Flow of Oil in Symbolic Protest," May 16, 1973.

34. *Ibid.*

35. "The Lure of Oil At Abu Dhabi," *New York Post,* April 5, 1973.

36. Leonard Mosley, *Power Play: Oil in the Middle East* (New York, 1973).

37. "The Danger of Doing Nothing," *New York Times,* June 28, 1973.

38. "Kissinger and The Arabs," New York *Post,* February 1, 1973.

39. Transcript, "Face the Nation."

40. "Fulbright Launches Strongest Attack on U.S. Policy Toward Israel," JTA *Daily News Bulletin,* May 31, 1973.

41. "Praise for Fulbright," New York *Daily News,* April 18, 1973.

10. Anti-Semitism in a Minority Community

1. Quoted in Robert G. Weisbord and Arthur Stein, *Bitter Sweet Encounter: Afro Americans and the American Jew* (Connecticut, 1970), p. 55.

2. Ibid., pp. 46, 56.

3. Frantz Fanon, *The Wretched of the Earth* (New York, 1963).

4. Quoted in C. Eric Lincoln, *The Black Muslims in America* (Boston, 1961) p. 166.

5. Malcolm Little, *The Autobiography of Malcolm X* (New York, 1965).

6. Quoted in Russell Sackett, "Plotting A War On Whitey," *Life Magazine,* June 10, 1966.

7. "Black Anti-Semitism," March 17, 1967.

8. *Liberator,* January 1966.

9. Ibid., April 1966.

10. Ibid., February 1966.

11. Quoted in Homer Bigart, "Baldwin Leaves Negro Monthly," *New York Times,* February 28, 1967.

12. "Readers' Forum," First Quarter 1967.

13. Quoted in William Borders, "CORE Disavows Racist Remark," *New York Times,* February 8, 1966.

14. February 5, 1966.

15. "Mayor Bars Brown At City Hall, Orders Report To F.B.I. And D.A." Mount Vernon *Daily Argus,* February 7, 1966.

16. William Borders, "CORE Board Member Quits Over Mt. Vernon Attack on Jews," *New York Times,* February 9, 1966.

17. Michael Stern, "Mt. Vernon Group Expelled by CORE," *New York Times,* May 28, 1966.

18. Will Maslow, executive director of the American Jewish Congress, in News Release of American Jewish Congress, February 8, 1966.

19. "Position of the Congress of Racial Equality on Anti-Semitism," issued March 1966.

20. September 19, 1970.

21. "Notes On People," *New York Times,* March 29, 1973.

22. Ibid., March 22, 1973.

23. Charles Mohr, "Amin, Calling Nixon 'Brilliant,' Asks Good Uganda-U.S. Ties," *New York Times,* April 5, 1973.

24. "Amin Praises Hitler For Killing of Jews," *New York Times,* September 13, 1972.

25. "'Protocols' in Uganda," London *Jewish Chronicle,* March 23, 1973.

26. Christopher Munnion, November 12, 1972.

27. "'Pan Africanism and black nationalism are one'—Roy Innis talks to Afroman U. O. Canada," January–February 1973.

28. "Negro Jew-Haters Spew Venom For Susskind," *B'nai B'rith Messenger,* October 28, 1966.

29. "Backlash To Affect Jewish Voters Also," *Jewish Post and Opinion,* October 28, 1966.

30. Richard Barr, "AJC Blasts Susskind Show As 'Fomenting Anti-Semitism,'" *World Journal Tribune,* October 10, 1966.

31. Editors note in response to letters to the editor, August 4 and August 11, 1966.

32. *The Quotable Karenga,* ed. Clyde Halisi and James Mtume (Los Angeles, 1967), p. 28.

33. Flyer received by ADL, January 20, 1967.

34. Based on report of ADL observer.

35. Ibid., P. 23.

36. July 1966.

37. Questions numbers 18 and 20.

38. The PLO booklet on which SNCC drew heavily in its June–July 1967, *Newsletter,* was entitled *Do You Know? Twenty Basic Questions About the Palestine Problem.* Another PLO propaganda booklet apparently used as a source by SNCC was Izzat Tannous' *The Enraging Story of Palestine and Its People,* produced in August 1965.

39. Quoted in Gene Roberts, "SNCC Charges Israeli Atrocities," *New York Times,* August 15, 1967.

40. "An Open Letter to SNCC. . . . by Theodore Bikel," printed by American Jewish Congress.

41. "What We Want." September 22, 1966.

42. "Letters to the Editor," December 1, 1966.

43. "Stokely Says CIA, Zionism In League," Santa Ana *Register,* September 22, 1967.

44. "Carmichael Back—Message Africa," March 18, 1971.

45. "Carmichael Says Politics 'Not Answer,'" Washington *Post,* October 18, 1972.

46. Tom Birns, "Carmichael denounces Zionism," February 1, 1973.

47. Transcript, February 10, 1973.

48. "Black Power Leaders Call for a Separate Nationhood," July 29, 1967.

49. "Rate of Negro Anti-Semitism Concerns Jewish Leaders," Long Island *Press,* August 13, 1967.

50. Robert Gruenberg, "Biafra Fails to Stir the U.S. Negro," October 17, 1968.

51. Warren Weaver, "Parley on New Politics Yields To Militant Negroes' Demands," *New York Times,* September 3, 1967.

52. *Ibid.*

53. Frank Lynn, "New Left Hits Israel, Viet War, Draft," *Newsday,* September 5, 1967.

54. Copy, Resolution on the Middle East—passed.

55. Renata Adler, "Letter From the Palmer House," *The New Yorker,* September 23, 1967.

56. September 4, 1967.

57. "Dr. King backs entity of Israel, calls anti-Semitism immoral," *Christian Science Monitor,* October 13, 1967.

58. *Facts On File,* March 12, 1972.

59. Letter from Absalam F. Jordan, Junior, field chairman, July 8, 1971.

60. Copy, Israel Resolution.

61. Congressional Black Caucus News Release, "Congressional Black Caucus Reaffirms Its Position On the State of Israel," March 21, 1972.

62. Letter to David Brody, regional director ADL, Washington, D.C., March 21, 1972.

63. NAACP News Release, "NAACP Withdraws From Black Political Group," May 16, 1972.

64. Sub-Resolution on Israel Adopted by the Continuations Committee of the National Black Political Convention, March 24, 1972.

65. Paul Delaney, "Black Convention Eases Busing and Israeli Stands," *New York Times,* May 20, 1972.

66. Imamu Sukumu, "African Congress happy over successful CAP convention," *Voice and Viewpoint,* September 13, 1972.

67. Tony Griggs, "Imamu Baraka 'rules' assembly," October 23, 1972.

68. "Projects Funded in 1970," A Report of IFCO 1970; "Partial Summary of Projects Funded By IFCO, 1970; "Foundation gives 100G to US, Afro Movements," New York *Amsterdam News,* July 1, 1972.

69. *Liberator,* January 1966; *Inner City Voice,* January 10, 1967.

70. "Black People!" *Evergreen Review,* December 1967.

71. *Ibid.*

72. Leonard Buder, "Negroes Urged At I.S. 201 To Aim for 'Self Defense.'" *New York Times,* February 22, 1968.

73. Imamu Amiri Baraka (LeRoi Jones), *Raise, Race, Rays, Raze* (New York, 1972).

74. "Cleaver, Arafat Hailed At Palestinian Rally," Deecember 28, 1969.

75. Jesse W. Lewis, Jr., "Cleaver Wants to Leave Algiers, Rejoin Panther 'Struggle' in U.S.," January 5, 1970.

76. "Panthers Against The Wall."

77. Statement of Black Panther Party To Palestinian Student Conference, Kuwait, February 13–17, 1971.

78. "Panthers Elected to Poverty Unit," Oakland *Tribune,* June 9, 1972.

79. Editorial, "A Revolutionary Means of Communication," *Right On,* December 4–18, 1971.

80. "Louisville Unites!" April 5, 1972.

81. "Anatomy of Roy Innis," May 31, 1972.

82. "Jordan Gets More U.S. Jets," February 17, 1973.

83. "No Half-Masts For Arabs," March 3, 1973.

84. April 21, 1973.

85. "Playboy Interview: Huey Newton—A Candid Conversation with the embattled leader of the black panther party."

86. Abass Rassoull, "Those Who Built a Mosque to Cause Harm."

87. George Thayer, *The Farther Shores of Politics—American Political Fringe Today* (New York, 1967), p. 307.

88. "Racial Strife," *Facts On File,* Thursday February 18–Wednesday February 24, 1965.

89. "Foreign policy issues effecting Blacks," August 11, 1972.

90. Shakil Ahmed Zia, *A History of Jewish Crimes* (Karachi, 1969), p. ix–x.

91. March 10, 1972; October 22, 1971; October 30, 1970; February 4, 1972.

92. January 22, 1971.

93. "The Accuser Will Be Cast Down!" May 12, 1972.

94. June 6, 1969; June 6, 1969; November 14, 1969; September 29, 1972; November 27, 1970; March 26, 1971.

95. October 16, 1970; December 25, 1970.

96. Nathaniel Lox, "Libyan Gov't reduces loan payments from Nation of Islam," October 20, 1972.

97. "Libya Bars $3 Million Loan To Black Muslims Group," Religious News Service, February 15, 1973.

98. Nathaniel Lox, "Muslim Nation of Abu Dhabi Unites to help nation of Islam," Qatar aids emerging Muslims in America," *Muhammad Speaks,* October 20, 1972; "Muslim World lines up to help Muhammud," *Muhammad Speaks,* July 21, 1972.

99. August 15, 1969; April 24, 1970; September 25, 1970; June 15, 1972.

100. "Messenger's Attacker Exposed," May 5, 1972.

101. "Israel Shares Guilt for Insane Massacre," June 16, 1972.

102. September 22, 1972.

103. "Libyan Air Tragedy," March 9, 1973.

104. Quoted in *The Militant,* March 7, 1969.

105. Quoted in "Wayne U. Officials Rebuke College Paper For Anti-Semitic Attitudes," Jewish Telegraphic Agency *Daily News Bulletin,* February 9, 1973.

106. Jacoby Sims, "Black student Convention in Chicago plans study, international solidarity," *People's World,* September 11, 1971.

107. Harold Cruse, *The Crisis of the Negro Intellectual* (New York, 1967).

108. Harold Cruse, *Rebellion Or Revolution* (New York, 1968).

109. Gary T. Marx, *Protest and Prejudice: A Study of Belief in the Black Community* (New York, 1967).

110. Gertrude Selznick and Stephen Steinberg, *The Tenacity of Prejudice* (New York, 1969).

111. Marx, *Protest and Prejudice,* "Postscript," 1969 revised edition.

112. Jeannye Thornton, "Black America today—who's in charge?" *The Christian Science Monitor,* March 17, 1973.

113. *Ibid.*

114. David Shipler, "City Study Backs Increase in Rents," New York *Times,* May 1, 1970.

11. The USSR, Western Europe, Latin America

1. William Korey, *The Soviet Cage—Anti-Semitism in Russia* (New York, 1973).

2. Quoted in "Soviet Anti-Semitism Is Now 'Respectable,'" *Jerusalem Post,* May 16, 1973.

3. *Jews in Eastern Europe* (periodical published in London by European Jewish Publications Ltd.), ed. Emanuel Litvinoff, November, 1967. (Notes 4 through 8 refer to material from Soviet publications cited in this November, 1967 issue. The dates given are those of the Soviet journals.)

4. June 15, 1967.

5. June 16, 1967.

6. June 23, 1967.

7. July 4, 1967.

8. July 5, 1967.

9. *Soviet Weekly,* July 6, 1967.

10. Quoted in William Korey, "Myths, Fantasies and Show Trials: Echos of the Past," *Perspectives on Soviet Jewry* (New York, 1971).

11. *Jews In Eastern Europe,* November, 1967.

12. Adolph Hitler, *My New Order,* ed. Raoul de Roussy de Sales (New York, 1941), p. 949.

13. *Beware Zionism!* Moscow: Political Literature Publishing House, 1969, quoted in "Selections from Soviet Publications and Mass Media," *Perspectives on Soviet Jewry,* p. 59.

14. P.5

15. Trofim Kichko, *Judaism and Zionism* (Kiev, 1968).

16. Quoted in "Whipping Up Anti-Semitism" *Jewish Observer and Middle East Review,* March 30, 1973.

17. "Jewish Circles Seriously Concerned Over New Soviet Anti-Zionist Film," Jewish Telegraphic Agency *Daily News Bulletin,* May 10, 1973.

18. "Eased Exit Vowed for Soviet Jews," *New York Times,* December 4, 1966.

19. Quoted in *A Hero for Our Time: The Trial and Fate of Boris Kochubiyevsky,* ed. Moshe Decter (New York, undated), pp. 34–35.
    The material in succeeding pages on the trials and imprisonment of Soviet Jews for their activities directed toward emigration to Israel or toward a Jewish religious and cultural renaissance in the Soviet Union (including, for example, the study of Hebrew) has been well documented within the past several years in many quarters, not the least of which is the intensive newspaper coverage of this ongoing story beginning with the December 1970 Leningrad trial that culminated in two death sentences, later commuted. Specific events, therefore, will not be documented in the text except when sources are quoted directly. Beginning with the Kochubiyevsky trial and the various petitions and letters that reached the West starting in 1968 and 1969, material on the condition of Soviet Jews has been issued periodically in pamphlet form by: the National Conference on Soviet Jewry (formerly the American Jewish Conference on Soviet Jewry); the American Jewish Com-

mittee, American Jewish Congress and Anti-Defamation League; the International Committee for the Defence of Human Rights in the USSR; the Academic Committee on Soviet Jewry; the Conference on the Status of Soviet Jews; the Information Division of the Ministry of Foreign Affairs, Jerusalem; the U.S. Department of State; and *Jews in Eastern Europe,* a periodical survey of events edited in London by Emanuel Litvinoff. Research papers, fact-finding reports and essays issued by these groups have included the work of recognized experts in the Soviet Jewry field, including Moshe Decter, William Korey, Hans Morgenthau and Abraham Brumberg, among many others. Information on the trial proceedings in various Soviet cities, accounts of the detention of Soviet Jewish activists and other details surrounding the issue have come from Soviet Jews themselves via phone calls to the USSR from the foregoing organizations as well as the Student Struggle for Soviet Jewry. In addition, several books published in recent years deal entirely with Soviet Jewry and encompass this period; among them are: *The Unredeemed: Anti-Semitism in the Soviet Union,* ed. Ronald I. Rubin; *Let My People Go: Today's Documentary Story of Soviet Jewry's Struggle to Be Free,* ed. Richard Cohen, and *The Soviet Cage* by William Korey.

20. *Jews in Eastern Europe,* August, 1970, p. 77.

21. December 30, 1970.

22. December 28, 1970.

23. Quoted in *Jews in Eastern Europe,* April, 1971, p. 35.

24. *Ibid.,* p. 42.

25. "Whipping Up Anti-Semitism" *Jewish Observer and Middle East Review,* March 30, 1973.

26. Quoted in "Prisoners In Mental Homes," *Focus On Soviet Jews,* (newsletter published in London), October, November 1971.

27. *Soviet Jews: Fact and Fiction,* p. 22.

28. Thomas B. Ross, "Soviets to Ease Emigration Tax on Most Jews," October 5, 1972.

29. Pamphlet, *Zionism Instrument of Imperialist Reaction* (Moscow, March–May, 1970).

30. *Ibid.*

31. Philippa Lewis, "A Crooked Exodus," November 17, 1972.

32. *Ibid.;* the monthly was *Oktyabr,* September, October 1972.

33. April 23, 1971.

34. Record of September 25, 1971 Security Council session (Document S/PV 1582), cited in William Korey, "Bigotry in the Hall of Brotherhood," *The American Zionist,* January, 1972.

35. *Ibid.*

36. *Ibid.*

37. "Malik Ridicules Israeli Delegate Over Observance," *American Examiner-Jewish Week,* September 14, 1972.

38. Nikita S. Khrushchev, *Khrushchev Remembers* (New York, 1970), quoted in Thomas B. Ross, "Anti-Semitism big in Russia, Khrushchev writes," Chicago *Sun-Times,* January 5, 1971.

39. Maurice Friedberg, "Anti-Semitism As a Policy Tool in the Soviet Union," *New Politics,* Fall, 1971.

40. *Ibid.*

41. *Ibid.*

42. Jonathan Randal, "Cracow Students Boycott Classes in Defiance of Polish Regime," *New York Times,* March 15, 1968.

43. "The Struggle in Poland: A Tangled Web," *Peoples World,* April 20, 1968.

44. Andrzej Werblan (a leading Party theoretician), *Miesiecynik Literacki,* June, 1968, quoted in Friedberg (see note 39).

45. "Forgive Them Not For They Knew What They Did," *New York Times Magazine,* October 24, 1965.

46. Joseph B. Schechtman, "Forgive Them Not—The Lesson of Poland," *The American Zionist,* November, 1968.

47. Paul Lendvai, *Anti-Semitism Without Jews* (New York, 1971).

48. Jack Maurice, "No Jewish Problem in Poland—Gierek," *Jerusalem Post,* October 3, 1972.

49. "German Publishers Honor Korczak," London *Jewish Chronicle,* October 6, 1972.

50. Quoted in Paul Lendvai, p. 262.

51. Friedberg, op. cit., p. 72.

52. *Ibid.*

53. *Ibid.,* p. 73.

54. *Ibid.,* p. 74.

55. Lendvai, op. cit., p. 297.

56. David Horowitz, "Palestinian Attacks Waldheim on the Refugees," *World Union Press* Syndicate, November 17, 1972.

57. Quoted in "British Press Critical," London *Jewish Chronicle,* November 3, 1972.

58. "West Germans Approve of Surrender to Terror," London *Jewish Chronicle,* November 3, 1972.

59. Grenville Janner, "Viennese with Mixed Feelings Would 'forgive and forget' slaughter of 'horrible people,'" *American Examiner-Jewish Week,* February 17, 1972.

60. *Ibid.*

61. *Ibid.*

62. Paul Hofmann, "Italian Neo-Fascists Are Linked to a Synagogue Fire in Padua," *New York Times,* April 30, 1973.

63. "Anti-Semitic Slant in Italian Television Series," London *Jewish Chronicle,* March 9, 1973.

64. "'Pro-Jewish' Priest Removed," JTA *Daily News Bulletin,* March 12, 1973.

65. *Ibid.*

66. "Le XXIX ème National de la LICA," *le droit de vivre,* January 1973.

67. Ze'ev Schul, "German Weekly Attacks Israel," *Jerusalem Post,* June 14, 1973.

68. *Ibid.*

69. Ze'ev Schul, "2nd 'Stern' piece on Israel as hostile as the first," *Jerusalem Post,* June 19, 1973.

70. "From Berlin to Amman and Back," *Encounter,* November, 1970.

71. Brian Arthur, "Germany Has 2,200 Arab Extremists, Supporters," *Jerusalem Post,* June 19, 1973.

72. Edward R. F. Sheehan, "The Mideast: Wrong Place for an Optimist,: *New York Times,* September 2, 1973.

73. September 23, 1972.

74. "Grim reports of repression in Israel-occupied lands," October 28, 1969, cited in "How pro-Arab bias affects British press," London *Jewish Chronicle,* November 14, 1969.

75. Reg Robinson, "MP's in Commons furore over 'dual loyalties' allegation," London *Jewish Chronicle,* December 22, 1972.

76. *Ibid.*

77. *Ibid.*

78. "Battle of the Bulldozers," April 29, 1972.

79. Letter to the editor, *Guardian,* May 20, 1972.

80. "Behind Black September," October 3, 1972.

81. August 5, 1972.

82. March 3, 1973.

83. Quoted in "Press divided on Israeli action," London *Jewish Chronicle,* March 2, 1973.

84. *Ibid.*

85. *Ibid.*

86. "Definition of 'Jew' Upheld," *New York Post,* July 6, 1973.

87. "Argentina, the World and the Jews," *Siglo XX,* Manuel Belgrano School, July 1971.

88. Memorandum of protest to Argentina's Minister of the Interior, General Francisco Imez from Delegacion De Asociaciones Israelitas Argentinas, February 11, 1970.

89. *Informativo DAIA,* September 15, 1971.

90. *Ibid.*

91. Natan Lerner, "The Anti-Semitic Radical Right in Argentina," World Jewish Congress, July 1965.

92. "Anti-Semitic Group Being Revived," JTA *Daily News Bulletin,* May. 24, 1973.

93. Flyer, Alianza Libertador Nacionalista, undated.

94. Orient News International Service, November 12, 1971.

95. "The Zionist Plan of Rabbi Gordon Must Be Investigated," February 16, 1972.

96. *Noticias,* February 3, 1972.

97. *Informativo DAIA,* March 15, 1972.

98. Newsletter of Congreso Judeo Latino Americano, April 1972.

99. "Anti-Semitic Campaign Stepped Up," JTA *Daily News Bulletin,* January 26, 1972.

100. Jonathan Kandell, "Military to Replace Civilians as Chile School Heads," New York *Times,* September 30, 1973.

101. "Leftists Win At University," *Times of the Americas,* October 3, 1973.

102. "Antisemitismo Por Culpa De Los Judios?" July 1972.

103. "Guerrillas Kill Argentina's Labor Leader," *New York Times,* September 26, 1973.

104. Flyer with imprint of ERP, undated; *Clarin,* May 29, 1973.

105. Nissim Elnecave, "Zionist Youth Boo Israeli," September 7, 1973.

106. *Cronica,* April 26, 1973.

107. *La Nacion,* July 1, 1973.

108. April 3, 1973.

109. *La Opinion,* June 14, 1973.

110. "'Argentina won't be anti-Semitic,' Campara says," *Jerusalem Post*, April 18, 1973.

111. May 7, 1973.

112. October 19, 1969.

113. Letter from Leonardo Lerner, member DAIA staff, to Morton Rosenthal, ADL, December 30, 1967.

114. Quoted in *Noticias*, September 14, 1972.

115. Flyer distributed at National University, Rosario, Argentina, July 27, 1973.

116. Morton M. Rosenthal, "Albandak's New Mission." ADL *Bulletin*, April 1972.

117. January 1970.

118. *La Tragedia Del Crestianismo En Israel* (Segunda Edicion) (Buenos Aires, C., early 1968).

119. *Ibid.*

120. *La Razon*, October 2.

121. October 8, 1971.

122. October 14, 1971.

123. October 20, 1971.

124. *Clarin*, October 14, 1971.

125. *Los Andes*, June 24, 1973; *Mendoza*, June 24, 1973.

126. *Informativo DAIA*, July 1973.

127. Speech delivered during ceremonies of the Diplomat's Day, April 1973.

128. "'Protocols' on sale," London *Jewish Chronicle*, July 6, 1973.

129. Murray Zuckoff, "Chilean Jewry Faces Uncertain Future," JTA *Daily News Bulletin*, September 13, 1973.

130. *La Segunda*, August 8, 1973.

131. Quoted in *El Siglo*, August 13, 1973.

132. "El Antisemitismo Traiciona Los Principios Deul PDC," *El Siglo*, August 31, 1973.

12. The Radical Right

1. Arnold Forster and Benjamin R. Epstein, *Danger on the Right* (New York, 1964).

2. Arnold Forster and Benjamin R. Epstein, *The Radical Right: Report on the John Birch Society and Its Allies* (New York, 1967).

3. John Birch Society *Bulletin,* September, 1972; *Homefront* (publication of Institute for American Democracy), August, 1973.

4. Elizabeth Duff, "Birch Society organizes new 'strike force' at Summer Youth Camps," *Boston Globe,* September 23, 1973; Lars-Erik Nelson, "Who's Afraid of the John Bircher?" *Boston Globe,* January 21, 1973.

5. Elizabeth Duff, loc cit.

6. Robert Welch, *The Neutralizers* (Boston, 1963).

7. Robert Welch, "Success Is In The Silences," John Birch Society *Bulletin,* March, 1972.

8. Editorial, "None Dare Call It Conspiracy," May 25, 1972.

9. Marguerite M. Woodman, "Letter to the Editor," Manchester (N.H.) *Union Leader,* June 29, 1972.

10. Memorandum to All Members of Chapters 876 and DAZO of the John Birch Society from Richard E. Woodin, Chapter leader, June 27, 1972.

11. Serialization begun on June 28, 1972 and continued chapter by chapter in subsequent issues.

12. Letter to John G. Schmitz from Harvey Schechter, Southern California regional director ADL, June 1, 1972.

13. June 19, 1972.

14. George Vecsey, "Schmitz Details Theory On Plots," *New York Times,* August 6, 1972.

15. Copy of platform adopted by the American Party.

16. ADL observer report.

17. "Birch candidate 'neutral' on the pro-Arab side," *American Examiner-Jewish Week,* September 7, 1972.

18. ADL observer report of John Schmitz statement at The American Party National Convention, August 3–5, 1972.

19. *The Summit Sun,* November 23, 1972.

20. January 20 and 27; February 3 and 10.

21. *America First* (The Mideast Problem in the Light of America's Traditional Policy of Non-Intervention), Summer, 1972.

22. Caption under photo of President Nixon and Henry Kissinger, Liberty Lobby's Election '72 Special, September, 1972.

23. Flyer, "Emergency P.S." September, 1973.

24. Bernard Gwertzman, "Varied Groups Urge Senate Panel to Reject Kissinger," *New York Times,* September 15, 1973; "Liberty Lobby Spearheads Hate Mail Against Dr. Kissinger," Jewish Telegraphic Agency *Daily News Bulletin,* September 10, 1973.

25. Copy of statement of Col. Curtis B. Dall before the Sentate Foreign Relations Committee hearings on nomination of Henry Kissinger as Secretary of State, September 14, 1973.

26. Bernard Gwertzman, loc cit.

27. *Ibid.*

13. The Hatemongers

1. "Lest We forget—In Case You Didn't Know—An Unbelievable Summary," Gerald L. K. Smith Newsletter.

2. "The Deadliest Issue Of The Century—The Threat of World War III," Gerald L. K. Smith Newsletter.

3. "The Coup d'Etat," Gerald L. K. Smith Newsletter.

4. "The Person Who Can Ignore The Following Summary Does Not Deserve The Title 'Patriotic American,'" Gerald L. K. Smith Newsletter.

5. "Watchman, What Of The Night? Are Americans On Guard?" Gerald L. K. Smith Newsletter.

6. "Front For Smith Haranguing Congressmen on Middle East," Jewish Telegraphic Agency *Daily News Bulletin,* May 14, 1973. Also see note 7.

7. "Blackmail Zionist Tyranny Threat of War," Gerald L. K, Smith Newsletter, June 26, 1973.

8. Pamphlet of Citizen's Congressional Committee containing photostatic copy of letter to members of Congress from Roland L. Morgan, Chairman, and the Congressional responses.

9. Letter to Jim Reed, president Mid-South Automobile Club, from Stuart Lewengrub, director southeastern regional office ADL, June 28, 1973. Letter to Stuart Lewengrub from Jim Reed, July 5, 1973.

10. Letter to Johanna Guzik, Editor, "Motor Travel," Automobile Club Publication from Irwin Suall, director domestic fact finding department, July 25, 1973; letter to Charles Gallagher, president AAA, from Irwin Suall, September 6, 1973.

11. "Thirty Years to Build an Ark," January 12, 1972.

12. Letter to NSRP supporters from Edward R. Fields, undated.

13. *Ibid.*

14. Quoted in "F.C.C. Won't Block Racist Ad In South," *New York Times,* August 4, 1972.

15. *Ibid.*

16. Forum for Senatorial Candidates, WSB-TV, August 1, 1972.

17. Petition filed with William B. Ray, Division of Complaints and Compliance, August 2, 1972.

18. Ruling FCC, Commissioners Robert E. Lee, Acting Chairman; H. Rex Lee and Wiley Acting as a Board, August 3, 1972.

19. "White Supremacist Wins; Ads Will Go On," *Daily News,* August 4, 1972.

20. "Stoner Polls 40,675 Votes—Jew ADL Rocked by Results," Personal News Letter, August 1972.

21. "$50,000 Cash Bond," *Jacksonville Daily News,* May 7, 1973.

22. Quoted in Fay Smulevitz Joyce, "Will The Hooded Knights Return?" *De-kalb* (Ill.) *New Era,* March 8, 1973.

23. Lois Landes, "'New Klan' Forgoes Old Masks," *Indiana Daily Student,* March 5, 1973.

24. David Lyon, "Plenty of Seats, Few Sheets," *Dayton Daily News,* August 6, 1973.

25. "Klan Chief in Mayor Race," *Houston Chronicle,* June 3, 1973.

26. Carolyn Bower, "Polk Rejects Klansman Rogers," *Orlando* (Florida) *Sentinel,* October 4, 1972.

27. "175 Attend KKK Rally in Field," February 10, 1973.

28. "College Students Shun Extremists," *New York Times,* February 7, 1971.

Epilogue

1. Robert Alden, "U.N. Condemns Israel for Forcing Down Arab Plane," *New York Times,* August 16, 1973.

2. *Ibid, ;* quotation of statement by Yosef Tekoah.

3. "Arab Guerrilla Units Are Set to Establish East Berlin Office," *New York Times,* August 19, 1973; East German government statement quoted.

4. *Ibid.*

5. "Israel Censured."

6. "Israel's Collision Course," *New York Post,* August 18, 1973.

7. CBS Radio transcript.

8. June 12, 1972.

9. CBS Radio transcript.

10. Terence Smith, September 30, 1973.

11. David Binder, "Kissinger Sworn, Praised by Nixon," *New York Times,* September 23, 1973.

12. Quoted in "Arabs Claim Kissinger Is Pro-Israel." *Newsday,* September 4, 1973.

13. *Ibid.*

14. "Algerians Say K. Is An Israeli," *Jerusalem Post,* August 27, 1973.

15. Robert Alden, "U.N.'s Anti-Israel Tone," *New York Times,* October 11, 1973.

16. "Vatican May Press Plea on Holy Places," *New York Times,* October 13, 1973.

17. Jack Nelson, "Fulbright Hit on 'Israeli Control' Remark," *New York Post,* October 27, 1973.

18. CBS Radio transcript of "Spectrum," October 15, 1973.

19. WCBS-TV transcript of "Middle East Madness," Sue Cott.

20. "U.S.-Soviet détente strained by war."

21. "Some Middle East facts," October 16, 1973.

22. Text by David R. Hunter, Shoreham Hotel, Washington, D.C.

23. Text of Middle East Resolution passed by Governing Board, October 15, 1973.

24. Text of Resolution on The Crisis in the Middle East.

Temple Israel

Minneapolis, Minnesota

In Honor of the Bar Mitzvah of

MICHAEL MALMON

September 30, 1974